Volume 1

Made in the United States
Text printed on recycled paper

Printed in the U.S.A.

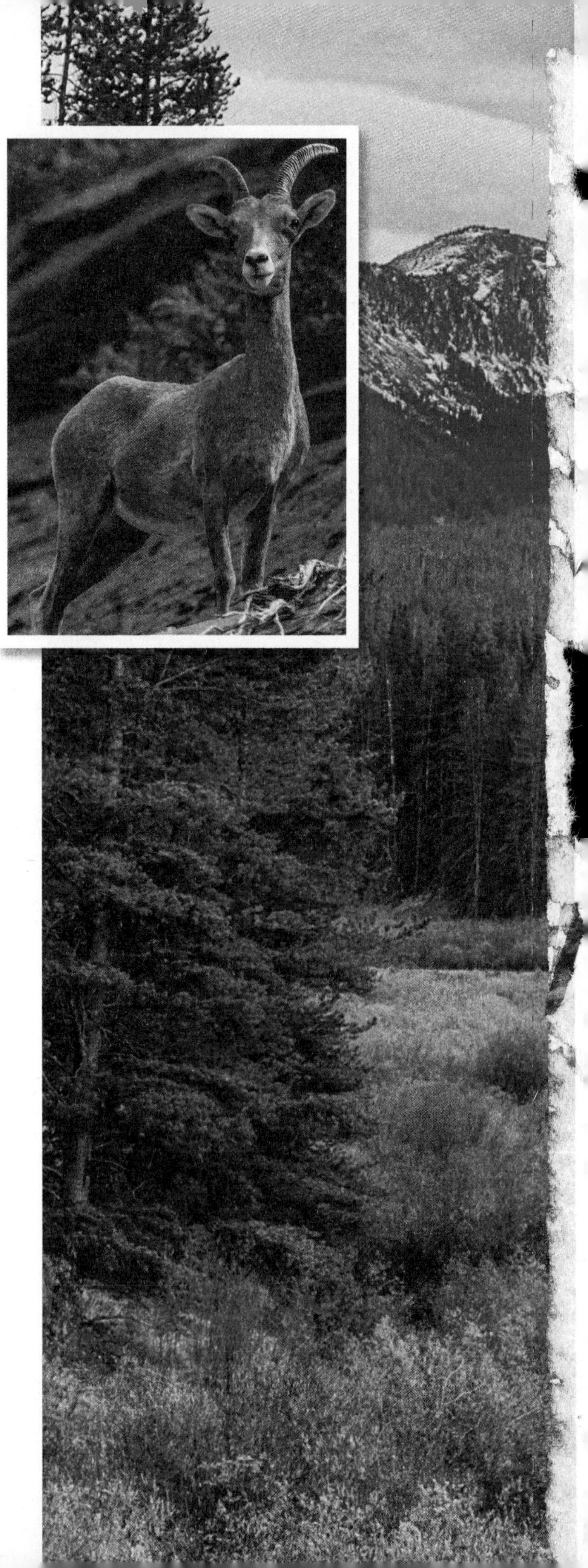

ISBN 978-0-544-43273-4

17 0868 21

4500827629 E F G

Dear Students and Families,

Welcome to **Go Math!**, Grade 2! In this exciting mathematics program, there are hands-on activities to do and real-world problems to solve. Best of all, you will write your ideas and answers right in your book. In **Go Math!**, writing and drawing on the pages helps you think deeply about what you are learning, and you will really understand math!

By the way, all of the pages in your **Go Math!** book are made using recycled paper. We wanted you to know that you can Go Green with **Go Math!**

Sincerely,

The Authors

Made in the United States
Text printed on recycled paper

Authors

Juli K. Dixon, Ph.D.
Professor, Mathematics Education
University of Central Florida
Orlando, Florida

Edward B. Burger, Ph.D.
President, Southwestern University
Georgetown, Texas

Steven J. Leinwand
Principal Research Analyst
American Institutes for Research (AIR)
Washington, D.C.

Contributor

Rena Petrello
Professor, Mathematics
Moorpark College
Moorpark, CA

Matthew R. Larson, Ph.D.
K-12 Curriculum Specialist for Mathematics
Lincoln Public Schools
Lincoln, Nebraska

Martha E. Sandoval-Martinez
Math Instructor
El Camino College
Torrance, California

English Language Learners Consultant

Elizabeth Jiménez
CEO, GEMAS Consulting
Professional Expert on English Learner Education
Bilingual Education and Dual Language
Pomona, California

VOLUME 1

Number Sense and Place Value

Critical Area Extending understanding of base-ten notation

Number Concepts 9

Domains Operations and Algebraic Thinking
Number and Operations in Base Ten

COMMON CORE STATE STANDARDS 2.OA.C.3, 2.NBT.A.2, 2.NBT.A.3

Critical Area

GO DIGITAL

Go online! Your math lessons are interactive. Use *i*Tools, Animated Math Models, the Multimedia *e*Glossary, and more.

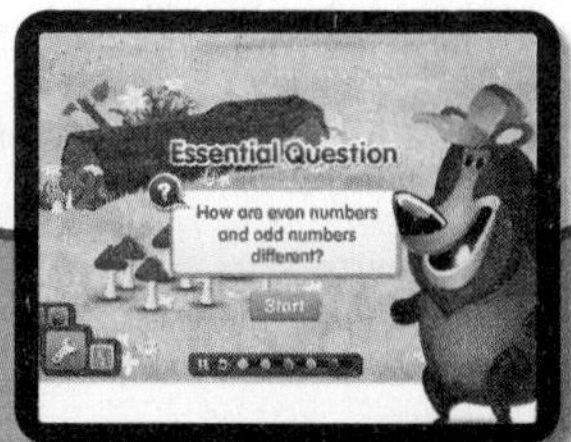

Chapter 1 Overview

In this chapter, you will explore and discover answers to the following **Essential Questions**:

- How do you use place value to find the values of numbers and describe numbers in different ways?
- How do you know the value of a digit?
- What are some different ways to show a number?
- How do you count by 1s, 5s, 10s, and 100s?

Personal Math Trainer
Online Assessment and Intervention

Chapter 2 Overview

In this chapter, you will explore and discover answers to the following **Essential Questions**:

- How can you use place value to model, write, and compare 3-digit numbers?
- How can you use blocks to show a 3-digit number?
- How can you write a 3-digit number in different ways?
- How can place value help you compare 3-digit numbers?

Addition and Subtraction

Critical Area Building fluency with addition and subtraction

3 Basic Facts and Relationships 159

Domain Operations and Algebraic Thinking
COMMON CORE STATE STANDARDS 2.OA.A.1, 2.OA.B.2, 2.OA.C.4

Critical Area

GO DIGITAL

Go online! Your math lessons are interactive. Use *i*Tools, Animated Math Models, the Multimedia *e*Glossary, and more.

Chapter 3 Overview

In this chapter, you will explore and discover answers to the following **Essential Questions**:

- How can you use patterns and strategies to find sums and differences for basic facts?
- What are some strategies for remembering addition and subtraction facts?
- How are addition and subtraction related?

Chapter 4 Overview

In this chapter, you will explore and discover answers to the following **Essential Questions**:

- How do you use place value to add 2-digit numbers, and what are some different ways to add 2-digit numbers?
- How do you make an addend a ten to help solve an addition problem?
- How do you record the steps when adding 2-digit numbers?
- What are some ways to add 3 numbers or 4 numbers?

Practice and Homework

Lesson Check and Spiral Review in every lesson

2-Digit Addition 233

Domains Operations and Algebraic Thinking
Number and Operations in Base Ten

COMMON CORE STATE STANDARDS 2.OA.A.1, 2.NBT.B.5, 2.NBT.B.6, 2.NBT.B.9

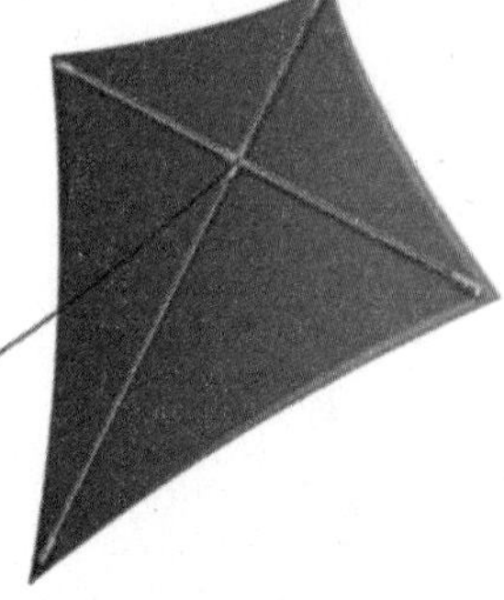

5 2-Digit Subtraction 313

Domains Operations and Algebraic Thinking
Number and Operations in Base Ten

COMMON CORE STATE STANDARDS 2.OA.A.1, 2.NBT.B.5

Chapter 5 Overview

In this chapter, you will explore and discover answers to the following **Essential Questions**:

- How do you use place value to subtract 2-digit numbers with and without regrouping?
- How can you break apart numbers to help solve a subtraction problem?
- What are the steps you use when you solve 2-digit subtraction problems?
- What are some different ways to model, show, and solve subtraction problems?

6 3-Digit Addition and Subtraction 387

Domain Number and Operations in Base Ten

COMMON CORE STATE STANDARDS 2.NBT.B.7, 2.NBT.B.9

Chapter 6 Overview

In this chapter, you will explore and discover answers to the following **Essential Questions**:

- What are some strategies for adding and subtracting 3-digit numbers?
- What are the steps when finding the sum in a 3-digit addition problem?
- What are the steps when finding the difference in a 3-digit subtraction problem?
- When do you need to regroup?

Critical Area

GO DIGITAL

Go online! Your math lessons are interactive. Use *i*Tools, Animated Math Models, the Multimedia *e*Glossary, and more.

Chapter 7 Overview

Essential Questions:

- How do you use the values of coins and bills to find the total value of a group of money, and how do you read times shown on analog and digital clocks?
- What are the names and values of the different coins?
- How can you tell the time on a clock by looking at the clock hands?

Chapter 8 Overview

Essential Questions:

- What are some of the methods and tools that can be used to estimate and measure length?
- What tools can be used to measure length and how do you use them?
- What units can be used to measure length and how do they compare with each other?
- How can you estimate the length of an object?

VOLUME 2

Measurement and Data

Common Core **Critical Area** Using standard units of measure

Chapter 9 Overview

In this chapter, you will explore and discover answers to the following **Essential Questions**:

- What are some of the methods and tools that can be used to estimate and measure length in metric units?
- What tools can be used to measure length in metric units and how do you use them?
- What metric units can be used to measure length and how do they compare with each other?
- If you know the length of one object, how can you estimate the length of another object?

Practice and Homework

Lesson Check and Spiral Review in every lesson

Chapter 10 Overview

In this chapter, you will explore and discover answers to the following **Essential Questions**:

- How do tally charts, picture graphs, and bar graphs help you solve problems?
- How are tally marks used to record data for a survey?
- How is a picture graph made?
- How do you know what the bars in a bar graph stand for?

Critical Area

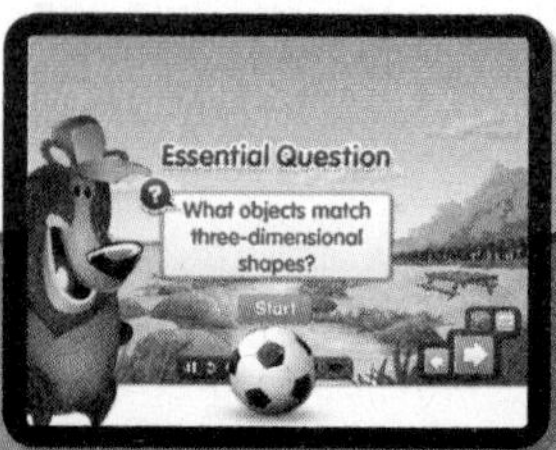

Go online! Your math lessons are interactive. Use *i*Tools, Animated Math Models, the Multimedia *e*Glossary, and more.

Chapter 11 Overview

In this chapter, you will explore and discover answers to the following **Essential Questions**:

- What are some two-dimensional shapes and three-dimensional shapes, and how can you show equal parts of shapes?
- How can you describe some two-dimensional and three-dimensional shapes?
- How can you describe equal parts of shapes?

Personal Math Trainer
Online Assessment and Intervention

Geometry and Fractions

Critical Area Describing and analyzing shapes

Whales

by John Hudson

CRITICAL AREA Extending understanding of base-ten notation

Common Core

Some scientists study whales. Different kinds of whales swim along the west coast of the United States of America.
A scientist sees 8 blue whales.
Blue whales are the largest animals on Earth.

Social Studies

Where is the United States of America on the map?

North America

Alaska

Canada

Pacific Ocean

Atlantic Ocean

United States of America

Mexico

N W E S

0 500 1,000 Miles
0 500 1,000 Kilometers

Map Legend
Border

The scientist also sees 13 humpback whales.
Humpback whales sing underwater.
Did the scientist see more humpback whales or more blue whales? more ______________ whales

Where is the Pacific Ocean on the map?

Whales also swim along the east coast of Canada and the United States of America. Pilot whales swim behind a leader, or a *pilot*. A scientist sees a group of 29 pilot whales.

Social Studies

Where is Canada on the map?

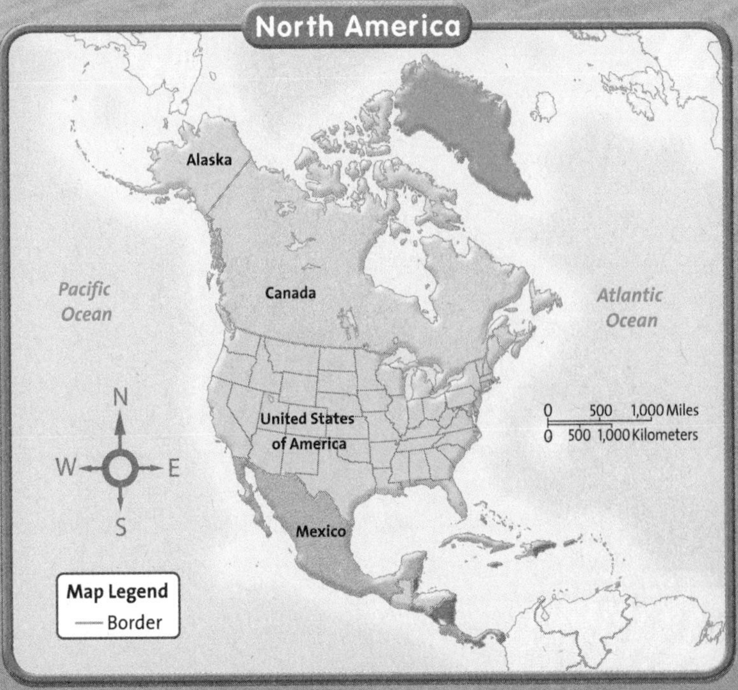

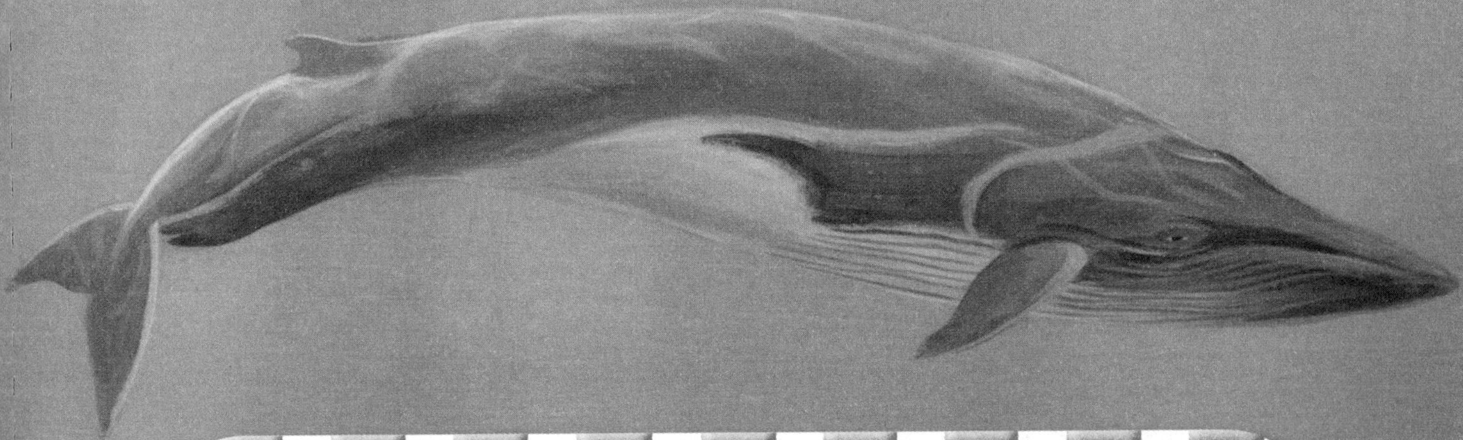

Fin whales are fast swimmers. They are the second-largest whales in the world. A scientist sees a group of 27 fin whales. How many tens are in the number 27?

_____ tens

Where is the Atlantic Ocean on the map?

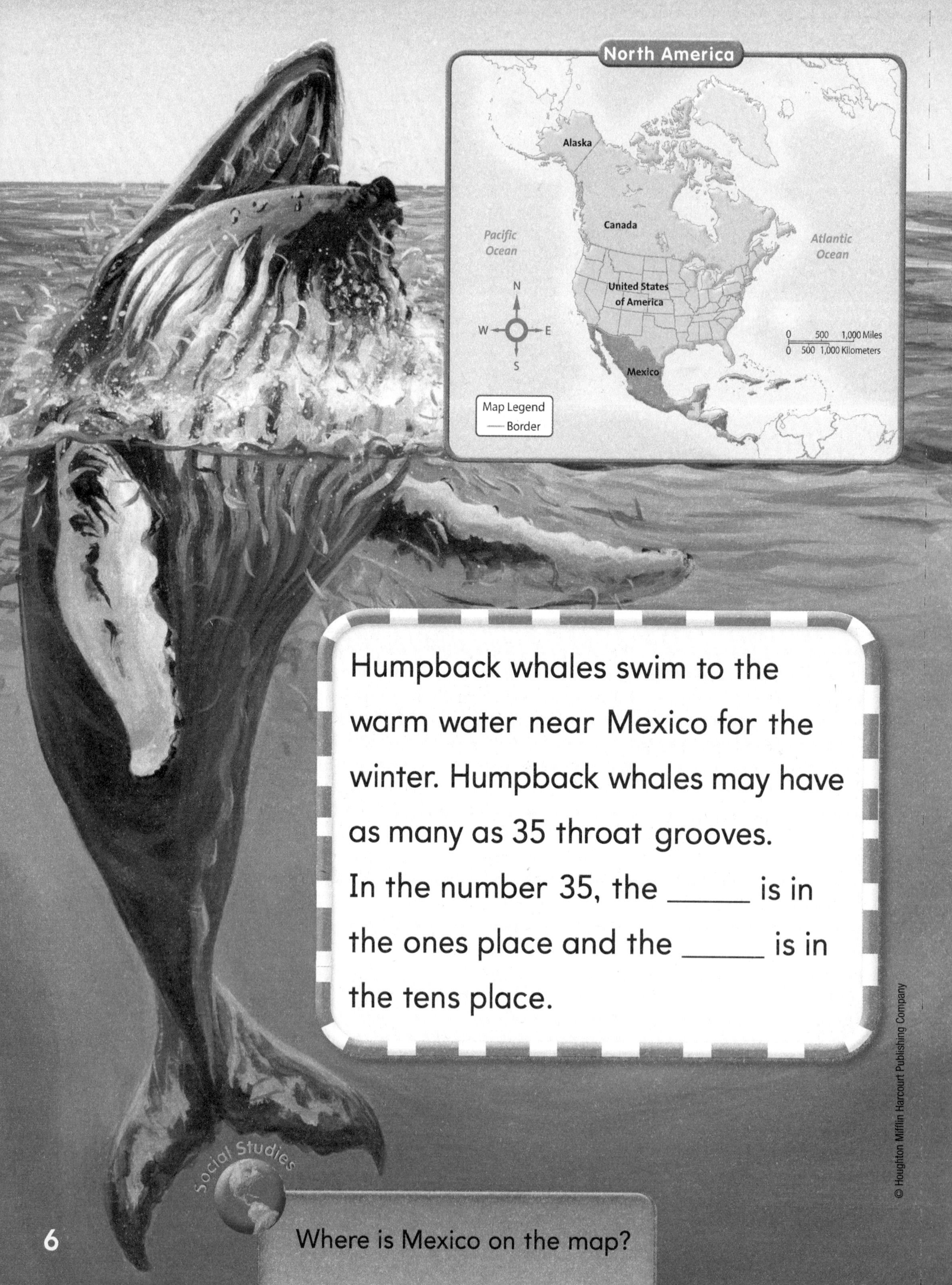

Humpback whales swim to the warm water near Mexico for the winter. Humpback whales may have as many as 35 throat grooves.

In the number 35, the _____ is in the ones place and the _____ is in the tens place.

Where is Mexico on the map?

Name ___________________________

Write About the Story

Look at the pictures. Draw and write your own story. Compare two numbers in your story.

Vocabulary Review

more	fewer
tens	greater than
ones	less than

WRITE Math

____

____

____

____

____

____

The Size of Numbers

The table shows how many young whales were seen by scientists.

Young Whales Seen	
Whale	**Number of Whales**
Humpback	34
Blue	13
Fin	27
Pilot	43

1. Which number of whales has a 4 in the tens place?

   ______

2. How many tens and ones describe the number of young blue whales seen?

   _____ ten _____ ones

3. Compare the number of young humpback whales and the number of young pilot whales seen. Write > or <.

   34 ◯ 43

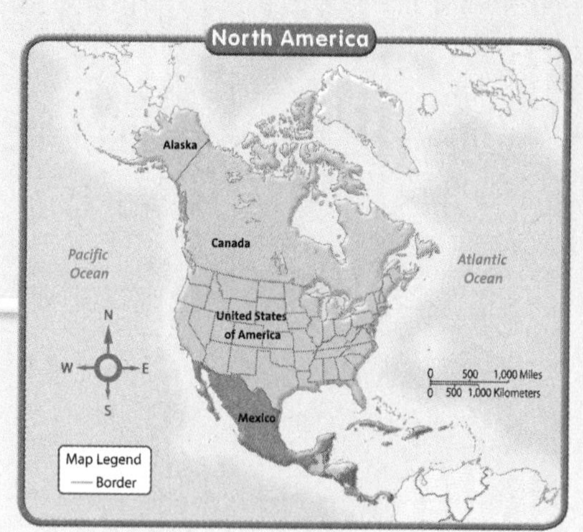

4. Compare the number of young fin whales and the number of young blue whales seen. Write > or <.

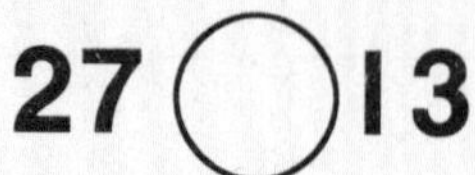

   27 ◯ 13

Write a story about a scientist watching sea animals. Use some 2-digit numbers in your story.

Chapter 1

Number Concepts

Curious about Math

At a farmers' market, many different fruits and vegetables are sold.

If there are 2 groups of 10 watermelons on a table, how many watermelons are there?

Name ______________________

Model Numbers to 20

Write the number that tells how many. (K.NBT.A.1)

1. ______

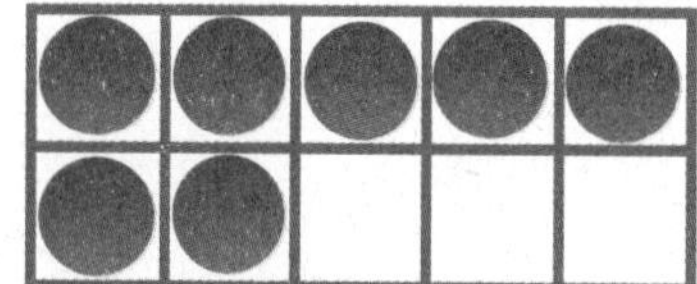

2. ______

Use a Hundred Chart to Count

Use the hundred chart. (1.NBT.A.1)

3. Count from 36 to 47. Which of the numbers below will you say? Circle them.

42 31 48 39 37

1	2	3	4	5	6	7	8	9	10
11	12	13	14	15	16	17	18	19	20
21	22	23	24	25	26	27	28	29	30
31	32	33	34	35	36	37	38	39	40
41	42	43	44	45	46	47	48	49	50
51	52	53	54	55	56	57	58	59	60
61	62	63	64	65	66	67	68	69	70
71	72	73	74	75	76	77	78	79	80
81	82	83	84	85	86	87	88	89	90
91	92	93	94	95	96	97	98	99	100

Tens

Write how many tens. Write the number. (1.NBT.B.2a, 1.NBT.B.2c)

4. ______ tens

______

5. 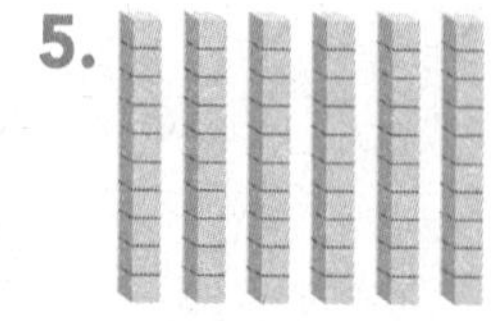

______ tens

______

This page checks understanding of important skills needed for success in Chapter 1.

Name ____________________________

Vocabulary Builder

Visualize It

Fill in the boxes of the graphic organizer.
Write sentences about **ones** and **tens**.

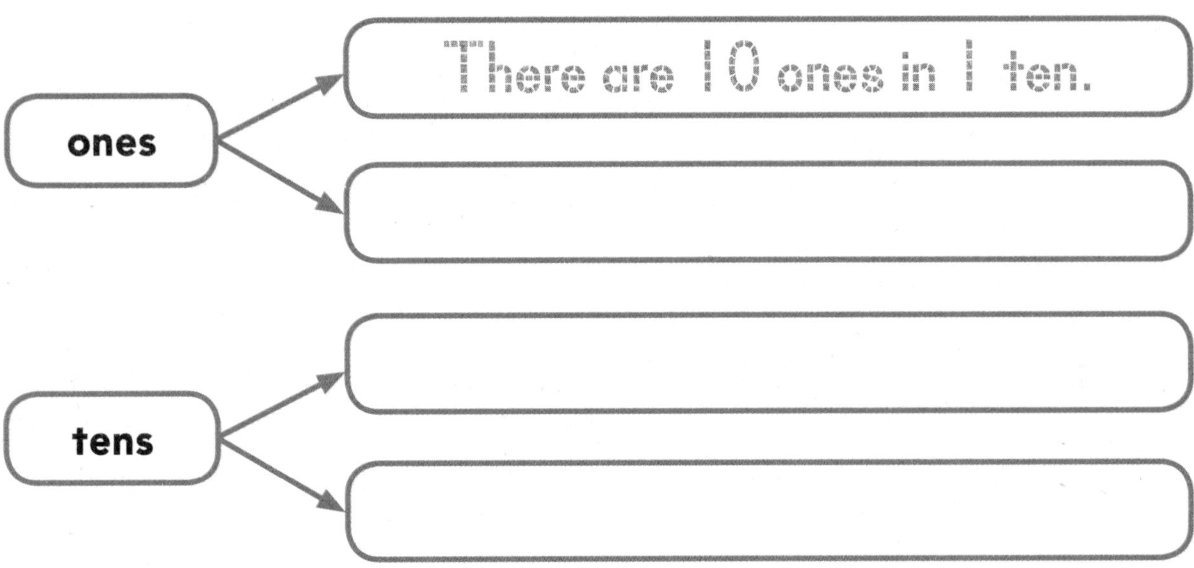

Understand Vocabulary

1. Start with 1. **Count on** by ones.

   1, ____, ____, ____, ____, ____

2. Start with 8. **Count back** by ones.

   8, ____, ____, ____, ____, ____

GO DIGITAL • Interactive Student Edition • Multimedia eGlossary

Game Three in a Row

Materials • 15 ● • 15 ○ • ▭ ▪

Play with a partner.

1. Choose a leaf. Read the number on the leaf. Use ▭ ▪ to model the number.
2. Your partner checks your model. If your model is correct, put your ● on the leaf.
3. Take turns. Try to get 3 ● in a row.
4. The first player with 3 ● in a row wins.

5	21	13	19	20
25	15	7	8	12
11	9	14	16	24
22	23	17	18	10

Chapter 1 Vocabulary

English	Spanish	Page
digit	dígito	15
doubles	dobles	19
even	par	22
is equal to (=)	es igual a	33
odd	impar	44
ones	unidades	45
plus (+)	más	49
ten	decena	61

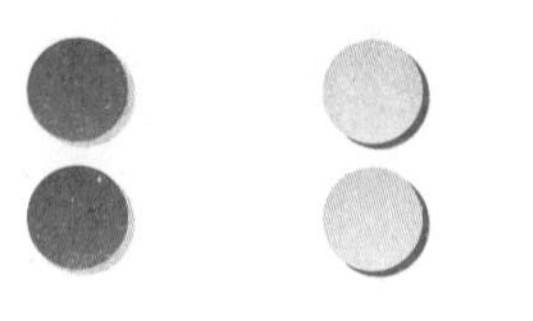

2 + 2 = 4

0, 1, 2, 3, 4, 5, 6, 7, 8, and 9 are **digits**.

2 plus 1 is equal to 3

2 + 1 = 3

Even numbers show pairs with no left over cubes.

10 ones = 1 ten

Odd numbers show pairs with one cube left over.

10 ones = 1 ten

2 plus 1 is equal to 3

2 + 1 = 3

Going to the Farmers Market

Word Box
digit
doubles
even numbers
is equal to (=)
odd numbers
ones
plus (+)
tens

For 2 to 4 players

Materials

- 1
- 1
- 1
- 1
- 1

How to Play

1. Put your in the START circle of the same color.
2. To get your out of START, you must roll a 6.
   - If you do not roll a 6, wait until your next turn.
   - If you roll a 6, move your to the circle of that same color on the path.
3. Once you have a on the path, toss the to take a turn. Move your that many.
4. If you land on a space with a question, answer the question. If your answer is correct, move ahead 1 space.
5. To reach FINISH, you need to move your up the path of the same color as the . The first player to reach FINISH wins.

Which number is equal to 12 + 7?

Which digit is in the ones place in 19?

How can you use doubles to add 4 and 5?

How can you tell when a number is even?

FINISH

Which digit is in the tens place in 45?

How can you tell when a number is odd?

What sign shows that one number is equal to another?

How many ones are in 24?

START

What does plus mean?

Which numbers are even? 32, 25, 15, 6

What does + mean?

How can you tell how many ones are in a number?

FINISH

Which numbers are odd? 13, 34, 22, 47

How can you tell how many tens are in a number?

How can you use doubles to add 9 and 8?

START

How many tens are in 37?

The Write Way

Reflect

Choose one idea. Write about it in the space below.

- Explain two things you know about even numbers and odd numbers.
- Write about all the different ways you can show 25.
- Tell how to count on by different amounts to 1,000.

Name ___________________________

Algebra • Even and Odd Numbers

Essential Question How are even numbers and odd numbers different?

Common Core **Operations and Algebraic Thinking—2.OA.C.3**
MATHEMATICAL PRACTICES
MP3, MP6, MP7

Use ▪ to show each number.

FOR THE TEACHER • Read the following problem. Beca has 8 toy cars. Can she put her cars in pairs on a shelf? Have children set pairs of cubes vertically on the ten frames. Continue the activity for the numbers 7 and 10.

MATHEMATICAL PRACTICES 6

When you make pairs for 7 and for 10, how are these models different? **Explain.**

Model and Draw

Count out cubes for each number. Make pairs.
Even numbers show pairs with no cubes left over.
Odd numbers show pairs with one cube left over.

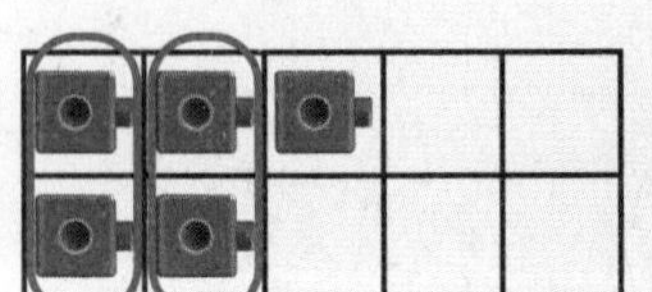

5 odd

8 even

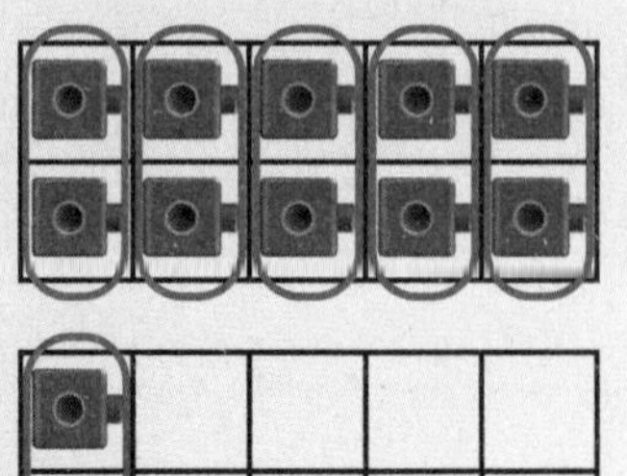

12 ______

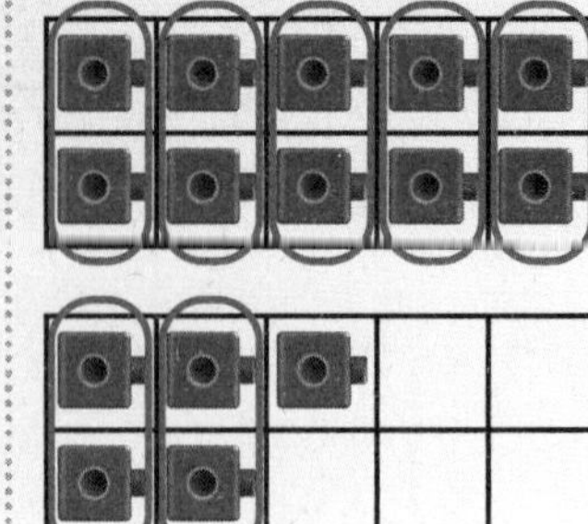

15 ______

Share and Show

Use cubes. Count out the number of cubes.
Make pairs. Then write **even** or **odd**.

1. 6 ______
2. 3 ______
3. 2 ______
4. 9 ______
5. 4 ______
6. 10 ______
7. 7 ______
8. 13 ______
9. 11 ______
10. 14 ______

Name ______________________________

On Your Own

Shade in the ten frames to show the number.
Circle **even** or **odd**.

11. 17

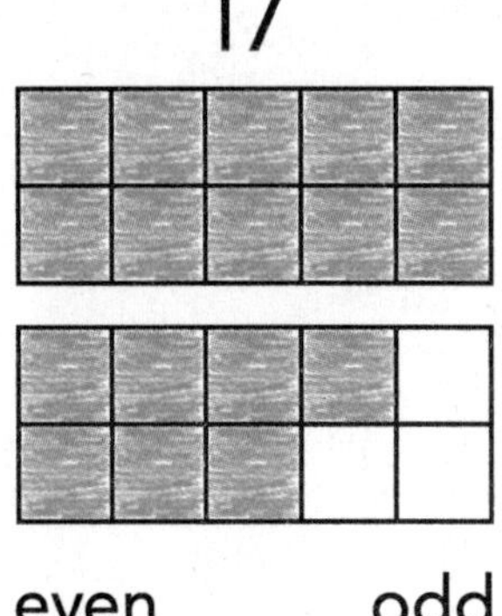

even odd

12. 16

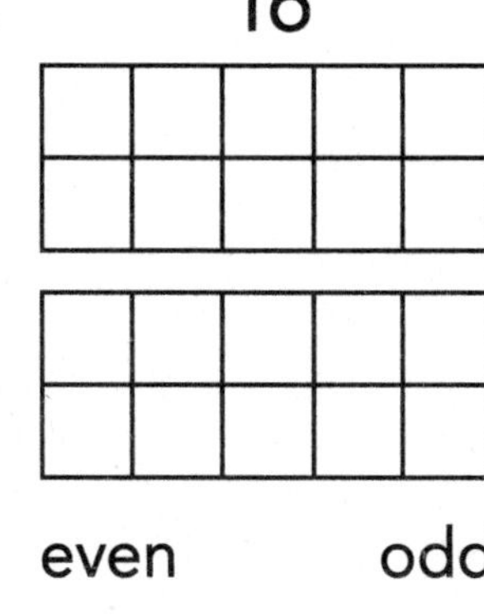

even odd

13. 19

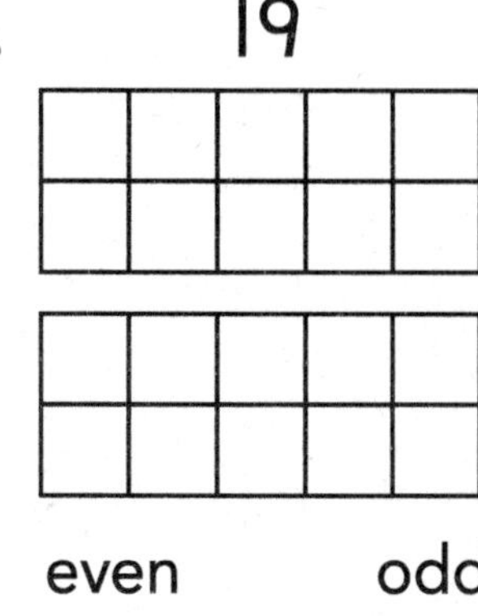

even odd

14. There are an even number of boys and an odd number of girls in Lena's class. How many boys and girls could be in her class? Show your work.

____

____

____

15. MATHEMATICAL PRACTICE 3 **Make Arguments**
Which two numbers in the box are even numbers?

________ and ________

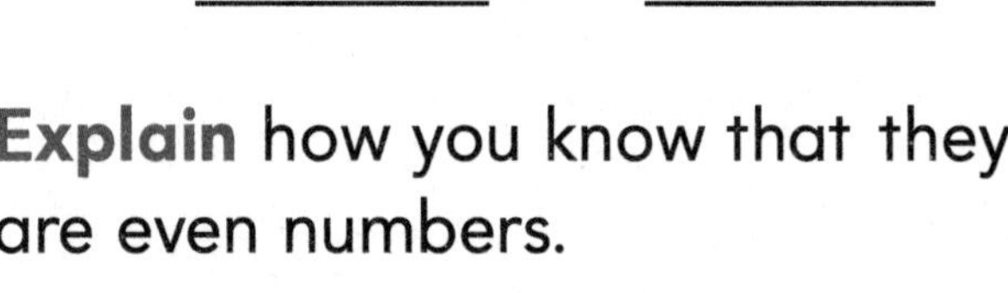

Explain how you know that they are even numbers.

____

____

____

Problem Solving • Applications  

16. THINKSMARTER Fill in the blanks to describe the groups of numbers. Write **even** or **odd**.

______________ **numbers** ______________ **numbers**

13 19 7

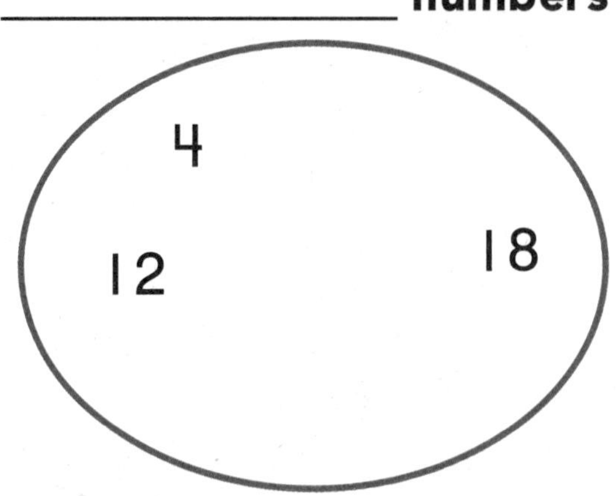

4 12 18

Write each of these numbers inside the correct loop.

5 **6** **10** **11** **24** **25**

17. THINKSMARTER Does each ten frame show an even number? Choose Yes or No.

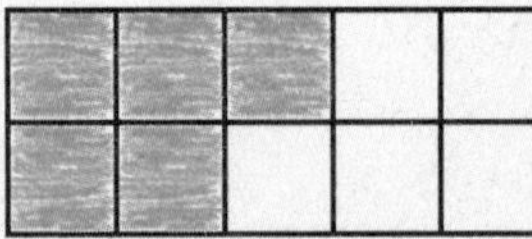

○ Yes ○ No

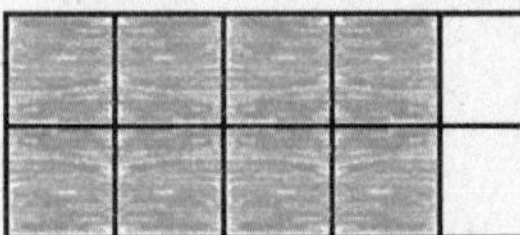

○ Yes ○ No

TAKE HOME ACTIVITY • Have your child show you a number, such as 9, using small objects and explain why the number is even or odd.

Name ______________________________

Algebra • Even and Odd Numbers

COMMON CORE STANDARD—2.OA.C.3
Work with equal groups of objects to gain foundations for multiplication.

Shade in the ten frames to show the number. Circle even or odd.

1. 

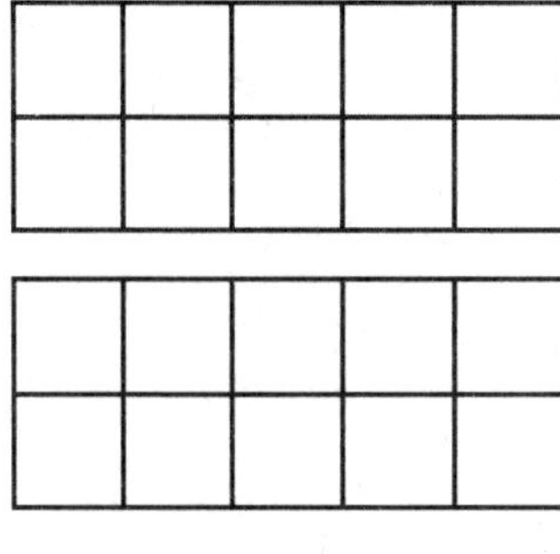

even odd

2. 18

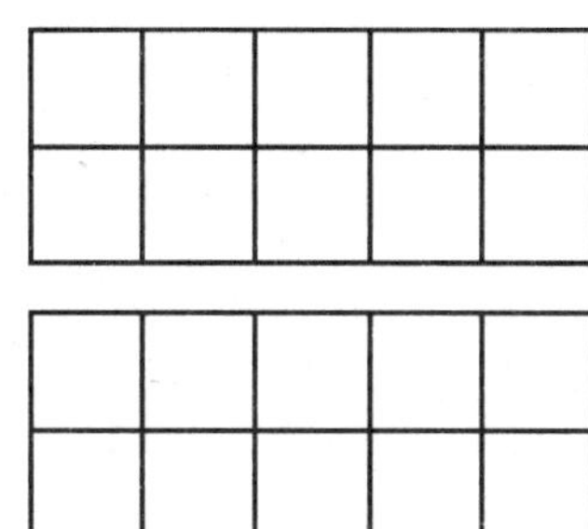

even odd

3. 11

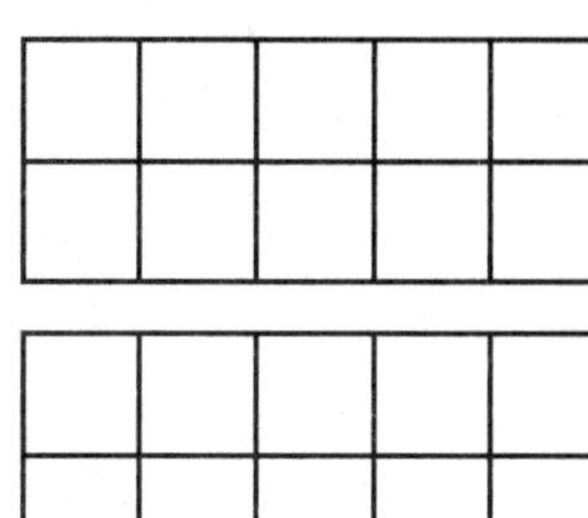

even odd

Problem Solving

4. Mr. Dell has an odd number of sheep and an even number of cows on his farm. Circle the choice that could tell about his farm.

9 sheep and 10 cows

10 sheep and 11 cows

8 sheep and 12 cows

5. WRITE Math Write two odd numbers and two even numbers. Explain how you know which numbers are even and which are odd.

Lesson Check (2.OA.C.3)

1. Circle the even number.

3 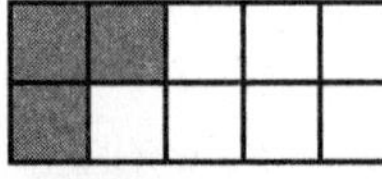

4 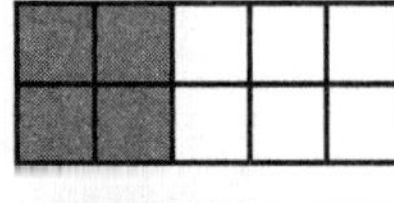

5

9

2. Circle the odd number.

2 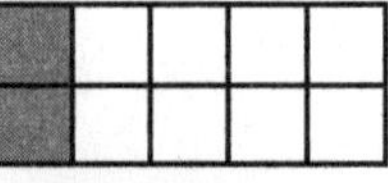

6 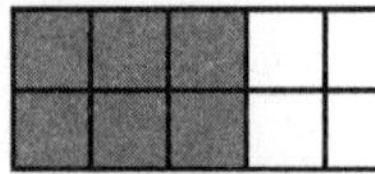

7 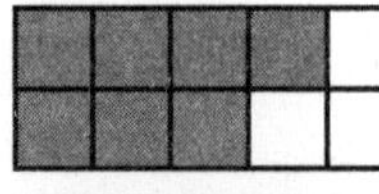

8 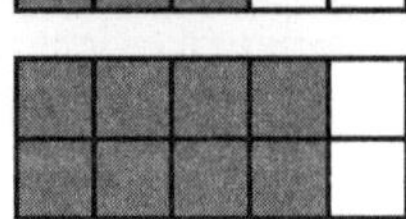

Spiral Review (2.OA.C.3)

3. Circle the odd number.

10 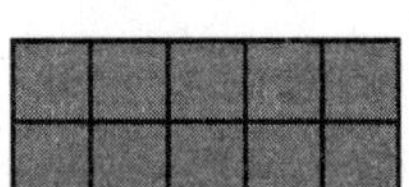

8 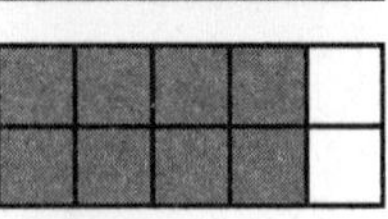

3 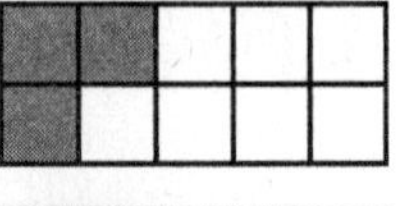

4 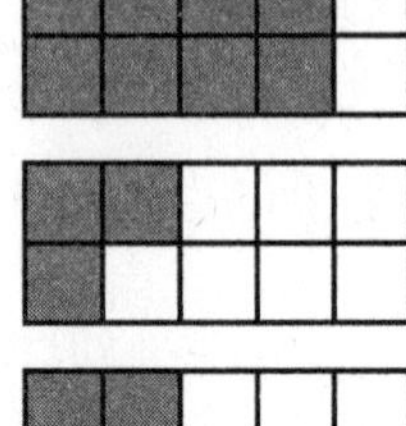

4. Circle the even number.

7 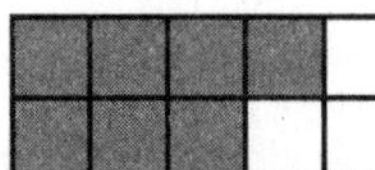

6 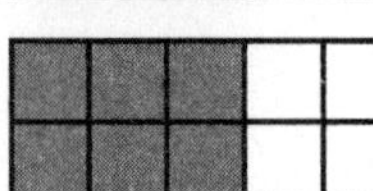

5 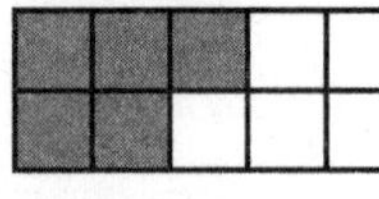

1 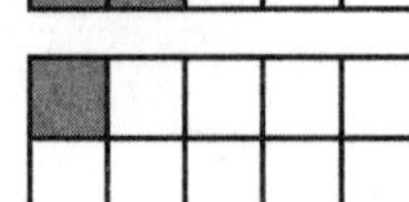

5. Circle the even number.

9 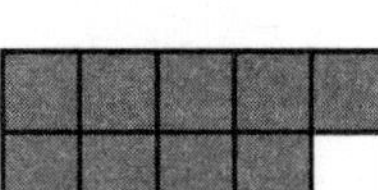

7 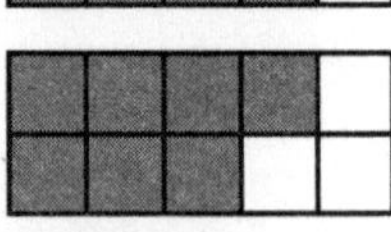

5 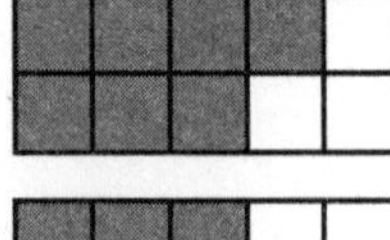

2 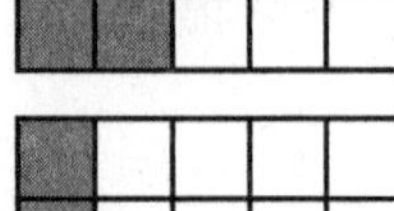

6. Circle the odd number.

1 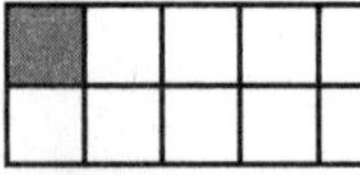

4 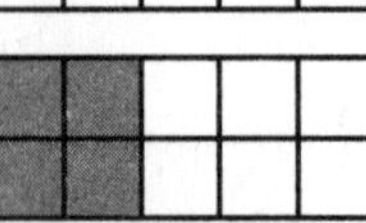

8 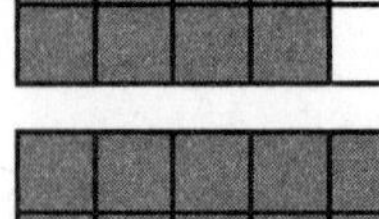

10

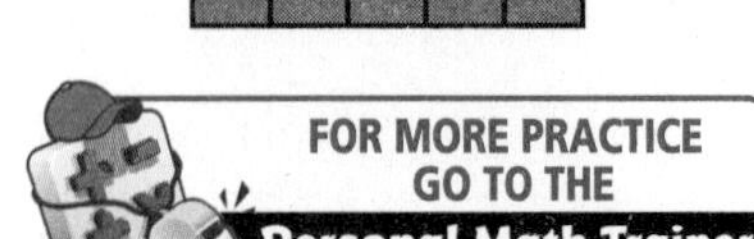

Name ______________________________

Algebra • Represent Even Numbers

Essential Question Why can an even number be shown as the sum of two equal addends?

Common Core **Operations and Algebraic Thinking—2.OA.C.3**

MATHEMATICAL PRACTICES
MP2, MP3, MP7, MP8

Listen and Draw

Make pairs with your cubes. Draw to show the cubes. Then write the numbers you say as you count to find the number of cubes.

______________________________ ________ cubes

FOR THE TEACHER • Give each small group of children a set of 10 to 15 connecting cubes. After children group their cubes into pairs, have them draw a picture of their cubes and write their counting sequence for finding the total number of cubes.

MATHEMATICAL PRACTICES 2

Use Reasoning
Explain how you know if a number modeled with cubes is an even number.

Model and Draw

An even number of cubes can be shown as two equal groups.

You can match each cube in the first group with a cube in the second group.

$6 = 3 + 3$

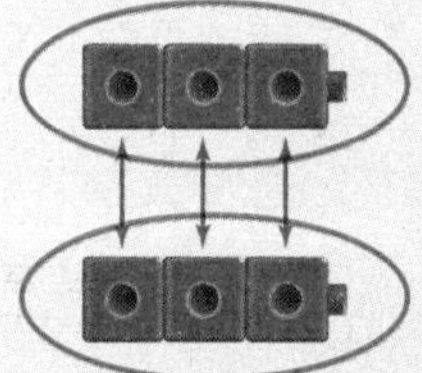

$10 = 5 + 5$

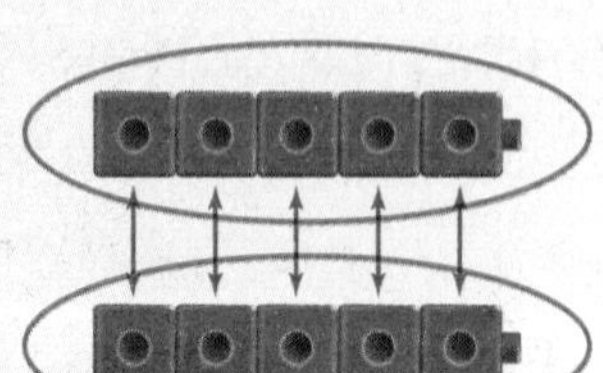

Share and Show

How many cubes are there in all? Complete the addition sentence to show the equal groups.

1. ____ = ____ + ____

2. ____ = ____ + ____

3. ____ = ____ + ____

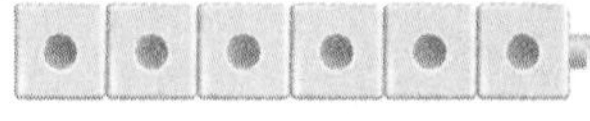

4. ____ = ____ + ____

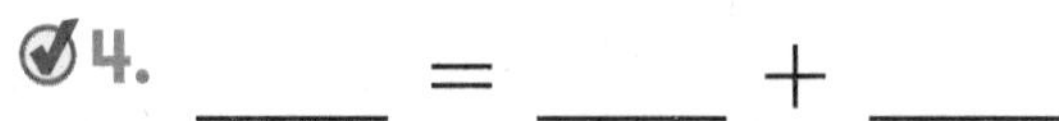

Name ____________________

On Your Own

Shade in the frames to show two equal groups for each number. Complete the addition sentence to show the groups.

5.  10

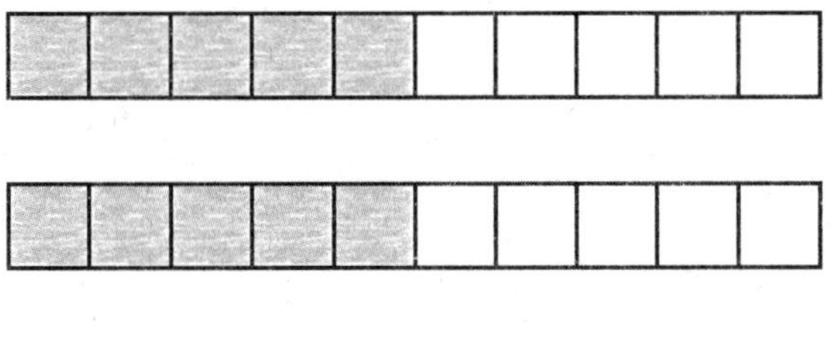

____ = ____ + ____

6.  16

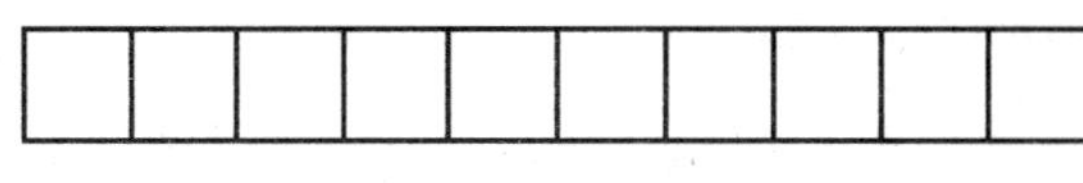

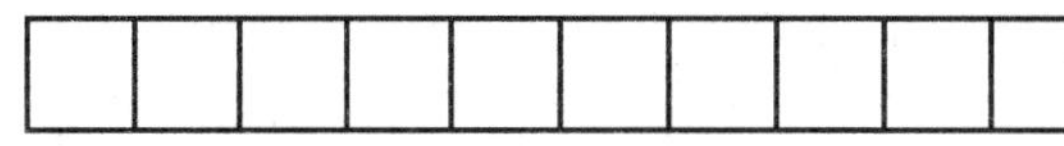

____ = ____ + ____

7. Elena and José have 18 postcards together. They each have the same number of postcards. How many postcards do Elena and José each have?

____ postcards

THINK SMARTER The number 7 is an odd number. Marc showed 7 with this addition sentence. Use Marc's way to show these odd numbers with addition sentences.

$7 = 3 + 3 + 1$

8. $5 =$ ____ + ____ + ____

9. $11 =$ ____ + ____ + ____

10. $9 =$ ____ + ____ + ____

11. $13 =$ ____ + ____ + ____

Problem Solving • Applications  

Solve. Write or draw to explain.

12. MATHEMATICAL PRACTICE 2 **Use Reasoning**
Jacob and Lucas each have the same number of shells. Together they have 16 shells. How many shells do Jacob and Lucas each have?

Jacob: _____ shells

Lucas: _____ shells

Personal Math Trainer

13. THINKSMARTER+ Choose an even number between 10 and 19. Draw a picture and then write a sentence to explain why it is an even number.

____

____

____

TAKE HOME ACTIVITY • Have your child explain what he or she learned in this lesson.

Name ______________________

Algebra • Represent Even Numbers

Common Core **COMMON CORE STANDARD—2.OA.C.3**
Work with equal groups of objects to gain foundations for multiplication.

Shade in the frames to show two equal groups for each number. Complete the addition sentence to show the groups.

1. 8

____ = ____ + ____

2. 18

____ = ____ + ____

3. 10

____ = ____ + ____

4. 14

____ = ____ + ____

5. 20

____ = ____ + ____

Problem Solving

Solve. Write or draw to explain.

6. The seats in a van are in pairs. There are 16 seats. How many pairs of seats are there?

____ pairs of seats

7. WRITE Math Draw or write to show that the number 18 is an even number.

Lesson Check (2.OA.C.3)

1. Circle the sum that is an even number.

9 + 9 = 18
9 + 8 = 17
8 + 7 = 15
6 + 5 = 11

2. Circle the sum that is an even number.

1 + 2 = 3
3 + 3 = 6
2 + 5 = 7
4 + 7 = 11

Spiral Review (2.OA.C.3)

3. Circle the even number.

7
9
10
13

4. Circle the odd number.

4
11
16
20

5. Ray has an odd number of cats. He also has an even number of dogs. Complete the sentence.

Ray has _____ cats and

_____ dogs.

6. Circle the sum that is an even number.

2 + 3 = 5
3 + 4 = 7
4 + 4 = 8
7 + 8 = 15

FOR MORE PRACTICE GO TO THE **Personal Math Trainer**

Name ______________________________

Understand Place Value

Essential Question How do you know the value of a digit?

Common Core **Number and Operations in Base Ten—2.NBT.A.3**
MATHEMATICAL PRACTICES
MP1, MP6

Listen and Draw Real World

Write the numbers. Then choose a way to show the numbers.

Tens	Ones

Tens	Ones

MATHEMATICAL PRACTICES 6

Explain why the value of 5 is different in the two numbers.

FOR THE TEACHER • Read the following problem. Have children write the numbers and describe how they chose to represent them. Gabriel collects baseball cards. The number of cards that he has is written with a 2 and a 5. How many cards might he have?

Model and Draw

0, 1, 2, 3, 4, 5, 6, 7, 8, and 9 are **digits**.
In a 2-digit number, you know the value of a digit by its place.

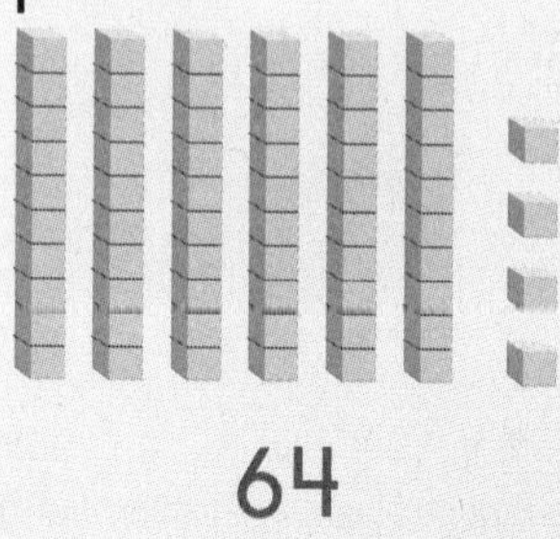

64

Tens	Ones
6	4

6 tens 4 ones

The digit **6** is in the tens place. It tells you there are 6 tens, or 60.

The digit 4 is in the ones place. It tells you there are 4 ones, or 4.

Share and Show

MATH BOARD

Circle the value of the red digit.

1. 26

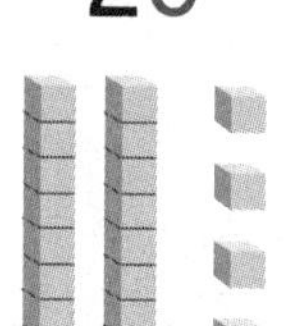
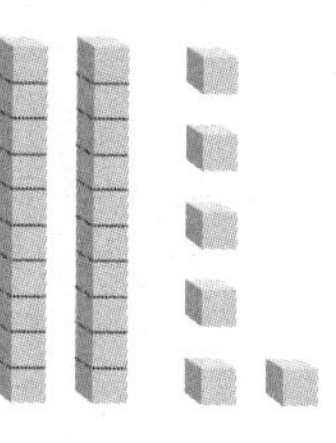

60 6

2. 58

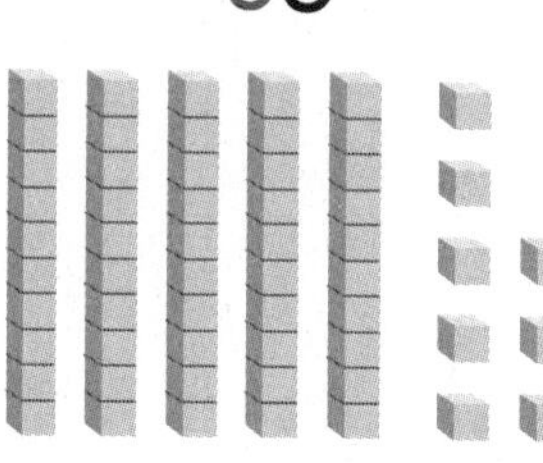

5 50

3. 40

40 4

4. 73

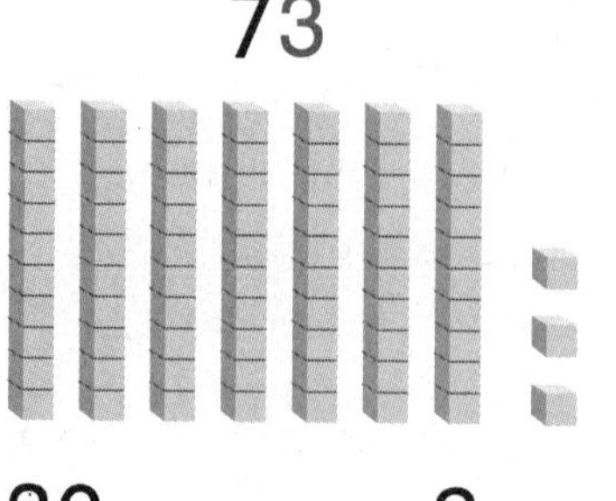

30 3

5. 24

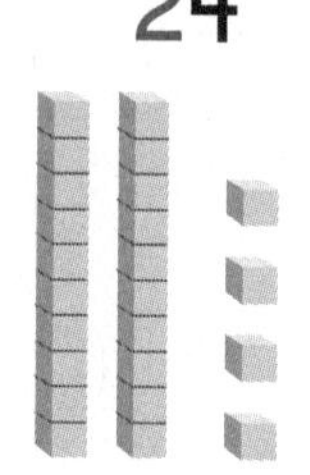
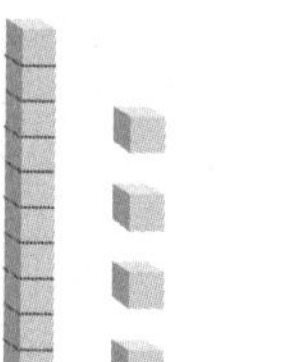

2 20

6. 61

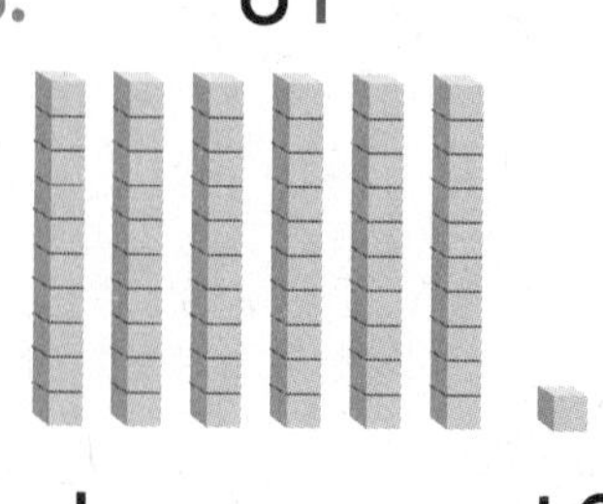

1 10

Name ________________________________

On Your Own

Circle the value of the red digit.

7. 51

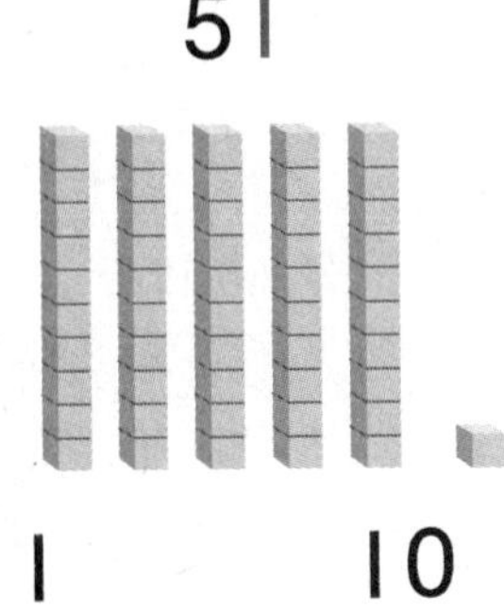

1 10

8. 49

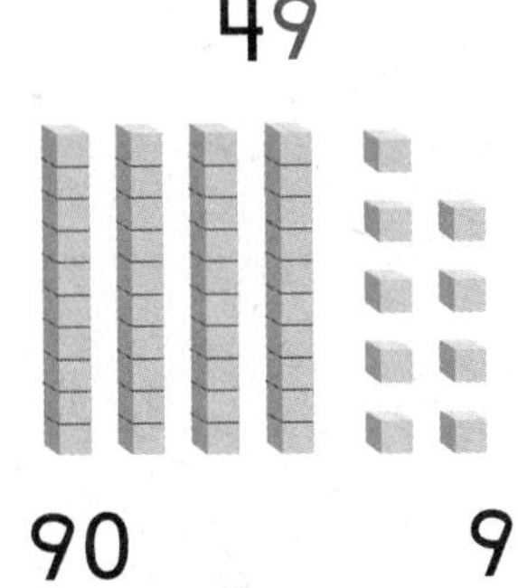

90 9

9. 70

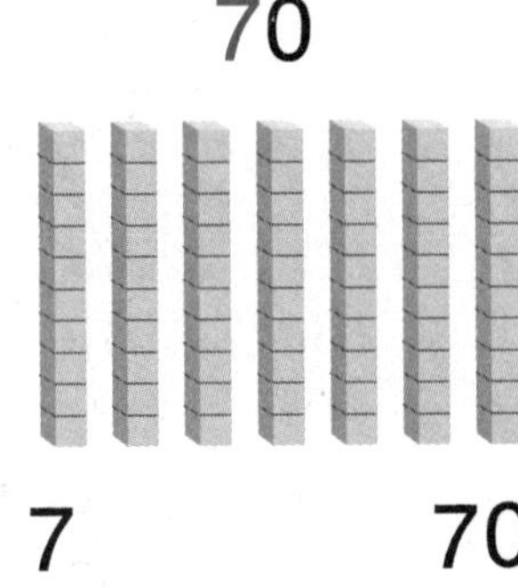

7 70

10. Phillip bought a puzzle. The number of puzzle pieces has the digit 6 in the ones place and the digit 3 in the tens place. How many puzzle pieces are in Phillip's puzzle?

_______ puzzle pieces

11. Noah baked apple pies. The number of apples he used has the digit 1 in the tens place and an even number less than 5 in the ones place. How many apples could Noah have used to bake apple pies?

_______ apples

12. THINK SMARTER Look at the digits of the numbers. Draw quick pictures for the missing blocks.

47

52

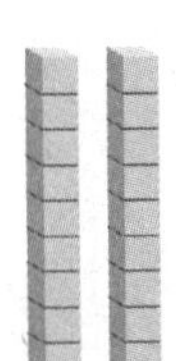

Problem Solving • Applications  

Write the 2-digit number that matches the clues.

13. My number has 8 tens.

The digit in the ones place is greater than the digit in the tens place.

My number is _______.

14. In my number, the digit in the ones place is double the digit in the tens place.

The sum of the digits is 3.

My number is _______.

15. MATHEMATICAL PRACTICE 1 Make Sense of Problems

In my number, both digits are even numbers.

The digit in the tens place is less than the digit in the ones place.

The sum of the digits is 6.

My number is _______.

16. THINKSMARTER What is the value of the digit 4 in the number 43?

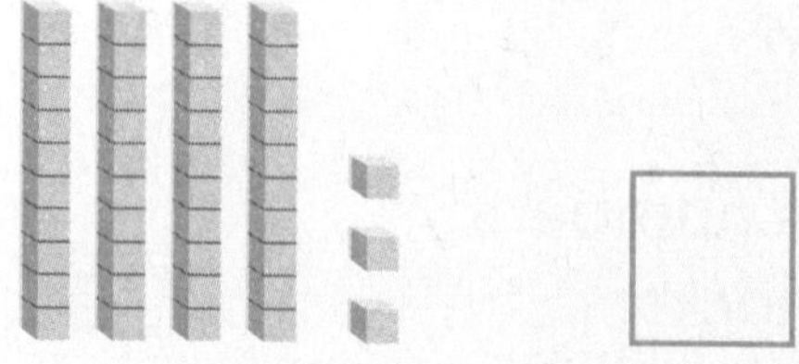

TAKE HOME ACTIVITY • Write the number 56. Have your child tell you which digit is in the tens place, which digit is in the ones place, and the value of each digit.

Name ______________________________

Understand Place Value

Common Core **COMMON CORE STANDARD—2.NBT.A.3**
Understand place value.

Circle the value of the underlined digit.

1. <u>2</u>3

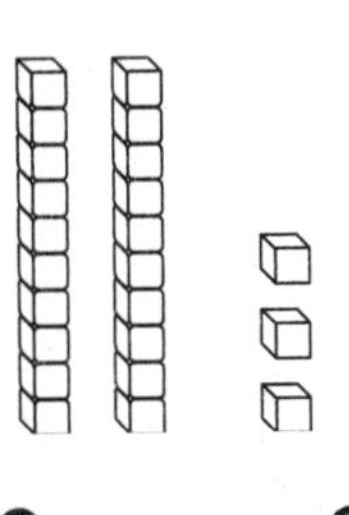

20 2

2. 4<u>8</u>

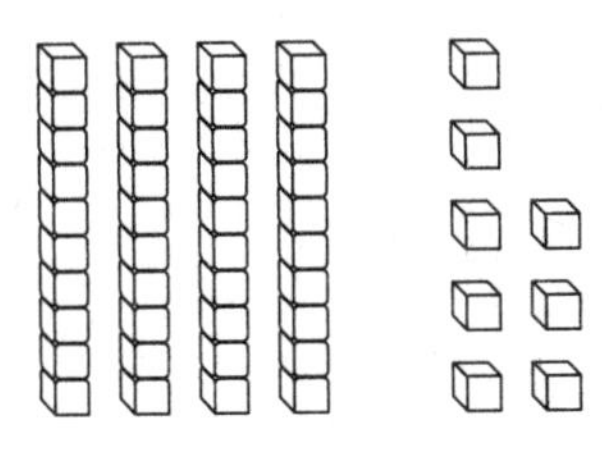

8 80

3. <u>1</u>8

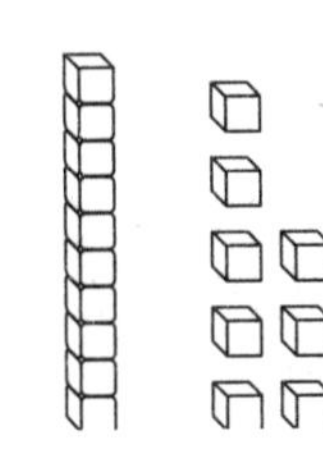

10 1

4. <u>4</u>3

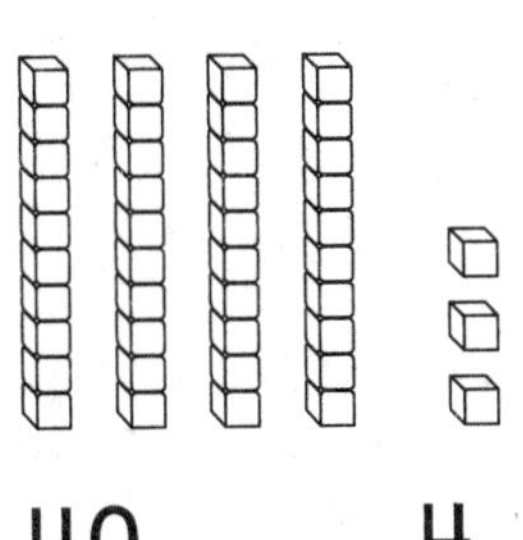

40 4

5. <u>5</u>4

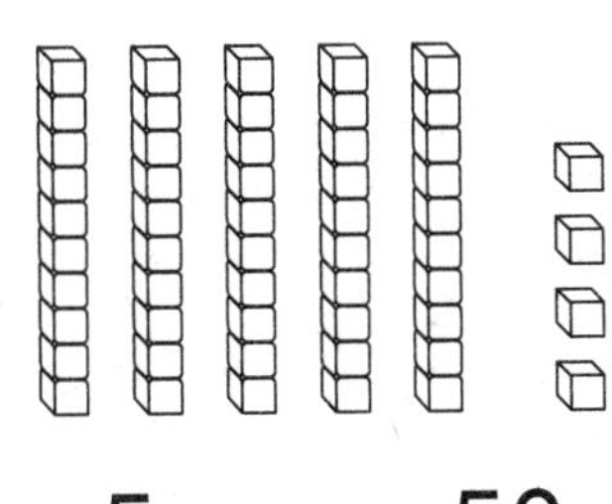

5 50

6. 6<u>5</u>

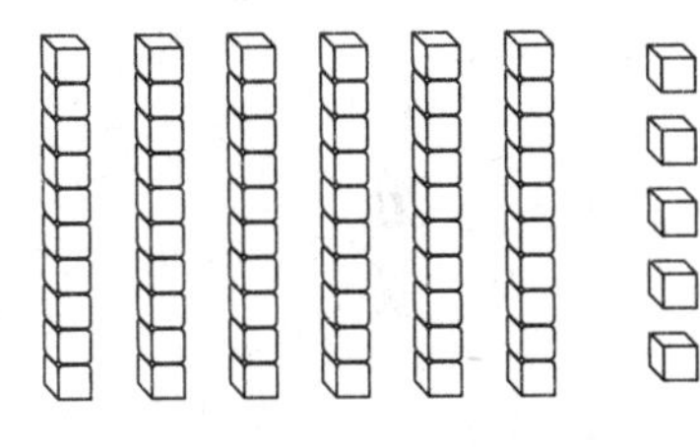

50 5

Problem Solving

Write the 2-digit number that matches the clues.

7. My number has a tens digit that is 8 more than the ones digit. Zero is not one of my digits.

My number is _____.

8. WRITE Math Draw a quick picture to show the number 76. Describe the value of each digit in this number.

Lesson Check (2.NBT.A.3)

1. What is the value of the underlined digit? Write the number.

$3\underline{2}$

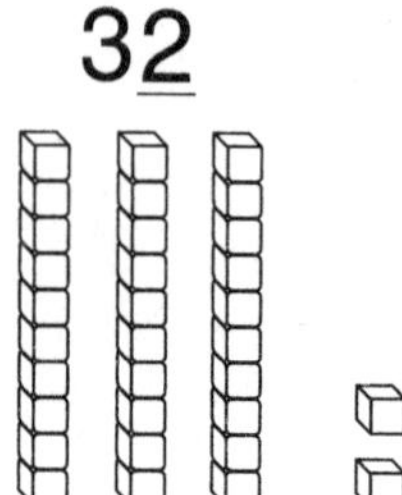

_____

2. What is the value of the underlined digit? Write the number.

$\underline{2}8$

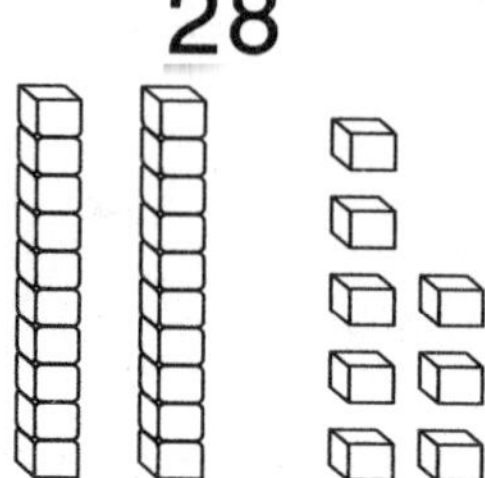

_____

Spiral Review (2.OA.C.3, 2.NBT.A.3)

3. What is the value of the underlined digit? Write the number.

$\underline{5}3$

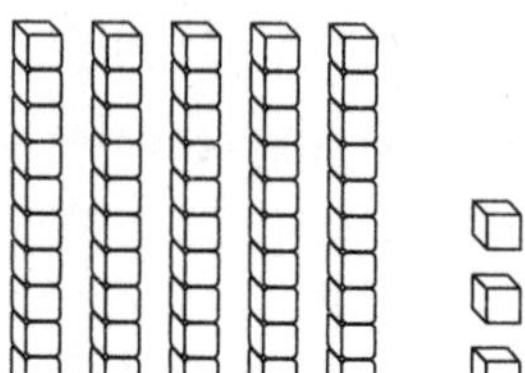

_____

4. What is the value of the underlined digit? Write the number.

$2\underline{4}$

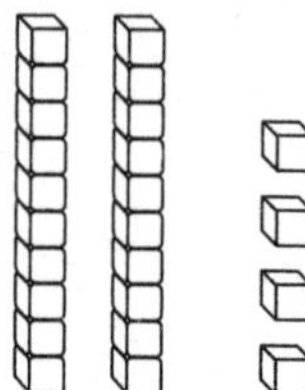

_____

5. Is the number of pens and pencils together even or odd? Write the number.
Circle even or odd.

2 pens + 3 pencils _____

even odd

6. Circle the sum that is an even number.

$5 + 2 =$ _____

$6 + 3 =$ _____

$7 + 4 =$ _____

$7 + 7 =$ _____

FOR MORE PRACTICE GO TO THE **Personal Math Trainer**

Name ______________________

Expanded Form

Essential Question How do you describe a 2-digit number as tens and ones?

Common Core **Number and Operations in Base Ten—2.NBT.A.3**
MATHEMATICAL PRACTICES
MP4, MP6

Use [tens block] [ones block] or *i*Tools to model each number.

Tens	Ones

Math Talk MATHEMATICAL PRACTICES 6

Explain how you know how many tens and ones are in the number 29.

FOR THE TEACHER • After you read the following problem, write 38 on the board. Have children model the number. Emmanuel put 38 stickers on his paper. How can you model 38 with blocks? Continue the activity for 83 and 77.

Model and Draw

What does 23 mean?

Tens	Ones

The 2 in 23 has a value of 2 tens, or 20.
The 3 in 23 has a value of 3 ones, or 3.

2 tens 3 ones

20 + 3

Share and Show MATH BOARD

Draw a quick picture to show the number.
Describe the number in two ways.

1. 37

_____ tens _____ ones

_____ + _____

2. 54

_____ tens _____ ones

_____ + _____

3. 16

_____ ten _____ ones

_____ + _____

4. 60

_____ tens _____ ones

_____ + _____

Name ______________________________

On Your Own

Draw a quick picture to show the number.
Describe the number in two ways.

5. 48

_______ tens _______ ones

_______ + _______

6. 31

_______ tens _______ one

_______ + _______

7. Riley has some toy dinosaurs. The number she has is one less than 50. Describe the number of toy dinosaurs in two ways.

____

____

Solve. Write or draw to explain.

8. THINK SMARTER Eric has 4 bags of 10 marbles and 6 single marbles. How many marbles does Eric have?

_______ marbles

Problem Solving • Applications

MATHEMATICAL PRACTICE 6 **Make Connections**

Use crayons. Follow the steps.

9. Start at 51 and draw a green line to 43.
10. Draw a blue line from 43 to 34.
11. Draw a red line from 34 to 29.
12. Then draw a yellow line from 29 to 72.

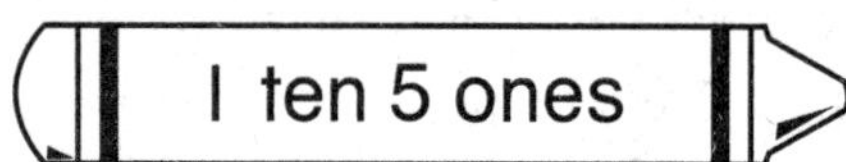

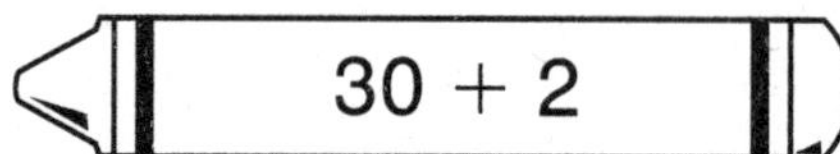

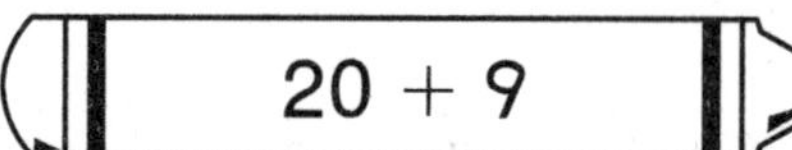

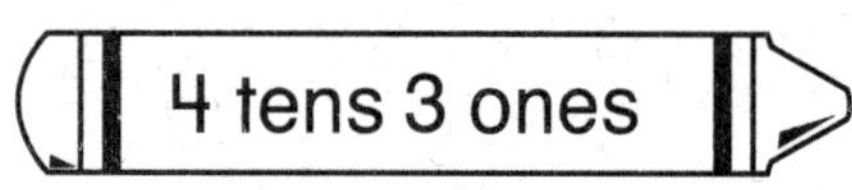

3 tens 4 ones

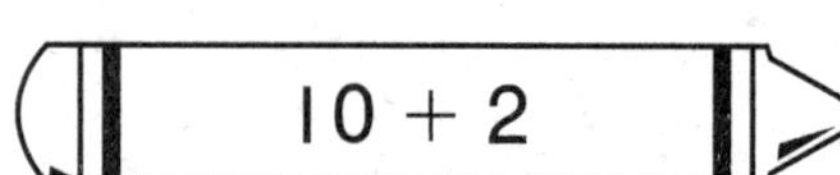

5 tens 1 one

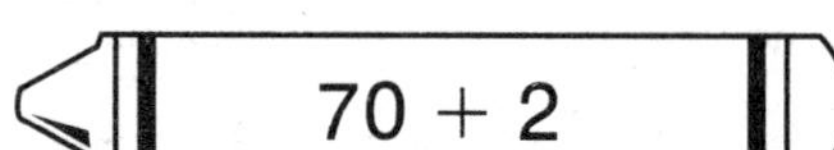

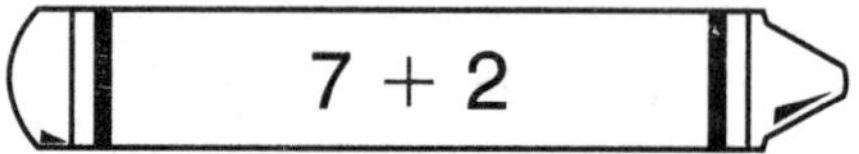

13. THINK SMARTER Draw a picture to show the number 26. Describe the number 26 in two ways.

________ tens ________ ones

________ + ________

TAKE HOME ACTIVITY • Ask your child to write 89 as tens plus ones. Then have him or her write 25 as tens plus ones.

Name ______________________

Expanded Form

Common Core COMMON CORE STANDARD—2.NBT.A.3
Understand place value.

Draw a quick picture to show the number. Describe the number in two ways.

1. 68

____ tens ____ ones

____ + ____

2. 21

____ tens ____ one

____ + ____

3. 70

____ tens ____ ones

____ + ____

4. 53

____ tens ____ ones

____ + ____

Problem Solving

5. Circle the ways to write the number shown by the model.

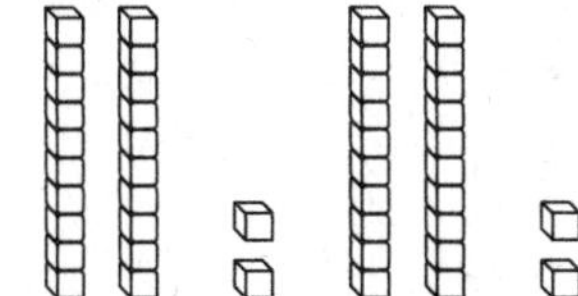

4 tens 6 ones	40 + 6	64
6 tens 4 ones	60 + 4	46

6. WRITE Math Explain how you know the values of the digits in the number 58.

____

____

Lesson Check (2.NBT.A.3)

1. Describe the number 92 in tens and ones.

_____ tens _____ ones

2. Describe the number 45 in tens and ones.

_____ tens _____ ones

Spiral Review (2.NBT.A.3)

3. What is the value of the underlined digit? Write the number.

$\underline{4}9$

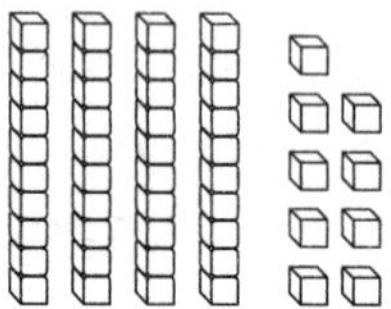

_____

4. What is the value of the underlined digit? Write the number.

$3\underline{4}$

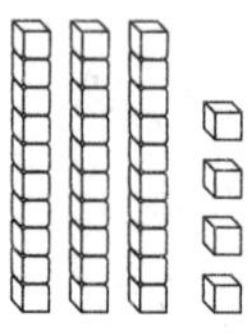

_____

5. Describe the number 76 in another way.

_____ tens _____ ones

6. Describe the number 52 in another way.

_____ tens _____ ones

Name ______________________________

Different Ways to Write Numbers

Essential Question What are different ways to write a 2-digit number?

Common Core **Number and Operations in Base Ten—2.NBT.A.3**

MATHEMATICAL PRACTICES **MP1, MP6**

Listen and Draw Real World

Write the number.
Then write it as tens and ones.

______ tens ______ ones

______ + ______

______ + ______

______ tens ______ ones

MATHEMATICAL PRACTICES

Analyze In 44, do both digits have the same value? Explain.

FOR THE TEACHER • Read the following problem. Taryn counted 53 books on the table. How many tens and ones are in 53? Continue the activity with the numbers 78, 35, and 40.

Model and Draw

A number can be written in different ways.

fifty-nine

5 tens 9 ones

50 + 9

59

ones	teen words	tens
0 zero	11 eleven	10 ten
1 one	12 twelve	20 twenty
2 two	13 thirteen	30 thirty
3 three	14 fourteen	40 forty
4 four	15 fifteen	50 fifty
5 five	16 sixteen	60 sixty
6 six	17 seventeen	70 seventy
7 seven	18 eighteen	80 eighty
8 eight	19 nineteen	90 ninety
9 nine		

Share and Show

Look at the examples above.
Then write the number another way.

1. thirty-two

____

2. 20 + 7

____

3. 63

_______ tens _______ ones

4. ninety-five

_______ + _______

5. 5 tens 1 one

____

6. seventy-six

_______ + _______

✓7. twenty-eight

_______ tens _______ ones

✓8. 8 tens 0 ones

____

Name ______________________________

On Your Own

Write the number another way.

9. 2 tens 4 ones

____

10. thirty

_______ tens _______ ones

11. eighty-five

____

12. 54

_______ + _______

13. Lee has a favorite number. The number has the digit 3 in the ones place and the digit 9 in the tens place. What is another way to write this number?

____

14. Dan's number has a digit greater than 5 in the ones place and a digit less than 5 in the tens place. What could be Dan's number?

____

THINKSMARTER Fill in the blanks to make the sentence true.

15. Sixty-seven is the same as _______ tens _______ ones.

16. 4 tens _______ ones is the same as _______ + _______.

17. 20 + _______ is the same as ______________________.

TAKE HOME ACTIVITY • Write 20 + 6 on a sheet of paper. Have your child write the 2-digit number. Repeat for 4 tens 9 ones.

Name ________________________________

Mid-Chapter Checkpoint

Concepts and Skills

Shade in the ten frames to show the number.
Circle **even** or **odd**. (2.OA.C.3)

1. 15

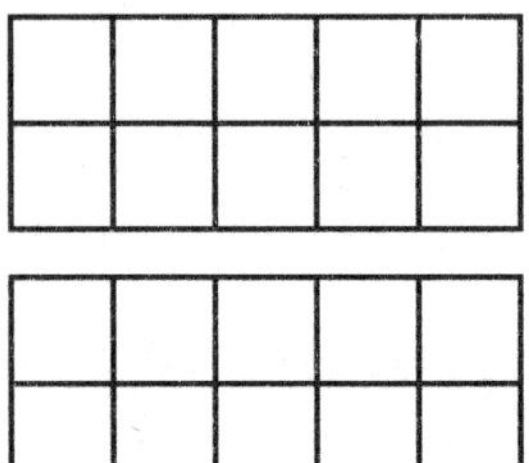

even odd

2. 18

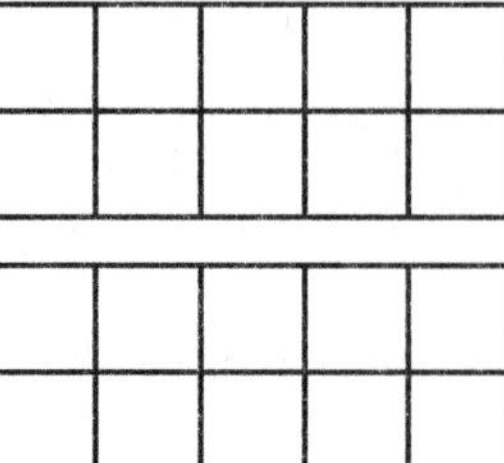

even odd

Draw a quick picture to show the number.
Describe the number in two ways. (2.NBT.A.3)

3. 35

_______ tens _______ ones

_______ + _______

4. 53

_______ tens _______ ones

_______ + _______

5. THINKSMARTER Write the number 42 in another way. (2.NBT.A.3)

____

Name ______________________

Different Ways to Write Numbers

Common Core **COMMON CORE STANDARD—2.NBT.A.3**
Understand place value.

Write the number another way.

1. 32

   ____ tens ____ ones

2. forty-one

   ____

3. 9 tens 5 ones

   ____

4. 80 + 3

   ____

5. 57

   ____ tens ____ ones

6. seventy-two

   ____ + ____

7. 60 + 4

   ____

8. 4 tens 8 ones

   ____

Problem Solving

9. A number has the digit 3 in the ones place and the digit 4 in the tens place. Which of these is another way to write this number? Circle it.

   3 + 4   40 + 3   30 + 4

10. WRITE Math Write the number 63 in four different ways.

Lesson Check (2.NBT.A.3)

1. Write 3 tens 9 ones in another way.

____

2. Write the number eighteen in another way.

____

Spiral Review (2.NBT.A.3)

3. Write the number 47 in tens and ones.

_____ tens _____ ones

4. Write the number 95 in words.

____

5. What is the value of the underlined digit? Write the number.

6<u>1</u>

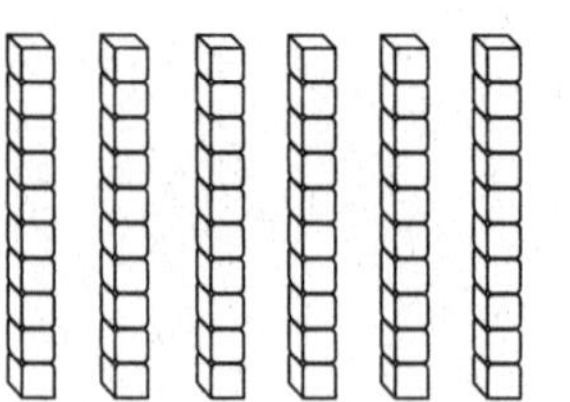

_____

6. What is the value of the underlined digit? Write the number.

<u>1</u>7

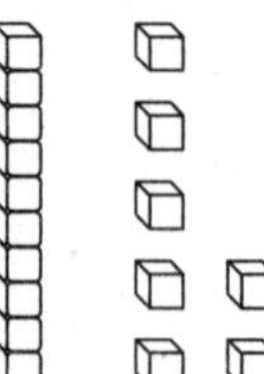

_____

FOR MORE PRACTICE GO TO THE Personal Math Trainer

Name ______________________________

Algebra • Different Names for Numbers

Essential Question How can you show the value of a number in different ways?

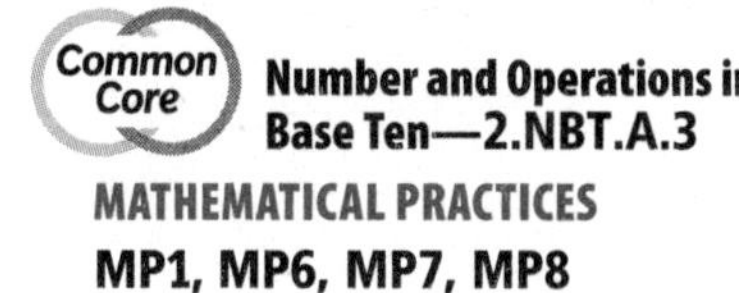

Listen and Draw

Use  to show the number different ways.
Record the tens and ones.

_______ tens _______ ones

_______ tens _______ ones

_______ tens _______ ones

FOR THE TEACHER • Read the following problem. Syed has 26 rocks. What are some different ways to show 26 with blocks? Have children start with 26 ones blocks. Then have them use base-ten blocks and record the number of tens and ones in each of their models.

Math Talk MATHEMATICAL PRACTICES 1

Describe how you can use addition to write the number 26.

Model and Draw

These are some different ways to show 32.

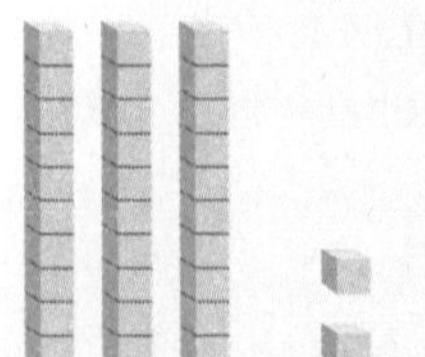

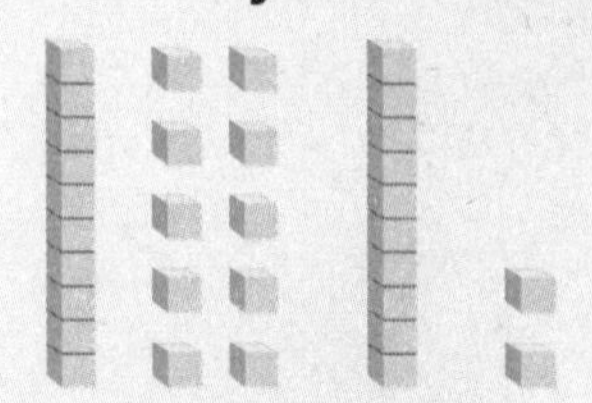

3 tens 2 ones	2 tens 12 ones	1 ten 22 ones
30 + 2	20 + 12	10 + 22

Share and Show 

The blocks show the numbers in different ways. Describe the blocks in two ways.

1. 28

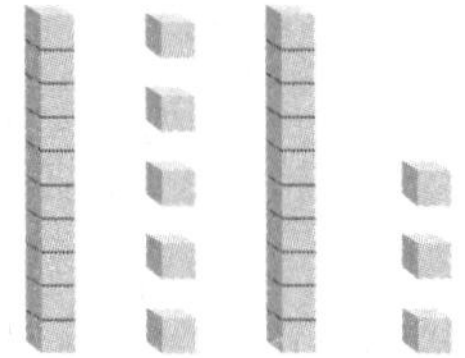

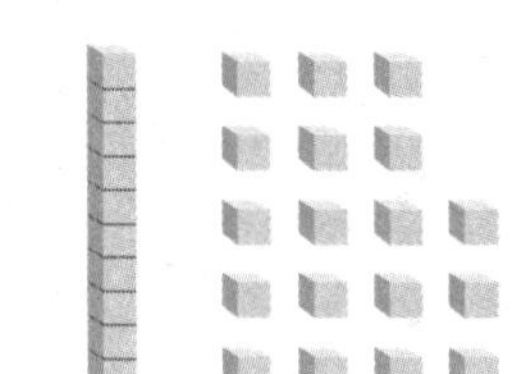

____ tens ____ ones	____ ten ____ ones	____ tens ____ ones
____ + ____	____ + ____	____ + ____

2. 35

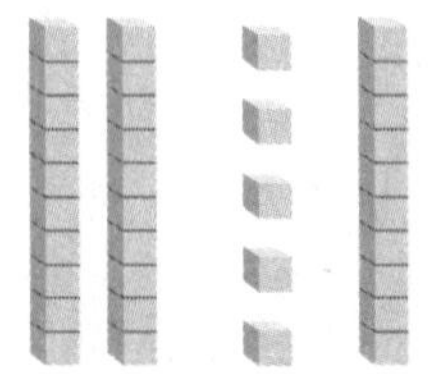

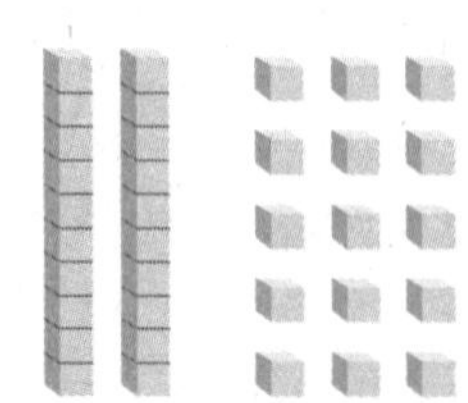

____ tens ____ ones	____ tens ____ ones	____ tens ____ ones
____ + ____	____ + ____	____ + ____

Name ______________________________

On Your Own

The blocks show the numbers in different ways.
Describe the blocks in two ways.

3. 43

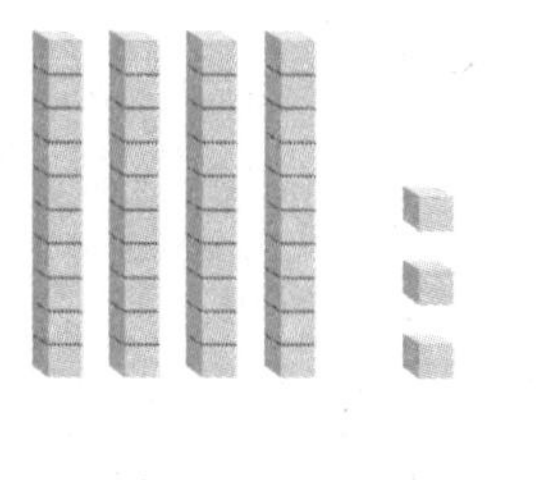

____ tens ____ ones

____ + ____

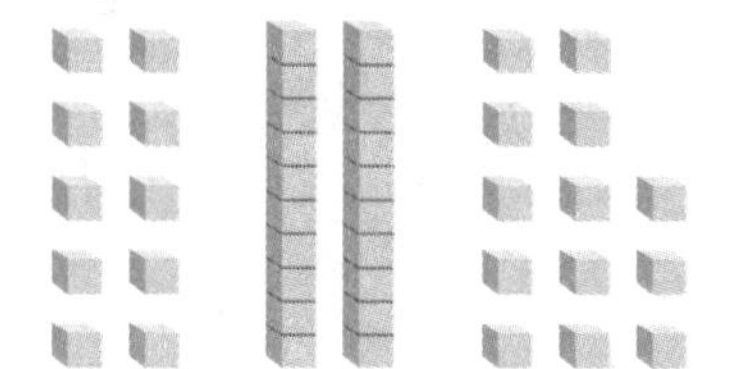

____ tens ____ ones

____ + ____

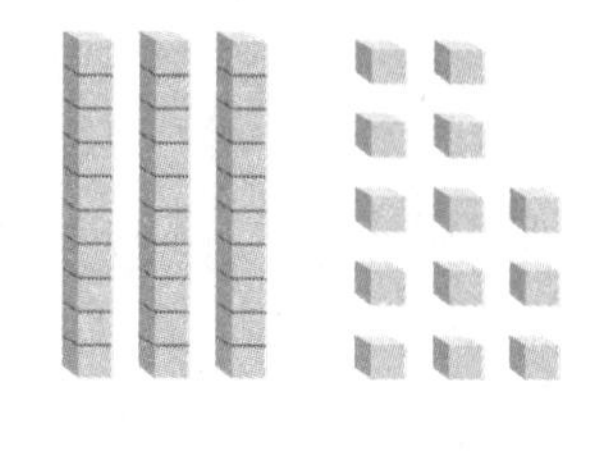

____ tens ____ ones

____ + ____

4. Roderick has 7 boxes of 10 cards and 4 single cards. How many cards does Roderick have?

________ cards

5. THINK SMARTER I have 2 bags of 10 oranges. I also have 24 single oranges. How many oranges do I have?

I have ______ oranges.

Draw a quick picture to show the number.

Problem Solving • Applications  

6. MATHEMATICAL PRACTICE 6 **Make Connections** Fill in the blanks to make each sentence true.

_______ tens _______ ones is the same as $90 + 3$.

2 tens 18 ones is the same as _______ + _______.

5 tens _______ ones is the same as _______ + 17.

7. GO DEEPER A number has the digit 4 in the ones place and the digit 7 in the tens place. Which of these show ways to write this number? Circle them.

$40 + 7$ $70 + 4$ seventy-four

4 tens 34 ones $4 + 7$ 4 tens 7 ones

8. THINK SMARTER Which of these is another way to show the number 42? Choose Yes or No for each.

1 ten 42 ones	○ Yes	○ No
$30 + 12$	○ Yes	○ No
2 tens 22 ones	○ Yes	○ No
3 tens 2 ones	○ Yes	○ No

TAKE HOME ACTIVITY • Write the number 45. Have your child write or draw two ways to show this number.

Name ______________________________

Algebra • Different Names for Numbers

COMMON CORE STANDARD—2.NBT.A.3
Understand place value.

The blocks show the number in different ways. Describe the blocks in two ways.

1. 24

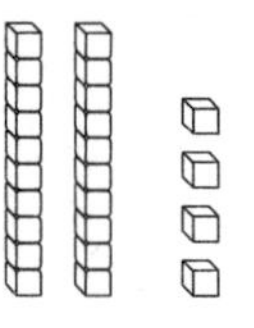

____ tens ____ ones

____ + ____

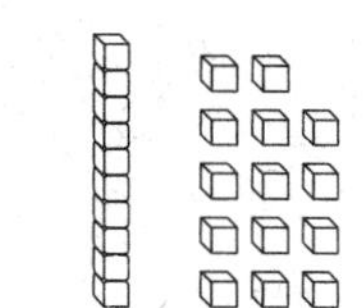

____ tens ____ ones

____ + ____

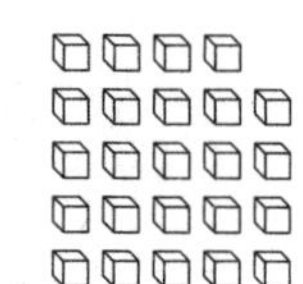

____ tens ____ ones

____ + ____

2. 36

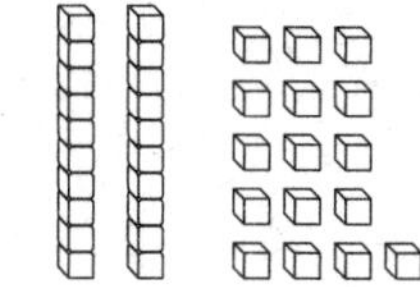

____ tens ____ ones

____ + ____

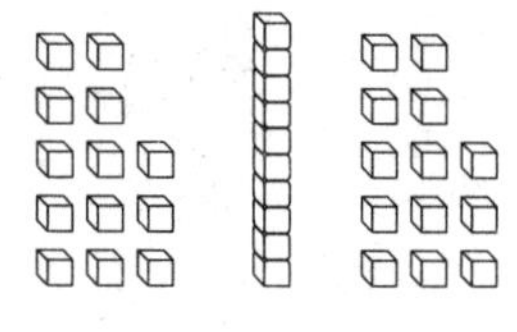

____ tens ____ ones

____ + ____

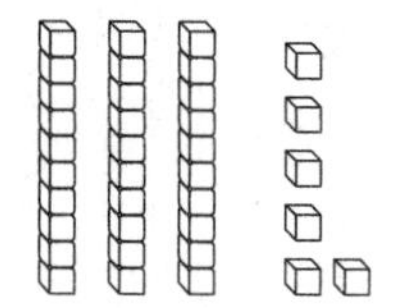

____ tens ____ ones

____ + ____

Problem Solving

3. Toni has these blocks. Circle the blocks that she could use to show 34.

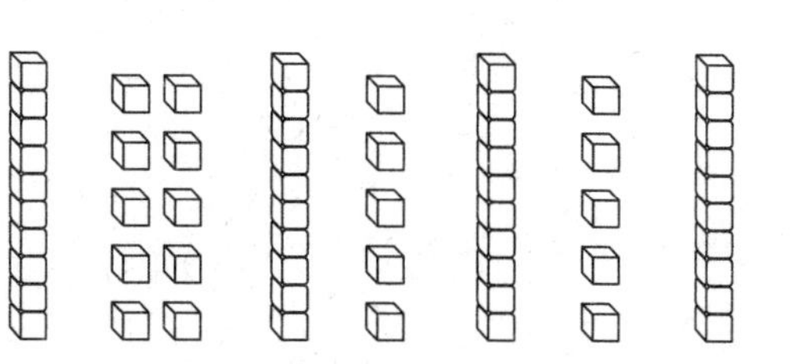

4. WRITE Math Draw quick pictures to show the number 38 in three different ways.

Lesson Check (2.NBT.A.3)

1. What number is shown with the blocks? Write the number.

2 tens 13 ones

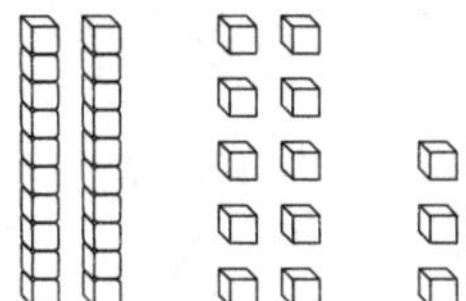

_____

2. What number is shown with the blocks? Write the number.

1 ten 16 ones

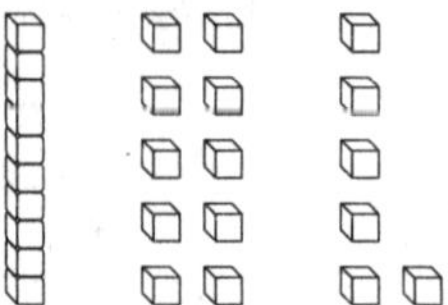

_____

Spiral Review (2.NBT.A.3)

3. What number is shown with the blocks? Write the number.

1 ten 17 ones

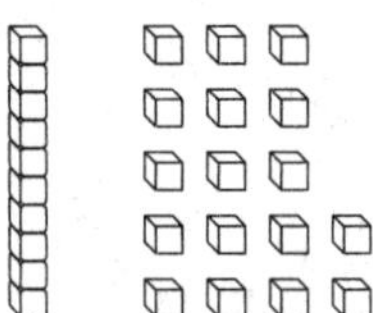

_____

4. What is the value of the underlined digit? Write the number.

2<u>9</u>

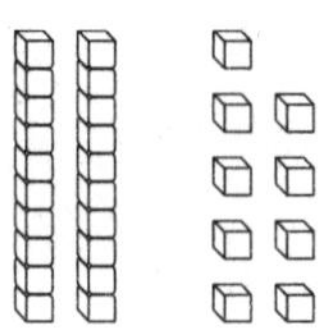

_____

5. Which is another way to write 9 tens 3 ones? Write the number.

_____

6. Describe the number 50 in tens and ones.

_____ tens _____ ones

FOR MORE PRACTICE GO TO THE Personal Math Trainer

Name ______________________

Problem Solving • Tens and Ones

Essential Question How does finding a pattern help you find all the ways to show a number with tens and ones?

Common Core **Number and Operations in Base Ten—2.NBT.A.3**
MATHEMATICAL PRACTICES
MP1, MP4, MP7

Gail needs to buy 32 pencils. She can buy single pencils or boxes of 10 pencils. What are all of the different ways Gail can buy 32 pencils?

Unlock the Problem (Real World)

What do I need to find?

ways Gail can buy
32 pencils

What information do I need to use?

She can buy single pencils or boxes of 10 pencils.

Show how to solve the problem.

Draw quick pictures for 32. Complete the chart.

Boxes of 10 pencils	Single pencils
3	2
2	12
1	
0	

HOME CONNECTION • Your child found a pattern in the different combinations of tens and ones. Using a pattern helps to make an organized list.

Try Another Problem

- What do I need to find?
- What information do I need to use?

Find a pattern to solve.

1. Sara has 36 crayons. She can pack them in boxes of 10 crayons or as single crayons. What are all of the ways Sara can pack the crayons?

Boxes of 10 crayons	Single crayons
3	6

2. Mr. Winter is putting away 48 chairs. He can put away the chairs in stacks of 10 or as single chairs. What are all of the ways Mr. Winter can put away the chairs?

Stacks of 10 chairs	Single chairs
4	8

Math Talk MATHEMATICAL PRACTICES 7

Look for Structure
Describe a pattern you can use to write the number 32.

Name ___________________________

Share and Show

Find a pattern to solve.

3. Philip is putting 25 markers into a bag. He can put the markers in the bag as bundles of 10 or as single markers. What are all of the ways Philip can put the markers in the bag?

Bundles of 10 markers	Single markers

4. Stickers are sold in packs of 10 stickers or as single stickers. Miss Allen wants to buy 33 stickers. What are all of the ways she can buy the stickers?

Packs of 10 stickers	Single stickers

5. THINKSMARTER Devin had 32 baseball cards. He gets 7 more cards. He can pack them in boxes of 10 cards or as single cards. What are all of the ways Devin can sort the cards?

Boxes of 10 cards	Single cards

On Your Own

Solve. Write or draw to explain.

6. MATHEMATICAL PRACTICE 7 **Look for Structure**
Lee can pack her toy cars in boxes of 10 cars or as single cars. Which of these is a way that she can pack her 24 toy cars? Circle your answer.

4 boxes of 10 cars and 2 single cars	1 box of 10 cars and 24 single cars	2 boxes of 10 cars and 4 single cars

Personal Math Trainer

7. THINKSMARTER+ Mr. Link needs 30 cups. He can buy them in packs of 10 cups or as single cups. What are all of the different ways he can buy the cups? Find a pattern to solve.

Packs of 10 cups	Single cups

Choose two of the ways from the chart. Explain how these two ways show the same number of cups.

TAKE HOME ACTIVITY • Have your child explain how he or she solved one of the exercises in this lesson.

Name ______________________

Problem Solving • Tens and Ones

Common Core **COMMON CORE STANDARD—2.NBT.A.3**
Understand place value.

Find a pattern to solve.

1. Ann is grouping 38 rocks. She can put them into groups of 10 rocks or as single rocks. What are the different ways Ann can group the rocks?

Groups of 10 rocks	Single rocks

2. Mr. Grant needs 30 pieces of felt. He can buy them in packs of 10 or as single pieces. What are the different ways Mr. Grant can buy the felt?

Packs of 10 pieces	Single pieces

3. WRITE Math Choose one of the problems above. Describe how you organized the answers.

____

____

____

____

____

____

Lesson Check (2.NBT.A.3)

1. Mrs. Chang is packing 38 apples. She can pack them in bags of 10 or as single apples. Complete the table to show another way Mrs. Chang can pack the apples.

Bags of 10 apples	Single apples
2	18
1	28
0	38

Spiral Review (2.NBT.A.3)

2. What is the value of the underlined digit? Write the number.

<u>5</u>4

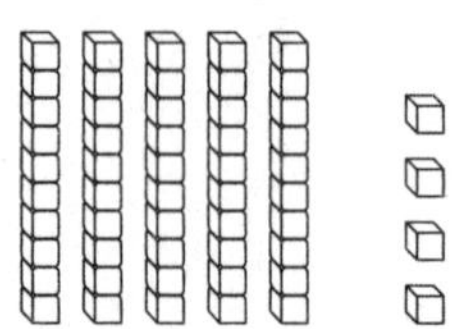

____

3. What number is shown with the blocks? Write the number.

2 tens 19 ones

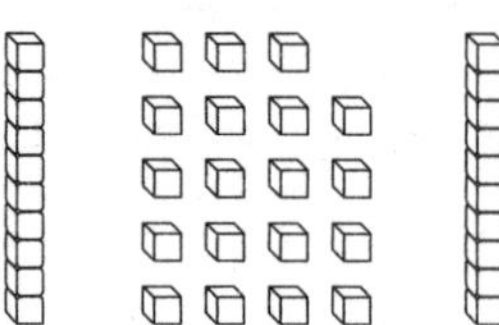

____

4. Write the number 62 in words.

____

5. What number can be written as 8 tens and 6 ones? Write the number.

____

FOR MORE PRACTICE GO TO THE Personal Math Trainer

Name ______________________

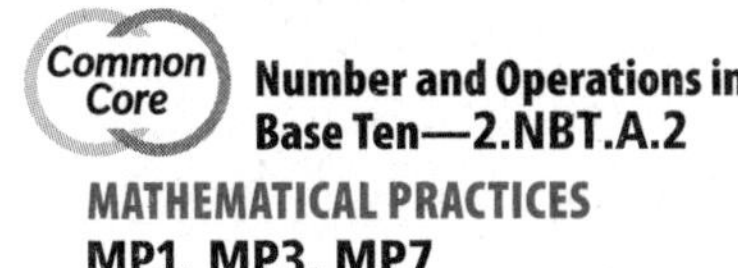

Counting Patterns Within 100

Essential Question How do you count by 1s, 5s, and 10s with numbers less than 100?

Common Core **Number and Operations in Base Ten—2.NBT.A.2**

MATHEMATICAL PRACTICES
MP1, MP3, MP7

Listen and Draw

Look at the hundred chart. Write the missing numbers.

1	2	3		5	6		8		10
11		13	14	15	16		18	19	20
	22	23	24		26	27	28	29	30
31	32		34	35	36		38	39	
41		43	44	45	46	47		49	50
51		53		55		57		59	60
	62		64	65	66	67	68		70
71	72	73	74		76		78	79	
81		83		85	86	87	88	89	90
	92		94	95	96		98		100

MATHEMATICAL PRACTICES 1

Describe some different ways to find the missing numbers in the chart.

FOR THE TEACHER • Have children complete the hundred chart to review counting to 100.

Model and Draw

You can count on by different amounts.
You can start counting with different numbers.

Count by ones.

1, 2, 3, 4, 5, 6, ____, ____

29, 30, 31, 32, 33, ____, ____, ____

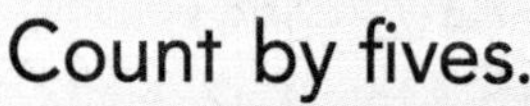

Count by fives.

5, 10, 15, 20, ____, ____, ____, ____

50, 55, 60, 65, ____, ____, ____, ____

Share and Show

Count by ones.

1. 15, 16, 17, ____, ____, ____, ____, ____

Count by fives.

2. 15, 20, 25, ____, ____, ____, ____, ____

3. 60, 65, ____, ____, ____, ____, ____

Count by tens.

4. 10, 20, ____, ____, ____, ____, ____

5. 30, 40, ____, ____, ____, ____, ____

Name ______________________________

On Your Own

Count by ones.

6. 77, 78, ______, ______, ______, ______, ______

Count by fives.

7. 35, 40, ______, ______, ______, ______, ______

Count by tens.

8. 20, 30, ______, ______, ______, ______, ______

9. Amber counts by fives to 50.
How many numbers will she say?

______ numbers

10. THINK SMARTER Dinesh counts by fives to 100.
Gwen counts by tens to 100.
Who will say more numbers? Explain.

____

____

____

____

____

Problem Solving • Applications  

MATHEMATICAL PRACTICE 1 Analyze

11. Andy counts by ones. He starts at 29 and stops at 45. Which of these numbers will he say? Circle them.

31 20 47 35 46 40 39

12. Camila counts by fives. She starts at 5 and stops at 50. Which of these numbers will she say? Circle them.

55 25 6 40 18 10 45

13. THINKSMARTER Grace starts at the number 40 and counts three different ways. Write to show how Grace counts.

Count by ones. 40, ____, ____, ____, ____, ____, ____

Count by fives. 40, ____, ____, ____, ____, ____, ____

Count by tens. 40, ____, ____, ____, ____, ____, ____

TAKE HOME ACTIVITY • With your child, practice counting by ones to 100, starting with numbers such as 58 or 62.

Name ____________________

Counting Patterns Within 100

COMMON CORE STANDARD—2.NBT.A.2
Understand place value.

Count by ones.

1. 58, 59, ____, ____, ____, ____, ____

Count by fives.

2. 45, 50, ____, ____, ____, ____, ____

3. 20, 25, ____, ____, ____, ____, ____

Count by tens.

4. 20, ____, ____, ____, ____, ____, ____

Count back by ones.

5. 87, 86, 85, ____, ____, ____

Problem Solving

6. Tim counts his friends' fingers by fives. He counts six hands. What numbers does he say?

5, ____, ____, ____, ____, ____

7. WRITE Math Count by 1s or 5s. Write the first five numbers you would count, starting at 15.

Lesson Check (2.NBT.A.2)

1. Count by fives.

70, ____, ____, ____, ____

2. Count by tens.

60, ____, ____, ____, ____

Spiral Review (2.OA.C.3, 2.NBT.A.2, 2.NBT.A.3)

3. Count back by ones.

21, ____, ____, ____, ____

4. A number has 2 tens and 15 ones. Write the number in words.

____

5. Describe the number 72 in tens and ones.

____ tens ____ ones

6. Find the sum. Is the sum even or odd? Write even or odd.

$9 + 9 =$ ____

____

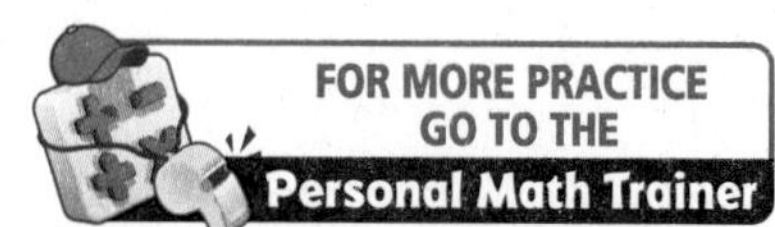

Name ______________________

Counting Patterns Within 1,000

Essential Question How do you count by 1s, 5s, 10s, and 100s with numbers less than 1,000?

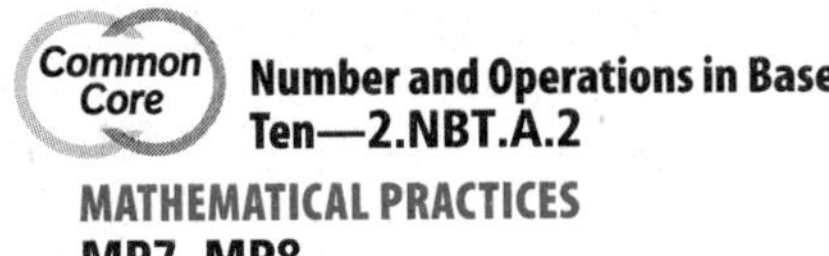

Number and Operations in Base Ten—2.NBT.A.2

MATHEMATICAL PRACTICES
MP7, MP8

Listen and Draw

Write the missing numbers in the chart.

401		403	404		406	407	408		410
411				415	416	417	418	419	
421	422	423	424	425		427	428	429	430
	432		434	435	436	437	438		
441	442	443	444		446	447		449	450
			454	455	456	457	458	459	460
461	462						468	469	470
	472	473	474	475	476	477		479	480
481	482		484	485	486				490
	492	493		495	496	497	498		

FOR THE TEACHER • Have children complete the number chart to practice counting with 3-digit numbers.

MATHEMATICAL PRACTICES 7

Look for Structure
What counting patterns could you use to complete the chart?

Model and Draw

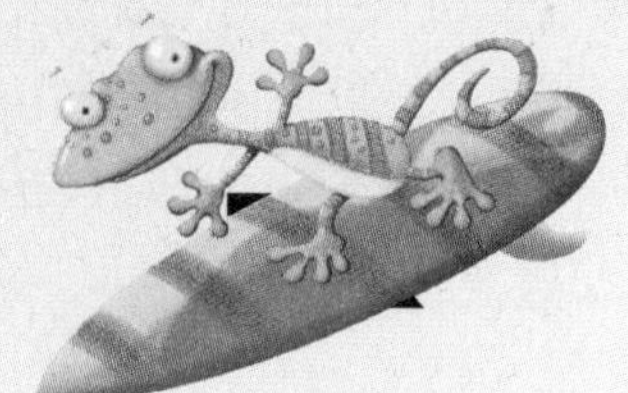

Counting can be done in different ways.
Use patterns to count on.

Count by fives.

95, 100, 105, 110, 115, ______, ______

140, 145, 150, 155, ______, ______, ______

Count by tens.

300, 310, 320, ______, ______, ______, ______

470, 480, 490, ______, ______, ______, ______

Share and Show

Count by fives.

1. 745, 750, 755, ______, ______, ______, ______

Count by tens.

2. 520, 530, 540, ______, ______, ______, ______

3. 600, 610, ______, ______, ______, ______, ______

Count by hundreds.

4. 100, 200, ______, ______, ______, ______, ______

5. 300, 400, ______, ______, ______, ______, ______

Name ______________________

On Your Own

Count by fives.

6. 215, 220, 225, ______, ______, ______, ______

7. 905, 910, ______, ______, ______, ______, ______

Count by tens.

8. 730, 740, 750, ______, ______, ______, ______

9. 160, 170, ______, ______, ______, ______, ______

Count by hundreds.

10. 200, 300, ______, ______, ______, ______, ______

11. THINK SMARTER Martin starts at 300 and counts by fives to 420. What are the last 6 numbers Martin will say?

______, ______, ______, ______, ______, ______

12. The book fair has 390 books. They have 5 more boxes with 10 books in each box. Count by tens. How many books are at the book fair.

______ books

Problem Solving • Applications

Look for a Pattern

13. Lisa counts by fives. She starts at 120 and stops at 175. Which of these numbers will she say? Circle them.

170 151 135

155 200 180

14. George counts by tens. He starts at 750 and stops at 830. Which of these numbers will he say? Circle them.

755 690 780

760 795 810

15. THINKSMARTER Carl counts by hundreds. Which of these show ways that Carl could count? Choose Yes or No for each.

100, 110, 120, 130, 140	○ Yes	○ No
100, 200, 300, 400, 500	○ Yes	○ No
500, 600, 700, 800, 900	○ Yes	○ No
300, 305, 310, 315, 320	○ Yes	○ No

TAKE HOME ACTIVITY • With your child, count by fives from 150 to 200.

Name ______________________

Counting Patterns Within 1,000

Common Core **COMMON CORE STANDARD—2.NBT.A.2**
Understand place value.

Count by fives.

1. 415, 420, ______, ______, ______, ______

2. 675, 680, ______, ______, ______, ______, ______

Count by tens.

3. 210, 220, ______, ______, ______, ______, ______

Count by hundreds.

4. 300, 400, ______, ______, ______, ______, ______

Count back by ones.

5. 953, 952, ______, ______, ______, ______, ______

Problem Solving

6. Lee has a jar of 100 pennies.
She adds groups of 10 pennies to the jar.
She adds 5 groups. What numbers does she say?

______, ______, ______, ______, ______

7. WRITE Math Count by fives from 135 to 175. Write these numbers and describe the pattern.

____

____

Lesson Check (2.NBT.A.2)

1. Count by tens.

160, ____, ____, ____, ____

2. Count by hundreds.

400, ____, ____, ____, ____

Spiral Review (2.NBT.A.2, 2.NBT.A.3)

3. Count by fives.

245, ____, ____, ____, ____

4. Count back by ones.

71, ____, ____, ____, ____

5. Describe 45 in another way.

____ tens ____ ones

6. Describe 7 tens 9 ones in another way.

____

Name ________________________________

Chapter 1 Review/Test

Personal Math Trainer
Online Assessment and Intervention

1. Does the ten frame show an even number? Choose Yes or No.

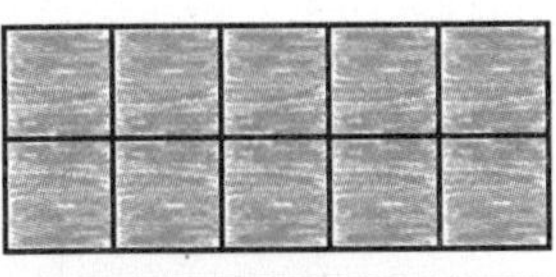

○ Yes ○ No

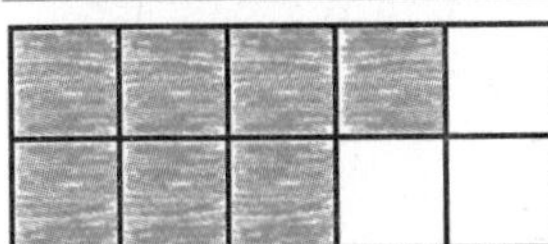

○ Yes ○ No

2. Write an even number between 7 and 16. Draw a picture and then write a sentence to explain why it is an even number.

____

____

3. What is the value of the digit 5 in the number 75?

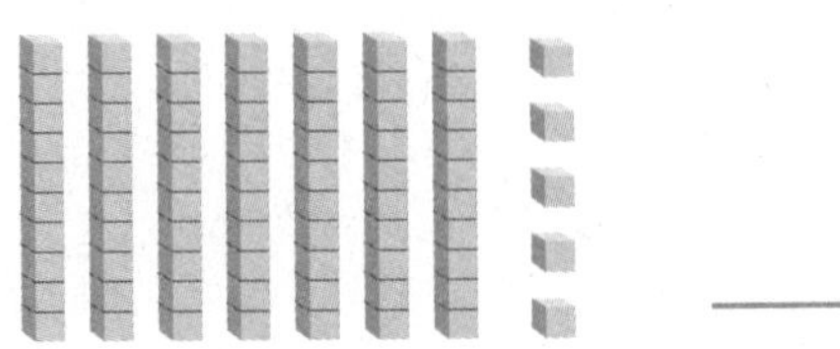

______

4. GO DEEPER Ted has an even number of yellow markers and an odd number of green markers. Choose all the groups of markers that could belong to Ted.

- ○ 8 yellow markers and 3 green markers
- ○ 3 yellow markers and 6 green markers
- ○ 4 yellow markers and 2 green markers
- ○ 6 yellow markers and 7 green markers

5. Jeff starts at 190 and counts by tens. What are the next 6 numbers Jeff will say?

190, ______, ______, ______, ______, ______, ______

6. Megan counts by ones to 10. Lee counts by fives to 20. Who will say more numbers? Explain.

____

____

____

Name ____________________

7. Draw a picture to show the number 43.

Describe the number 43 in two ways.

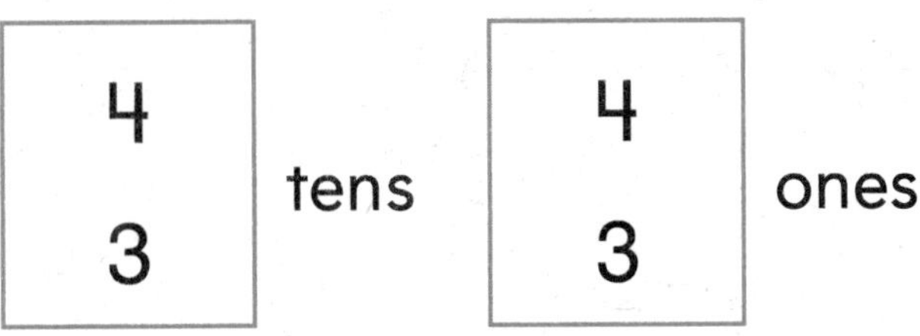

______ + ______

8. Jo lives on Maple Road. Her address has the digit 2 in the ones place and the digit 4 in the tens place. What is Jo's address?

______ Maple Road

9. Do the numbers show counting by fives? Choose Yes or No.

76, 77, 78, 79, 80	○ Yes	○ No
20, 30, 40, 50, 60	○ Yes	○ No
70, 75, 80, 85, 90	○ Yes	○ No
35, 40, 45, 50, 55	○ Yes	○ No

Personal Math Trainer

10. THINK SMARTER + Mrs. Payne needs 35 notepads. She can buy them in packs of 10 notepads or as single pads. What are all the different ways Mrs. Payne can buy the notepads? Find a pattern to solve.

Packs of 10 notepads	Single notepads

Choose two of the ways from the chart. Explain how these two ways show the same number of notepads.

11. Ann has a favorite number. It has a digit less than 4 in the tens place. It has a digit greater than 6 in the ones place. Could the number be Ann's number? Choose Yes or No.

30 + 9	○ Yes	○ No
sixty-seven	○ Yes	○ No
2 tens 8 ones	○ Yes	○ No

Write another number that could be Ann's favorite. ______

Chapter 2

Numbers to 1,000

Curious about Math

The White House has 412 doors and 147 windows. Look at the digit 1 in each of these numbers. How do the values of these digits compare?

Name ______________________________

Identify Numbers to 30

Write how many. (K.NBT.A.1)

1. 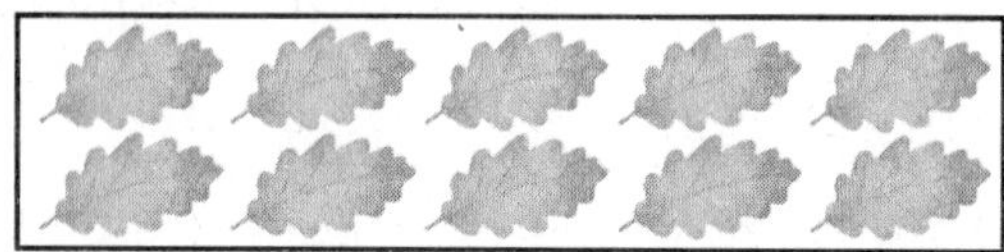

____ leaves

2. 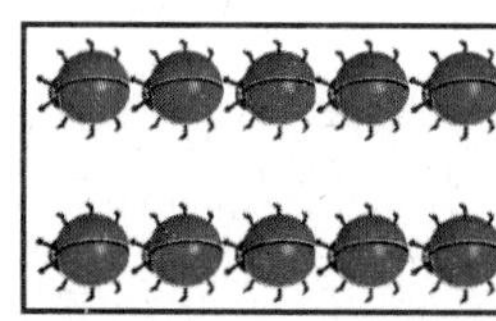 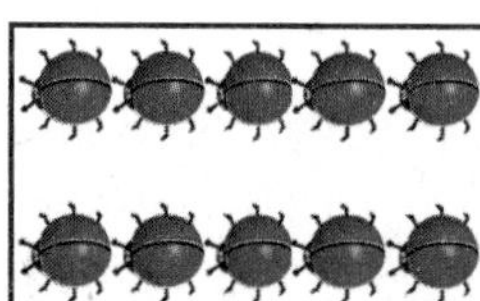 

____ bugs

Place Value: 2-Digit Numbers

Circle the value of the red digit. (2.NBT.A.3)

3. 47

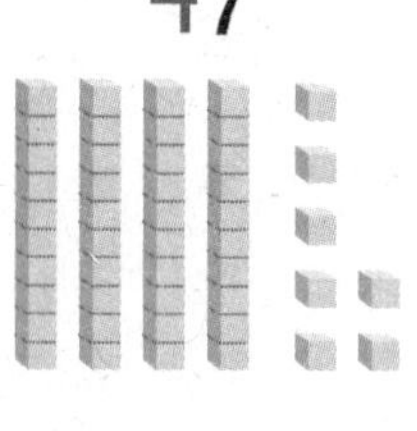

40 4

4. 84

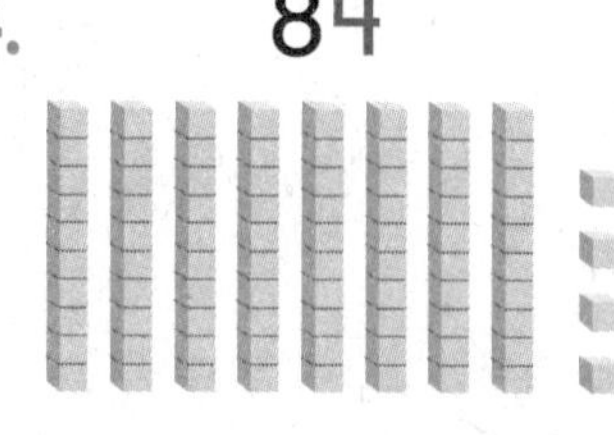

4 40

5. 65

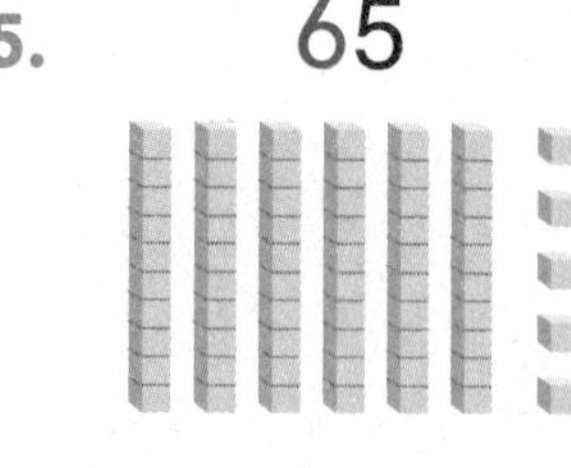

6 60

Compare 2-Digit Numbers Using Symbols

Compare. Write >, <, or =. (1.NBT.B.3)

6. 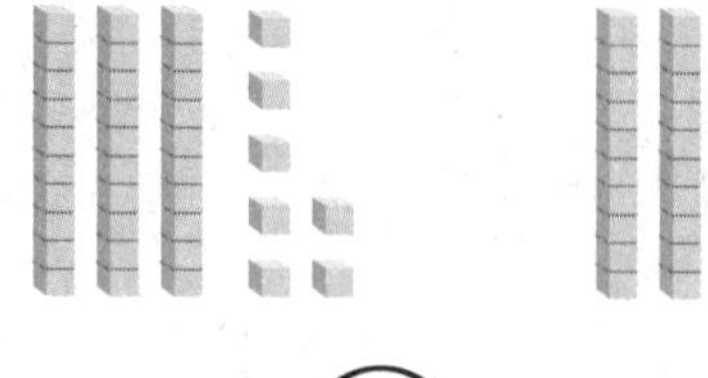

37 ◯ 42

7. 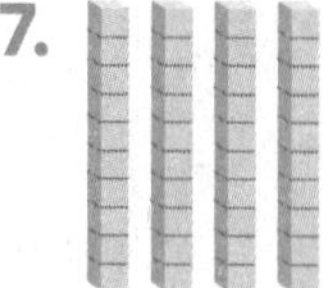
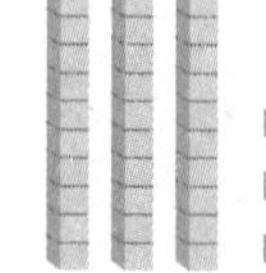

40 ◯ 33

This page checks understanding of important skills needed for success in Chapter 2.

Name ______________________________

Review Words

more
fewer
digits
tens
ones

Vocabulary Builder

Visualize It

Fill in the boxes of the graphic organizer.
Write sentences using **fewer** and **more.**

fewer
- 9 pens is fewer than 11 pens.
-

more
-
-

Understand Vocabulary

Use the review words. Complete the sentences.

1. 3 and 9 are ________________ in the number 39.

2. 7 is in the ________________ place in the number 87.

3. 8 is in the ________________ place in the number 87.

GO DIGITAL
- Interactive Student Edition
- Multimedia eGlossary

Chapter 2

Game Fish for Digits

Materials

- 12 ● • 12 ○ • 1 🎲

Play with a partner.

1. Name a place for a digit. You can say **tens place** or **ones place**. Toss the 🎲.
2. Match the number on the 🎲 and the place that you named with a fish.
3. Put a ● on that fish. Take turns.
4. Match all the fish. The player with more ● on the board wins.

14

56 12

46 25

23

32 53 65

61 41 34

Chapter 2 Vocabulary

English	Spanish	Page
compare	comparar	8
digit	dígito	15
hundred	centena	31
is equal to (=)	es igual a	33
is greater than (>)	es mayor que (>)	34
is less than (<)	es menor que (<)	35
ten	decena	61
thousand	millar	64

0, 1, 2, 3, 4, 5, 6, 7, 8, and 9 are **digits**.

Use these symbols when you **compare**: >, <, =.

241 > 234

123 < 128

247 = 247

2	plus	1	is equal to	3
2	+	1	=	3

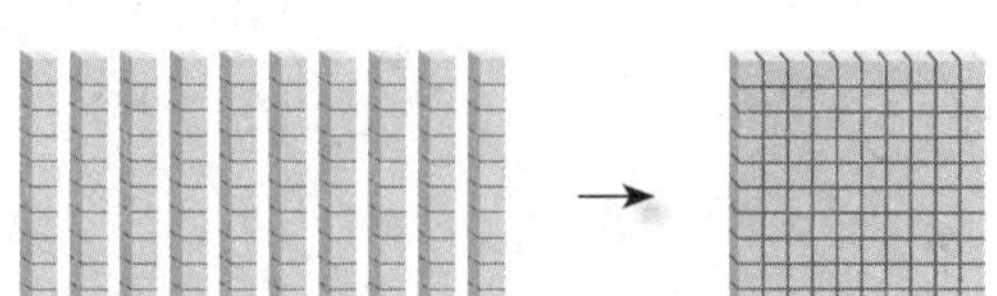

There are 10 tens in 1 **hundred**.

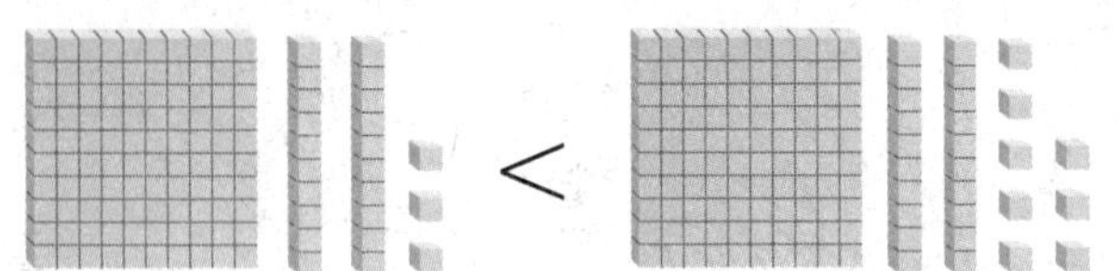

123 **is less than** 128.

123 < 128

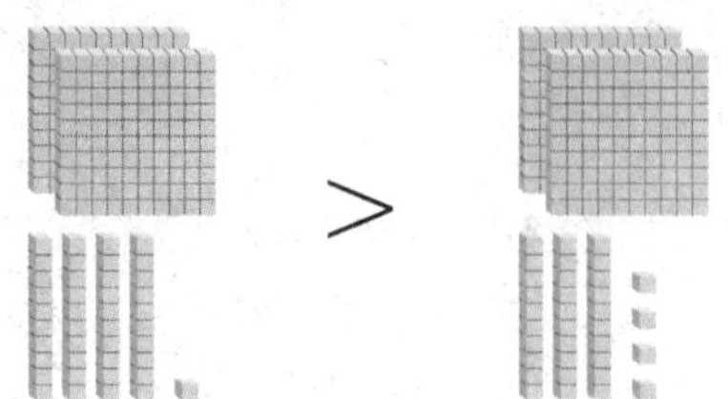

241 **is greater than** 234.

241 > 234

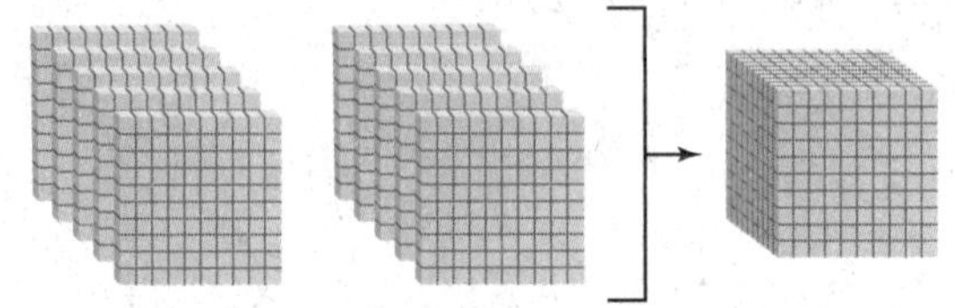

There are 10 hundreds in 1 **thousand**.

10 ones = 1 ten

Guess the Word

Word Box
compare
digit
hundred
is equal to (=)
is greater than (>)
is less than (<)
ten
thousand

For 3 to 4 players

Materials

- timer

How to Play

1. Take turns to play.
2. Choose a math word, but do not say it aloud.
3. Set the timer for 1 minute.
4. Give a one-word clue about your word. Give each player one chance to guess your word.
5. If nobody guesses correctly, repeat Step 4 with a different clue. Repeat until a player guesses the word or time runs out.
6. The first player to guess the word gets 1 point. If the player can use the word in a sentence, he or she gets 1 more point. Then that player gets a turn.
7. The first player to score 5 points wins.

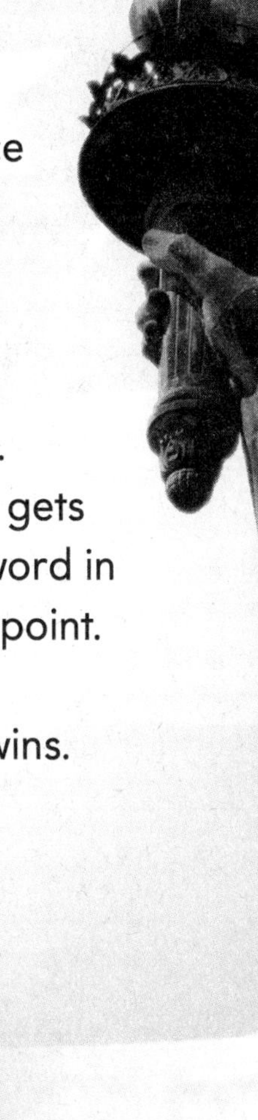

The Write Way

Reflect

Choose one idea. Write about it in the space below.

- Draw and write about all the different ways you can show the number 482. Use a separate piece of paper for your drawing.
- Explain how to compare two numbers.
- Write sentences that include at least two of these terms.

digit **is equal to** **hundred** **thousand**

Name ____________________

Group Tens as Hundreds

Essential Question How do you group tens as hundreds?

Common Core **Number and Operations in Base Ten—2.NBT.A.1a, 2.NBT.A.1b**

MATHEMATICAL PRACTICES
MP6, MP7, MP8

Listen and Draw Real World

Circle groups of ten. Count the groups of ten.

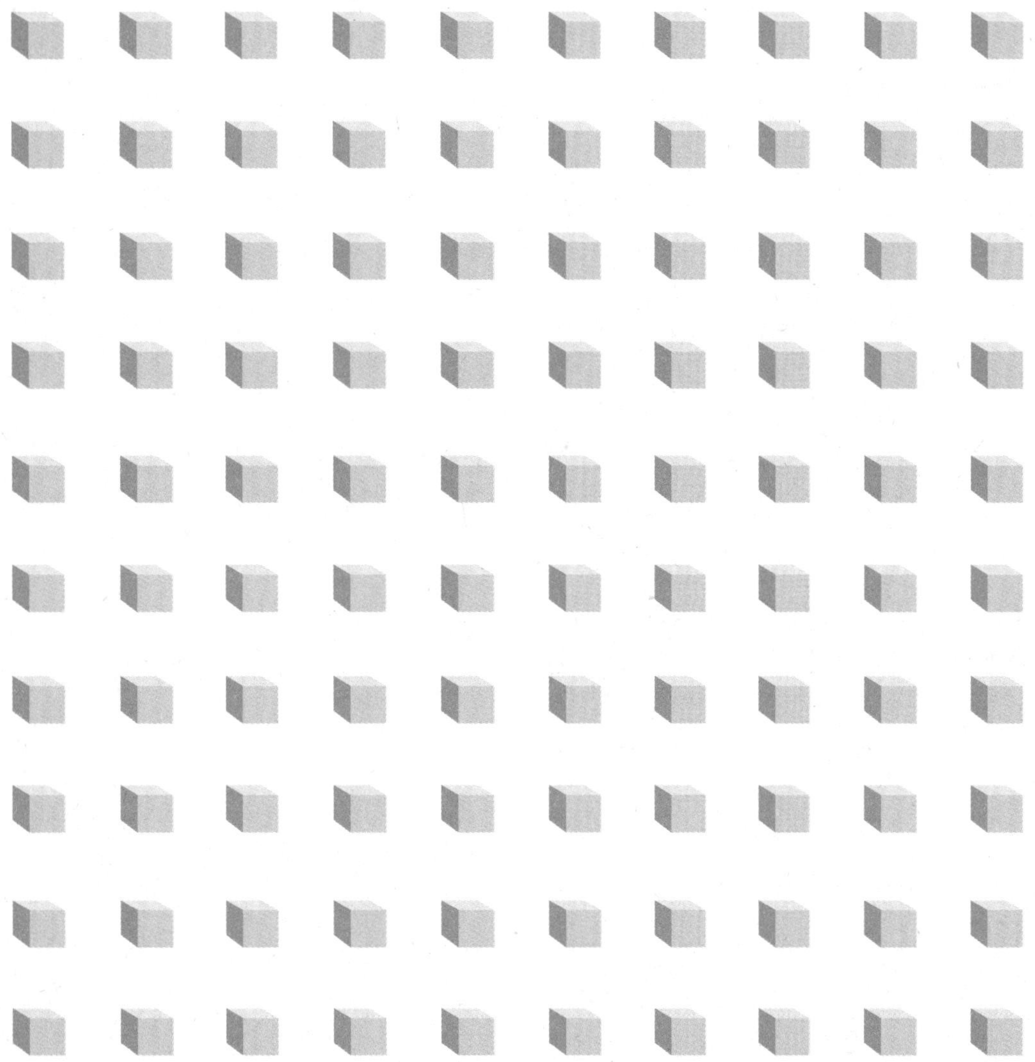

MATHEMATICAL PRACTICES 6

Describe How many ones are in 3 tens? How many ones are in 7 tens? Explain.

FOR THE TEACHER • Read the following problem and have children group ones blocks to solve. Marco has 100 cards. How many groups of 10 cards can he make?

Model and Draw

10 tens is the same as 1 **hundred**.

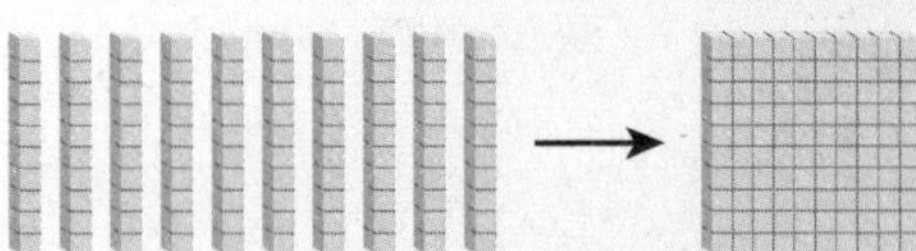

10 tens

1 hundred

100

Share and Show

MATH BOARD

Write how many tens. Circle groups of 10 tens.
Write how many hundreds. Write the number.

1. 

20 tens

_____ hundreds

_____

2. 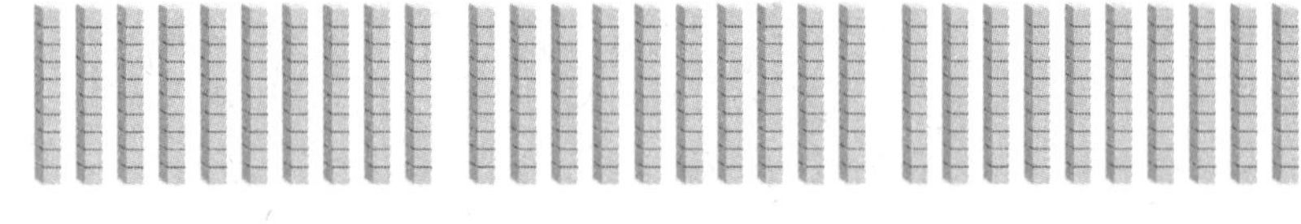

_____ tens

_____ hundreds

_____

3. 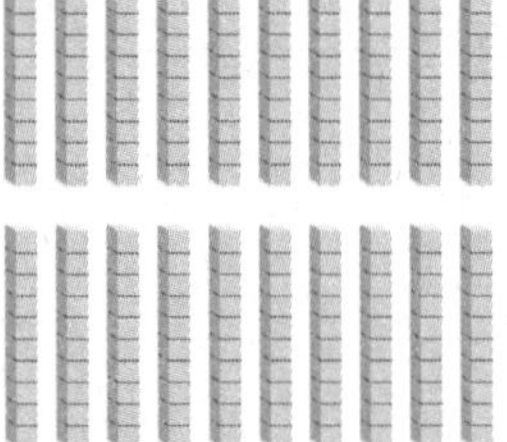

_____ tens

_____ hundreds

_____

4. 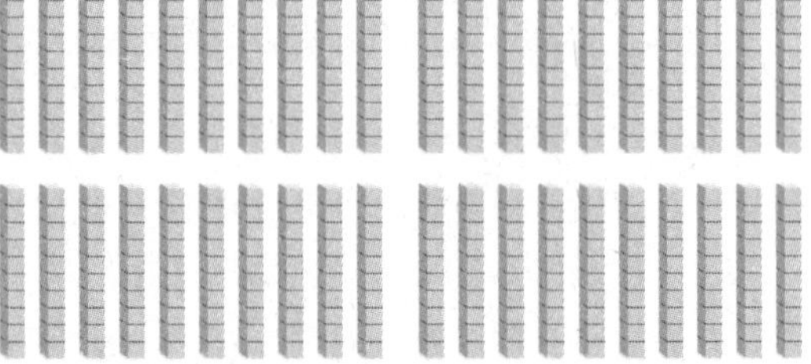

_____ tens

_____ hundreds

_____

Name ______________________________

On Your Own

Write how many tens. Circle groups of 10 tens.
Write how many hundreds. Write the number.

5. 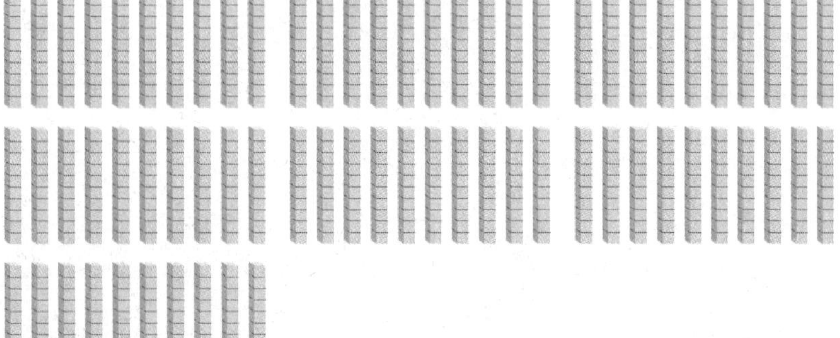

_______ tens

_______ hundreds

____

6. 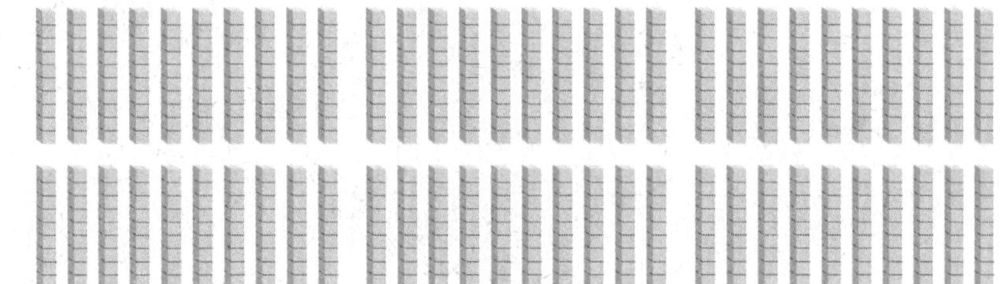

_______ tens

_______ hundreds

____

7. 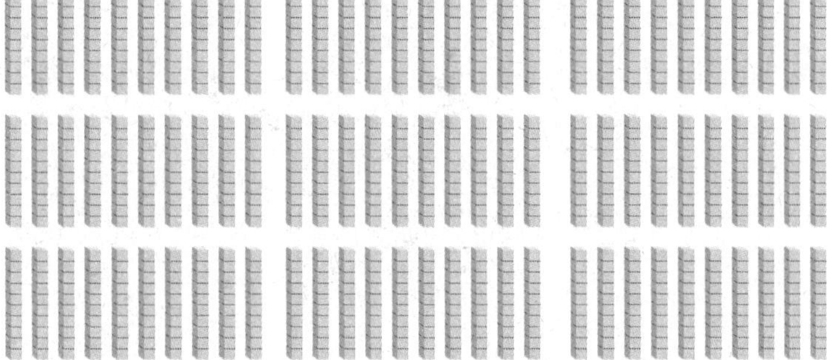

_______ tens

_______ hundreds

____

8. THINK SMARTER Wally has 400 cards.
How many stacks of 10 cards can he make?

_______ stacks of 10 cards

Problem Solving • Applications  

Solve. Write or draw to explain.

9. Mrs. Martin has 80 boxes of paper clips. There are 10 paper clips in each box. How many paper clips does she have?

_______ paper clips

10. THINKSMARTER Pencils are sold in boxes of 10 pencils. Mr. Lee needs 100 pencils. He has 40 pencils. How many boxes of 10 pencils should he buy?

_____ boxes of 10 pencils

Draw a picture to explain your answer.

TAKE HOME ACTIVITY • Ask your child to draw a quick picture of 20 tens and then tell you how many hundreds there are.

Name ______________________________

Group Tens as Hundreds

Common Core **COMMON CORE STANDARDS— 2.NBT.A.1a. 2.NBT.A.1b**
Understand place value.

Write how many tens. Circle groups of 10 tens. Write how many hundreds. Write the number.

1. 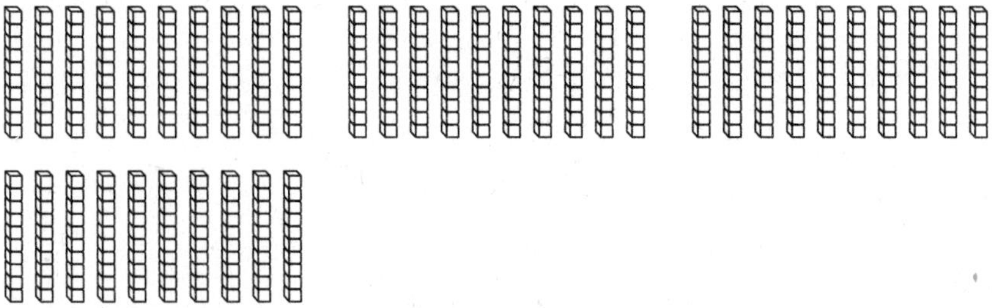 ______ tens

______ hundreds

______

2. 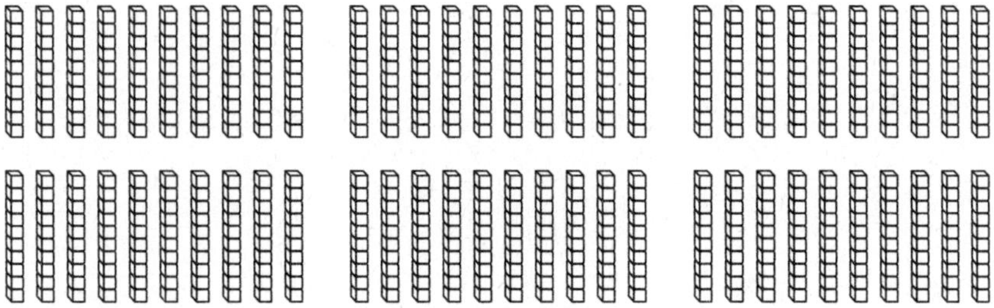 ______ tens

______ hundreds

______

Problem Solving Real World

Solve. Write or draw to explain.

3. Farmer Gray has 30 flowerpots. He plants 10 seeds in each pot. How many seeds does he plant?

______ seeds

4. WRITE Math Ella has 50 stacks of ten pennies in each stack. Describe how to find how many pennies Ella has in all.

____

____

____

____

Lesson Check (2.NBT.A.1a, 2.NBT.A.1b)

1. Mai has 40 tens. Write how many hundreds. Write the number.

____

_____

2. There are 80 tens. Write how many hundreds. Write the number.

____

_____

Spiral Review (2.OA.C.3, 2.NBT.A.2, 2.NBT.A.3)

3. Write the number equal to 5 tens and 13 ones.

____

4. Count by fives.

5, 10, 15

_____, _____, _____, _____

5. Carlos has 58 pencils. What is the value of the digit 5 in this number?

____

6. Circle the sum that is an even number.

$2 + 3 = 5$

$4 + 4 = 8$

$5 + 6 = 11$

$8 + 7 = 15$

FOR MORE PRACTICE GO TO THE Personal Math Trainer

Name ______________________________

Explore 3-Digit Numbers

Essential Question How do you write a 3-digit number for a group of tens?

Common Core **Number and Operations in Base Ten—2.NBT.A.1**

MATHEMATICAL PRACTICES **MP1, MP7, MP8**

Listen and Draw Real World

Circle groups of blocks to show hundreds. Count the hundreds.

_______ hundreds

_______ straws

Math Talk MATHEMATICAL PRACTICES

Analyze Describe how the number of hundreds would be different if there were 10 more bundles of straws.

FOR THE TEACHER • Read the following problem and have children circle groups of tens blocks to solve. Mrs. Rodriguez has 30 bundles of straws. There are 10 straws in each bundle. How many straws does Mrs. Rodriguez have?

Model and Draw

What number is shown with 11 tens?

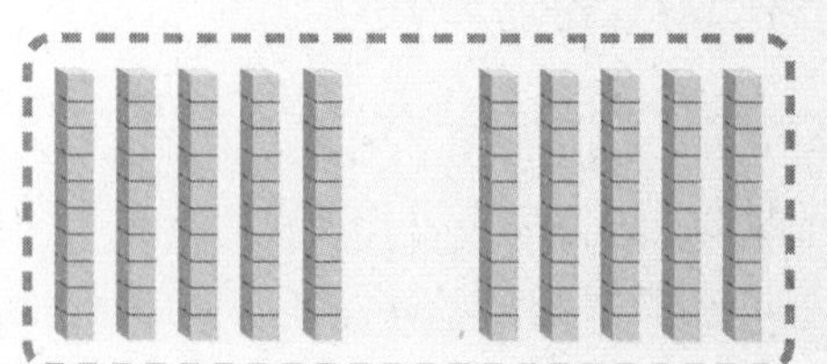

11 tens

1 hundred 1 ten

110

In the number 110, there is a 1 in the hundreds place and a 1 in the tens place.

Share and Show

Circle tens to make 1 hundred. Write the number in different ways.

1. 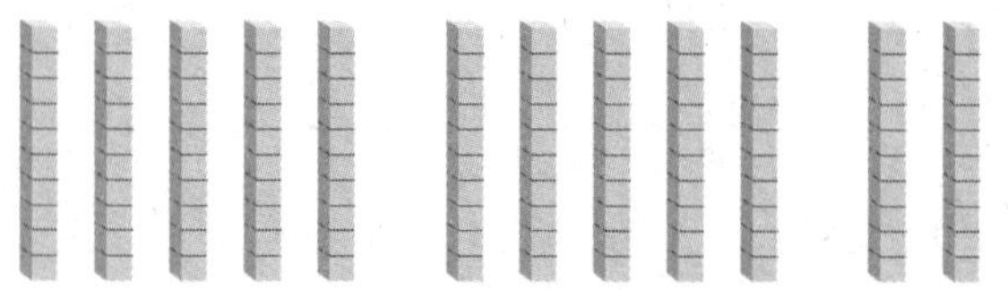

____ tens

____ hundred ____ tens

____

✓2. 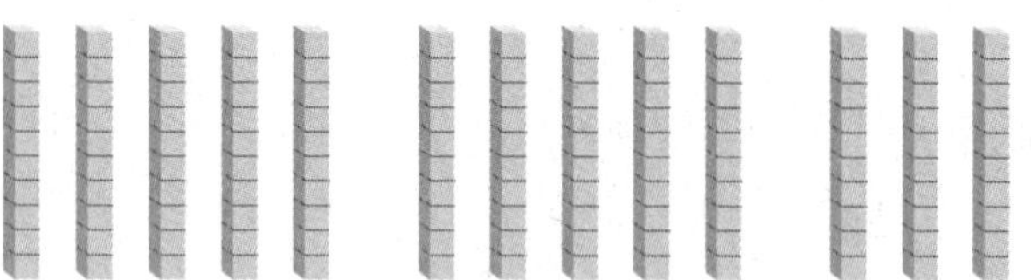

____ tens

____ hundred ____ tens

____

✓3. 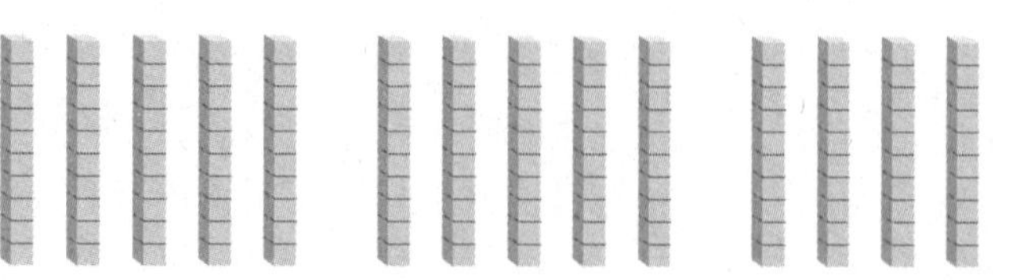

____ tens

____ hundred ____ tens

____

Name ____________________

On Your Own

Circle tens to make 1 hundred. Write the number in different ways.

4. 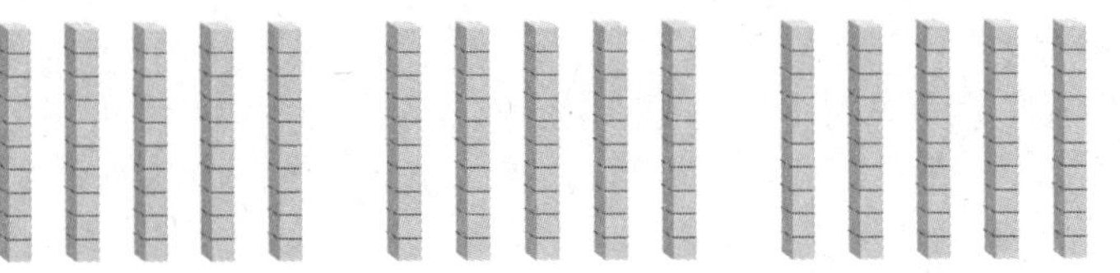

____ tens

____ hundred ____ tens

____

5. 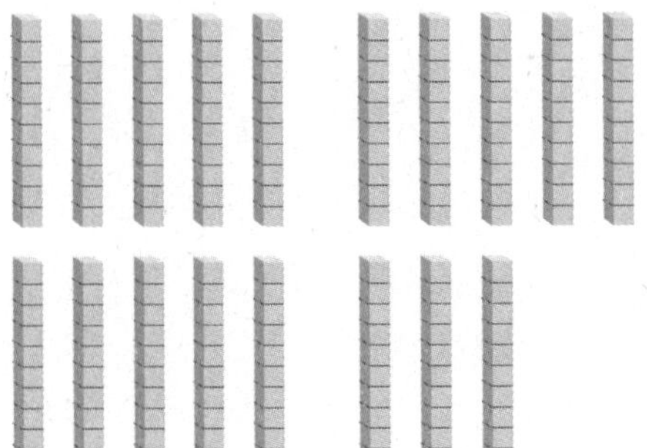

____ tens

____ hundred ____ tens

____

6. GO DEEPER Saul has 130 baseball cards. How many baseball cards does he need to get so that he will have 200 baseball cards in all?

____ baseball cards

7. THINK SMARTER Kendra has 120 stickers. 10 stickers fill a page. How many pages can she fill?

____ pages

Problem Solving • Applications

Solve. Write or draw to explain.

8. MATHEMATICAL PRACTICE 1 **Analyze** There are 16 boxes of crackers. There are 10 crackers in each box. How many crackers are in the boxes?

_______ crackers

9. GO DEEPER Simon makes 8 towers of 10 blocks each. Ron makes 9 towers of 10 blocks each. How many blocks did they use?

_______ blocks

10. THINK SMARTER Ed has 150 marbles. How many bags of 10 marbles does he need to get so that he will have 200 marbles in all?

_______ bags of 10 marbles

TAKE HOME ACTIVITY • Have your child draw 110 Xs by drawing 11 groups of 10 Xs.

Name ______________________________

Explore 3-Digit Numbers

Common Core — **COMMON CORE STANDARD—2.NBT.A.1**
Understand place value.

Circle tens to make 1 hundred. Write the number in different ways.

1.

_____ tens

_____ hundred _____ tens

_____

2.

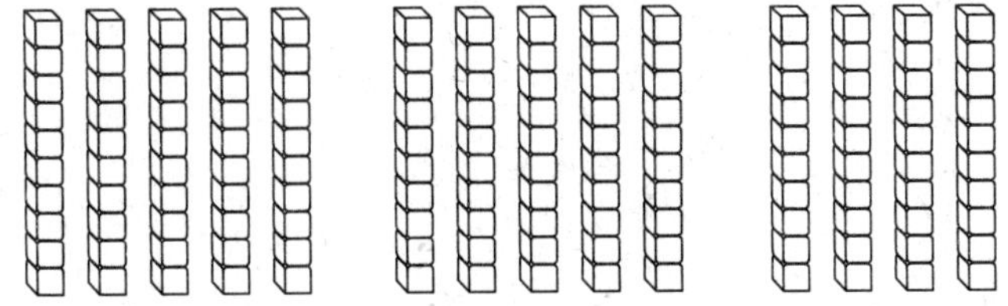

_____ tens

_____ hundred _____ tens

_____

Problem Solving

Solve. Write or draw to explain.

3. Millie has a box of 1 hundred cubes. She also has a bag of 70 cubes. How many trains of 10 cubes can she make?

_____ trains of 10 cubes

4. WRITE Math Draw or write to explain why 1 hundred 4 tens and 14 tens name the same amount.

____

____

____

Lesson Check (2.NBT.A.1)

1. Circle tens to make 1 hundred. Write the number a different way.

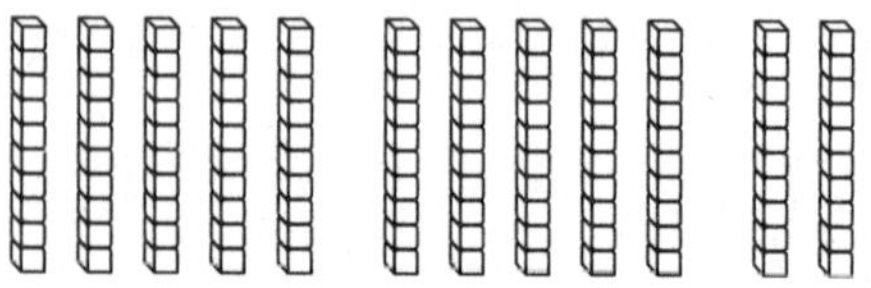

_____ tens

_____ hundred _____ tens

_____

2. Circle tens to make 1 hundred. Write the number a different way.

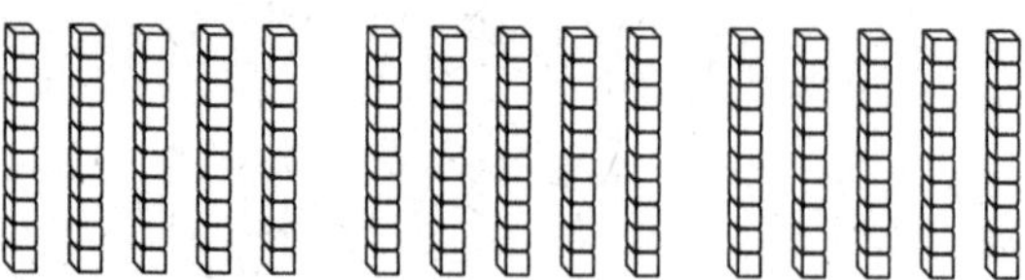

_____ tens

_____ hundred _____ tens

_____

Spiral Review (2.OA.C.3, 2.NBT.A.3)

3. Circle the odd number.

18   10

9   4

4. Write the number equal to 2 tens 15 ones.

____

5. Describe the number 78 in two different ways.

_____ tens + _____ ones

_____ + _____

6. Write the number 55 in another way.

____

Name ______________________________

Model 3-Digit Numbers

Essential Question How do you show a 3-digit number using blocks?

Number and Operations in Base Ten—2.NBT.A.1

MATHEMATICAL PRACTICES
MP1, MP4, MP7

Listen and Draw Real World

Use [tens block]. Draw to show what you did.

Math Talk MATHEMATICAL PRACTICES 1

If Jack had 14 tens, how many hundreds and tens would he have? **Explain**

FOR THE TEACHER • Read the following problem. Jack has 12 tens blocks. How many hundreds and tens does Jack have? Have children show Jack's blocks and then draw quick pictures. Then have children circle 10 tens and solve the problem.

Model and Draw

In the number 348, the 3 is in the hundreds place, the 4 is in the tens place, and the 8 is in the ones place.

Write how many hundreds, tens, and ones.

3 hundreds + 4 tens + 8 ones

Show the number 348 using blocks.

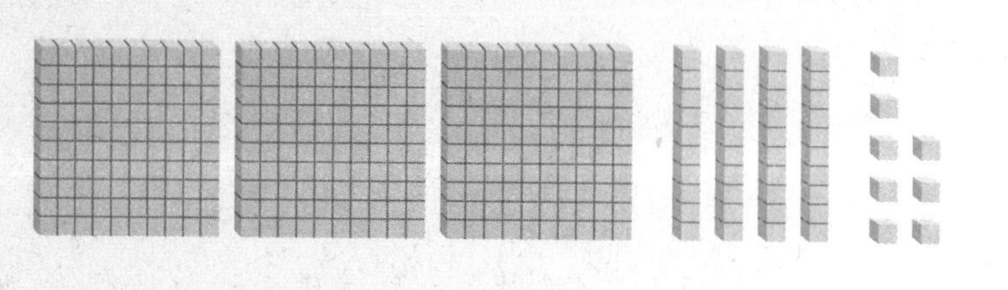

Draw a quick picture.

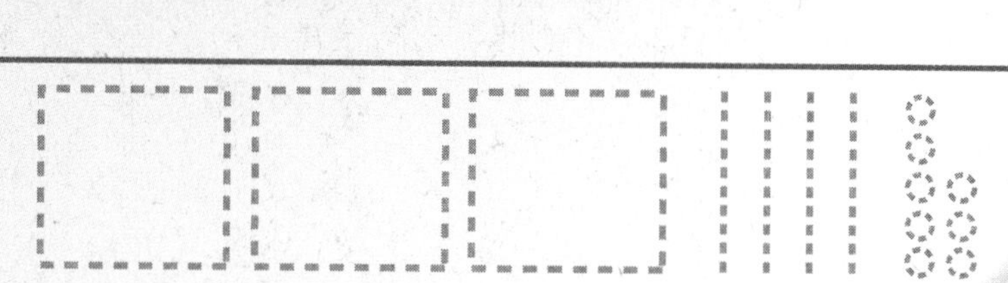

Share and Show

MATH BOARD

Write how many hundreds, tens, and ones.

Show with . Then draw a quick picture.

1. 234

___ hundreds + ___ tens + ___ ones

2. 156

___ hundred + ___ tens + ___ ones

Name ______________________________

On Your Own

Write how many hundreds, tens, and ones.

Show with [hundred block] [ten rod] [one cube]. Then draw a quick picture.

3. 125

___ hundred + ___ tens + ___ ones

4. 312

___ hundreds + ___ ten + ___ ones

5. 245

___ hundreds + ___ tens + ___ ones

6. 103

___ hundred + ___ tens + ___ ones

7. THINK SMARTER Lexi needs 144 beads. A large box holds 100 beads. A medium box holds 10 beads. A small box holds 1 bead. Lexi already had 1 large box and 4 small boxes. How many medium boxes of beads does she need?

_______ medium boxes

Problem Solving • Applications

8. THINK SMARTER How are the numbers 342 and 324 alike? How are they different?

____

____

____

____

MATHEMATICAL PRACTICE 4 Model with Mathematics

Write the number for the clue.

9. A model for my number has 2 hundreds blocks, no tens blocks, and 3 ones blocks.

My number is ________.

10. A model for my number has 3 hundreds blocks, 5 tens blocks, and no ones blocks.

My number is ________.

11. THINK SMARTER There are 2 boxes of 100 pencils and some single pencils on the table. Choose all the numbers that show how many pencils could be on the table.

- ○ 200
- ○ 106
- ○ 203
- ○ 207

TAKE HOME ACTIVITY • Write the number 438. Have your child tell you the values of the digits in the number 438.

Name ____________________

Model 3-Digit Numbers

Common Core **COMMON CORE STANDARD—2.NBT.A.1**
Understand place value.

Write how many hundreds, tens, and ones.
Show with  **. Then draw a quick picture.**

1. 118

Hundreds	Tens	Ones

2. 246

Hundreds	Tens	Ones

Problem Solving Real World

3. Write the number that matches the clues.

- My number has 2 hundreds.
- The tens digit is 9 more than the ones digit.

Hundreds	Tens	Ones

My number is ________.

4. WRITE Math Write a 3-digit number using digits 2, 9, 4. Draw a quick picture to show the value of your number.

Lesson Check (2.NBT.A.1)

1. What number is shown with these blocks?

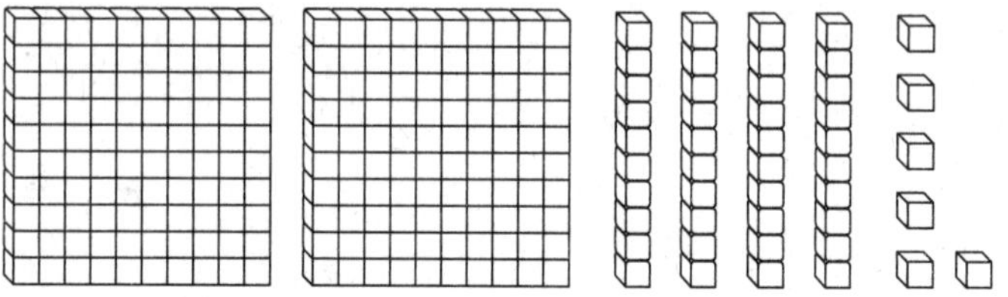

Hundreds	Tens	Ones

____

Spiral Review (2.OA.C.3, 2.NBT.A.1a, 2.NBT.A.1b, 2.NBT.A.3)

2. Write the number with the same value as 28 tens.

____

3. Describe 59 in two other ways.

_____ tens _____ ones

_____ + _____

4. Circle the odd number.

11 12

18 20

5. Write the number equal to 7 tens and 3 ones.

____

FOR MORE PRACTICE GO TO THE Personal Math Trainer

Name ______________________________

Hundreds, Tens, and Ones

Essential Question How do you write the 3-digit number that is shown by a set of blocks?

Number and Operations in Base Ten—2.NBT.A.1, 2.NBT.A.3

MATHEMATICAL PRACTICES
MP1, MP7, MP8

Listen and Draw

Write the number of hundreds, tens, and ones. Then draw a quick picture.

Hundreds	Tens	Ones

Hundreds	Tens	Ones

MATHEMATICAL PRACTICES 1

Describe how the two numbers are alike. **Describe** how they are different.

FOR THE TEACHER • Read the following to children. Sebastion has 243 yellow blocks. How many hundreds, tens, and ones are in this number? Repeat for 423 red blocks.

Model and Draw

Write how many hundreds, tens, and ones there are in the model. What are two ways to write this number?

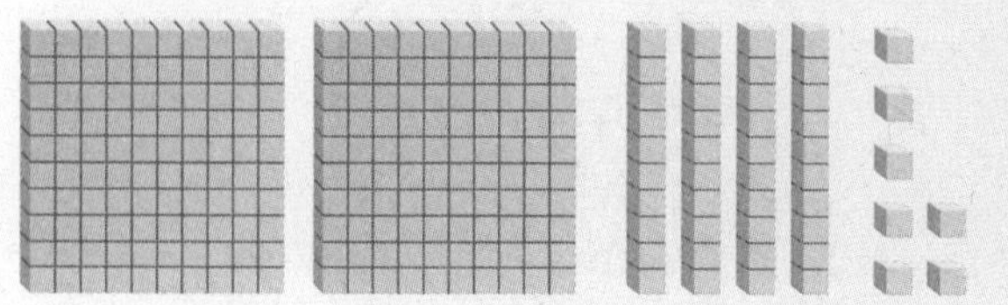

Hundreds	Tens	Ones
2	4	7

247

200 + 40 + 7

Share and Show

Write how many hundreds, tens, and ones are in the model. Write the number in two ways.

1. 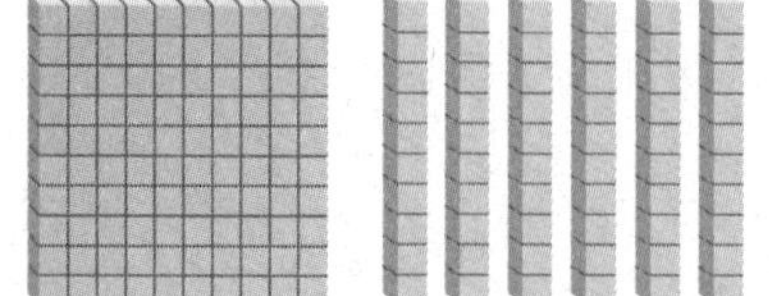

Hundreds	Tens	Ones

______

______ + ______ + ______

✓ 2. 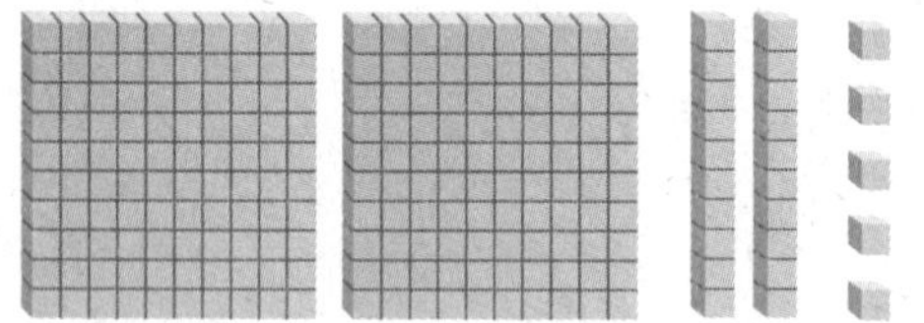

Hundreds	Tens	Ones

______

______ + ______ + ______

✓ 3. 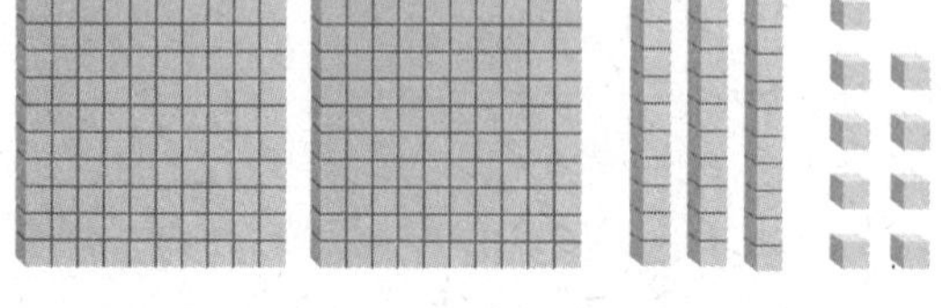

Hundreds	Tens	Ones

______

______ + ______ + ______

Name ___________________________

On Your Own

Write how many hundreds, tens, and ones are in the model. Write the number in two ways.

4. 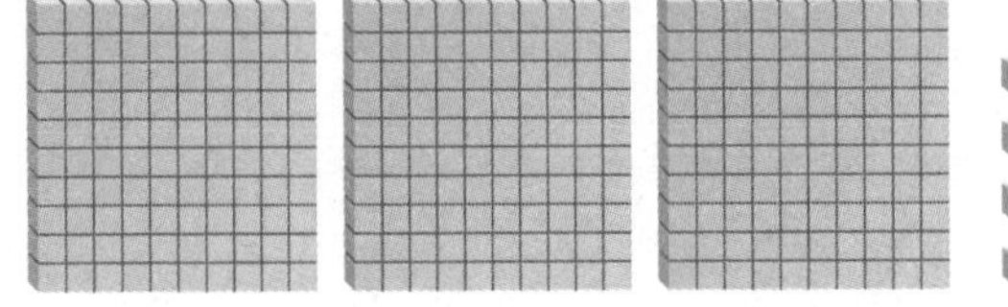

Hundreds	Tens	Ones

______

______ + ______ + ______

5. 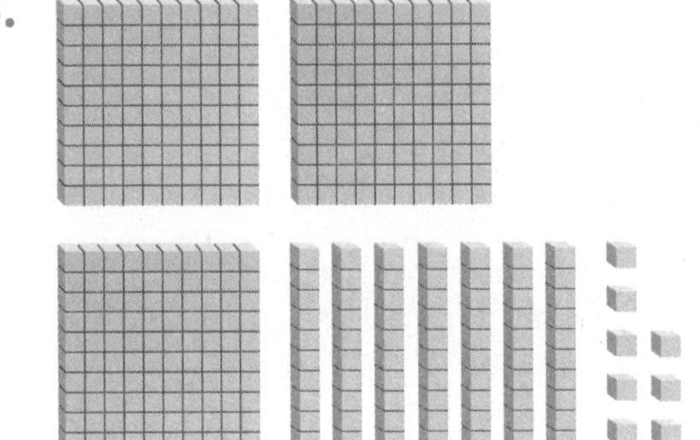

Hundreds	Tens	Ones

______

______ + ______ + ______

6. 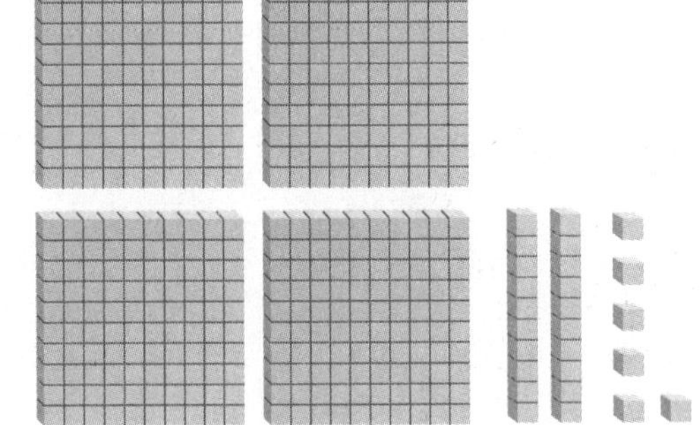

Hundreds	Tens	Ones

______

______ + ______ + ______

Solve. Write or draw to explain.

7. THINK SMARTER A model for my number has 4 ones blocks, 5 tens blocks, and 7 hundreds blocks. What number am I?

______

Problem Solving • Applications  

8. GO DEEPER The hundreds digit of my number is greater than the tens digit. The ones digit is less than the tens digit. What could my number be? Write it in two ways.

_______ + _______ + _______

____

9. THINK SMARTER Karen has these bags of marbles. How many marbles does Karen have?

_______ marbles

Explain how you used the picture to find the number of marbles Karen has.

____

____

____

TAKE HOME ACTIVITY • Say a 3-digit number, such as 546. Have your child draw a quick picture for that number.

Name ______________________

Hundreds, Tens, and Ones

Common Core **COMMON CORE STANDARD—2.NBT.A.1, 2.NBT.A.3** *Understand place value.*

Write how many hundreds, tens, and ones are in the model. Write the number in two ways.

1. 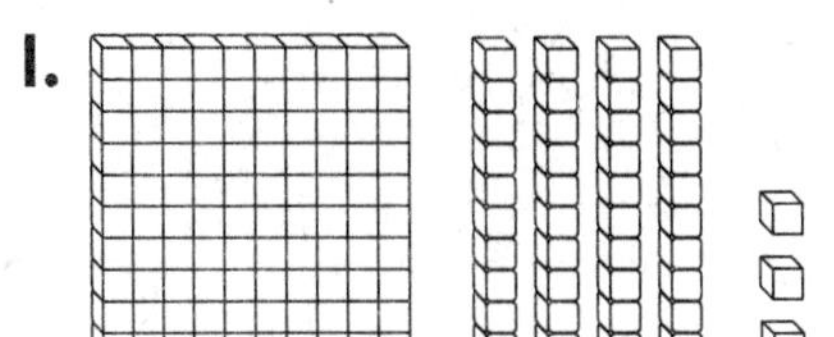

Hundreds	Tens	Ones

______

______ + ______ + ______

2. 

Hundreds	Tens	Ones

______

______ + ______ + ______

Problem Solving Real World

3. Write the number that answers the riddle. Use the chart. A model for my number has 6 ones blocks, 2 hundreds blocks, and 3 tens blocks. What number am I?

Hundreds	Tens	Ones

______

4. WRITE Math Write a number that has a zero in the tens place. Draw a quick picture for your number.

Lesson Check (2.NBT.A.1)

1. Write the number 254 as a sum of hundreds, tens, and ones.

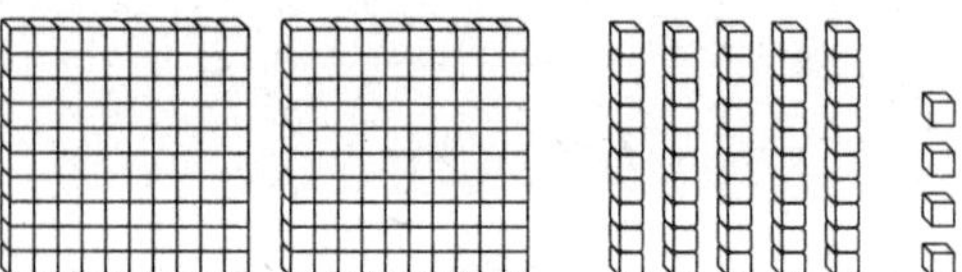

____ + ____ + ____

2. Write the number 307 as a sum of hundreds, tens, and ones.

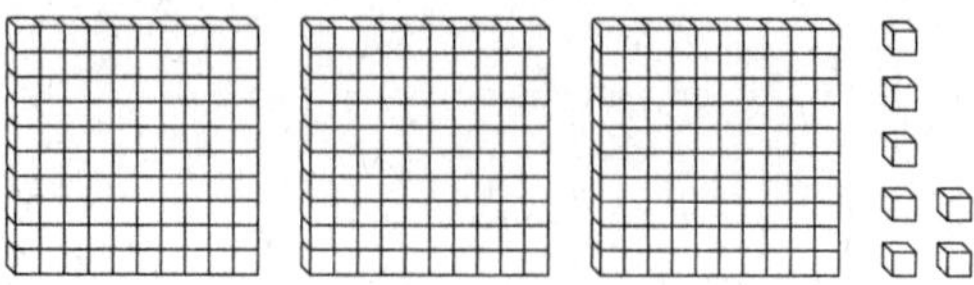

____ + ____ + ____

Spiral Review (2.OA.C.3. 2.NBT.A.1a, 2.NBT.A.1b, 2.NBT.A.3)

3. Describe 83 in two other ways.

____ tens ____ ones

____ + ____

4. Write 86 in words.

____

5. Write the number with the same value as 32 tens.

____

6. Circle the odd number.

2 6

10 17

FOR MORE PRACTICE GO TO THE Personal Math Trainer

Name ____________________

Place Value to 1,000

Essential Question How do you know the values of the digits in numbers?

Common Core **Number and Operations in Base Ten—2.NBT.A.1**

MATHEMATICAL PRACTICES
MP1, MP3, MP6, MP7

Listen and Draw Real World

Write the numbers. Then draw quick pictures.

________ sheets of color paper

Hundreds	Tens	Ones

________ sheets of plain paper

Hundreds	Tens	Ones

Math Talk MATHEMATICAL PRACTICES 1

Describe how 5 tens is different from 5 hundreds.

FOR THE TEACHER • Read the following. There are 245 sheets of color paper in the closet. There are 458 sheets of plain paper by the table. Have children write each number and draw quick pictures to show the numbers.

Model and Draw

The place of a digit in a number tells its value.

327	The 3 in 327 has a value of 3 hundreds, or 300. The 2 in 327 has a value of 2 tens, or 20. The 7 in 327 has a value of 7 ones, or 7.

There are 10 hundreds in 1 **thousand**.

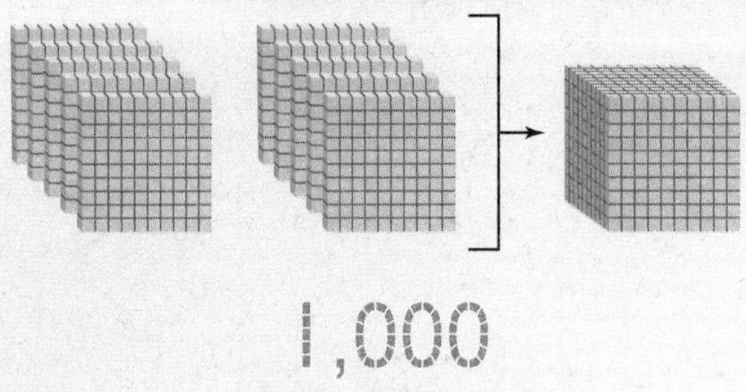

1,000

The 1 is in the thousands place and has a value of 1 thousand.

Share and Show

Circle the value or the meaning of the red digit.

1. 702	2 ones	2 tens	2 hundreds
✓2. 459	500	50	5
✓3. 362	3 hundreds	3 tens	3 ones

Name ________________________

On Your Own

Circle the value or the meaning of the red digit.

4. 549	400	40	4
5. 607	7 ones	7 tens	7 hundreds
6. 1,000	1 one	1 hundred	1 thousand
7. 914	90	900	9,000

8. THINKSMARTER The value of the ones digit in George's favorite number is 2. The value of the hundreds digit is 600 and the value of the tens digit is 90. Write George's favorite number.

____

9. GO DEEPER Write the number that matches the clues.

- The value of my hundreds digit is 300.
- The value of my tens digit is 0.
- The value of my ones digit is an even number greater than 7.

The number is ________.

Problem Solving • Applications

10. THINK SMARTER Ty is making a Venn diagram. Where in the diagram should he write the other numbers?

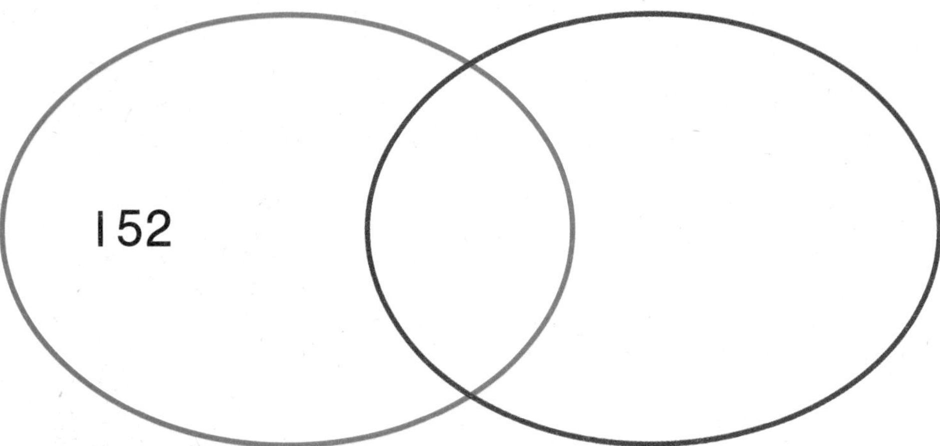

~~152~~
215
454
257
352
205
250

11. MATHEMATICAL PRACTICE 3 **Apply** Describe where 752 should be written in the diagram. Explain your answer.

____

____

____

12. THINK SMARTER + Fill in the bubble next to all the numbers that have the digit 4 in the tens place.

- ○ 764
- ○ 149
- ○ 437
- ○ 342

TAKE HOME ACTIVITY • Ask your child to write 3-digit numbers, such as "a number with 2 hundreds" and "a number with a 9 in the ones place."

Name ______________________

Place Value to 1,000

Common Core **COMMON CORE STANDARD—2.NBT.A.1**
Understand place value.

Circle the value or the meaning of the underlined digit.

1. 33̲7 (underlined: 3 in tens place)	3	30	300
2. 46̲2̲ (underlined: 2)	200	20	2
3. 5̲72 (underlined: 5)	5	50	500
4. 567 (underlined: 7)	7 ones	7 tens	7 hundreds
5. 462 (underlined: 4)	4 hundreds	4 ones	4 tens

Problem Solving Real World

6. Write the 3-digit number that answers the riddle.

- I have the same hundreds digit as ones digit.
- The value of my tens digit is 50.
- The value of my ones digit is 4. The number is ________.

7. WRITE Math What is the value of 5 in 756? Write and draw to explain how you know.

____

____

Lesson Check (2.NBT.A.1)

1. What is the value of the underlined digit?

<u>3</u>15

____

2. What is the meaning of the underlined digit?

6<u>4</u>8

_____ tens

Spiral Review (2.OA.C.3, 2.NBT.A.1, 2.NBT.A.3)

3. What number can be written as 40 + 5?

____

4. What number has the same value as 14 tens?

____

5. Write the number described by 1 ten 16 ones.

____

6. Circle the even number.

7 16

21 25

FOR MORE PRACTICE GO TO THE **Personal Math Trainer**

Name ______________________

Number Names

Essential Question How do you write 3-digit numbers using words?

Common Core **Number and Operations in Base Ten—2.NBT.A.3**
MATHEMATICAL PRACTICES
MP2, MP6, MP7

Listen and Draw

Write the missing numbers in the chart. Then find and circle the word form of these numbers below.

	12	13		15	16	17	18	19	20
21	22	23	24	25	26	27	28		30
31	32	33	34		36	37	38	39	40
41	42	43	44	45		47	48	49	50
51		53	54	55	56	57	58	59	60

forty-one ninety-two fourteen

eleven thirty-five forty-six

fifty-three twenty-nine fifty-two

Math Talk MATHEMATICAL PRACTICES 6

Explain Describe how to use words to write the number with a 5 in the tens place and a 7 in the ones place.

HOME CONNECTION • In this activity, your child reviewed the word form of numbers less than 100.

Model and Draw

You can use words to write 3-digit numbers.
First, look at the hundreds digit. Then, look at the tens digit and ones digit together.

245

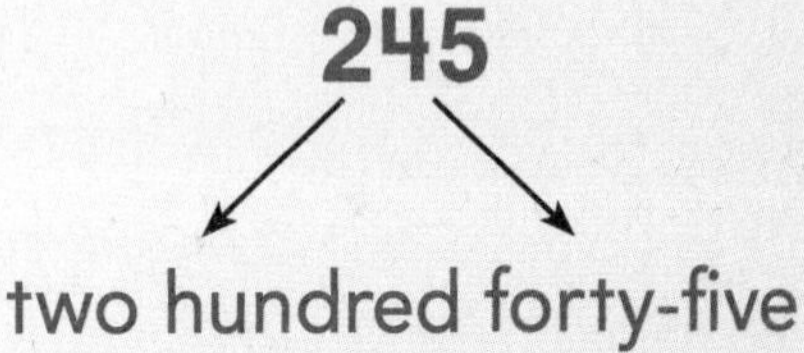

two hundred forty-five

713

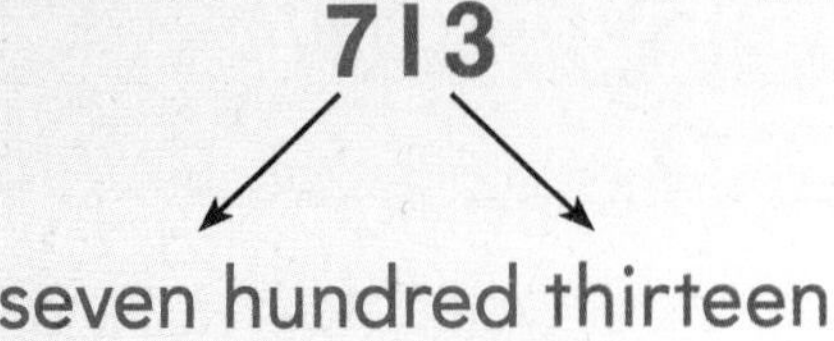

seven hundred thirteen

Share and Show

Write the number using words.

1. 506

five hundred six

____

2. 189

____

3. 328

____

Write the number.

4. four hundred fifteen

____

5. two hundred ninety-one

____

6. six hundred three

____

7. eight hundred forty-seven

____

Name ______________________

On Your Own

Write the number.

8. seven hundred seventeen

______

9. three hundred ninety

______

Write the number using words.

10. 568

____

11. 321

____

12. GO DEEPER My 3-digit number has a 4 in the hundreds place. It has a greater digit in the tens place than in the ones place. The sum of the digits is 6.

What is my number? ______________________

Write the number using words. ______________________

13. THINK SMARTER Alma counts two hundred sixty-eight leaves. Which is another way to write this number? Circle your answer.

$2 + 6 + 8$

$200 + 60 + 8$

$2 + 60 + 8$

Problem Solving • Applications

Connect Symbols and Words

Circle the answer for each problem.

14. Derek counts one hundred ninety cars. Which is another way to write this number?

    119

    190

    910

15. Beth counted three hundred fifty-six straws. Which is another way to write this number?

    $3 + 5 + 6$

    $30 + 50 + 60$

    $300 + 50 + 6$

16. THINKSMARTER There are 537 chairs at the school. Write this number using words.

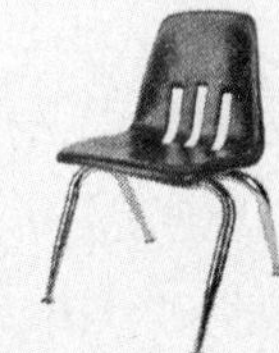

____

Show the number in two other ways.

Hundreds	Tens	Ones

_______ + _______ + _______

TAKE HOME ACTIVITY • Ask your child to write the number 940 using words.

Name ______________________

Number Names

Common Core **COMMON CORE STANDARD—2.NBT.A.3**
Understand place value.

Write the number.

1. two hundred thirty-two ______

2. five hundred forty-four ______

3. one hundred fifty-eight ______

4. nine hundred fifty ______

5. four hundred twenty ______

6. six hundred seventy-eight ______

Write the number using words.

7. 317

____

Problem Solving

Circle the answer.

8. Six hundred twenty-six children attend Elm Street School. Which is another way to write this number?

266 626 662

9. WRITE Math Write a 3-digit number using the digits 5, 9, and 2. Then write your number using words.

____

Lesson Check (2.NBT.A.3)

1. Write the number 851 in words.

____

2. Write the number two hundred sixty using numbers.

____

Spiral Review (2.NBT.A.1, 2.NBT.A.2)

3. Write a number with the digit 8 in the tens place.

____

4. Write the number shown with these blocks.

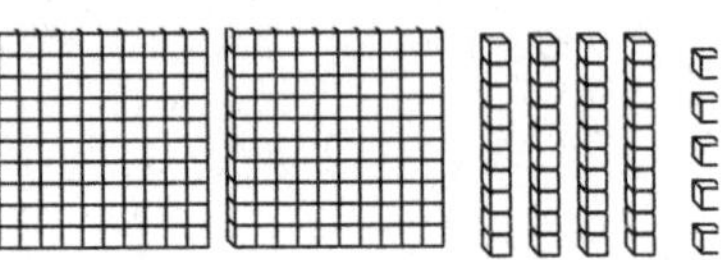

____

5. Count by fives.

650, 655,

_____, _____, _____

6. Sam has 128 marbles. How many hundreds are in this number?

_____ hundred

FOR MORE PRACTICE GO TO THE **Personal Math Trainer**

Name ______________________________

Different Forms of Numbers

Essential Question What are three ways to write a 3-digit number?

Common Core Number and Operations in Base Ten—2.NBT.A.3
MATHEMATICAL PRACTICES MP6, MP7

Listen and Draw Real World

Write the number. Use the digits to write how many hundreds, tens, and ones.

____ hundreds ____ tens ____ ones

____ hundreds ____ tens ____ ones

____ hundreds ____ tens ____ one

FOR THE TEACHER • Read the following: Evan has 426 marbles. How many hundreds, tens, and ones are in 426? Continue the activity for 204 and 341.

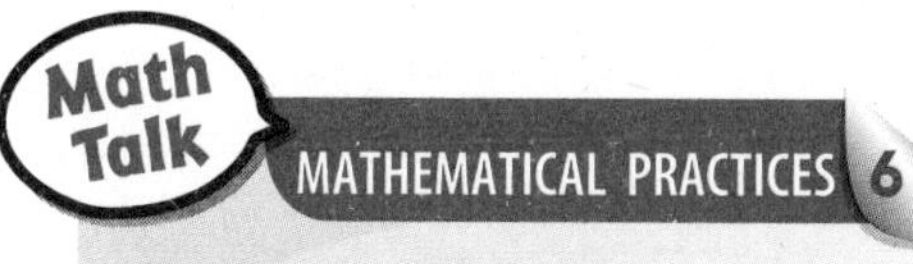

How many hundreds are in 368? **Explain.**

Model and Draw

You can use a quick picture to show a number.
You can write a number in different ways.

five hundred thirty-six

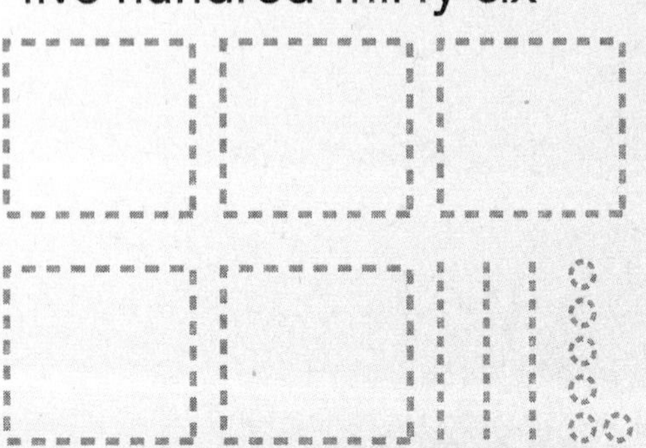

5 hundreds 3 tens 6 ones

500 + 30 + 6

536

Share and Show

Read the number and draw a quick picture.
Then write the number in different ways.

1. four hundred seven

____ hundreds ____ tens ____ ones

______ + ______ + ______

______

2. three hundred twenty-five

____ hundreds ____ tens ____ ones

______ + ______ + ______

______

3. two hundred fifty-three

____ hundreds ____ tens ____ ones

______ + ______ + ______

______

Name ______________________________

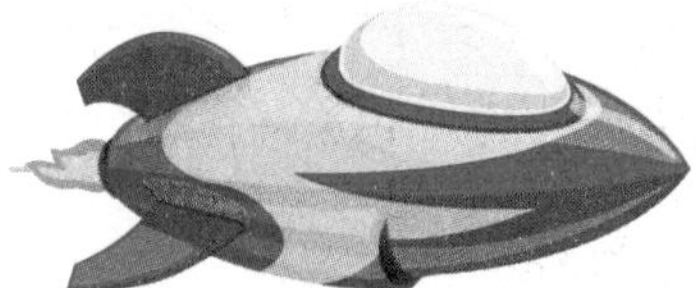

On Your Own

Read the number and draw a quick picture. Then write the number in different ways.

4. one hundred seventy-two

____ hundred ____ tens ____ ones

______ + ______ + ______

______

5. three hundred forty-six

____ hundreds ____ tens ____ ones

______ + ______ + ______

______

6. THINK SMARTER Think of a 3-digit number with a zero in the ones place. Use words to write that number.

____

7. THINK SMARTER Ellen used these blocks to show 452. What is wrong? Cross out blocks and draw quick pictures for missing blocks.

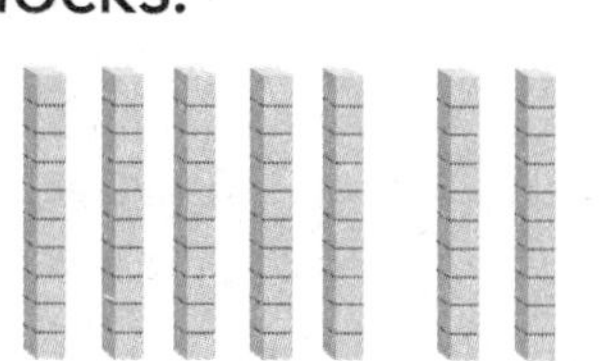

TAKE HOME ACTIVITY • Ask your child to show the number 315 in three different ways.

Name ______________________________

Concepts and Skills

Circle tens to make 1 hundred. Write the number in different ways. (2.NBT.A.3)

1. 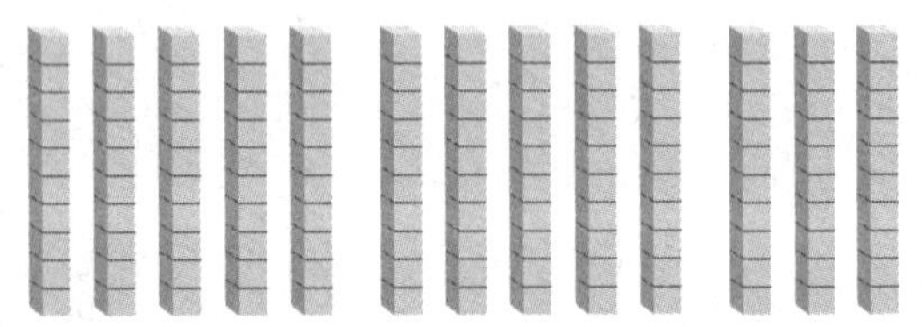

_____ tens

_____ hundred _____ tens

____

Write how many hundreds, tens, and ones are in the model. Write the number in two ways. (2.NBT.A.1)

2. 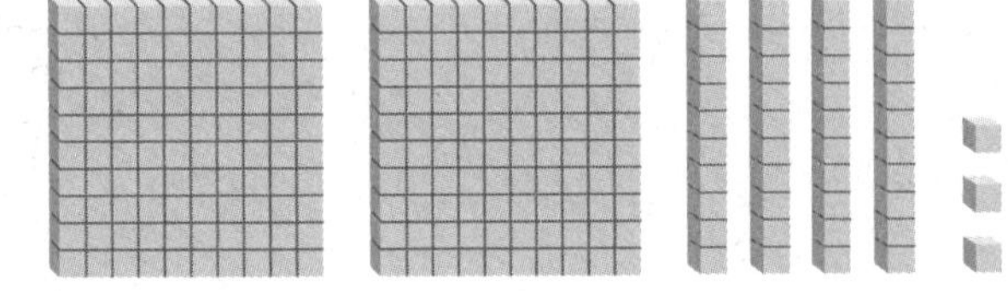

Hundreds	Tens	Ones

____

______ + ______ + ______

Circle the value or the meaning of the red digit. (2.NBT.A.1)

3. 528 | 5 | 50 | 500

4. 674 | 4 ones | 4 tens | 4 hundreds

5. THINK SMARTER Write the number six hundred forty-five in another way. (2.NBT.A.3)

____

Name ______________________________

Different Forms of Numbers

Practice and Homework
Lesson 2.7

Common Core **COMMON CORE STANDARD—2.NBT.A.3**
Understand place value.

Read the number and draw a quick picture. Then write the number in different ways.

1. two hundred fifty-one

____ hundreds ____ tens ____ one

______ + ______ + ______

______

2. three hundred twelve

____ hundreds ____ ten ____ ones

______ + ______ + ______

______

Problem Solving

Write the number another way.

3. 200 + 30 + 7

____

4. 895

____

5. WRITE Math Draw a quick picture of 3 hundreds, 5 tens, and 7 ones. What number does your quick picture show? Write it in three different ways.

Lesson Check (2.NBT.A.1)

1. Write the number 392 as hundreds, tens, and ones.

_____ hundreds _____ tens _____ ones

2. What is another way to write the number 271?

_____ hundreds _____ tens _____ one

Spiral Review (2.NBT.A.1, 2.NBT.A.3)

3. What is the value of the underlined digit?

<u>5</u>6

____

4. What number is shown with these blocks?

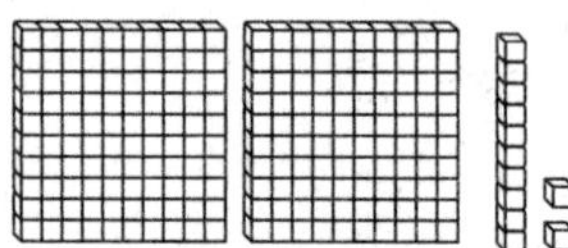

____

5. What is another way to write the number 75?

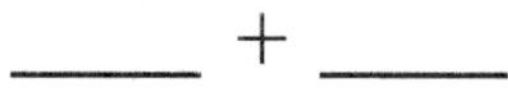

6. What number can be written as 60 + 3?

____

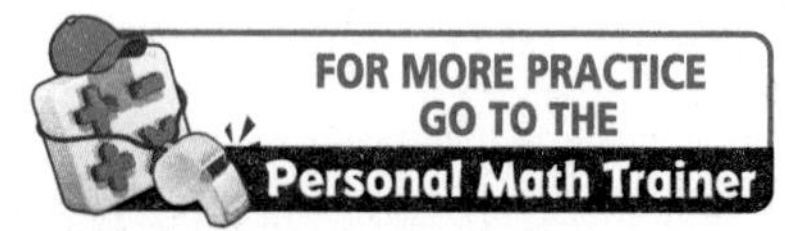

Name ______________________________

Algebra • Different Ways to Show Numbers

Essential Question How can you use blocks or quick pictures to show the value of a number in different ways?

Common Core Number and Operations in Base Ten—2.NBT.A.3
MATHEMATICAL PRACTICES
MP3, MP4, MP7

Listen and Draw Real World

Draw quick pictures to solve.
Write how many tens and ones.

_______ tens _______ ones

_______ tens _______ ones

FOR THE TEACHER • Read this problem to children. Mrs. Peabody has 35 books on a cart to take to classrooms. She can use boxes that each hold 10 books. She can also place single books on the cart. What are two different ways she can put the books on the cart?

MATHEMATICAL PRACTICES 4

Model Describe how you found different ways to show 35 books.

Model and Draw

Here are two ways to show 148.

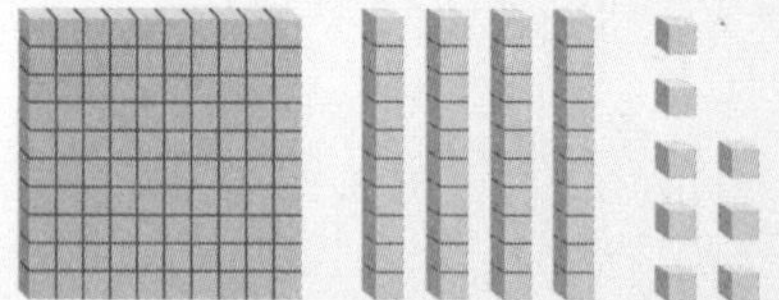

Hundreds	Tens	Ones
1	4	8

Hundreds	Tens	Ones
0	14	8

Share and Show

Use quick pictures to show the number a different way. Write two ways to show how many hundreds, tens, and ones.

1. 213

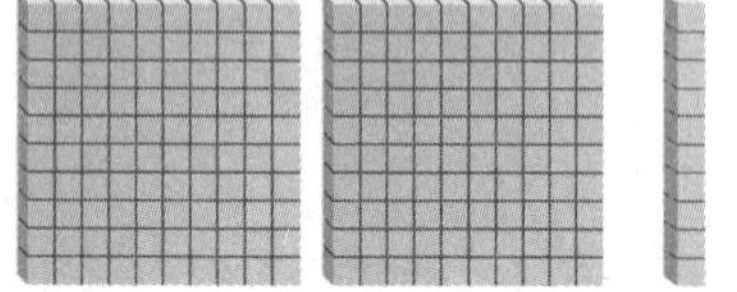

Hundreds	Tens	Ones

Hundreds	Tens	Ones

2. 132

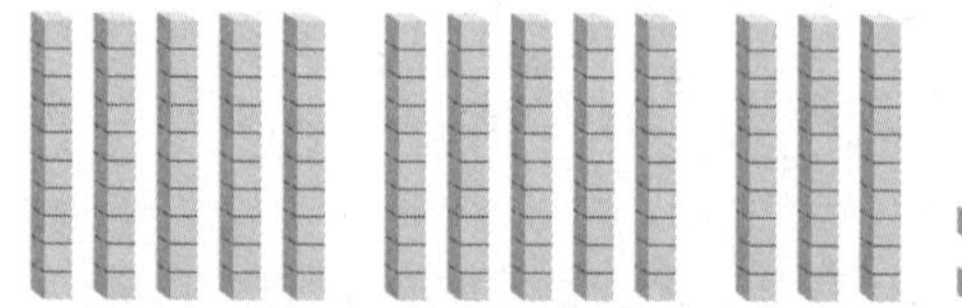

Hundreds	Tens	Ones

Hundreds	Tens	Ones

Name ______________________________

On Your Own

Use quick pictures to show the number a different way. Write two ways to show how many hundreds, tens, and ones.

3. 144

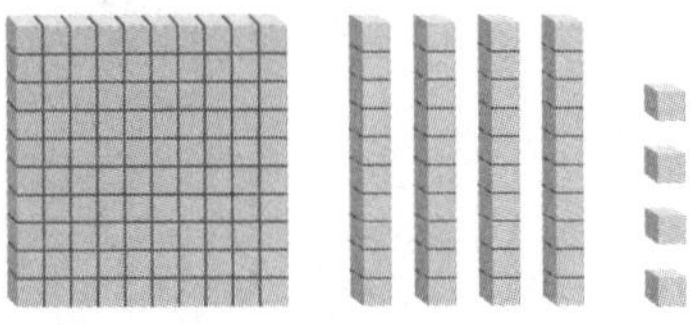

Hundreds	Tens	Ones

Hundreds	Tens	Ones

4. 204

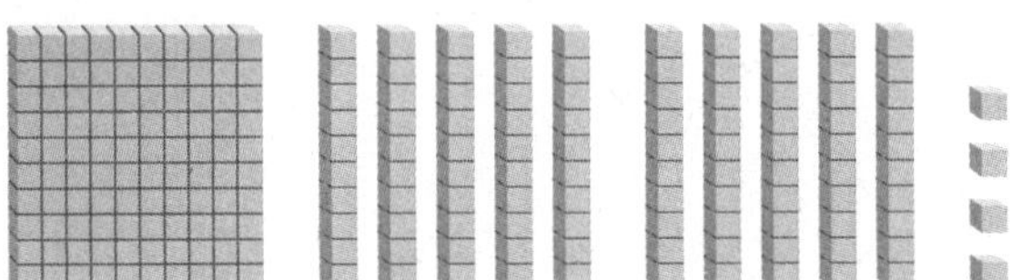

Hundreds	Tens	Ones

Hundreds	Tens	Ones

5. MATHEMATICAL PRACTICE 3 **Make Arguments**
Sue said that 200 + 20 + 23 is the same as 200 + 30 + 3. Is she correct? Explain.

____

____

____

Problem Solving • Applications 

Marbles are sold in boxes, in bags, or as single marbles. Each box has 10 bags of marbles in it. Each bag has 10 marbles in it.

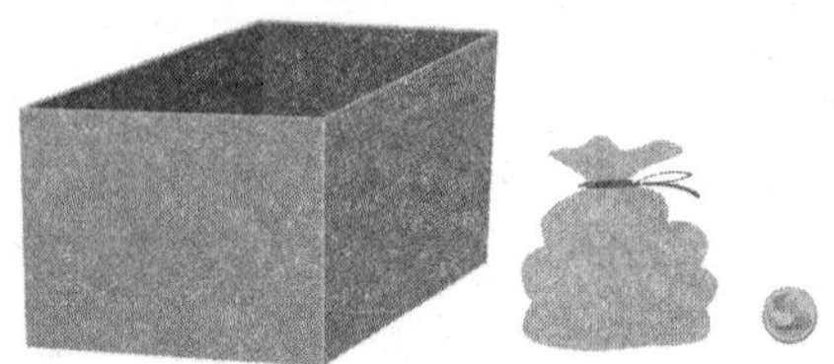

6. THINKSMARTER Draw pictures to show two ways to buy 324 marbles.

Use the marble information above.

7. THINKSMARTER There is only one box of marbles in the store. There are many bags of marbles and single marbles. Draw a picture to show a way to buy 312 marbles.

How many boxes, bags, and single marbles did you show?

____

____

TAKE HOME ACTIVITY • Write the number 156. Have your child draw quick pictures of two ways to show this number.

Name ________________________________

Algebra • Different Ways to Show Numbers

Common Core **COMMON CORE STANDARD—2.NBT.A.3**
Understand place value.

Write how many hundreds, tens, and ones are in the model.

1. 135

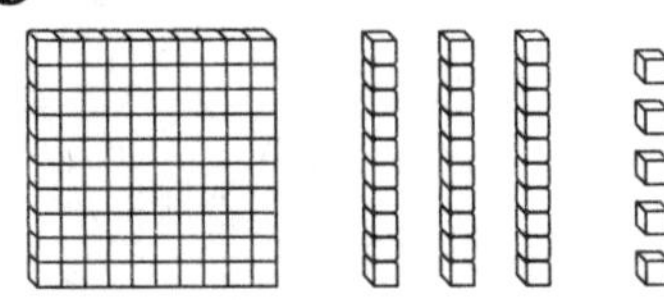

Hundreds	Tens	Ones

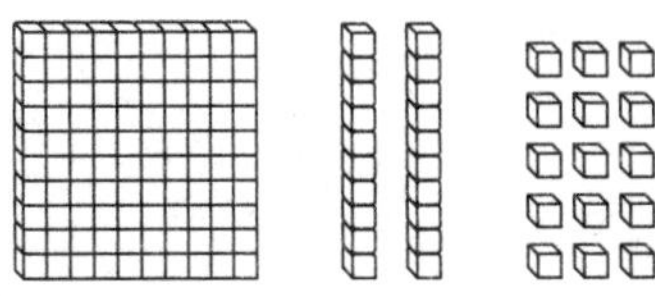

Hundreds	Tens	Ones

Problem Solving

Markers are sold in boxes, packs, or as single markers. Each box has 10 packs. Each pack has 10 markers.

2. Draw pictures to show two ways to buy 276 markers.

3. WRITE Math Draw quick pictures to show the number 326.

Lesson Check (2.NBT.A.3)

1. Write the number that can be shown with this many hundreds, tens, and ones.

Hundreds	Tens	Ones
1	2	18

______

2. Write the number that can be shown with this many hundreds, tens, and ones.

Hundreds	Tens	Ones
2	15	6

______

Spiral Review (2.NBT.A.3)

3. What number can be written as 6 tens 2 ones?

______

4. What number can be written as $30 + 2$?

______

5. Write the number 584 in words.

______

6. Write the number 29 in words.

______

FOR MORE PRACTICE GO TO THE Personal Math Trainer

Name ______________________________

Count On and Count Back by 10 and 100

Essential Question How do you use place value to find 10 more, 10 less, 100 more, or 100 less than a 3-digit number?

Common Core **Number and Operations in Base Ten—2.NBT.B.8**
MATHEMATICAL PRACTICES
MP1, MP7

Listen and Draw Real World

Draw quick pictures for the numbers.

Girls

Hundreds	Tens	Ones

Boys

Hundreds	Tens	Ones

Math Talk MATHEMATICAL PRACTICES 1

Describe how the two numbers are different.

FOR THE TEACHER • Tell children that there are 342 girls at Center School. Have children draw quick pictures for 342. Then tell them that there are 352 boys at the school. Have them draw quick pictures for 352.

Model and Draw

You can show 10 less or 10 more than a number by changing the digit in the tens place.

10 less than 264

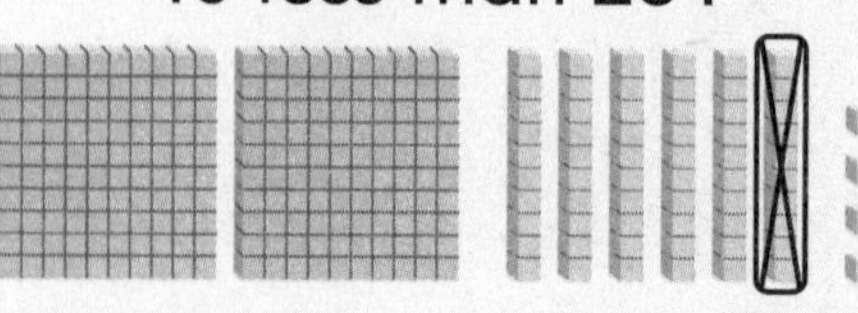

Hundreds	Tens	Ones
2	5	4

10 more than 264

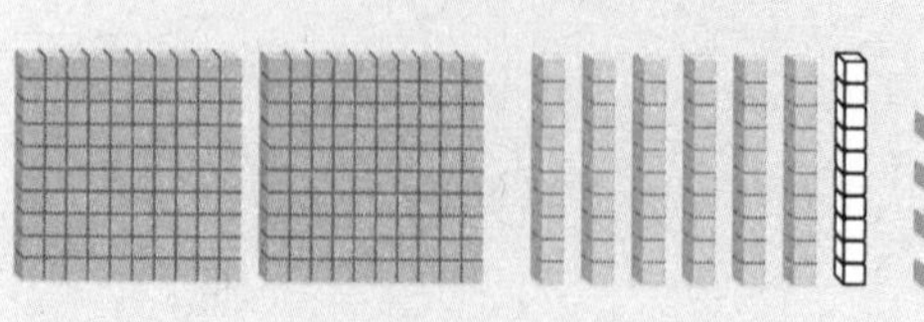

Hundreds	Tens	Ones
2	7	4

You can show 100 less or 100 more than a number by changing the digit in the hundreds place.

100 less than 264

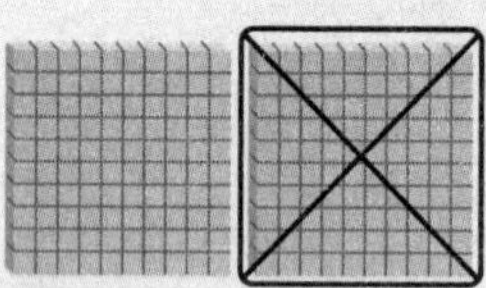

Hundreds	Tens	Ones
1	6	4

100 more than 264

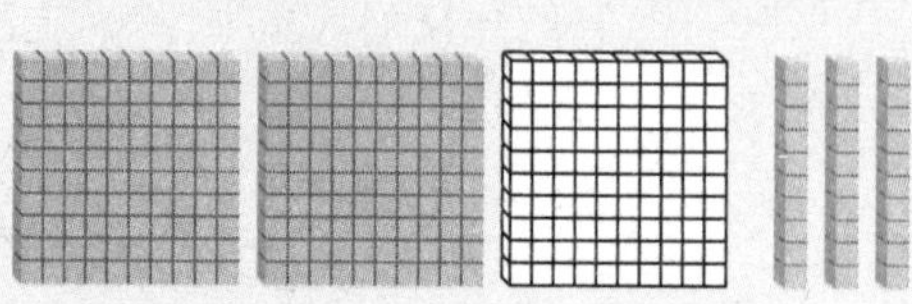

Hundreds	Tens	Ones
3	6	4

Share and Show

Write the number.

1. 10 more than 648 ______

2. 100 less than 513 ______

3. 100 more than 329 ______

4. 10 less than 827 ______

Name ______________________________

On Your Own

Write the number.

5. 10 more than 471

______

6. 10 less than 143

______

7. 100 more than 555

______

8. 100 less than 757

______

9. 100 more than 900

______

10. 10 less than 689

______

11. 100 less than 712

______

12. 10 less than 254

______

13. THINK SMARTER Kyla wrote the riddle below. Fill in the blanks to make the sentence true.

______ is 10 less than 948 and 10 more than ______.

14. THINK SMARTER Rick has 10 more crayons than Lori. Lori has 136 crayons. Tom has 10 fewer crayons than Rick. How many crayons does each child have?

Rick: ______ crayons

Tom: ______ crayons

Lori: ______ crayons

Problem Solving • Applications

Analyze Relationships

15. Juan's book has 248 pages. This is 10 more pages than there are in Kevin's book. How many pages are in Kevin's book?

_______ pages

16. There are 217 pictures in Tina's book. There are 100 fewer pictures in Mark's book. How many pictures are in Mark's book?

_______ pictures

17. GO DEEPER Use the clues to answer the question.

- Shawn counts 213 cars.
- Maria counts 100 fewer cars than Shawn.
- Jayden counts 10 more cars than Maria.

How many cars does Jayden count? _______ cars

18. THINK SMARTER Rico has 235 stickers. Gabby has 100 more stickers than Rico. Thomas has 10 fewer stickers than Gabby. Write the number of stickers each child has.

_______ Rico _______ Gabby _______ Thomas

TAKE HOME ACTIVITY • Write the number 596. Have your child name the number that is 100 more than 596.

Name ______________________

Count On and Count Back by 10 and 100

Common Core **COMMON CORE STANDARD—2.NBT.B.8** *Use place value understanding and properties of operations to add and subtract.*

Write the number.

1. 10 more than 451

____

2. 10 less than 770

____

3. 100 more than 367

____

4. 100 less than 895

____

5. 10 less than 812

____

6. 100 more than 543

____

7. 10 more than 218

____

8. 100 more than 379

____

Problem Solving

Solve. Write or draw to explain.

9. Sarah has 128 stickers. Alex has 10 fewer stickers than Sarah. How many stickers does Alex have?

________ stickers

10. WRITE Math Choose any 3-digit number. Describe how to find the number that is 10 more.

____

Lesson Check (2.NBT.B.8)

1. Write the number that is 10 less than 526.

____

2. Write the number that is 100 more than 487.

____

Spiral Review (2.NBT.A.1, 2.NBT.A.3)

3. Write another way to describe 14 tens.

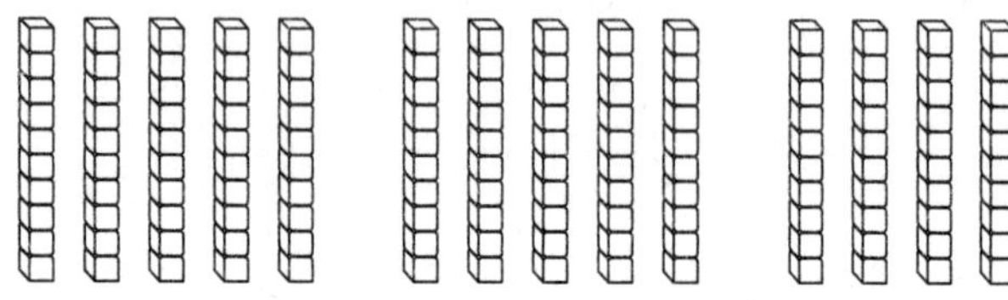

_____ hundred _____ tens

4. What is the value of the underlined digit?

5<u>8</u>7

____

5. What number can be written as 30 + 5?

____

6. What number can be written as 9 tens and 1 one?

____

FOR MORE PRACTICE GO TO THE Personal Math Trainer

Name ______________________________

Algebra • Number Patterns

Essential Question How does place value help you identify and extend counting patterns?

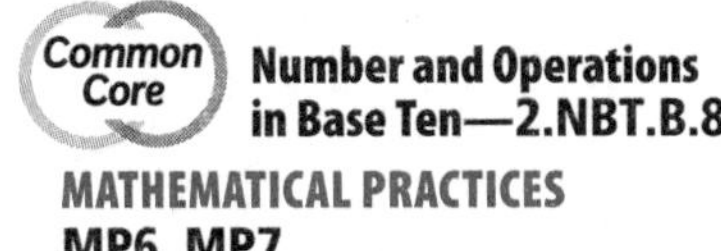

Number and Operations in Base Ten—2.NBT.B.8

MATHEMATICAL PRACTICES
MP6, MP7

Listen and Draw Real World

Shade the numbers in the counting pattern.

801	802	803	804	805	806	807	808	809	810
811	812	813	814	815	816	817	818	819	820
821	822	823	824	825	826	827	828	829	830
831	832	833	834	835	836	837	838	839	840
841	842	843	844	845	846	847	848	849	850
851	852	853	854	855	856	857	858	859	860
861	862	863	864	865	866	867	868	869	870
871	872	873	874	875	876	877	878	879	880
881	882	883	884	885	886	887	888	889	890
891	892	893	894	895	896	897	898	899	900

FOR THE TEACHER • Read the following problem and discuss how children can use a counting pattern to solve. At Blossom Bakery, 823 muffins were sold in the morning. In the afternoon, four packages of 10 muffins were sold. How many muffins were sold that day?

Math Talk MATHEMATICAL PRACTICES 7

Look for Structure
What number is next in the counting pattern you see? Explain.

Model and Draw

Look at the digits in the numbers. What two numbers are next in the counting pattern?

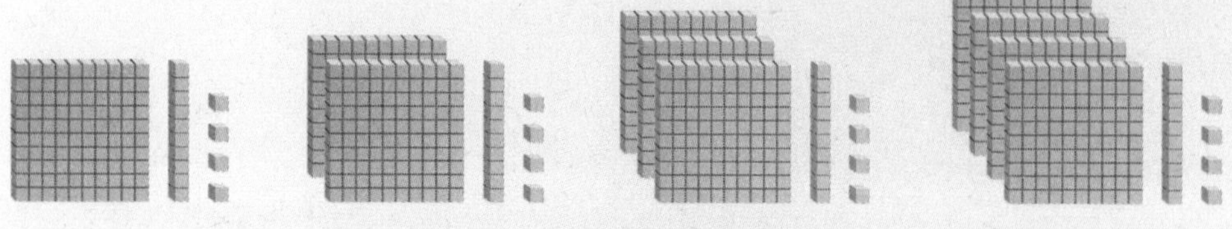

114, 214, 314, 414, 

The ____________ digit changes by one each time.

The next two numbers are ______ and ______.

Share and Show 

Look at the digits to find the next two numbers.

1. 137, 147, 157, 167, ■, ■

   The next two numbers are ______ and ______.

2. 245, 345, 445, 545, ■, ■

   The next two numbers are ______ and ______.

3. 421, 431, 441, 451, ■, ■

   The next two numbers are ______ and ______.

4. 389, 489, 589, 689, ■, ■

   The next two numbers are ______ and ______.

Name ______________________________

On Your Own

Look at the digits to find the next two numbers.

5. 193, 293, 393, 493, ■, ■

The next two numbers are ________ and ________.

6. 484, 494, 504, 514, ■, ■

The next two numbers are ________ and ________.

7. 500, 600, 700, 800, ■, ■

The next two numbers are ________ and ________.

8. 655, 665, 675, 685, ■, ■

The next two numbers are ________ and ________.

9. THINK SMARTER Mark read 203 pages. Laney read 100 more pages than Mark. Gavin read 10 fewer pages than Laney. How many pages did Gavin read?

________ pages

Problem Solving • Applications  

Solve.

10. GO DEEPER There were 135 buttons in a jar. After Robin put more buttons into the jar, there were 175 buttons in the jar. How many groups of 10 buttons did she put into the jar?

_______ groups of 10 buttons

Explain how you solved the problem.

____

____

____

____

11. THINK SMARTER Write the next number in each counting pattern.

162, 262, 362, 462, _______

347, 357, 367, 377, _______

609, 619, 629, 639, _______

TAKE HOME ACTIVITY • With your child, take turns writing number patterns in which you count on by tens or by hundreds.

Name ______________________________

Algebra • Number Patterns

Common Core **COMMON CORE STANDARD—2.NBT.B.8**
Use place value understanding and properties of operations to add and subtract.

Look at the digits to find the next two numbers.

1. 232, 242, 252, 262, ☐, ☐

   The next two numbers are ________ and ________.

2. 185, 285, 385, 485, ☐, ☐

   The next two numbers are ________ and ________.

3. 428, 528, 628, 728, ☐, ☐

   The next two numbers are ________ and ________.

4. 654, 664, 674, 684, ☐, ☐

   The next two numbers are ________ and ________.

Problem Solving

5. What are the missing numbers in the pattern?

   431, 441, 451, 461, ☐, 481, 491, ☐

   The missing numbers are ________ and ________.

6. WRITE Math How can you tell when a pattern shows counting on by tens?

   ____

   ____

Lesson Check (2.NBT.B.8)

1. What is the next number in this pattern?

453, 463, 473, 483, ____

2. What is the next number in this pattern?

295, 395, 495, 595, ____

Spiral Review (2.NBT.A.1, 2.NBT.A.3)

3. Write the number seven hundred fifty-one with digits.

____

4. What is the value of the underlined digit?

<u>1</u>95

____

5. What is another way to write 56?

____ tens ____ ones

6. Write the number 43 in tens and ones.

____ tens ____ ones

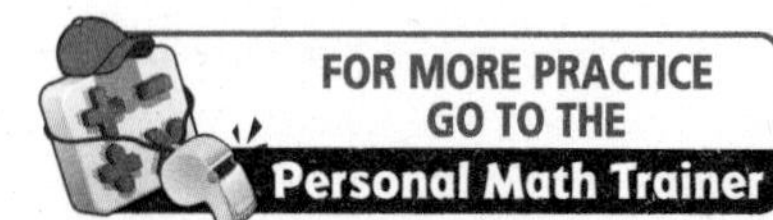

Name ____________________

Problem Solving • Compare Numbers

Essential Question How can you make a model to solve a problem about comparing numbers?

Common Core **Number and Operations in Base Ten—2.NBT.A.4**
MATHEMATICAL PRACTICES
MP1, MP2, MP3, MP4

Children bought 217 boxes of chocolate milk and 188 boxes of plain milk. Did they buy more boxes of chocolate milk or plain milk?

Unlock the Problem

Hands On

What do I need to find?

if the children bought more boxes of chocolate milk or plain milk

What information do I need to use?

________ boxes of chocolate milk

________ boxes of plain milk

Show how to solve the problem.
Model the numbers. Draw quick pictures of your models.

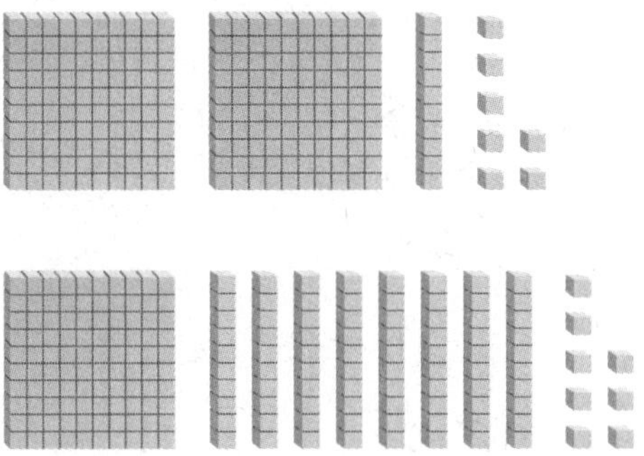

The children bought more boxes of ____________ milk.

HOME CONNECTION • Your child used base-ten blocks to represent the numbers in the problem. These models were used as a tool for comparing numbers to solve the problem.

Try Another Problem

Model the numbers. Draw quick pictures to show how you solved the problem.

- What do I need to find?
- What information do I need to use?

1. At the zoo, there are 137 birds and 142 reptiles. Are there more birds or more reptiles at the zoo?

more ________________

2. Tom's book has 105 pages. Delia's book has 109 pages. Whose book has fewer pages?

________________ book

MATHEMATICAL PRACTICES 3

Compare Explain what you did to solve the second problem.

Name ______________________________

Model the numbers. Draw quick pictures to show how you solved the problem.

3. Mary's puzzle has 164 pieces. Jake's puzzle has 180 pieces. Whose puzzle has more pieces?

_______________ puzzle

4. There are 246 people at the game. There are 251 people at the museum. At which place are there fewer people?

at the _______________

5. There are 131 crayons in a box. There are 128 crayons in a bag. Are there more crayons in the box or in the bag?

in the _______________

6. There are 308 books in the first room. There are 273 books in the second room. In which room are there fewer books?

in the _______________ room

Problem Solving • Applications 

7. THINKSMARTER There are 748 children at Dan's school. There are 651 children at Karen's school. There are 763 children at Jason's school. Which school has more than 759 children?

_______________ school

8. MATHEMATICAL PRACTICE 1 **Analyze** There are 136 crayons in a box. Use the digits 4, 1, and 2 to write a number that is greater than 136.

____

9. THINKSMARTER Becky has 134 stamps. Sara has 129 stamps. Who has more stamps?

____

Sara buys 10 more stamps. Who has more stamps now?

____

Draw quick pictures to show the stamps Becky and Sara have now.

TAKE HOME ACTIVITY • Ask your child to explain how he or she solved one of the problems on this page.

Name ______________________________

Problem Solving • Compare Numbers

Common Core **COMMON CORE STANDARD—2.NBT.A.4**
Understand place value.

Model the numbers. Draw quick pictures to show how you solved the problem.

1. Lauryn has 128 marbles. Kristin has 118 marbles. Who has more marbles?

   ____

2. Nick has 189 trading cards. Kyle has 198 trading cards. Who has fewer cards?

   ____

3. A piano has 36 black keys and 52 white keys. Are there more black keys or white keys on a piano?

   ____

4. WRITE Math Draw to show how you can use models to compare 345 and 391.

Lesson Check (2.NBT.A.4)

1. Gina has 245 stickers. Circle the number less than 245.

   285 254
   245 239

2. Carl's book has 176 pages. Circle the number greater than 176.

   203 174
   168 139

Spiral Review (2.NBT.A.1, 2.NBT.A.3)

3. Write 63 as a sum of tens and ones.

   ________ + ________

4. Write the number 58 in tens and ones.

   ________ tens ________ ones

5. Mr. Ford drove 483 miles during his trip. How many hundreds are in this number?

   ____

6. Write 20 in words.

   ____

FOR MORE PRACTICE GO TO THE Personal Math Trainer

Name ___________________________

Algebra • Compare Numbers

Essential Question How do you compare 3-digit numbers?

Common Core **Number and Operations in Base Ten—2.NBT.A.4**
MATHEMATICAL PRACTICES
MP1, MP2, MP6, MP8

Listen and Draw Real World

Draw quick pictures to solve the problem.

More ______________ were at the park.

Math Talk MATHEMATICAL PRACTICES 6

Explain how you compared the numbers.

FOR THE TEACHER • Read the following problem and have children draw quick pictures to compare the numbers. There were 125 butterflies and 132 birds at the park. Were there more butterflies or more birds at the park?

Model and Draw

Use place value to **compare** numbers. Start by looking at the digits in the greatest place value position first.

> is greater than
< is less than
= is equal to

Hundreds	Tens	Ones
4	8	3
5	7	0

4 hundreds < 5 hundreds

483 (<) 570

Hundreds	Tens	Ones
3	5	2
3	4	6

The hundreds are equal.

5 tens > 4 tens

352 (>) 346

Share and Show

Compare the numbers. Write >, <, or =.

1.

Hundreds	Tens	Ones
2	3	9
1	7	9

239 ◯ 179

2.

Hundreds	Tens	Ones
4	3	5
4	3	7

435 ◯ 437

3. 764
674

764 ◯ 674

4. 519
572

519 ◯ 572

Name ______________________________

On Your Own

Compare the numbers. Write >, <, or =.

5. 378
504

378 ◯ 504

6. 821
821

821 ◯ 821

7. 560
439

560 ◯ 439

8. 934
943

934 ◯ 943

THINK SMARTER Write the 3-digit numbers and compare the numbers. Use >, <, or =.

9. 400 + 70 + 5
400 + 70 + 5

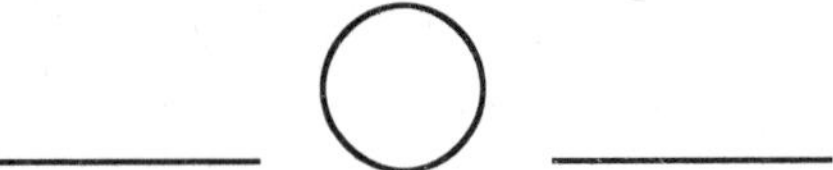

_____ ◯ _____

10. 700 + 30 + 6
600 + 80 + 7

_____ ◯ _____

MATHEMATICAL PRACTICE 2 **Use Reasoning** Write a 3-digit number in the box that makes the comparison true.

11. 526 < ☐

12. 319 > ☐

13. ☐ > 782

14. ☐ < 131

Problem Solving • Applications

Solve. Write or draw to explain.

15. THINKSMARTER Mrs. York has 300 red stickers, 50 blue stickers, and 8 green stickers. Mr. Reed has 372 stickers. Who has more stickers?

____

16. 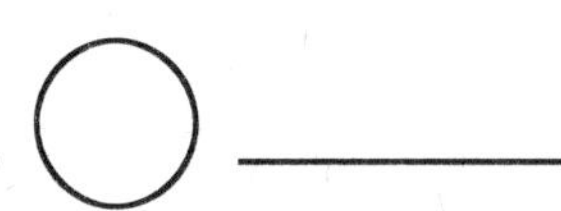 Analyze Jasmine has some number cards. Use the digits on these cards to make two 3-digit numbers. Use each digit only once. Compare the numbers.

1	2	5
6	3	8

_____ ◯ _____

17. THINKSMARTER+ Is the comparison true? Choose Yes or No.

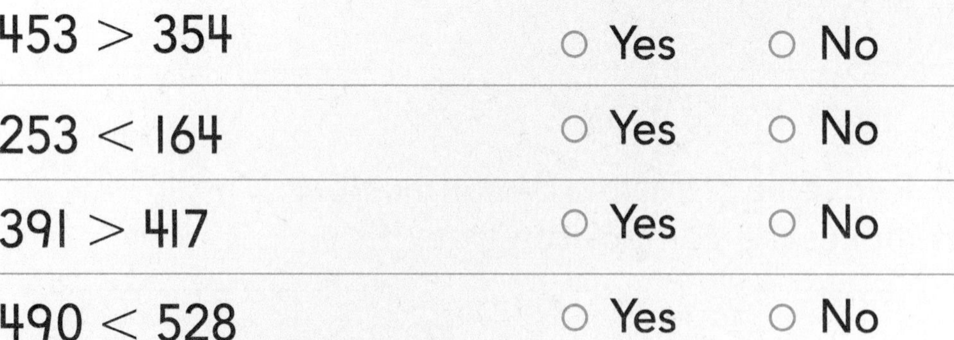

453 > 354	○ Yes	○ No
253 < 164	○ Yes	○ No
391 > 417	○ Yes	○ No
490 < 528	○ Yes	○ No

TAKE HOME ACTIVITY • Have your child explain how to compare the numbers 281 and 157.

Name ______________________________

Algebra • Compare Numbers

COMMON CORE STANDARD—2.NBT.A.4
Understand place value.

Compare the numbers. Write $>$, $<$, or $=$.

1. 489
605

489 ◯ 605

2. 719
719

719 ◯ 719

3. 370
248

370 ◯ 248

4. 645
654

645 ◯ 654

5. 205
250

205 ◯ 250

6. 813
781

813 ◯ 781

Problem Solving

Solve. Write or draw to explain.

7. Toby has 178 pennies.
Bella has 190 pennies.
Who has more pennies?

__________ has more pennies.

8. WRITE Math Explain how comparing 645 and 738 is different from comparing 645 and 649.

____

____

Lesson Check (2.NBT.A.4)

1. Write >, <, or = to compare.

315 ◯ 351

2. Write >, <, or = to compare.

401 ◯ 399

Spiral Review (2.OA.C.3, 2.NBT.A.1, 2.NBT.A.1a, 2.NBT.A.1b, 2.NBT.A.2)

3. What number has the same value as 50 tens?

____

4. Write a number with an 8 in the hundreds place.

____

5. Ned counts by fives. He starts at 80. Which number should he say next?

____

6. Mr. Dean has an even number of cats and an odd number of dogs. Show how many dogs and cats he might have.

6 cats and _____ dogs

FOR MORE PRACTICE GO TO THE **Personal Math Trainer**

Name ____________________

Chapter 2 Review/Test

1. Do the choices show a way to represent the blocks? Choose Yes or No.

3 hundreds	○ Yes	○ No
30 ones	○ Yes	○ No
30 hundreds	○ Yes	○ No
30 tens	○ Yes	○ No

2. Robin has 180 stickers. How many pages of 10 stickers does she need so that she will have 200 stickers in all?

_______ pages of stickers

3. Sanjo has 348 marbles. Harry has 100 fewer marbles than Sanjo. Ari has 10 more marbles than Harry. Write the number of marbles each child has.

_______ Sanjo   _______ Ari   _______ Harry

GO DIGITAL Assessment Options Chapter Test

4. Write the next number in each counting pattern.

214, 314, 414, 514, ______

123, 133, 143, 153, ______

Personal Math Trainer

5. THINKSMARTER+ Is the comparison true? Choose Yes or No.

$787 < 769$	○ Yes	○ No
$405 > 399$	○ Yes	○ No
$396 > 402$	○ Yes	○ No
$128 < 131$	○ Yes	○ No

6. GO DEEPER Cody is thinking of the number 627. Write Cody's number in words.

____

Show Cody's number in two other ways.

Hundreds	Tens	Ones

______ + ______ + ______

Name ___

7. Matty needs 200 buttons. Amy gives her 13 bags with 10 buttons in each bag. How many buttons does she need now?

_____ buttons

8. There are 4 boxes of 100 sheets of paper and some single sheets of paper in the closet. Choose all the numbers that show how many sheets of paper could be in the closet.

- ○ 348
- ○ 324
- ○ 406
- ○ 411

9. Blocks are sold in boxes, in bags, or as single blocks. Each box has 10 bags in it. Each bag has 10 blocks in it. Tara needs 216 blocks. Draw a picture to show a way to buy 216 blocks.

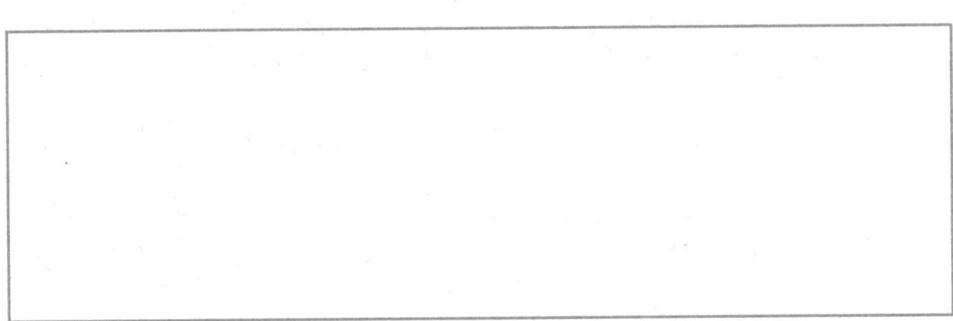

How many boxes, bags, and single blocks did you show?

___

___

10. Dan and Hannah collect toy cars. Dan has 132 cars. Hannah has 138 cars. Who has more cars? ______

Dan gets 10 more cars. Hannah gets 3 more cars. Who has more cars now? ______

Draw quick pictures to show how many cars Dan and Hannah have now.

Dan's Cars	Hannah's Cars

11. Choose all the numbers that have the digit 2 in the tens place.

- ○ 721
- ○ 142
- ○ 425
- ○ 239

12. Ann has 239 shells. Write the number in words.

____

Basic Facts and Relationships

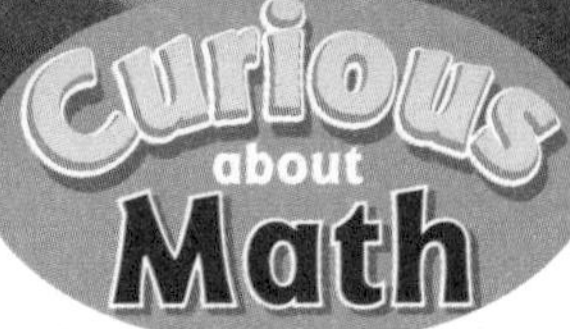

Parrot fish live near coral reefs in tropical ocean waters. They use their sharp teeth to scrape food off of the coral.

Suppose 10 parrot fish are eating at a coral reef. 3 of the fish swim away. How many fish are still eating?

Name ____________________

Use Symbols to Add

Use the picture. Use + and = to complete the addition sentence. (K.OA.A.5)

1.  

3 ◯ 1 ◯ 4

2.  

2 ◯ 3 ◯ 5

Sums to 10

Write the sum. (1.OA.C.6)

3. $\begin{array}{r} 4 \\ +\ 3 \\ \hline \end{array}$

4. $\begin{array}{r} 5 \\ +\ 0 \\ \hline \end{array}$

5. $\begin{array}{r} 2 \\ +\ 7 \\ \hline \end{array}$

6. $\begin{array}{r} 6 \\ +\ 2 \\ \hline \end{array}$

7. $\begin{array}{r} 9 \\ +\ 1 \\ \hline \end{array}$

Doubles and Doubles Plus One

Write the addition sentence. (1.OA.C.6)

8.  

____ ◯ ____ ◯ ____

9.  

____ ◯ ____ ◯ ____

This page checks understanding of important skills needed for success in Chapter 3.

Name ____________________

Vocabulary Builder

Review Words
addition
subtraction
plus
minus
equals
count on
count back

Visualize It

Sort the review words in the graphic organizer.

Addition Words **Subtraction** Words

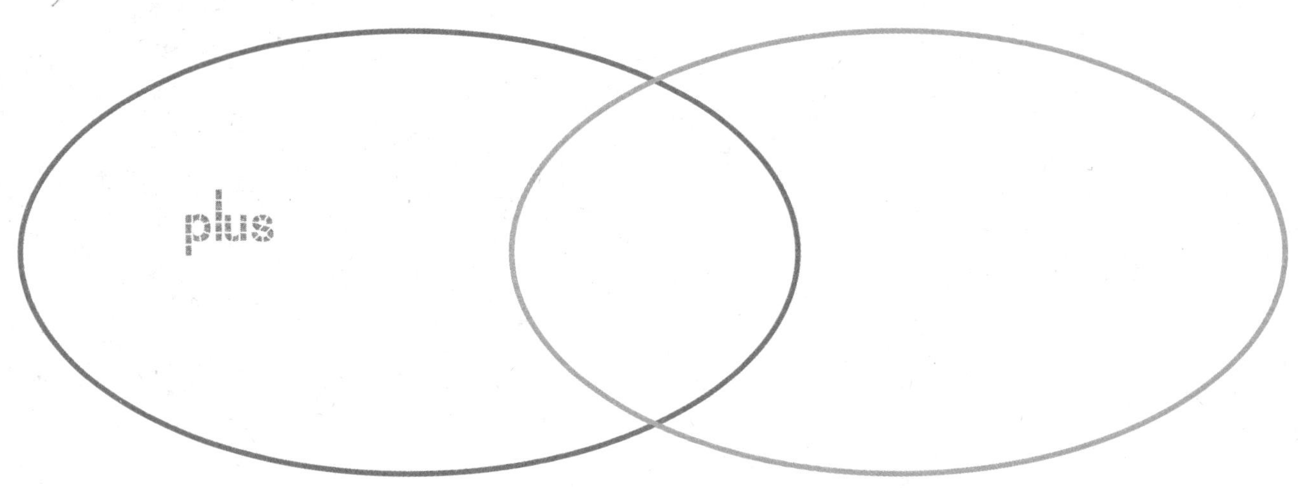

Understand Vocabulary

1. Circle the **addition** sentence. $3 + 6 = 9$ $9 - 6 = 3$

2. Circle the **subtraction** sentence. $8 + 2 = 10$ $10 - 2 = 8$

3. Circle the **count on** fact. $5 - 1 = 4$ $4 + 1 = 5$

4. Circle the **count back** fact. $8 - 2 = 6$ $6 + 2 = 8$

GO DIGITAL • Interactive Student Edition • Multimedia eGlossary

Chapter 3

Game Caterpillar Chase

Materials

- 1 [cube]
- 1 [cube]
- 1 [number cube]

Play with a partner.

1. Put your cube on START.
2. Toss the [number cube], and move that many spaces.
3. Say the sum or difference. Your partner checks your answer.
4. Take turns. The first person to get to FINISH wins.

FINISH | $7 + 3$ | $3 - 1$ | $3 + 4$ | $6 - 0$ | $5 + 2$

$2 + 4$

$1 + 6$ | $4 - 1$ | $3 + 0$ | $6 - 3$ | $5 - 2$

$5 - 5$

$7 - 4$ | $3 + 5$ | $0 + 4$ | $7 - 5$ | $2 + 3$ | $5 - 3$

START

$4 + 4$ | $6 - 1$ | $2 + 2$ | $5 + 3$ | $8 - 2$

Chapter 3 Vocabulary

addend sumando 1	**difference** diferencia 14
digit dígito 15	**even** par 22
is equal to (=) es igual a 33	**odd** impar 44
sum suma o total 59	**ten** decena 61

5 − 3 = 2

difference

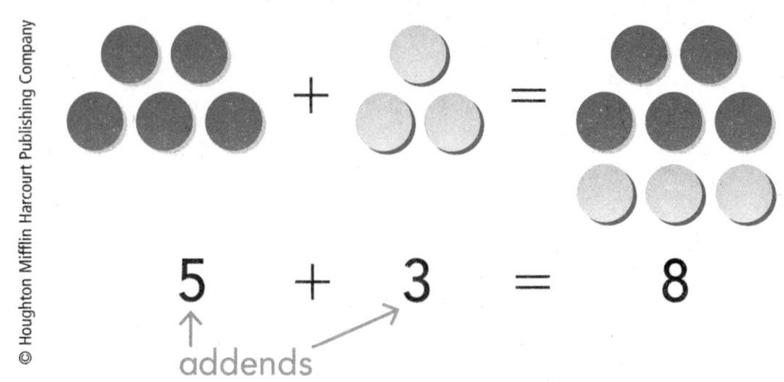

5 + 3 = 8

addends

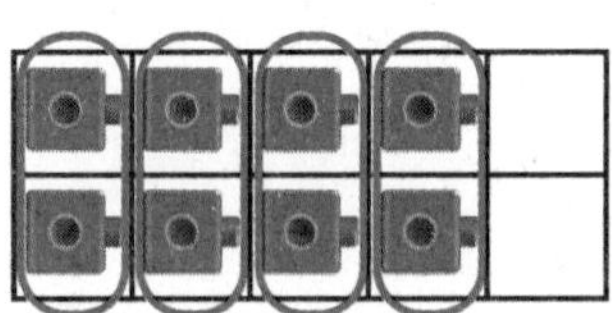

Even numbers show pairs with no left over cubes.

0, 1, 2, 3, 4, 5, 6, 7, 8, and 9 are **digits**.

Odd numbers show pairs with one cube left over.

2 plus 1 is equal to 3

2 + 1 = 3

10 ones = 1 ten

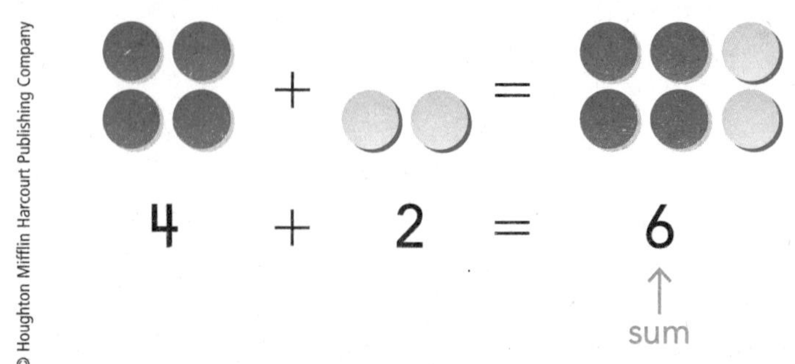

4 + 2 = 6

sum

Going to a Coral Reef

Word Box
addends
difference
digit
even numbers
is equal to (=)
odd numbers
sum
tens

For 2 players

Materials

- 1
- 1
- 1

How to Play

1. Each player chooses a and puts it on START.
2. Toss the to take a turn. Move your that many spaces around the track to the right.
3. If you land on these squares:
   White Space Tell the meaning of the math word or use it in a sentence. If you are correct, jump to the next space with that word.
   Green Space Follow the directions on the space. If there are no directions, stay where you are.
4. The first player to reach FINISH wins.

HOW TO PLAY

1. Each player chooses a and puts it on START.
2. Toss the to take a turn. Move your that many spaces around the track to the right.
3. If you land on these squares:
   White Space Tell the meaning of the math word or use it in a sentence. If you are correct, jump to the next space with that word.
   Green Space Follow the directions on the space. If there are no directions, stay where you are.
4. The first player to reach FINISH wins.

MATERIALS • 1 • 1 • 1

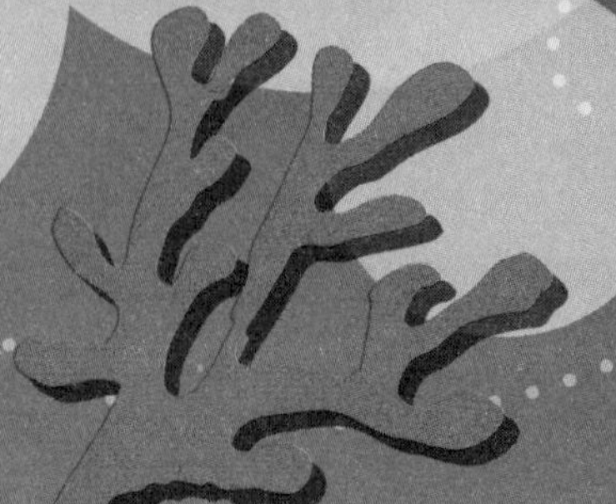

FINISH | sum | odd numbers | even numbers | addends

sum | addends | Go back to | difference | tens

odd numbers | even numbers | digit | is equal to

digit | numbers | odd numbers | sum | addends

is equal to | tens | Go back to | addends | sum

START | tens | is equal to | digit | even numbers

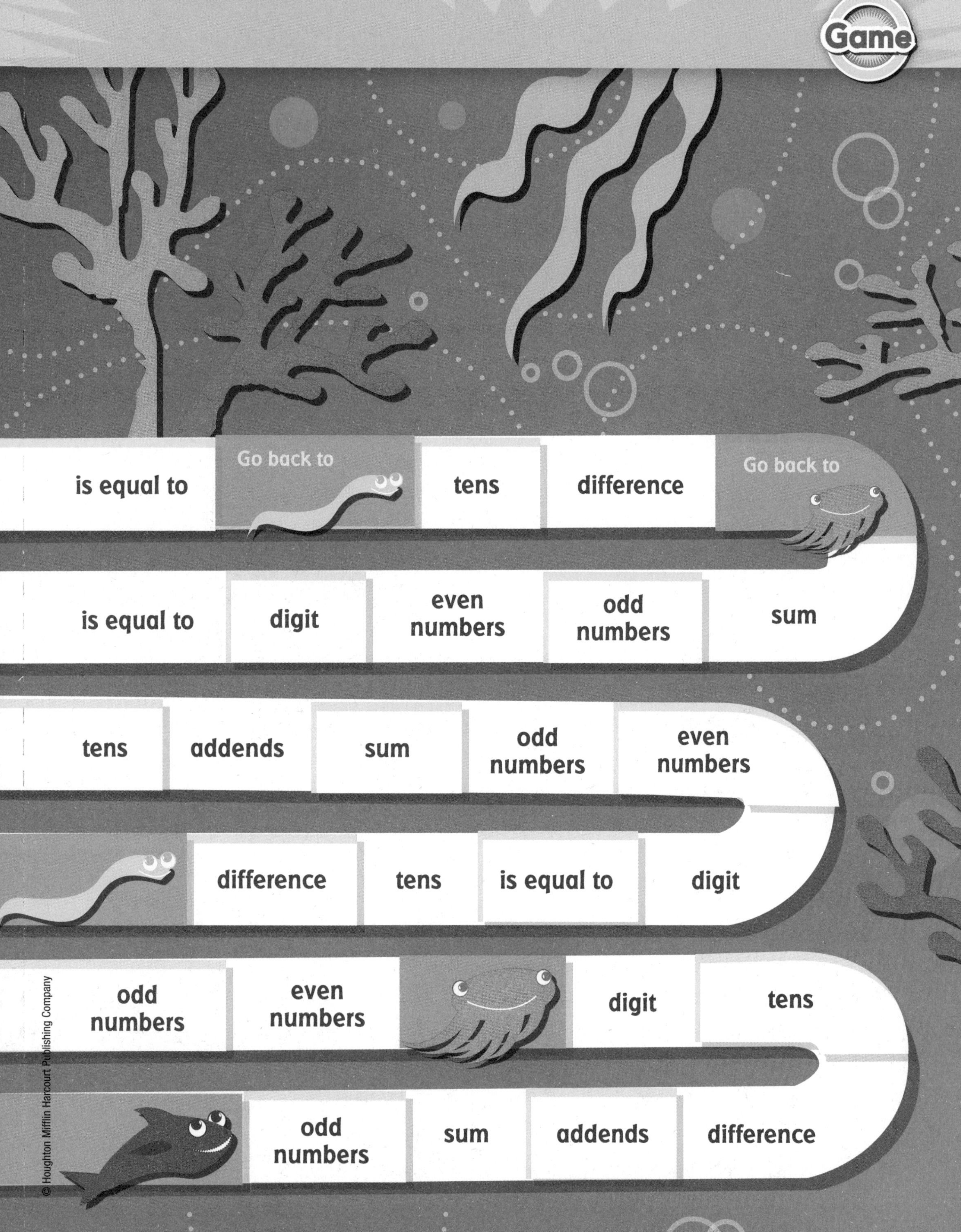
is equal to
Go back to
tens
difference
Go back to
is equal to
digit
even numbers
odd numbers
sum
tens
addends
sum
odd numbers
even numbers
difference
tens
is equal to
digit
odd numbers
even numbers
digit
tens
odd numbers
sum
addends
difference

The Write Way

Reflect

Choose one idea. Write about it in the space below.

- Think about what you did in math class today. Complete this sentence:

  I learned that I _____.

- Write your own story problem that uses addition. Then ask a partner to solve the problem.

- Use the words *addends* and *sum* to explain how to solve this problem:

  7 + 5 = _____.

Name ______________________

Use Doubles Facts

Essential Question How can you use doubles facts to find sums for near doubles facts?

Common Core **Operations and Algebraic Thinking—2.OA.B.2**
MATHEMATICAL PRACTICES
MP1, MP4, MP7

Listen and Draw Real World

Draw a picture to show the problem. Then write an addition sentence for the problem.

______ toy cars

Math Talk MATHEMATICAL PRACTICES 4

Represent Explain why 4 + 4 = 8 is called a doubles fact.

FOR THE TEACHER • Read this problem and have children draw a picture for the problem. Nathan has 6 toy cars. Alisha gives him 6 more toy cars. How many toy cars does Nathan have now? After children write an addition sentence, have them name other doubles facts that they know.

Model and Draw

You can use doubles facts to find sums for other facts.

$3 + 4 = ?$

↓

$3 + 3 + 1 = ?$

$3 + 3 = 6$

$6 + 1 = 7$

So, $3 + 4 =$ ______.

$7 + 6 = ?$

↓

$7 + 7 - 1 = ?$

$7 + 7 = 14$

$14 - 1 = 13$

So, $7 + 6 =$ ______.

Share and Show

Write a doubles fact you can use to find the sum. Write the sum.

1. $2 + 3 =$ ______

   ______ + ______ = ______

2. $4 + 5 =$ ______

   ______ + ______ = ______

3. $4 + 3 =$ ______

   ______ + ______ = ______

4. $6 + 7 =$ ______

   ______ + ______ = ______

5. $5 + 6 =$ ______

   ______ + ______ = ______

6. $8 + 7 =$ ______

   ______ + ______ = ______

Name ____________________

On Your Own

Write a doubles fact you can use to find the sum. Write the sum.

7. 5 + 4 = ______

______ + ______ = ______

8. 6 + 5 = ______

______ + ______ = ______

9. 6 + 7 = ______

______ + ______ = ______

10. 7 + 8 = ______

______ + ______ = ______

11. 8 + 9 = ______

______ + ______ = ______

12. 5 + 6 = ______

______ + ______ = ______

13. 7 + 6 = ______

______ + ______ = ______

14. 9 + 8 = ______

______ + ______ = ______

15. THINK SMARTER Mr. Norris wrote a doubles fact. It has a sum greater than 6. The numbers that he added are each less than 6. What fact might he have written?

____

Problem Solving • Applications

Solve. Write or draw to explain.

16. MATHEMATICAL PRACTICE 1 **Analyze**
Andrea has 8 red buttons and 9 blue buttons. How many buttons does Andrea have?

_______ buttons

17. GO DEEPER Henry sees 3 rabbits. Callie sees double that number of rabbits. How many more rabbits does Callie see than Henry?

_______ more rabbits

18. THINK SMARTER Could you use the doubles fact to find the sum for 4 + 5? Choose Yes or No.

4 + 4 = 8	○ Yes	○ No
5 + 5 = 10	○ Yes	○ No
9 + 9 = 18	○ Yes	○ No

TAKE HOME ACTIVITY • Ask your child to write three different doubles facts with sums less than 17.

Name ______________________

Use Doubles Facts

COMMON CORE STANDARD—2.OA.B.2
Add and subtract within 20.

Write a doubles fact you can use to find the sum. Write the sum.

1. 2 + 3 = ____

____ + ____ = ____

2. 7 + 6 = ____

____ + ____ = ____

3. 3 + 4 = ____

____ + ____ = ____

4. 8 + 9 = ____

____ + ____ = ____

Problem Solving

Solve. Write or draw to explain.

5. There are 4 ants on a log. Then 5 ants crawl onto the log. How many ants are on the log now?

______ ants

6. WRITE Math Draw or write to show two ways to use a doubles fact to find 6 + 7.

____

____

Lesson Check (2.OA.B.2)

1. Write a doubles fact you can use to find the sum. Write the sum.

   4 + 3 = ____

   ____ + ____ = ____

2. Write a doubles fact you can use to find the sum. Write the sum.

   6 + 7 = ____

   ____ + ____ = ____

Spiral Review (2.OA.C.3, 2.NBT.A.1, 2.NBT.A.3, 2.NBT.A.4)

3. There are 451 children in Lia's school. Write a number greater than 451.

   ____

4. What number is shown with these blocks?

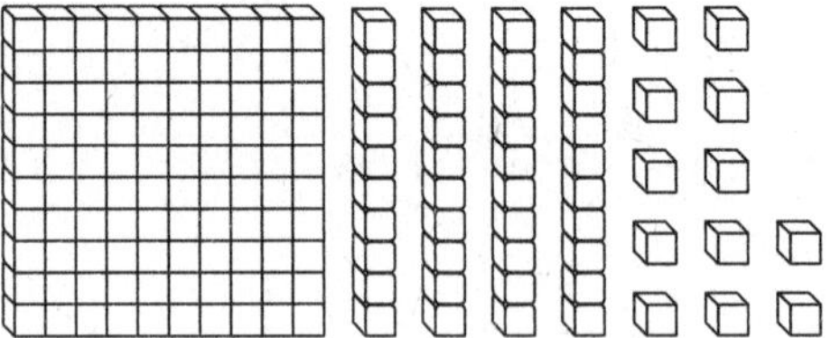

   ____

5. Write a number with the digit 8 in the tens place.

   ____

6. Circle the sum that is an even number.

   2 + 3 = 5
   3 + 4 = 7
   4 + 5 = 9
   6 + 6 = 12

FOR MORE PRACTICE GO TO THE Personal Math Trainer

Name ______________________________

Practice Addition Facts

Essential Question What are some ways to remember sums?

Operations and Algebraic Thinking—2.OA.B.2

MATHEMATICAL PRACTICES
MP1, MP7, MP8

Listen and Draw Real World

Draw pictures to show the problems.

____

____

FOR THE TEACHER • Read the following two problems. Have children draw a picture and write a number sentence for each. On Monday, Tony saw 3 dogs and 6 cats. How many animals did he see? On Tuesday, Tony saw 6 dogs and 3 cats. How many animals did he see?

MATHEMATICAL PRACTICES 1

Analyze Explain how the two problems are alike. Explain how they are different.

Model and Draw

These are some ways to remember facts.

You can count on 1, 2, or 3.

$6 + 1 = \underline{7}$

$6 + 2 = \underline{8}$

$6 + 3 = \underline{9}$

Changing the order of the **addends** does not change the sum.

$\underline{8} = 2 + 6$

$\underline{8} = 6 + 2$

Share and Show

Write the sums.

1. $4 + 4 = \_\_\_\_$

   $4 + 5 = \_\_\_\_$

2. $5 + 0 = \_\_\_\_$

   $2 + 0 = \_\_\_\_$

3. $3 + 8 = \_\_\_\_$

   $8 + 3 = \_\_\_\_$

4. $\_\_\_\_ = 5 + 5$

   $\_\_\_\_ = 5 + 4$

5. $5 + 7 = \_\_\_\_$

   $7 + 5 = \_\_\_\_$

6. $\_\_\_\_ = 7 + 7$

   $\_\_\_\_ = 7 + 8$

7. $\_\_\_\_ = 3 + 7$

   $\_\_\_\_ = 7 + 3$

8. $9 + 3 = \_\_\_\_$

   $3 + 9 = \_\_\_\_$

9. $\_\_\_\_ = 6 + 6$

   $\_\_\_\_ = 6 + 5$

Name ____________________

On Your Own

Write the sums.

10. $7 + 1 =$ ____

$1 + 7 =$ ____

11. ____ $= 4 + 0$

____ $= 9 + 0$

12. $5 + 5 =$ ____

$5 + 4 =$ ____

13. $8 + 2 =$ ____

$2 + 8 =$ ____

14. $3 + 3 =$ ____

$3 + 4 =$ ____

15. $7 + 8 =$ ____

$8 + 7 =$ ____

16. ____ $= 4 + 1$

____ $= 1 + 4$

17. $0 + 7 =$ ____

$0 + 6 =$ ____

18. $8 + 8 =$ ____

$8 + 9 =$ ____

19. $5 + 3 =$ ____

$3 + 5 =$ ____

20. ____ $= 9 + 9$

____ $= 9 + 8$

21. $6 + 7 =$ ____

$7 + 6 =$ ____

22. THINK SMARTER Sam painted 3 pictures. Ellie painted twice as many pictures as Sam. How many pictures did they paint altogether?

________ pictures

Problem Solving • Applications 

Solve. Write or draw to explain.

23. GO DEEPER Chloe draws 8 pictures. Reggie draws 1 more picture than Chloe. How many pictures do they draw?

_______ pictures

24. MATHEMATICAL PRACTICE 1 **Analyze** Joanne made 9 clay bowls last week. She made the same number of clay bowls this week. How many clay bowls did she make in two weeks?

_______ clay bowls

Personal Math Trainer

25. THINKSMARTER+ There are 9 raisins in the bowl. Devon puts 8 more raisins in the bowl. Complete the addition sentence to find how many raisins are in the bowl now.

_______ + _______ = _______

_______ raisins

TAKE HOME ACTIVITY • Ask your child to write several addition facts that he or she knows.

Name ______________________

Practice Addition Facts

Common Core **COMMON CORE STANDARD—2.OA.B.2**
Add and subtract within 20.

Write the sums.

1. 9 + 1 = ____ 1 + 9 = ____	**2.** 7 + 6 = ____ 6 + 7 = ____	**3.** 8 + 0 = ____ 5 + 0 = ____
4. ____ = 7 + 9 ____ = 9 + 7	**5.** 4 + 4 = ____ 4 + 5 = ____	**6.** 9 + 9 = ____ 9 + 8 = ____
7. 8 + 8 = ____ 8 + 7 = ____	**8.** 2 + 2 = ____ 2 + 3 = ____	**9.** ____ = 6 + 3 ____ = 3 + 6
10. 6 + 6 = ____ 6 + 7 = ____	**11.** ____ = 0 + 7 ____ = 0 + 9	**12.** 5 + 5 = ____ 5 + 6 = ____

Solve. Write or draw to explain.

13. Jason has 7 puzzles. Quincy has the same number of puzzles as Jason. How many puzzles do they have altogether?

____ puzzles

14. WRITE Math Write or draw to explain a way to find each sum: 6 + 7, 8 + 4, 2 + 9.

____

Lesson Check (2.OA.B.2)

1. What is the sum?

$8 + 7 =$ ____

2. What is the sum?

$2 + 9 =$ ____

Spiral Review (2.NBT.A.2, 2.NBT.A.3, 2.NBT.A.4, 2.NBT.B.8)

3. Write another way to describe 43.

____ + ____

4. Write the number that is 100 more than 276.

____

5. Count by tens.

20, 30, 40, ____, ____, ____

6. Write <, >, or = to compare.

127 ____ 142

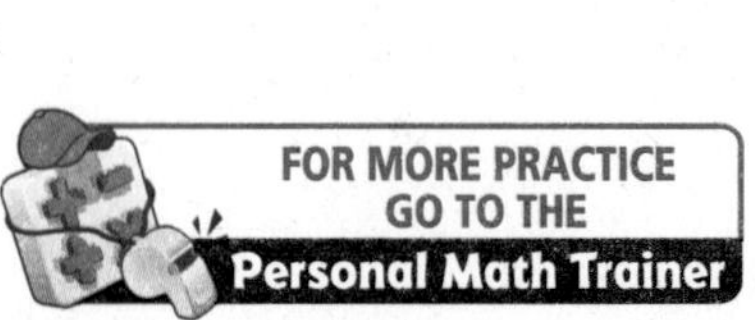

Name ______________________________

Algebra • Make a Ten to Add

Essential Question How is the make a ten strategy used to find sums?

Common Core **Operations and Algebraic Thinking—2.OA.B.2**

MATHEMATICAL PRACTICES
MP1, MP7, MP8

Listen and Draw Real World

Write the fact below the ten frame when you hear the problem that matches the model.

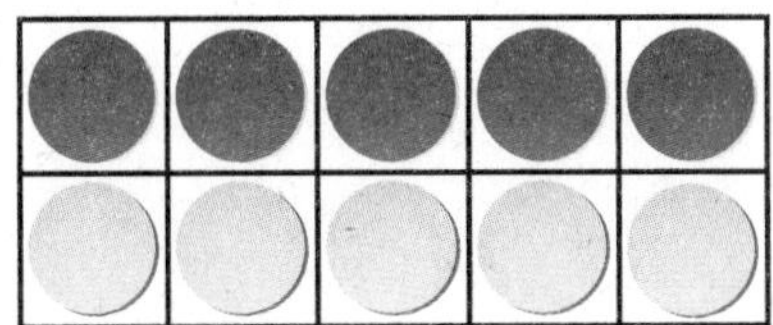

____

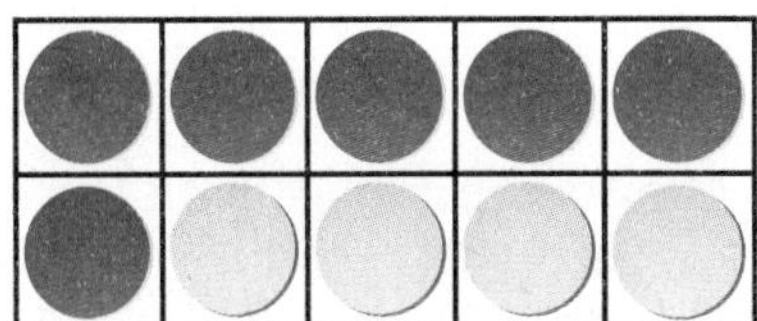

____

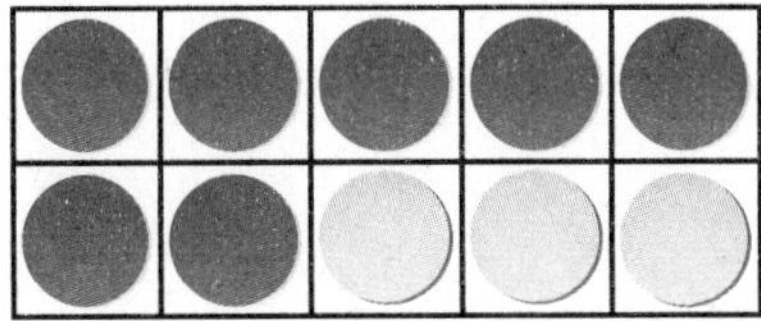

____

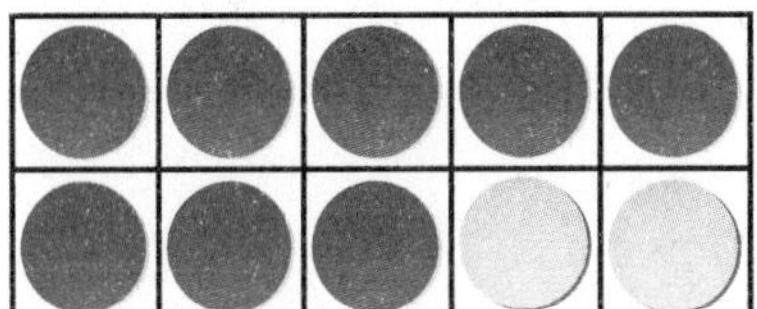

____

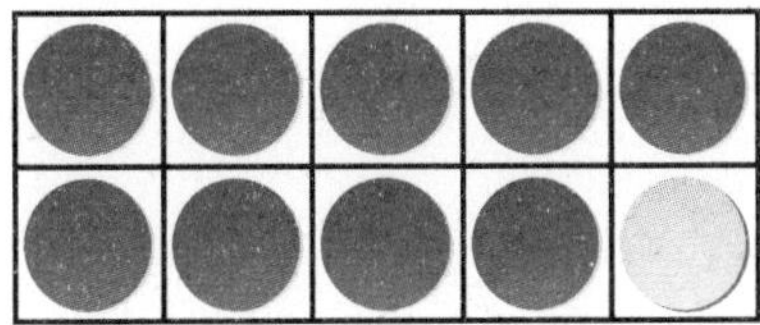

____

FOR THE TEACHER • Read the following problem. There are 6 large dogs and 4 small dogs. How many dogs are there? Have children find the ten frame that models the problem and write the addition sentence. Repeat by revising the story for each addition fact represented by the other ten frames.

Math Talk — MATHEMATICAL PRACTICES 7

Look for Structure Describe a pattern you see in these make a ten facts.

Model and Draw

$7 + 5 = ?$

You need to add 3 to 7 to make a ten. Break apart 5 as 3 and 2.

7 + 5

7 + 3 + 2

10 + 2 = 12

So, 7 + 5 = ______.

Share and Show

Show how you can make a ten to find the sum. Write the sum.

1. 8 + 3 = ______
   2 1
   10 + ______ = ______

2. 2 + 9 = ______
   1 1
   10 + ______ = ______

3. 8 + 5 = ______
   10 + ______ = ______

4. 4 + 7 = ______
   10 + ______ = ______

5. 3 + 9 = ______
   10 + ______ = ______

6. 7 + 6 = ______
   10 + ______ = ______

Name ______________________

On Your Own

Show how you can make a ten to find the sum.
Write the sum.

7. 4 + 9 = ____

3 1

10 + ____ = ____

8. 9 + 8 = ____

1 7

10 + ____ = ____

9. 8 + 6 = ____

10 + ____ = ____

10. 5 + 9 = ____

10 + ____ = ____

11. 7 + 9 = ____

10 + ____ = ____

12. 8 + 4 = ____

10 + ____ = ____

13. GO DEEPER Alex is thinking of a doubles fact. The sum is greater than the sum of 7 + 7 but less than the sum of 8 + 9. What fact is Alex thinking of?

____ + ____ = ____

14. THINK SMARTER There were 5 bees in a hive. How many more bees need to go in the hive for there to be 14 bees?

____ more bees

Problem Solving • Applications

Solve. Write or draw to explain.

15. MATHEMATICAL PRACTICE 1 **Analyze** There are 9 large bicycles at the store. There are 6 small bicycles at the store. How many bicycles are at the store?

_______ bicycles

16. GO DEEPER Max is thinking of a doubles fact. It has a sum that is greater than the sum of 6 + 4 but less than the sum of 8 + 5. What fact is Max thinking of?

_______ + _______ = _______

17. THINK SMARTER Natasha had 8 shells. Then she found 5 more shells. Draw to show how to find the number of shells Natasha has now.

How many shells does she have now? _______ shells

TAKE HOME ACTIVITY • Ask your child to name pairs of numbers that have a sum of 10. Then have him or her write the addition sentences.

Name ____________________

Algebra • Make a Ten to Add

COMMON CORE STANDARD—2.OA.B.2
Add and subtract within 20.

Show how you can make a ten to find the sum. Write the sum.

1. 9 + 7 = ____

10 + ____ = ____

2. 8 + 5 = ____

10 + ____ = ____

3. 8 + 6 = ____

10 + ____ = ____

4. 3 + 9 = ____

10 + ____ = ____

5. 8 + 7 = ____

10 + ____ = ____

6. 6 + 5 = ____

10 + ____ = ____

Problem Solving Real World

Solve. Write or draw to explain.

7. There are 9 children on the bus. Then 8 more children get on the bus. How many children are on the bus now?

____ children

8. WRITE Math Describe how you can use the make a ten strategy to find the sum 7 + 9.

____

Lesson Check (2.OA.B.2)

1. Circle the fact with the same sum as 8 + 7.

10 + 3
10 + 4
10 + 5
10 + 6

2. Write a fact with the same sum as 7 + 5.

____ + ____

Spiral Review (2.OA.C.3, 2.NBT.A.3)

3. Write the number shown by 200 + 10 + 7.

____

4. Circle the odd number.

2 4 6 7

5. What is the value of the underlined digit?

<u>6</u>5

____

6. What is another way to write the number 47?

____ tens ____ ones

Name ______________________

Algebra • Add 3 Addends

Essential Question How do you add three numbers?

Common Core **Operations and Algebraic Thinking—2.OA.B.2** *Also 2.NBT.B.5*
MATHEMATICAL PRACTICES
MP1, MP7, MP8

Listen and Draw

Write the sum of each pair of addends.

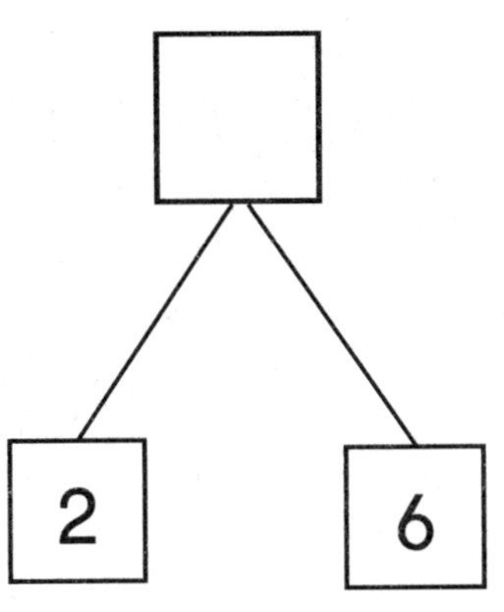

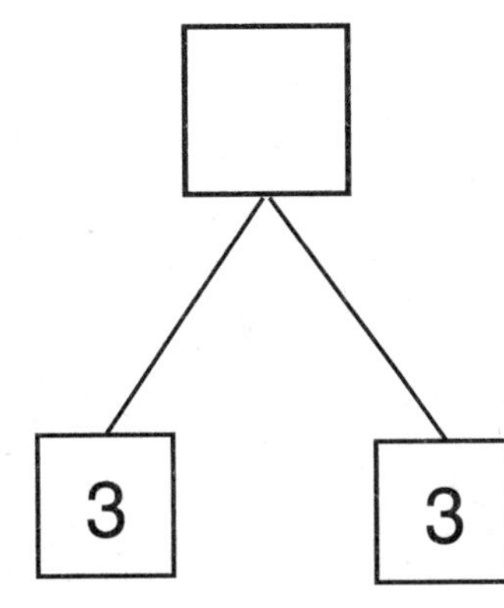

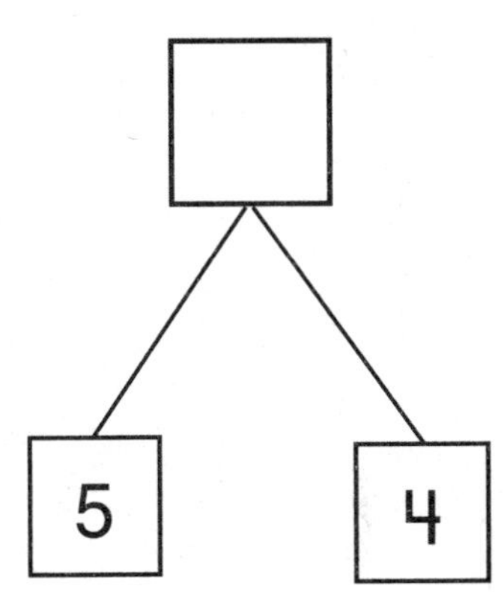

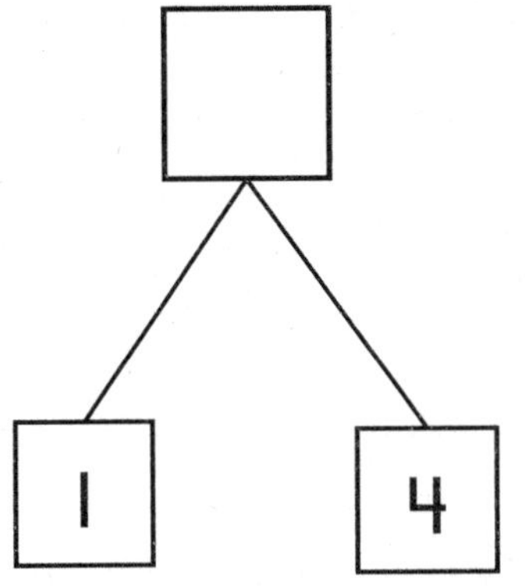

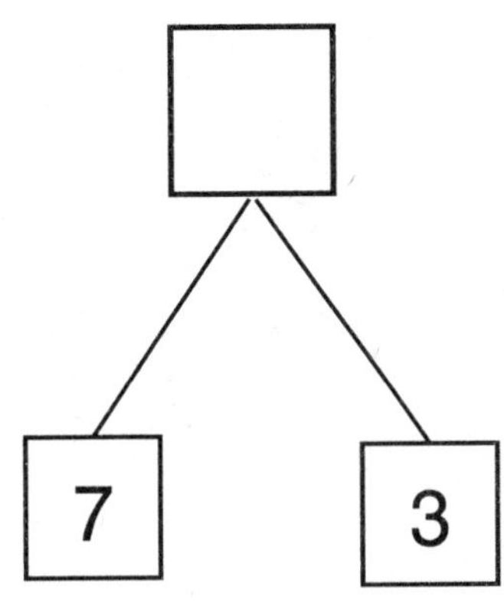

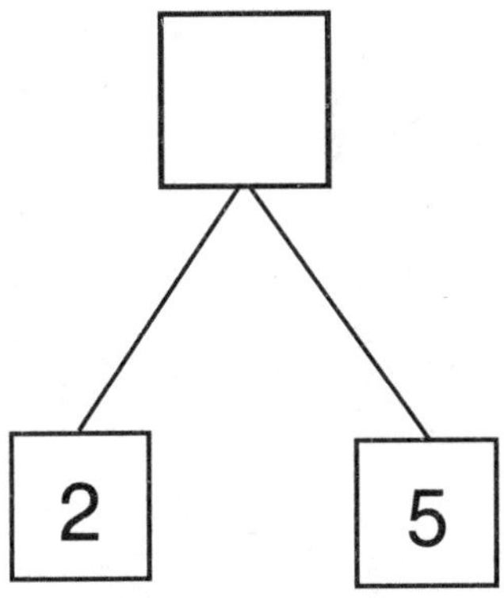

MATHEMATICAL PRACTICES 1

Describe how you found the sum of 5 and 4.

FOR THE TEACHER • After children have recorded the sum of each pair of addends, have them share their answers and discuss the strategies used.

Model and Draw

You can group numbers in different ways to add.

Choose two addends.
Look for facts you know.

$3 + 2 + 7 = ?$

$5 + 7 = $ 12

$3 + 2 + 7 = ?$

$3 + 9 = $ ______

$3 + 2 + 7 = ?$

$10 + 2 = $ ______

Share and Show

MATH BOARD

Solve two ways. Circle the two addends you add first.

1. $1 + 8 + 2 = $ ______ $1 + 8 + 2 = $ ______

2. $7 + 3 + 3 = $ ______ $7 + 3 + 3 = $ ______

3. $4 + 2 + 4 = $ ______ $4 + 2 + 4 = $ ______

4. $2 + 8 + 2 = $ ______ $2 + 8 + 2 = $ ______

5.
$$\begin{array}{r} 3 \\ 2 \\ +\ 6 \\ \hline \end{array} \qquad \begin{array}{r} 3 \\ 2 \\ +\ 6 \\ \hline \end{array}$$

6.
$$\begin{array}{r} 7 \\ 0 \\ +\ 2 \\ \hline \end{array} \qquad \begin{array}{r} 7 \\ 0 \\ +\ 2 \\ \hline \end{array}$$

Name ______________________________

On Your Own

Solve two ways. Circle the two addends you add first.

7. 4 + 1 + 6 = _______ 4 + 1 + 6 = _______

8. 4 + 3 + 3 = _______ 4 + 3 + 3 = _______

9. 1 + 5 + 3 = _______ 1 + 5 + 3 = _______

10. 6 + 4 + 4 = _______ 6 + 4 + 4 = _______

11. 5 + 5 + 5 = _______ 5 + 5 + 5 = _______

12. 7 + 0 + 6 = _______ 7 + 0 + 6 = _______

13.
$$\begin{array}{r} 5 \\ 3 \\ +\ 4 \\ \hline \end{array} \qquad \begin{array}{r} 5 \\ 3 \\ +\ 4 \\ \hline \end{array}$$

14.
$$\begin{array}{r} 4 \\ 2 \\ +\ 5 \\ \hline \end{array} \qquad \begin{array}{r} 4 \\ 2 \\ +\ 5 \\ \hline \end{array}$$

MATHEMATICAL PRACTICE 7 **Look for Structure**

Write the missing addend.

15.
$$\begin{array}{r} 5 \\ 5 \\ +\ \square \\ \hline 14 \end{array}$$

16.
$$\begin{array}{r} 4 \\ \square \\ +\ 4 \\ \hline 12 \end{array}$$

17.
$$\begin{array}{r} 3 \\ \square \\ +\ 7 \\ \hline 11 \end{array}$$

18.
$$\begin{array}{r} 5 \\ 3 \\ +\ \square \\ \hline 13 \end{array}$$

Problem Solving • Applications

Choose a way to solve.
Write or draw to explain.

19. THINKSMARTER Nick, Alex, and Sophia eat 15 raisins in all. Nick and Alex each eat 4 raisins. How many raisins does Sophia eat?

_______ raisins

20. MATHEMATICAL PRACTICE 1 **Analyze**
There are 5 green grapes and 4 red grapes in a bowl. Eli puts 4 more grapes in the bowl. How many grapes are in the bowl now?

_______ grapes

21. THINKSMARTER Mrs. Moore bought 4 small apples, 6 medium apples, and 3 large apples. How many apples did she buy?

_______ apples

TAKE HOME ACTIVITY • Have your child describe two ways to add 3, 6, and 2.

Name ______________________________

Algebra • Add 3 Addends

COMMON CORE STANDARD—2.OA.B.2
Add and subtract within 20.

Solve two ways. Circle the two addends you add first.

1. 2 + 3 + 7 = ____ 2 + 3 + 7 = ____

2. 5 + 3 + 3 = ____ 5 + 3 + 3 = ____

3. 4 + 5 + 4 = ____ 4 + 5 + 4 = ____

4. $\begin{array}{r} 5 \\ 4 \\ +\ 5 \\ \hline \end{array}$ $\begin{array}{r} 5 \\ 4 \\ +\ 5 \\ \hline \end{array}$

5. $\begin{array}{r} 6 \\ 3 \\ +\ 4 \\ \hline \end{array}$ $\begin{array}{r} 6 \\ 3 \\ +\ 4 \\ \hline \end{array}$

Problem Solving

Choose a way to solve. Write or draw to explain.

6. Amber has 2 red crayons, 5 blue crayons, and 4 yellow crayons. How many crayons does she have?

____ crayons

7. WRITE Math Write or draw to explain two ways you can find the sum of 3 + 4 + 5.

____

Lesson Check (2.OA.B.2)

1. What is the sum of
$2 + 4 + 6$?

____

2. What is the sum of
$5 + 4 + 2$?

____

Spiral Review (2.NBT.A.1a, 2.NBT.A.1b, 2.NBT.A.3, 2.NBT.A.4, 2.NBT.B.8)

3. Write $>$, $<$, or $=$ to compare.

688 ____ 648

4. What number can be written as 4 tens 2 ones?

____

5. What number has the same value as 50 tens?

____

6. What is the next number in the pattern?

420, 520, 620, 720, ____

FOR MORE PRACTICE GO TO THE **Personal Math Trainer**

Name ______________________________

Algebra • Relate Addition and Subtraction

Essential Question How are addition and subtraction related?

Common Core **Operations and Algebraic Thinking—2.OA.B.2**
MATHEMATICAL PRACTICES
MP2, MP6, MP8

Listen and Draw Real World

Complete the bar model to show the problem.

8	7

______

______ soccer balls

______	7

15

______ soccer balls

FOR THE TEACHER • Read the following problems. Have children complete the bar model for each. The soccer team has 8 red balls and 7 yellow balls. How many soccer balls does the team have? The soccer team has 15 balls inside the locker room. The children took the 7 yellow balls outside. How many soccer balls were inside?

MATHEMATICAL PRACTICES 6

Explain how the bar models for the problems are alike and how they are different.

Model and Draw

You can use addition facts to remember **differences**. Related facts have the same whole and parts.

Think of the addends in an addition fact to find the difference for a related subtraction fact.

6	7

13

$6 + 7 = \underline{13}$

____	7

13

$13 - 7 =$ ____

Share and Show

Write the sum and the difference for the related facts.

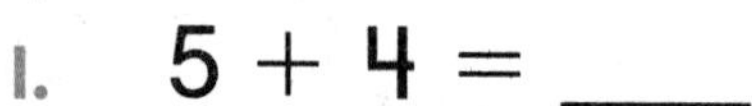

1. $5 + 4 =$ ____
   $9 - 4 =$ ____

2. $2 + 7 =$ ____
   $9 - 2 =$ ____

3. $3 + 8 =$ ____
   $11 - 8 =$ ____

4. $5 + 8 =$ ____
   $13 - 5 =$ ____

5. ____ $= 1 + 8$
   ____ $= 9 - 1$

6. $9 + 9 =$ ____
   $18 - 9 =$ ____

7. ____ $= 8 + 7$
   ____ $= 15 - 8$

8. $4 + 7 =$ ____
   $11 - 7 =$ ____

9. $7 + 5 =$ ____
   $12 - 7 =$ ____

Name ______________________________

On Your Own

Write the sum and the difference for the related facts.

10. $4 + 3 =$ ____
$7 - 3 =$ ____

11. $2 + 6 =$ ____
$8 - 6 =$ ____

12. $6 + 4 =$ ____
$10 - 6 =$ ____

13. $7 + 3 =$ ____
$10 - 7 =$ ____

14. $8 + 6 =$ ____
$14 - 6 =$ ____

15. ____ $= 3 + 9$
____ $= 12 - 9$

16. $6 + 5 =$ ____
$11 - 5 =$ ____

17. $7 + 7 =$ ____
$14 - 7 =$ ____

18. $9 + 6 =$ ____
$15 - 9 =$ ____

19. $5 + 9 =$ ____
$14 - 9 =$ ____

20. ____ $= 4 + 8$
____ $= 12 - 4$

21. $9 + 7 =$ ____
$16 - 7 =$ ____

MATHEMATICAL PRACTICE 6 Make Connections

Write a related subtraction fact for each addition fact.

22. $7 + 8 = 15$

____

23. $5 + 7 = 12$

____

24. $6 + 7 = 13$

____

25. $9 + 8 = 17$

____

Problem Solving • Applications

WRITE Math

Solve. Write or draw to explain.

26. Trevor has 7 kites. Pam has 4 kites. How many more kites does Trevor have than Pam?

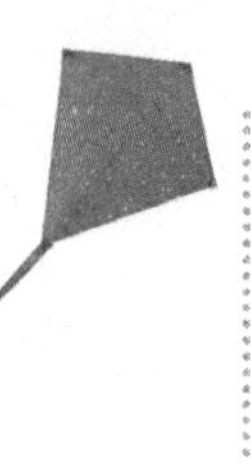

_______ more kites

27. THINK SMARTER Mr. Sims has a bag of 7 pears and a bag of 6 pears. His family eats 5 pears. How many pears does he have now?

_______ pears

28. THINK SMARTER Elin counts 7 geese in the water and some geese on the shore. There are 16 geese in all. Draw a picture to show the two groups of geese.

Write a number sentence that can help you find how many geese are on the shore.

____

How many geese are on the shore? _______ geese

TAKE HOME ACTIVITY • Ask your child to name some subtraction facts that he or she knows well.

Name ______________________________

Practice Subtraction Facts

Essential Question What are some ways to remember differences?

Common Core **Operations and Algebraic Thinking—2.OA.B.2**
MATHEMATICAL PRACTICES
MP1, MP3

Use Gina's model to answer the question.

Gina's Model

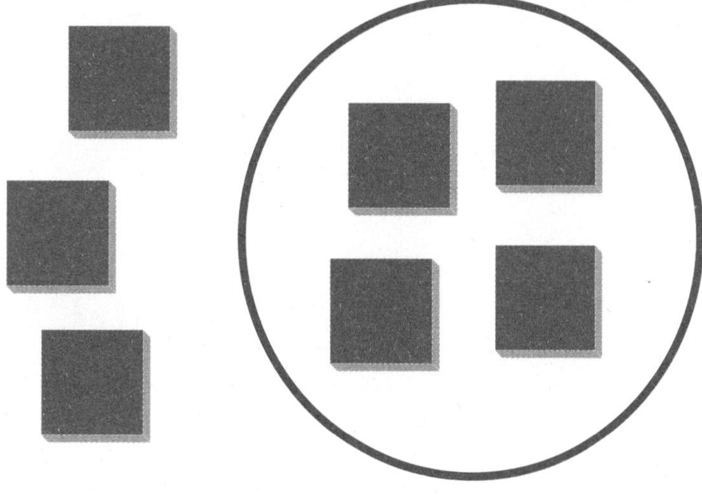

______________________ ______________________

______________________ ______________________

FOR THE TEACHER • Tell children that Gina put 4 color tiles inside the circle and then put 3 color tiles outside the circle. Then ask: What addition fact could be written for Gina's model? Repeat with stories for the three facts that are related to this addition fact.

MATHEMATICAL PRACTICES 3

Compare Strategies Explain how the different facts for Gina's model are related.

Model and Draw

These are some ways to find differences.

You can count back by 1, 2, or 3.

7 − 2 = ____

Start with 7.
Say: 6, 5.

9 − 3 = ____

Start with 9.
Say: 8, 7, 6.

You can think about a missing addend to subtract.

8 − 5 = ■ 5 + 3 = 8

So, 8 − 5 = ____.

Share and Show

Write the difference.

1. 6 − 4 = ____
2. 10 − 7 = ____
3. ____ = 5 − 2
4. 14 − 6 = ____
5. ____ = 8 − 4
6. 11 − 3 = ____
7. ____ = 7 − 5
8. 10 − 4 = ____
9. 5 − 0 = ____
10. 13 − 9 = ____
11. 9 − 3 = ____
12. ____ = 7 − 6
13. 12 − 3 = ____
14. 6 − 3 = ____
15. 9 − 5 = ____
16. 10 − 6 = ____
17. ____ = 8 − 3
18. 13 − 5 = ____

Name ____________________

On Your Own

Write the difference.

19. 11 − 2 = ____

20. 9 − 7 = ____

21. ____ = 7 − 4

22. 12 − 5 = ____

23. 8 − 6 = ____

24. ____ = 7 − 0

25. ____ = 10 − 5

26. 15 − 8 = ____

27. 13 − 7 = ____

28. 10 − 8 = ____

29. 8 − 5 = ____

30. ____ = 9 − 6

31. ____ = 9 − 4

32. 11 − 8 = ____

33. 12 − 7 = ____

34. THINK SMARTER
Write the differences.
Then write the next fact
in the pattern.

10 − 1 = ____	12 − 9 = ____	18 − 9 = ____
8 − 1 = ____	13 − 9 = ____	17 − 8 = ____
6 − 1 = ____	14 − 9 = ____	16 − 7 = ____
4 − 1 = ____	15 − 9 = ____	15 − 6 = ____
____________	____________	____________

TAKE HOME ACTIVITY • With your child, practice saying subtraction facts from this lesson.

Name ____________________

Mid-Chapter Checkpoint

Concepts and Skills

Write the sum. (2.OA.B.2)

1. 3 + 6 = ____
2. 8 + 0 = ____
3. 7 + 7 = ____
4. 9 + 4 = ____
5. ____ = 5 + 6
6. 2 + 8 = ____
7. 3 + 7 + 2 = ____
8. 4 + 4 + 6 = ____

Show how you can make a ten to find the sum.
Write the sum. (2.OA.B.2)

9. 9 + 7 = ____

   10 + ____ = ____

10. 6 + 8 = ____

   10 + ____ = ____

Write the sum and the difference for the related facts. (2.OA.B.2)

11. 5 + 4 = ____

    9 − 4 = ____

12. 3 + 9 = ____

    12 − 9 = ____

13. 8 + 7 = ____

    15 − 8 = ____

14. THINK SMARTER Lily has 6 toys cars. Yong has 5 toy cars. How many toy cars do they have? (2.OA.B.2)

____ toy cars

Name ______________________

Practice Subtraction Facts

Common Core **COMMON CORE STANDARD—2.OA.B.2**
Add and subtract within 20.

Write the difference.

1. 15 − 9 = ____	**2.** 10 − 2 = ____	**3.** ____ = 13 − 5
4. 14 − 7 = ____	**5.** 10 − 8 = ____	**6.** 12 − 7 = ____
7. ____ = 10 − 3	**8.** 16 − 7 = ____	**9.** 8 − 4 = ____
10. 11 − 5 = ____	**11.** 13 − 6 = ____	**12.** ____ = 12 − 9
13. 16 − 9 = ____	**14.** ____ = 11 − 9	**15.** 12 − 8 = ____

Problem Solving

Solve. Write or draw to explain.

16. Mr. Li has 16 pencils. He gives 9 pencils to some students. How many pencils does Mr. Li have now?

____ pencils

17. WRITE Math Write or draw to explain two different ways to find the difference for 12 − 3.

____

Lesson Check (2.OA.B.2)

1. Write the difference.

$13 - 6 =$ ____

2. Write the difference.

$12 - 3 =$ ____

Spiral Review (2.NBT.A.1, 2.NBT.A.1a, 2.NBT.A.1b, 2.NBT.A.2, 2.NBT.A.3)

3. What is the value of the underlined digit?

6<u>2</u>5

____

4. Count by fives.

405, ____, ____, ____

5. Devin has 39 toy blocks. What is the value of the digit 9 in this number?

____

6. Which number has the same value as 20 tens?

____

FOR MORE PRACTICE GO TO THE **Personal Math Trainer**

Name ______________________________

Use Ten to Subtract

Essential Question How does getting to 10 in subtraction help when finding differences?

Common Core **Operations and Algebraic Thinking—2.OA.B.2** *Also 2.MD.B.6*
MATHEMATICAL PRACTICES
MP5, MP7, MP8

Listen and Draw Real World

Circle to show the amount you subtract for each problem.

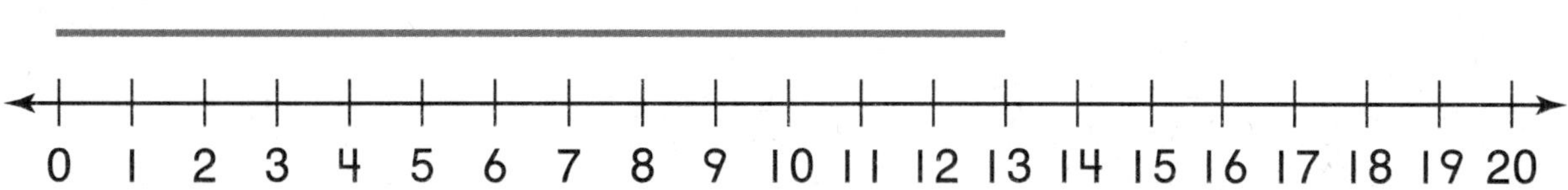

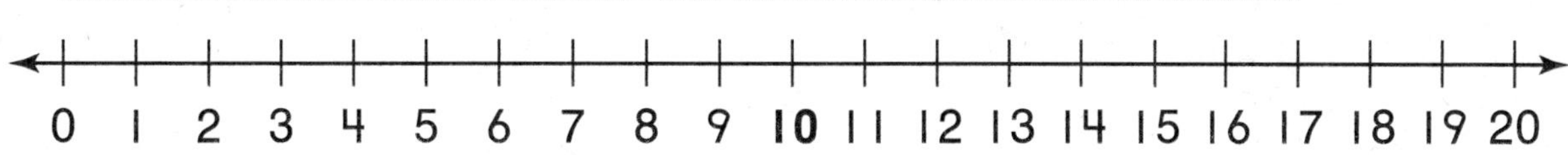

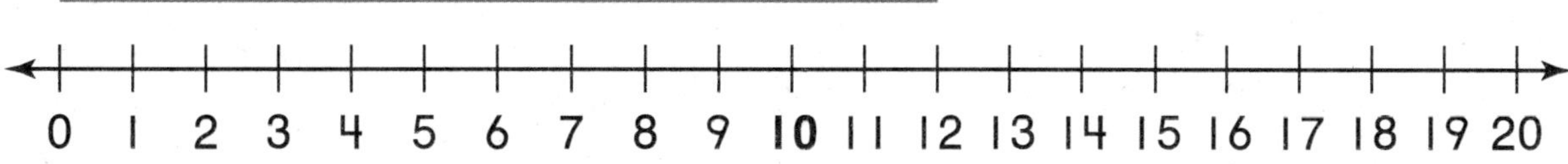

FOR THE TEACHER • Read the following problem. Deveron has 13 crayons. He gives 3 crayons to Tyler. How many crayons does Deveron have now? Have children circle the part of the blue line segment that shows what is subtracted from the total. Repeat for two more problems.

MATHEMATICAL PRACTICES 7

Look for Structure
Describe a pattern in the three problems and answers.

Model and Draw

You can subtract in steps to use a tens fact.

14 − 6 = ?

4 2

Subtract in steps:
14 - 4 = 10
10 - 2 = 8

- 2   - 4

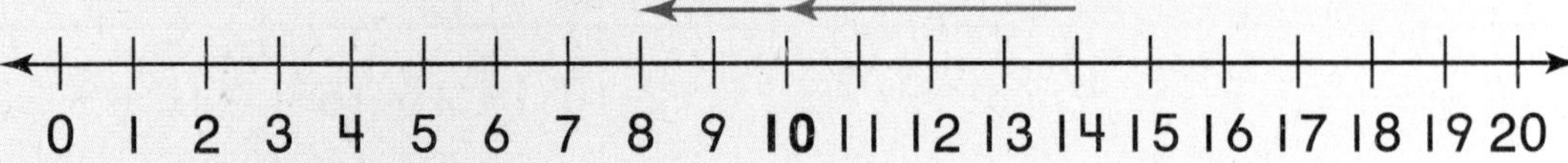

So, 14 − 6 = 8.

Share and Show

Show the tens fact you used. Write the difference.

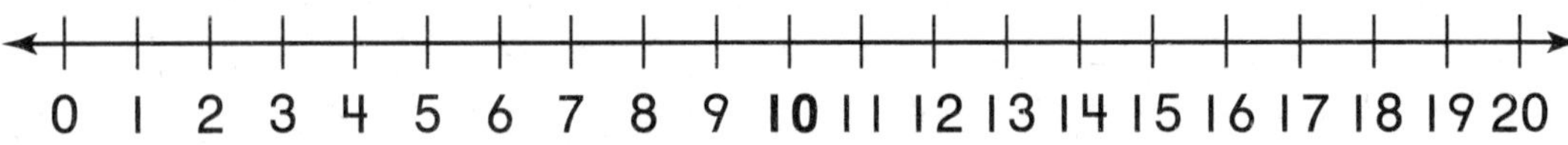

1. 12 − 5 = ____

2 3

10 − ____ = ____

2. 11 − 6 = ____

1 5

10 − ____ = ____

3. 15 − 7 = ____

10 − ____ = ____

4. 13 − 7 = ____

10 − ____ = ____

Name ________________________________

On Your Own

Show the tens fact you used. Write the difference.

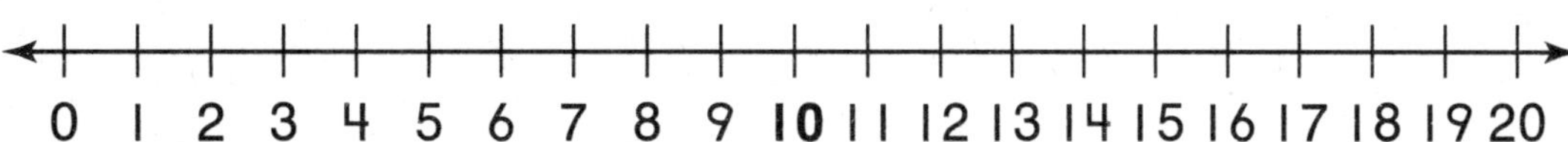

5. 13 − 5 = ____

10 − ____ = ____

6. 15 − 6 = ____

10 − ____ = ____

7. 12 − 8 = ____

10 − ____ = ____

8. 14 − 8 = ____

10 − ____ = ____

9. GO DEEPER Chris had 15 stickers. He gave Ann and Suzy each the same number of stickers. Now Chris has 7 stickers. How many stickers did he give to each girl?

____ stickers

Solve. Write or draw to explain.

10. THINK SMARTER Beth has a box of 16 crayons. She gives 3 crayons to Jake and 7 crayons to Wendy. How many crayons does Beth have now?

____ crayons

Problem Solving • Applications

WRITE Math

GO DEEPER Write number sentences that use both addition and subtraction. Use each choice only once.

~~9 − 2~~
~~3 + 4~~
1 + 4
14 − 6
5 + 4
15 − 6
10 − 5
4 + 4

11. 9 − 2 = 3 + 4
    7 = 7

12. ________ = ________

13. ________ = ________

14. ________ = ________

15. THINK SMARTER Does the number sentence have the same difference as 15 − 7 = ■? Choose Yes or No.

10 − 6 = ■	○ Yes	○ No
10 − 2 = ■	○ Yes	○ No
10 − 4 = ■	○ Yes	○ No

TAKE HOME ACTIVITY • Ask your child to name pairs of numbers that have a difference of 10. Then have him or her write the number sentences.

Name ______________________

Use Ten to Subtract

Common Core

COMMON CORE STANDARD—2.OA.B.2
Add and subtract within 20.

Show the tens fact you used.
Write the difference.

1. 14 − 6 = ____

10 − ____ = ____

2. 12 − 7 = ____

10 − ____ = ____

3. 13 − 7 = ____

10 − ____ = ____

4. 15 − 8 = ____

10 − ____ = ____

Problem Solving Real World

Solve. Write or draw to explain.

5. Carl read 15 pages on Monday night and 9 pages on Tuesday night. How many more pages did he read on Monday night than on Tuesday night?

____ more pages

6. WRITE Math Describe how to use a tens fact to find the difference for 15 − 8.

____

Lesson Check (2.OA.B.2)

1. Show the tens fact you used. Write the difference.

12 − 6 = ____

10 − 4 = ____

2. Show the tens fact you used. Write the difference.

13 − 8 = ____

10 − 5 = ____

Spiral Review (2.OA.B.2, 2.NBT.A.4)

3. Write a related subtraction fact for 7 + 3 = 10.

____

4. Joe has 8 trucks. Carmen has 1 more truck than Joe. How many trucks do they have now?

____ trucks

5. There were 276 people on an airplane. Write a number greater than 276.

____

6. Write >, <, or = to compare.

537 ____ 375

Name ____________________

Algebra • Use Drawings to Represent Problems

Common Core **Operations and Algebraic Thinking—2.OA.A.1**
MATHEMATICAL PRACTICES
MP1, MP4, MP6

Essential Question How are bar models used to show addition and subtraction problems?

Listen and Draw Real World

Complete the bar model to show the problem.
Complete the number sentence to solve.

_____ + _____ = _____ _____ pennies

_____ − _____ = _____ _____ pennies

Math Talk MATHEMATICAL PRACTICES 6

Explain how the problems are alike and how they are different.

FOR THE TEACHER • Read each problem and have children complete the bar models. Hailey has 5 pennies in her pocket and 7 pennies in her wallet. How many pennies does she have? Blake has 12 pennies in his bank. He gives 5 pennies to his sister. How many pennies does he have now?

Model and Draw

You can use bar models to show problems.

Ben eats 14 crackers. Ron eats 6 crackers. How many more crackers does Ben eat than Ron?

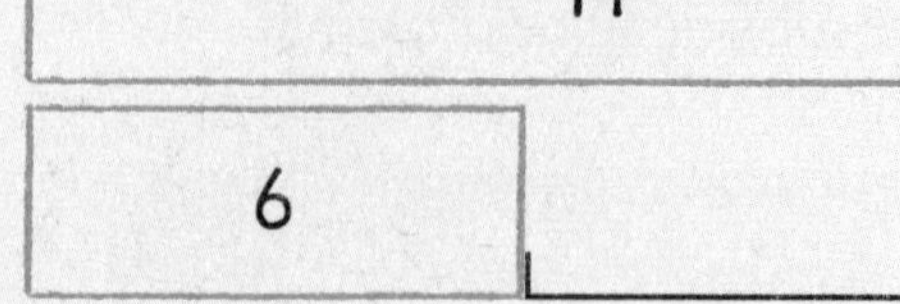

14 − 6 = 8

_____ more crackers

Suzy had 14 cookies. She gave 6 cookies to Grace. How many cookies does Suzy have now?

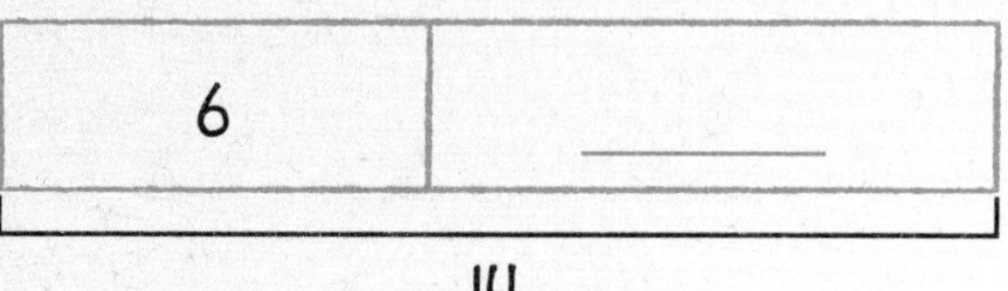

_____ cookies

Share and Show

Complete the bar model. Then write a number sentence to solve.

1. Mr. James bought 15 plain bagels and 9 raisin bagels. How many more plain bagels than raisin bagels did he buy?

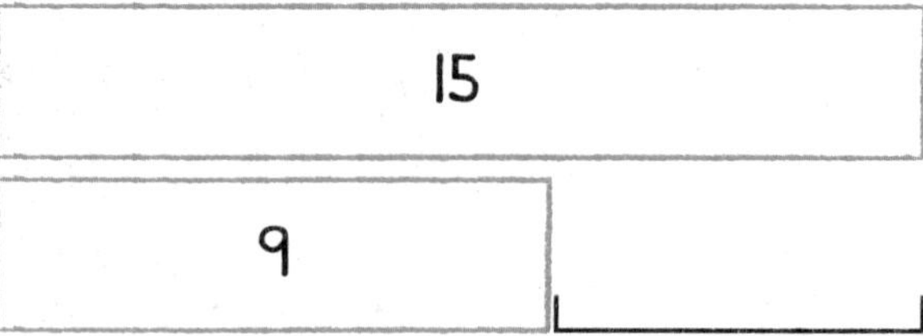

_____ more plain bagels

Name ___

On Your Own

Complete the bar model. Then write a number sentence to solve.

2. Cole has 5 books about dogs and 6 books about cats. How many books does Cole have?

5	6

___

___

___ books

3. THINK SMARTER Anne has 16 blue clips and 9 red clips. How many more blue clips than red clips does she have?

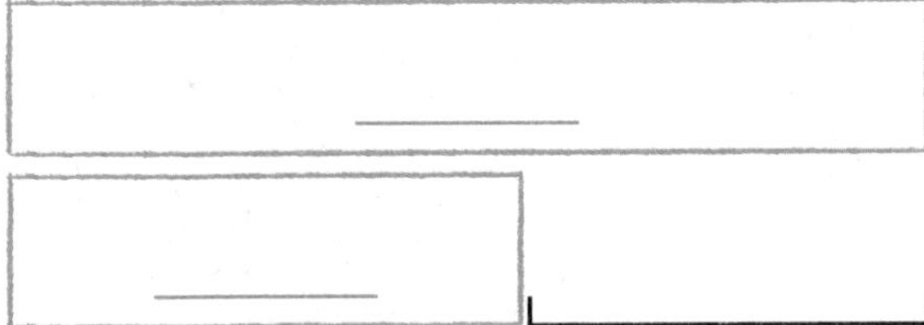

___

___

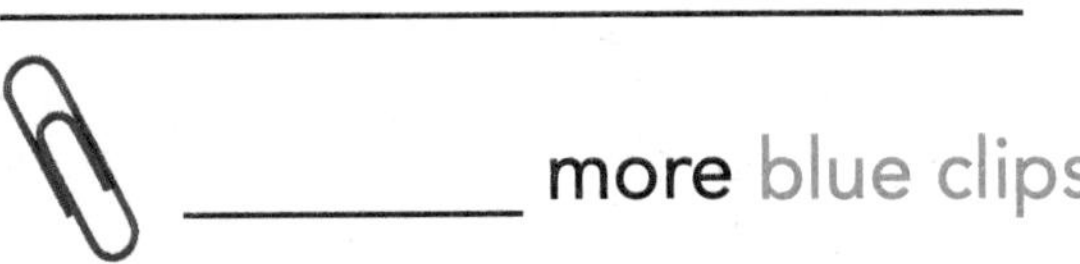

___ more blue clips

4. GO DEEPER Fill in the blank. Then label the bar model and solve.

Miss Gore had 18 pencils. She gave ____ pencils to Erin. How many pencils does Miss Gore have now?

___	___

___

___ pencils

Problem Solving • Applications

Use the information in the table to solve. Write or draw to explain.

Jenna's Flowers	
Flowers	**Number**
roses	6
tulips	8
daisies	11

5. Jenna put all of the roses and all of the tulips into a vase. How many flowers did she put into the vase?

_______ flowers

6. THINKSMARTER Four of the daisies are white. The other daisies are yellow. How many daisies are yellow?

_______ yellow daisies

7. THINKSMARTER Rita counts 4 frogs in the grass and some other frogs in the water. There are 10 frogs in all. How many frogs are in the water? Draw a picture and write a number sentence to solve.

____

_______ frogs are in the water.

TAKE HOME ACTIVITY • Ask your child to describe what he or she learned in this lesson.

Name ______________________

Algebra • Use Drawings to Represent Problems

Common Core **COMMON CORE STANDARD—2.OA.A.1**
Represent and solve problems involving addition and subtraction.

Complete the bar model. Then write a number sentence to solve.

1. Adam had 12 trucks. He gave 4 trucks to Ed. How many trucks does Adam have now?

____	4

12

____

____ trucks

2. Grandma has 14 red roses and 7 pink roses. How many more red roses than pink roses does she have?

14	
7	____

____

____ more red roses

3. WRITE Math Explain how you used the bar model in Exercise 2 to solve the problem

____

____

Lesson Check (2.OA.A.1)

1. Complete the bar model. Then solve. Abby has 16 grapes. Jason has 9 grapes. How many more grapes does Abby have than Jason?

16	
9	____

____

____ more grapes

Spiral Review (2.OA.B.2, 2.NBT.A.3)

2. Write a subtraction fact with the same difference as $16 - 7$.

____

3. What is the difference?

$18 - 9 =$ ____

4. What is another way to write $300 + 20 + 5$?

____

5. What is the value of the underlined digit?

<u>2</u>8

____

FOR MORE PRACTICE GO TO THE Personal Math Trainer

Name ______________________________

Algebra • Use Equations to Represent Problems

Essential Question How are number sentences used to show addition and subtraction situations?

Common Core Operations and Algebraic Thinking—2.OA.A.1

MATHEMATICAL PRACTICES MP1, MP2, MP4

Listen and Draw

Write a story problem that could be solved using this bar model.

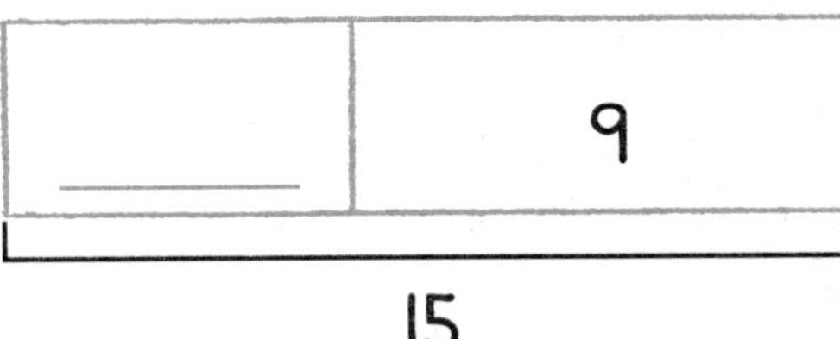

____

____

____

____

____

FOR THE TEACHER • Discuss with children how this bar model can be used to represent an addition or a subtraction situation.

Math Talk MATHEMATICAL PRACTICES 2

Would you add or subtract to solve your story problem? **Explain.**

Model and Draw

A number sentence can be used to show a problem.

There were some girls and 4 boys at the park. There were 9 children in all. How many girls were at the park?

$\blacksquare + 4 = 9$

Think: $5 + 4 = 9$

So, there were __5__ girls at the park.

The ■ is a placeholder for the missing number.

Share and Show MATH BOARD

Write a number sentence for the problem.
Use a ■ for the missing number. Then solve.

1. There were 14 ants on the sidewalk. Then 6 ants went into the grass. How many ants were still on the sidewalk?

____

_____ ants

2. There were 7 big dogs and 4 little dogs at the park. How many dogs were at the park?

____

_____ dogs

Name ______________________________

On Your Own

Write a number sentence for the problem.
Use a ■ for the missing number. Then solve.

3. A group of children were flying 13 kites. Some kites were put away. Then the children were flying 7 kites. How many kites were put away?

____

______ kites

4. There are 18 boys at the field. 9 of the boys are playing soccer. How many boys are not playing soccer?

____

______ boys

5. MATHEMATICAL PRACTICE 2 **Use Reasoning** Matthew found 9 acorns. Greg found 6 acorns. How many acorns did the two boys find?

____

______ acorns

6. THINKSMARTER There were some ducks in a pond. Four more ducks joined them. Then there were 12 ducks in the pond. How many ducks were in the pond at first?

______ ducks

Problem Solving • Applications

Read the story. Write or draw to show how you solved the problems.

At camp, 5 children are playing games and 4 children are making crafts. 5 other children are having a snack.

7. How many children are at camp?

_____ children

8. GO DEEPER Suppose 7 more children arrive at camp and join the children playing games. How many more children are playing games than children not playing games?

_____ more children

Personal Math Trainer

9. THINK SMARTER+ Ashley had 9 crayons. She gave 4 crayons to her brother. How many crayons does Ashley have now? Write a number sentence for the problem. Use ■ for the missing number. Then solve.

____

Ashley has _____ crayons now.

TAKE HOME ACTIVITY • Ask your child to explain how he or she solved one of the problems on this page.

Name ______________________

Algebra • Use Equations to Represent Problems

COMMON CORE STANDARD—2.OA.A.1
Represent and solve problems involving addition and subtraction.

Write a number sentence for the problem. Use a ■ for the missing number. Then solve.

1. There were 15 apples in a bowl. Dan used some apples to make a pie. Now there are 7 apples in the bowl. How many apples did Dan use?

____

____ apples

2. Amy has 16 gift bags. She fills 8 gift bags with whistles. How many gift bags are not filled with whistles?

____

____ gift bags

Problem Solving

Write or draw to show how you solved the problem.

3. Tony has 7 blue cubes and 6 red cubes. How many cubes does he have?

____ cubes

4. WRITE Math Write a story problem for the addition sentence 7 + ■ = 9. Solve the story problem.

____

____

____

Lesson Check (2.OA.A.1)

1. Fred peeled 9 carrots. Nancy peeled 6 carrots. How many fewer carrots did Nancy peel than Fred?

   _____ fewer carrots

2. Omar has 8 marbles. Joy has 7 marbles. How many marbles do they have together?

   _____ marbles

Spiral Review (2.OA.B.2, 2.NBT.A.1)

3. What is the sum?

   $8 + 8 =$ _____

4. What is the sum?

   $5 + 4 + 3 =$ _____

5. What number has the same value as 1 hundred 7 tens?

   _____

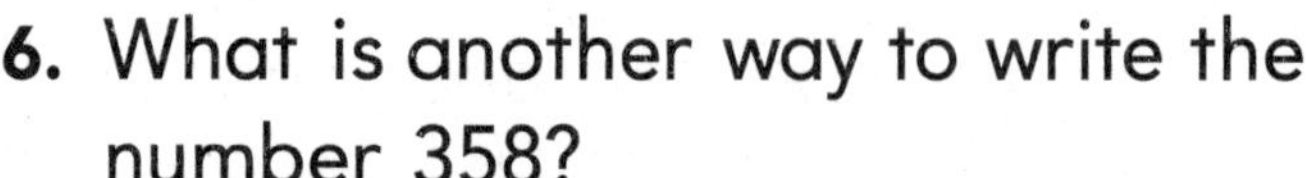

6. What is another way to write the number 358?

   _____ hundreds _____ tens _____ ones

FOR MORE PRACTICE GO TO THE Personal Math Trainer

Name ______________________

Problem Solving • Equal Groups

Essential Question How can acting it out help when solving a problem about equal groups?

Common Core **Operations and Algebraic Thinking—2.OA.C.4**
MATHEMATICAL PRACTICES
MP1, MP5, MP7

Theo puts his stickers in 5 rows.
There are 3 stickers in each row.
How many stickers does Theo have?

Unlock the Problem

Hands On

What do I need to find?

how many stickers
Theo has

What information do I need to use?

5 rows of stickers

3 stickers in each row

Show how to solve the problem.

_______ stickers

HOME CONNECTION • Your child used counters to act out the problem. Counters are a concrete tool that helps children act out the problem.

Try Another Problem

Act out the problem.
Draw to show what you did.

- What do I need to find?
- What information do I need to use?

1. Maria puts all of her postcards in 4 rows. There are 3 postcards in each row. How many postcards does Maria have? _______ postcards

2. Jamal puts 4 toys in each box. How many toys will he put in 4 boxes? _______ toys

MATHEMATICAL PRACTICES 7

Explain how acting it out and skip counting helped you solve the second problem.

Name ____________________

Share and Show

Act out the problem.
Draw to show what you did.

3. Mr. Fulton puts 3 bananas on each tray. How many bananas are on 4 trays?

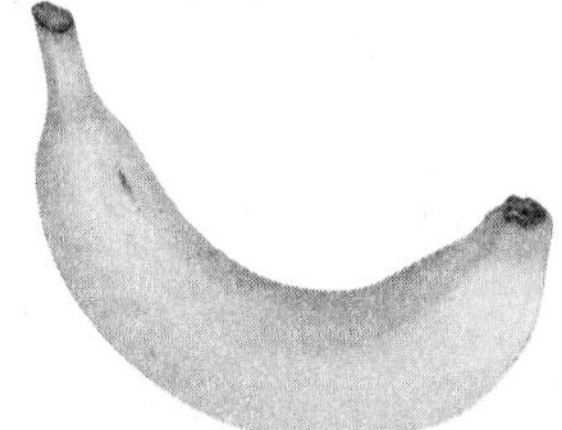

_______ bananas

4. There are 3 rows of apples. There are 5 apples in each row. How many apples are there?

_______ apples

5. THINK SMARTER There are 4 plates. Dexter puts 2 grapes on each plate. Then he puts 2 grapes on each of 6 more plates. How many grapes in all does he put on the plates?

_______ grapes

Problem Solving • Applications

6. MATHEMATICAL PRACTICE 6 Make Connections
Angela used these counters to act out a problem.

Write a problem about equal groups that Angela could have modeled with these counters.

____

____

____

7. THINK SMARTER Max and 4 friends get books from the library. Each person gets 3 books. Draw a picture to show the groups of books.

How many books did they get?

________ books

TAKE HOME ACTIVITY • Ask your child to explain how he or she solved one of the problems in this lesson.

Name ______

Problem Solving • Equal Groups

Common Core **COMMON CORE STANDARD—2.OA.C.4**
Work with equal groups of objects to gain foundations for multiplication.

Act out the problem.
Draw to show what you did.

1. Mr. Anderson has 4 plates of cookies. There are 5 cookies on each plate. How many cookies are there?

____ cookies

2. Ms. Trane puts some stickers in 3 rows. There are 2 stickers in each row. How many stickers does Ms. Trane have?

____ stickers

3. WRITE Math Draw 3 rows with 2 counters in each row. Write a word problem that can be acted out using these counters.

______

______

Lesson Check (2.OA.C.4)

1. Jaime puts 3 oranges on each tray. How many oranges does he put on 5 trays?

   _____ oranges

2. Maurice has 4 rows of toys with 4 toys in each row. How many toys does he have?

   _____ toys

Spiral Review (2.OA.A.1, 2.OA.B.2, 2.OA.C.3)

3. Jack has 12 pencils and 7 pens. How many more pencils than pens does he have?

   _____ pencils

4. Laura has 9 apples. Jon has 6 apples. How many apples do they have together?

   _____ apples

5. Circle the even number.

   1 3 5 8

6. What is the sum?

   $7 + 9 =$ _____

FOR MORE PRACTICE GO TO THE Personal Math Trainer

Name ______________________

Algebra • Repeated Addition

Essential Question How can you write an addition sentence for problems with equal groups?

Common Core **Operations and Algebraic Thinking—2.OA.C.4**
MATHEMATICAL PRACTICES
MP1, MP4, MP6

Listen and Draw (Real World)

Use counters to model the problem.
Then draw a picture of your model.

FOR THE TEACHER • Read the following problem and have children first model the problem with counters and then draw a picture of their models. Clayton has 3 rows of cards. There are 5 cards in each row. How many cards does Clayton have?

Math Talk — MATHEMATICAL PRACTICES 1

Describe how you found the number of counters in your model.

Model and Draw

You can use addition to find the total amount when you have equal groups.

3 rows of 4

Write: 4 + 4 + 4 = ____

____ in all

Share and Show

Find the number of shapes in each row.
Complete the addition sentence to find the total.

1.

3 rows of ____

____ + ____ + ____ = ____

2.

4 rows of ____

____ + ____ + ____ + ____ = ____

3.

5 rows of ____

____ + ____ + ____ + ____ + ____ = ____

Name ___________________________

On Your Own

Find the number of shapes in each row.
Complete the addition sentence to find the total.

4. 

2 rows of ____

____ + ____ = ____

5. 

3 rows of ____

____ + ____ + ____ = ____

6. 

4 rows of ____

__ + __ + __ + __ = ____

7. 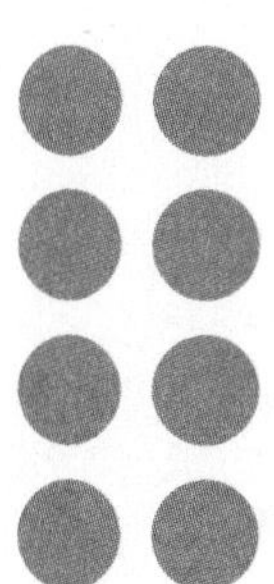

4 rows of ____

__ + __ + __ + __ = ____

8. 

5 rows of ____

____ + ____ + ____ + ____ + ____ = ____

Problem Solving • Applications

Solve. Write or draw to explain.

9. THINK SMARTER There are 6 photos on the wall. There are 2 photos in each row. How many rows of photos are there?

_______ rows

10. GO DEEPER Mrs. Chen makes 5 rows of 2 chairs and 2 rows of 3 chairs. How many chairs does Mrs. Chen use?

_______ chairs

11. THINK SMARTER Find the number of counters in each row. Complete the number sentence to find the total number of counters.

____ + ____ + ____ = ____

_______ counters

TAKE HOME ACTIVITY • Have your child use small objects to make 2 rows with 4 objects in each row. Then have your child find the total number of objects.

Name ________________________________

Algebra • Repeated Addition

COMMON CORE STANDARD—2.OA.C.4
Work with equal groups of objects to gain foundations for multiplication.

Find the number of shapes in each row. Complete the addition sentence to find the total.

1.

3 rows of ____

____ + ____ + ____ = ____

2.

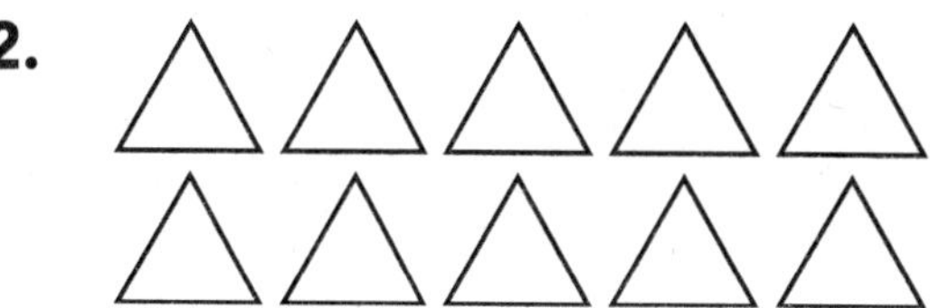

2 rows of ____

____ + ____ = ____

Problem Solving

Solve. Write or draw to explain.

3. A classroom has 3 rows of desks. There are 5 desks in each row. How many desks are there altogether?

____ desks

4. WRITE Math Explain how to write an addition sentence for a picture of 4 rows with 3 items in each row.

____

____

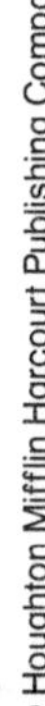

Lesson Check (2.OA.C.4)

1. A scrapbook has 4 pages. There are 2 stickers on each page. How many stickers are there?

   ____ stickers

2. Ben makes 5 rows of coins. He puts 3 coins in each row. How many coins are there?

   ____ coins

Spiral Review (2.OA.B.2, 2.NBT.A.2, 2.NBT.A.3)

3. There are 5 apples and 4 oranges. How many pieces of fruit are there?

   ____ pieces

4. Count by tens.

   40, ____, ____, ____, ____

5. Write the number 260 using words.

   ____

6. Write a fact with the same sum as 7 + 5.

   ____

FOR MORE PRACTICE GO TO THE Personal Math Trainer

Name ______________________________

1. Erin puts 3 small cans, 4 medium cans, and 5 large cans on a shelf. How many cans does she put on the shelf?

_______ cans

2. Fill in the bubble next to all the doubles facts you could use to find the sum of $3 + 2$?

- ○ $2 + 2$
- ○ $5 + 5$
- ○ $3 + 3$
- ○ $1 + 1$

3. Does the number sentence have the same difference as $14 - 6 = ■$? Choose Yes or No.

$10 - 1 = ■$	○ Yes	○ No
$10 - 2 = ■$	○ Yes	○ No
$10 - 3 = ■$	○ Yes	○ No
$10 - 4 = ■$	○ Yes	○ No

GO DIGITAL Assessment Options Chapter Test

4. Mr. Brown sold 5 red backpacks and 8 blue backpacks. Write the number sentence. Show how you can make a ten to find the sum. Write the sum.

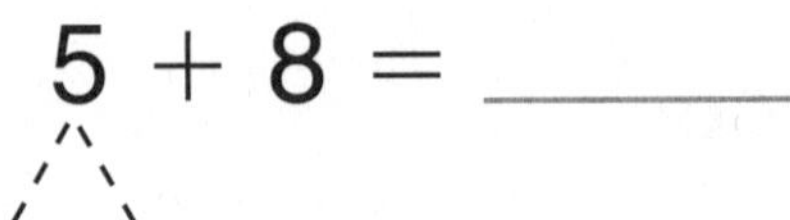

$5 + 8 =$ ______

$10 +$ ______ $=$ ______

5. Find the number of shapes in each row.

3 rows of ______

Complete the addition sentence to find the total.

______ $+$ ______ $+$ ______ $=$ ______

6. Tanya and 2 friends put rocks on the table. Each person put 2 rocks on the table. Draw a picture to show the groups of rocks.

How many rocks did they put on the table?

______ rocks

Name ______________________________

7. THINKSMARTER+ Lily sees 15 tan puppies and 8 white puppies at the pet store. How many more tan puppies than white puppies does she see? Draw a picture and write a number sentence to solve.

____

______ more tan puppies

8. Mark counts 6 ducks in a pond and some ducks on the grass. There are 14 ducks in all. Draw a picture to show the two groups of ducks.

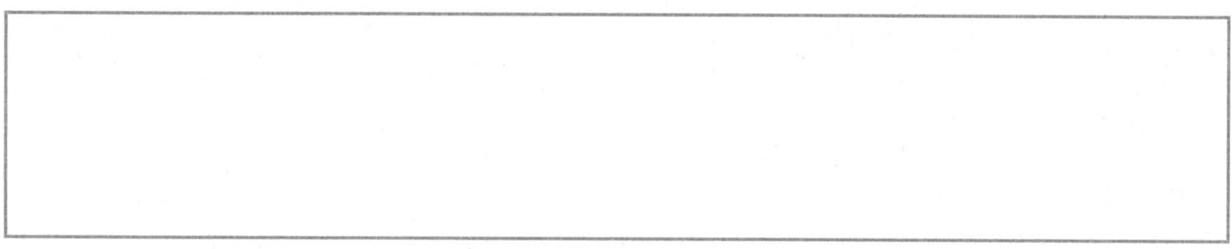

Write a number sentence that can help you find how many ducks are on the grass.

______ + ______ = ______

How many ducks are on the grass? ______ ducks

9. There are 8 peaches in a basket. Mrs. Dalton puts 7 more peaches in the basket. Complete the addition sentence to find how many peaches are in the basket now.

______ + ______ = ______

______ peaches

10. GO DEEPER Use the numbers on the tiles to write the differences.

Then write the next fact in the pattern.

4	5	6	7

$12 - 6 =$ ______

$12 - 7 =$ ______

$12 - 8 =$ ______

____

$11 - 6 =$ ______

$12 - 6 =$ ______

$13 - 6 =$ ______

____

11. Jose wanted to share 18 strawberries with his brother equally. Draw a picture to show how Jose can share the strawberries.

How many strawberries will Jose receive?

______ strawberries

12. Hank has 13 grapes. He gives 5 grapes to his sister. How many grapes does Hank have now? Write a number sentence for the problem. Use ■ for the missing number. Then solve.

____

______ grapes

Chapter 4

2-Digit Addition

Curious about Math

The keys of a modern piano are made from wood or plastic. A modern piano has 36 black keys and 52 white keys. How many keys is this in all?

Name ______________________________

Addition Patterns

Add 2. Complete each addition sentence. (1.OA.A.1)

1. 1 + 2 = 3
2. 2 + ____ = ____
3. 3 + ____ = ____
4. 4 + ____ = ____
5. 5 + ____ = ____
6. 6 + ____ = ____

Addition Facts

Write the sum. (1.OA.C.6)

7. $\begin{array}{r} 7 \\ +\ 3 \\ \hline \end{array}$

8. $\begin{array}{r} 8 \\ +\ 8 \\ \hline \end{array}$

9. $\begin{array}{r} 6 \\ +\ 7 \\ \hline \end{array}$

10. $\begin{array}{r} 4 \\ +\ 4 \\ \hline \end{array}$

11. $\begin{array}{r} 9 \\ +\ 5 \\ \hline \end{array}$

12. $\begin{array}{r} 8 \\ +\ 7 \\ \hline \end{array}$

Tens and Ones

Write how many tens and ones for each number. (1.NBT.B.2b)

13. 43

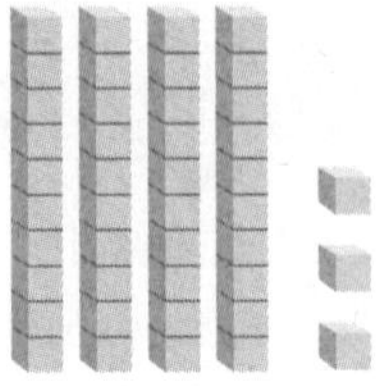

____ tens ____ ones

14. 68

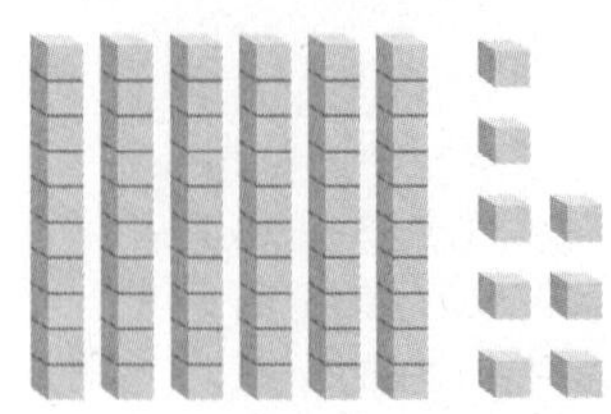

____ tens ____ ones

This page checks understanding of important skills needed for success in Chapter 4.

Name ______________________

Review Words
sum
addend
digit
tens
ones

Vocabulary Builder

Visualize It

Use review words to fill in the graphic organizer.

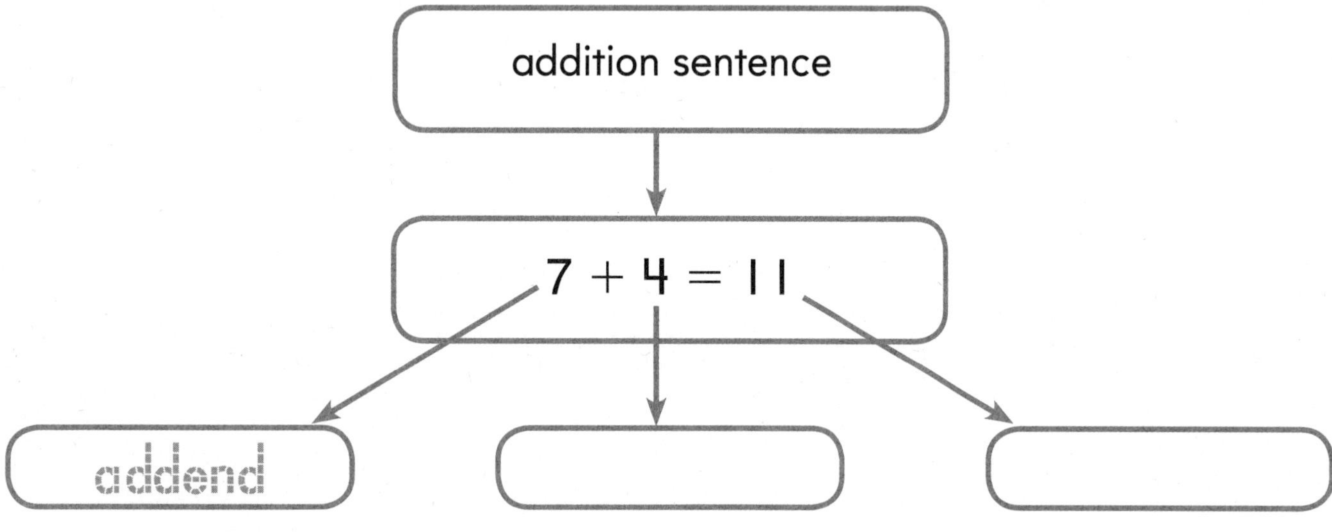

Understand Vocabulary

1. Write a number with the **digit** 3 in the **tens** place. ______

2. Write a number with the **digit** 5 in the **ones** place. ______

3. Write a number that has the same **digit** in the **tens** place and in the **ones** place. ______

4. Write a number with **digits** that have a **sum** of 8. ______

GO DIGITAL • Interactive Student Edition • Multimedia eGlossary

Game: What is the Sum?

Materials

- 12 ●
- 12 ○
- 1 🎲

Play with a partner.

1. Put your ● on START.
2. Toss the 🎲. Move that many spaces.
3. Say the sum. Your partner checks your answer.
4. If your answer is correct, find that number in the middle of the board. Put one of your ● on that number.
5. Take turns until both players reach FINISH. The player with more ● on the board wins.

START

$\begin{array}{r} 2 \\ +7 \\ \hline \end{array}$ $\begin{array}{r} 6 \\ +5 \\ \hline \end{array}$ $\begin{array}{r} 3 \\ +9 \\ \hline \end{array}$ $\begin{array}{r} 0 \\ +7 \\ \hline \end{array}$ $\begin{array}{r} 8 \\ +6 \\ \hline \end{array}$

$\begin{array}{r} 6 \\ +2 \\ \hline \end{array}$

$\begin{array}{r} 8 \\ +7 \\ \hline \end{array}$

$\begin{array}{r} 5 \\ +1 \\ \hline \end{array}$ $\begin{array}{r} 4 \\ +6 \\ \hline \end{array}$ $\begin{array}{r} 2 \\ +2 \\ \hline \end{array}$ $\begin{array}{r} 7 \\ +9 \\ \hline \end{array}$ $\begin{array}{r} 9 \\ +9 \\ \hline \end{array}$ $\begin{array}{r} 5 \\ +8 \\ \hline \end{array}$

$\begin{array}{r} 1 \\ +4 \\ \hline \end{array}$

$\begin{array}{r} 9 \\ +8 \\ \hline \end{array}$

FINISH

7	18	9	11	15
13	6	17	8	10
16	4	12	14	5

Chapter 4 Vocabulary

column columna 7	**digit** dígito 15
hundred centena 31	**is equal to (=)** es igual a 33
ones unidades 45	**regroup** reagrupar 56
sum suma o total 59	**ten** decena 61

0, 1, 2, 3, 4, 5, 6, 7, 8, and 9 are **digits**.

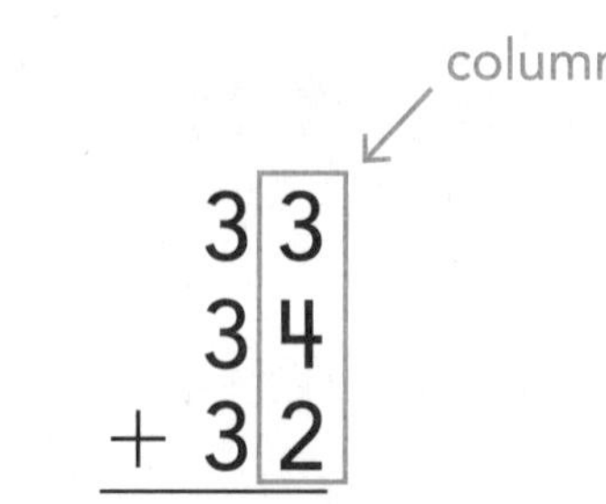

2 plus 1 is equal to 3

$2 + 1 = 3$

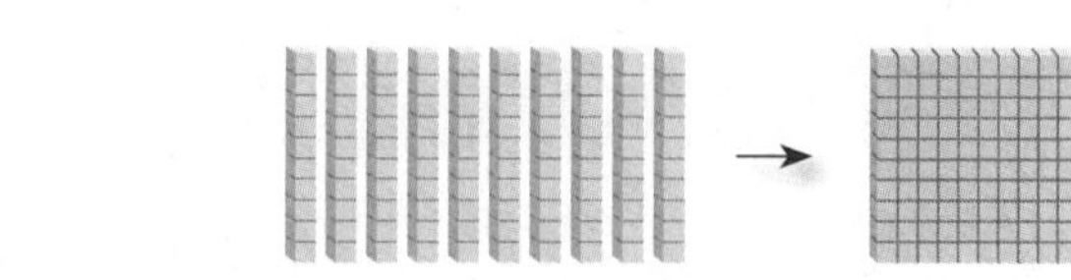

There are 10 tens in 1 **hundred**.

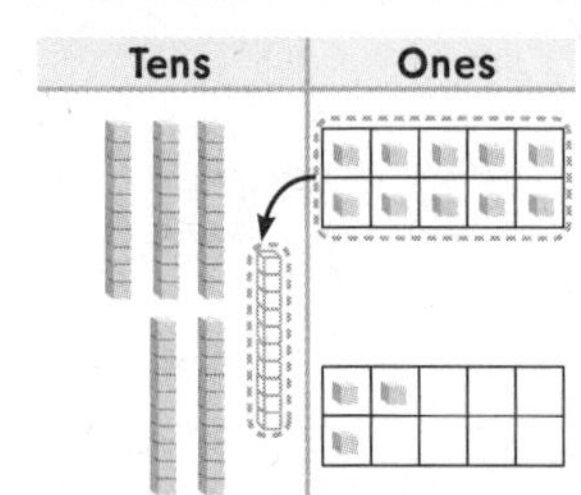

You can trade 10 ones for 1 ten to **regroup**.

10 ones = 1 ten

10 ones = 1 ten

$4 + 2 = 6$

sum

Matchup

Word Box
column
digit
hundred
is equal to (=)
ones
regroup
sum
tens

For 2 to 3 players

Materials

- 1 set of word cards

How to Play

1. Put the cards face-down in rows. Take turns to play.
2. Choose two cards. Turn the cards face-up.
   - If the cards match, keep the pair and take another turn.
   - If the cards do not match, turn them over again.
3. The game is over when all cards have been matched. The players count their pairs. The player with the most pairs wins.

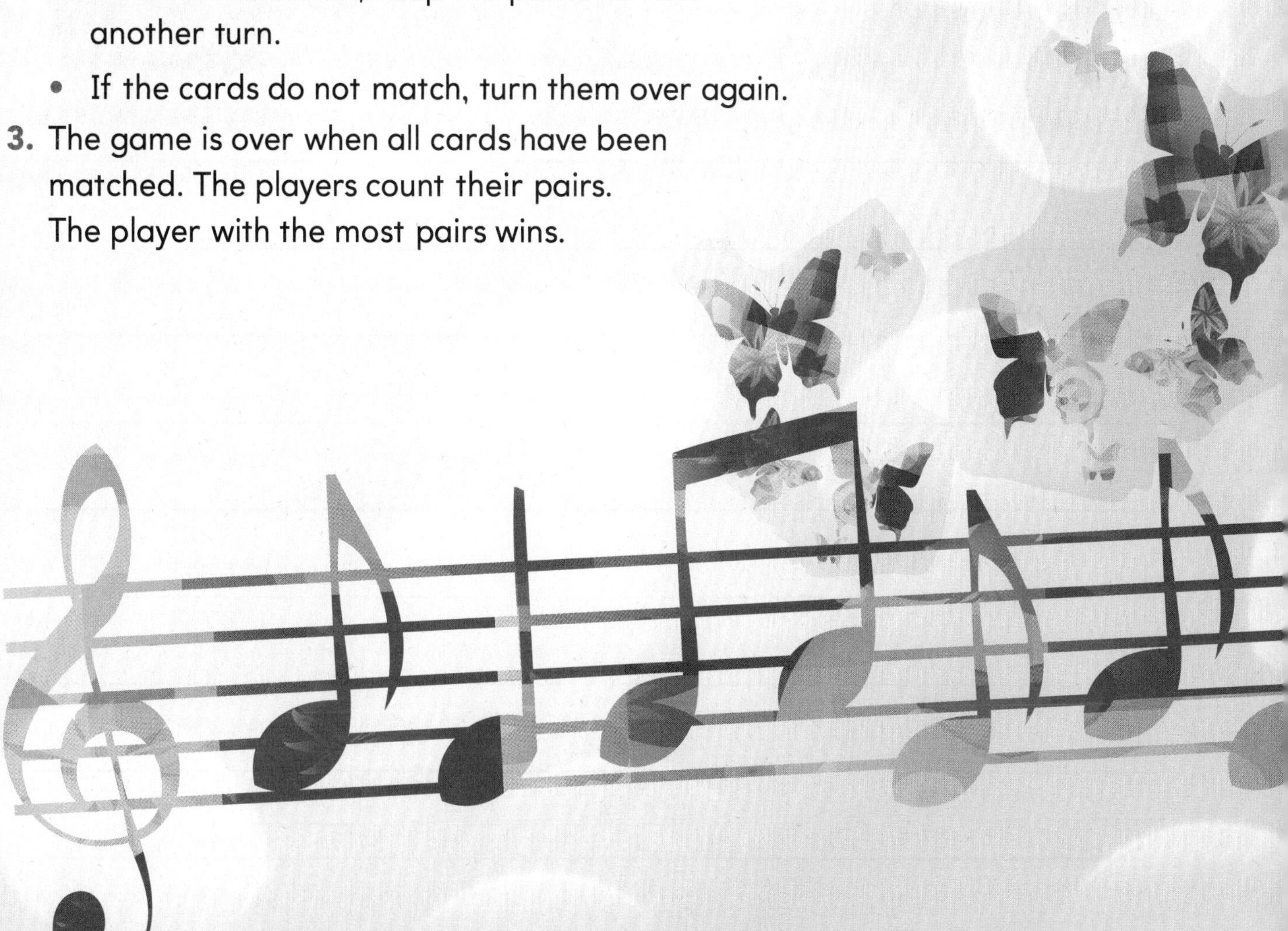

The Write Way

Reflect

Choose one idea. Write about it in the space below.

- Explain how drawing quick pictures helps you add 2-digit numbers.
- Tell about all the different ways you can add 2-digit numbers.
- Write three things you know about regrouping.

Name ________________________________

Break Apart Ones to Add

Essential Question How does breaking apart a number make it easier to add?

Common Core **Number and Operations in Base Ten—2.NBT.B.5**

MATHEMATICAL PRACTICES
MP1, MP4, MP6

Use . Draw to show what you did.

FOR THE TEACHER • Read the following problem. Have children use blocks to solve. Griffin read 27 books about animals and 6 books about space. How many books did he read?

Math Talk MATHEMATICAL PRACTICES 6

Describe what you did with the blocks.

Model and Draw

Break apart ones to make a ten.
Use this as a way to add.

$27 + 8 =$ ___?___

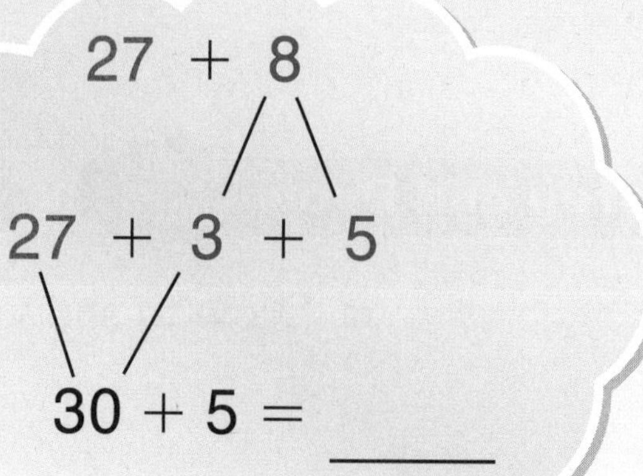

$27 + 8 =$ ______

Share and Show

Draw quick pictures. Break apart ones to make a ten. Then add and write the sum.

1. $15 + 7 =$ ______

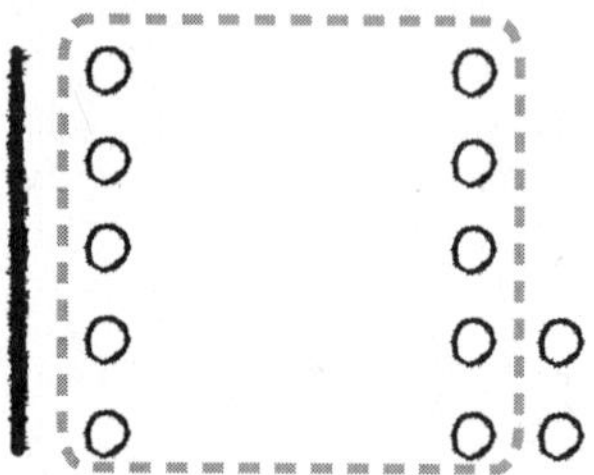

2. $26 + 5 =$ ______

3. $37 + 8 =$ ______

4. $28 + 6 =$ ______

Name ______________________________

On Your Own

Break apart ones to make a ten. Then add and write the sum.

5. 23 + 9 = ______

6. 48 + 5 = ______

7. 18 + 5 = ______

8. 33 + 9 = ______

9. 27 + 6 = ______

10. 49 + 4 = ______

11. GO DEEPER Alex sets up 32 small tables and 9 large tables in a room. Then he sets up 5 more large tables along a wall. How many tables does Alex set up?

______ tables

12. THINK SMARTER Bruce sees 29 oak trees and 4 maple trees at the park. Then he sees double the number of pine trees as maple trees. How many trees does Bruce see?

Math on the Spot

______ trees

Problem Solving • Applications  

Solve. Write or draw to explain.

13. GO DEEPER Megan has 38 animal pictures, 5 people pictures, and 3 insect pictures. How many pictures does she have?

_______ pictures

14. MATHEMATICAL PRACTICE 1 Analyze
Jamal has a box with 22 toy cars in it. He puts 9 more toy cars into the box. Then he takes 3 toy cars out of the box. How many toy cars are in the box now?

_______ toy cars

15. THINK SMARTER Dan has 16 pencils. Quentin gives him 5 more pencils. Choose all the ways you can use to find how many pencils Dan has in all.

○ 16 + 5
○ 16 + 4 + 1
○ 16 − 5

TAKE HOME ACTIVITY • Say a number from 0 to 9. Have your child name a number to add to yours to have a sum of 10.

Name ______________________________

Break Apart Ones to Add

COMMON CORE STANDARD—2.NBT.B.5
Use place value understanding and properties of operations to add and subtract.

Break apart ones to make a ten. Then add and write the sum.

1. $62 + 9 =$ ____	2. $27 + 7 =$ ____
3. $28 + 5 =$ ____	4. $17 + 8 =$ ____
5. $57 + 6 =$ ____	6. $23 + 9 =$ ____
7. $39 + 7 =$ ____	8. $26 + 5 =$ ____
9. $13 + 8 =$ ____	10. $18 + 7 =$ ____

Problem Solving

Solve. Write or draw to explain.

11. Jimmy had 18 toy airplanes. His mother bought him 7 more toy airplanes. How many toy airplanes does he have now?

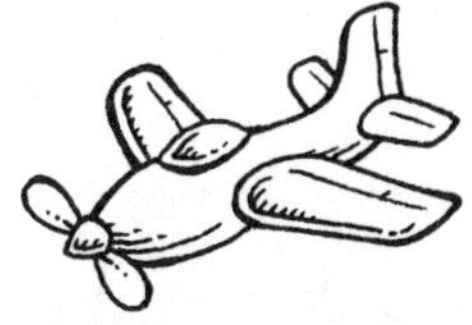

____ toy airplanes

12. WRITE Math Explain how you would find the sum of $46 + 7$.

____

____

Lesson Check (2.NBT.B.5)

1. What is the sum?

$26 + 7 = \_\_\_\_$

2. What is the sum?

$15 + 8 = \_\_\_\_$

Spiral Review (2.OA.A.1, 2.OA.B.2, 2.NBT.A.3)

3. Hannah has 4 blue beads and 8 red beads. How many beads does Hannah have?

$4 + 8 = \_\_\_\_$ beads

4. Rick had 4 stickers. Then he earned 2 more. How many stickers does he have now?

$4 + 2 = \_\_\_\_$ stickers

5. What is the sum?

$4 + 5 + 4 = \_\_\_\_$

6. Write 281 using hundreds, tens, and ones.

____ hundreds ____ tens ____ one

FOR MORE PRACTICE GO TO THE Personal Math Trainer

Name ______________________________

Use Compensation

Essential Question How can you make an addend a ten to help solve an addition problem?

Common Core **Number and Operations in Base Ten—2.NBT.B.5**
MATHEMATICAL PRACTICES
MP1, MP4, MP6

Listen and Draw Real World

Draw quick pictures to show the problems.

MATHEMATICAL PRACTICES 1

Analyze Describe how you found how many stickers Tyrone has.

FOR THE TEACHER • Have children draw quick pictures to solve this problem. Kara has 47 stickers. She buys 20 more stickers. How many stickers does she have now? Repeat for this problem. Tyrone has 30 stickers and buys 52 more stickers. How many stickers does he have now?

Model and Draw

Take ones from an addend to make the other addend the next tens number.

Adding can be easier when one of the addends is a tens number.

$25 + 48 = ?$

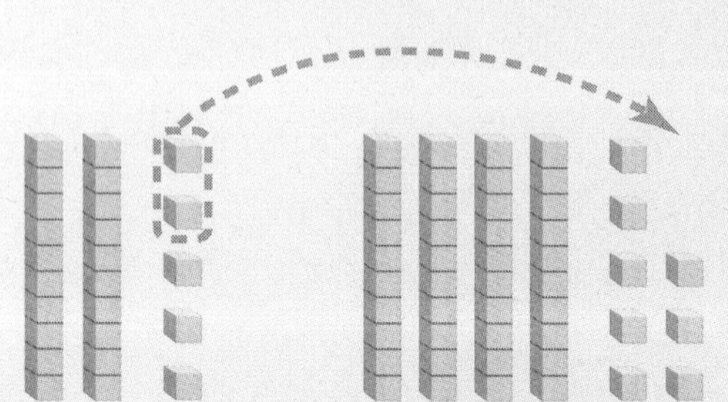

23 + 50 = ____

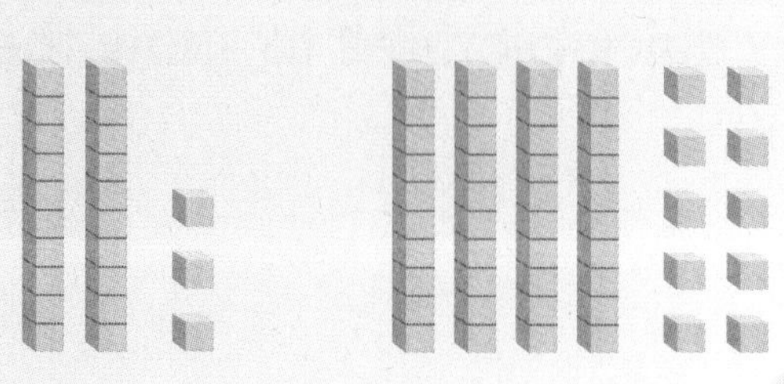

Share and Show

Show how to make one addend the next tens number. Complete the new addition sentence.

1. $37 + 25 = ?$

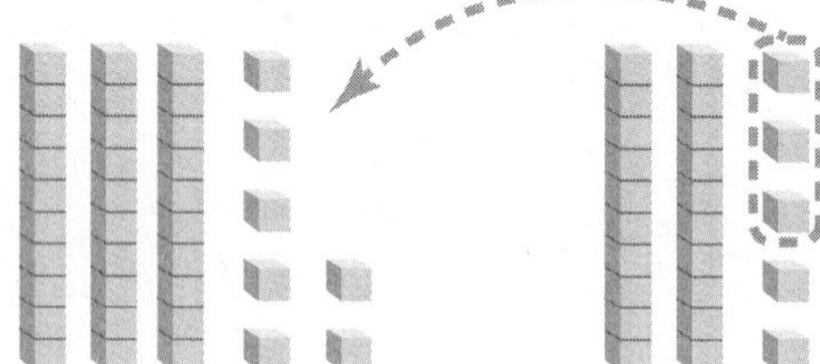

40 + ____ = ____

2. $27 + 46 = ?$

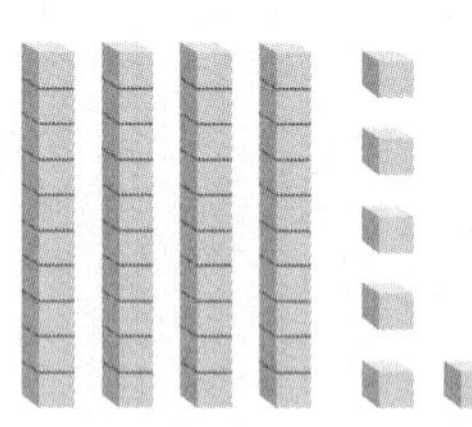

____ + ____ = ____

3. $14 + 29 = ?$

____ + ____ = ____

Name ____________________

On Your Own

Show how to make one addend the next tens number. Complete the new addition sentence.

4. 18 + 13 = ?

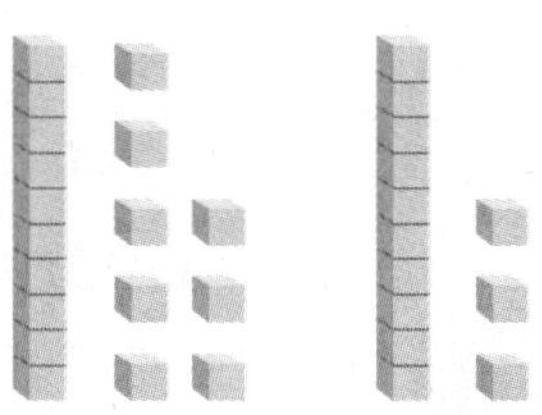

____ + ____ = ____

5. 24 + 18 = ?

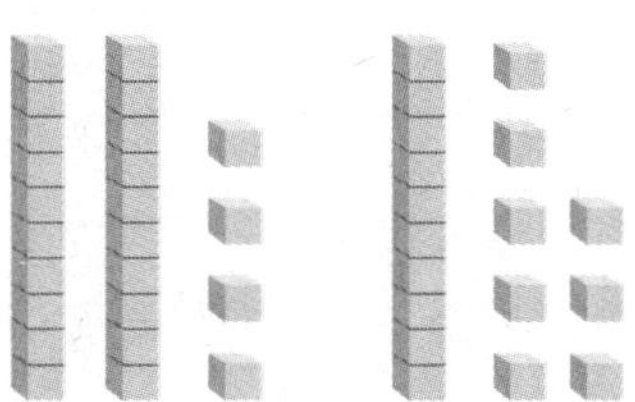

____ + ____ = ____

6. GO DEEPER Lee finds 44 shells. Wayne finds 39 shells. How many shells do they still need if they want 90 shells in all?

____ shells

Solve. Write or draw to explain.

7. THINK SMARTER Zach finds 38 sticks. Kelly finds 27 sticks. How many more sticks do the two children still need if they want 70 sticks in all?

____ more sticks

Problem Solving • Applications

Solve. Write or draw to explain.

8. MATHEMATICAL PRACTICE 6 **Make Connections** The chart shows the leaves that Philip collected. He wants a collection of 52 leaves, using only two colors. Which two colors of leaves should he use?

Leaves Collected	
Color	**Number**
green	27
brown	29
yellow	25

_____________ and _____________

9. THINK SMARTER Ava has 39 sheets of white paper. She has 22 sheets of green paper. Draw a picture and write to explain how to find the number of sheets of paper Ava has.

Ava has ________ sheets of paper.

TAKE HOME ACTIVITY • Have your child choose one problem on this page and explain how to solve it in another way.

Name ______________________

Use Compensation

Common Core **COMMON CORE STANDARD—2.NBT.B.5**
Use place value understanding and properties of operations to add and subtract.

Show how to make one addend the next tens number. Complete the new addition sentence.

1. 15 + 37 = ?

____ + ____ = ____

2. 22 + 49 = ?

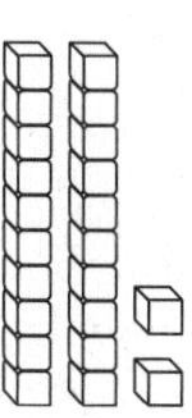

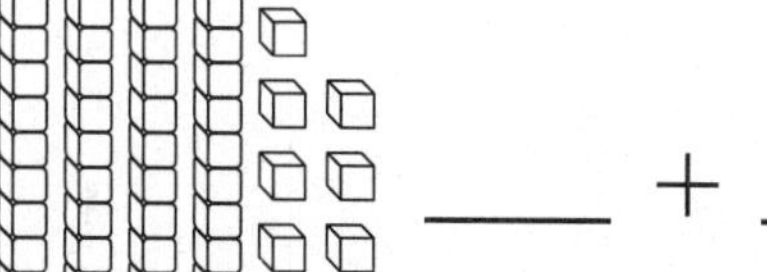

____ + ____ = ____

3. 38 + 26 = ?

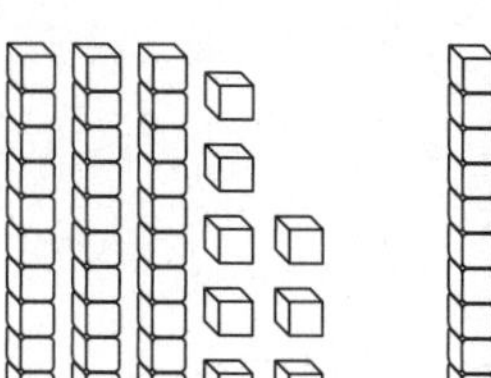

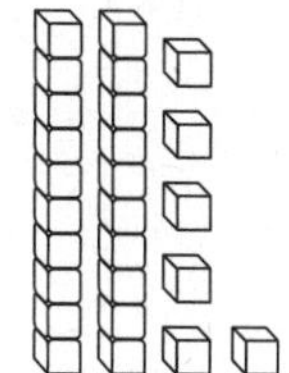

____ + ____ = ____

Problem Solving

Solve. Write or draw to explain.

4. The oak tree at the school was 34 feet tall. Then it grew 18 feet taller. How tall is the oak tree now?

____ feet tall

5. WRITE Math Explain why you would make one of the addends a tens number when solving an addition problem.

____

____

Lesson Check (2.NBT.B.5)

1. What is the sum?

$18 + 25 =$ ____

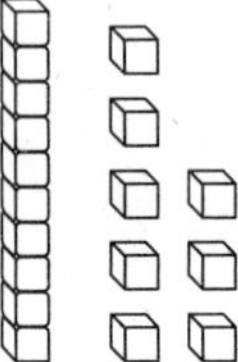

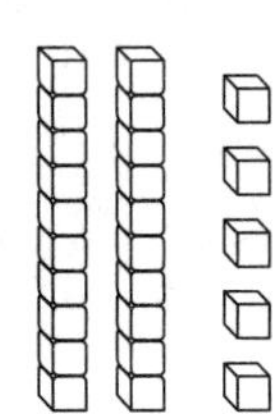

2. What is the sum?

$27 + 24 =$ ____

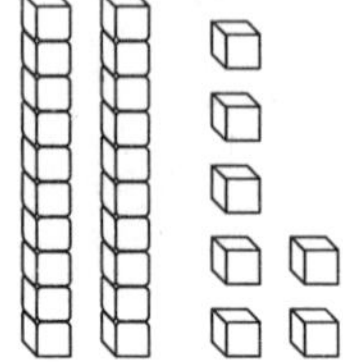

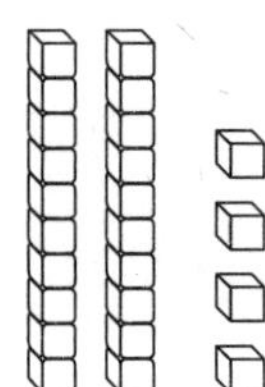

Spiral Review (2.OA.B.2, 2.OA.C.3)

3. Circle the even number.

27 14 11 5

4. Andrew sees 4 fish. Kim sees double that number of fish. How many fish does Kim see?

____ fish

5. Write a related subtraction fact for $7 + 6 = 13$.

____

6. What is the sum?

$2 + 8 =$ ____

FOR MORE PRACTICE GO TO THE **Personal Math Trainer**

Name ______________________________

Break Apart Addends as Tens and Ones

Essential Question How do you break apart addends to add tens and then add ones?

Common Core Number and Operations in Base Ten—2.NBT.B.5
MATHEMATICAL PRACTICES MP1, MP6, MP8

Listen and Draw

Write the number. Then write the number as tens plus ones.

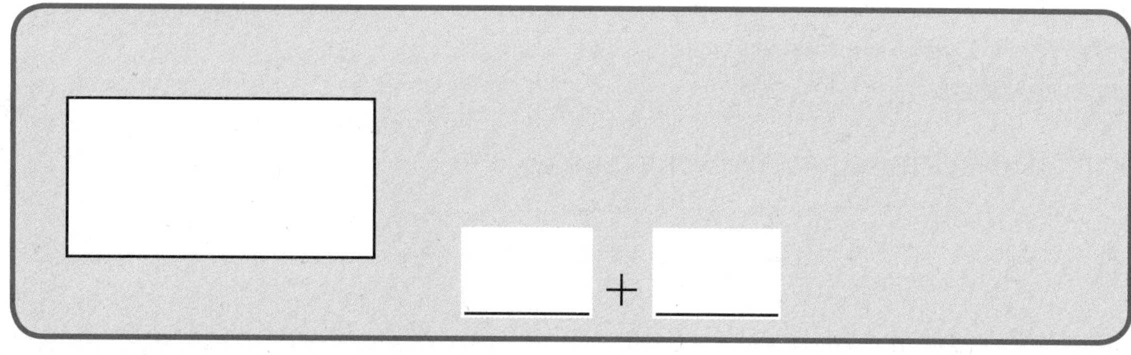

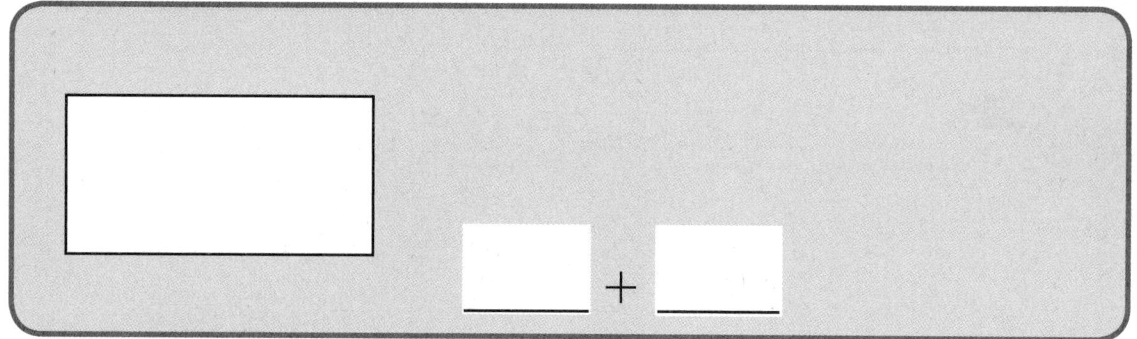

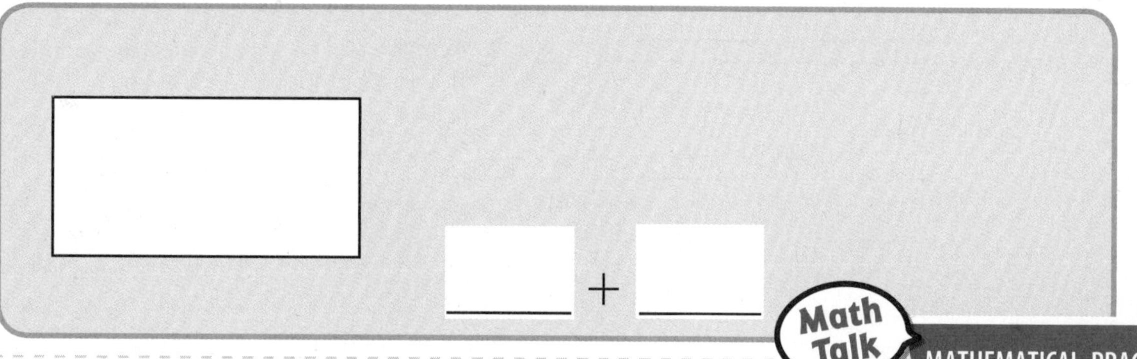

FOR THE TEACHER • Direct children's attention to the orange box. Have children write 25 inside the large rectangle. Then ask children to write 25 as tens plus ones. Repeat the activity for 36 and 42.

Math Talk MATHEMATICAL PRACTICES 1

What is the value of the 6 in the number 63? **Explain** how you know.

Model and Draw

Break apart the addends into tens and ones.
Add the tens and add the ones.
Then find the total sum.

$$\begin{array}{r} 27 \\ +48 \\ \hline \end{array} \quad \begin{array}{l} \longrightarrow 20 + 7 \\ \longrightarrow 40 + 8 \\ \hline \end{array}$$

60 + 15 = ____

60 + 15
(15 breaks into 10 and 5)
70 + 5 = ____

Share and Show

Break apart the addends to find the sum.

1. 35 → ____ + ____
   +54 → ____ + ____
   ____ + ____ = ____

2. 43 → ____ + ____
   +29 → ____ + ____
   ____ + ____ = ____

3. 56 → ____ + ____
   +38 → ____ + ____
   ____ + ____ = ____

Name ______________________________

On Your Own

Break apart the addends to find the sum.

4. 14 → ____ + ____

+23 → ____ + ____

____ + ____ = ____

5. 37 → ____ + ____

+45 → ____ + ____

____ + ____ = ____

6. GO DEEPER Chris read 15 pages of his book. Tony read 4 more pages than Chris. How many pages did Chris and Tony read?

____ pages

7. THINK SMARTER Julie read 18 pages of her book in the morning. She read the same number of pages in the afternoon. How many pages did she read?

____ pages

Problem Solving • Applications

Write or draw to explain.

8. MATHEMATICAL PRACTICE 1 **Make Sense of Problems** Len has 35 baseball cards. The rest of his cards are basketball cards. He has 58 cards in all. How many basketball cards does he have?

_______ basketball cards

9. MATHEMATICAL PRACTICE 1 **Evaluate** Tomás has 17 pencils. He buys 26 more pencils. How many pencils does Tomás have now?

_______ pencils

Personal Math Trainer

10. THINKSMARTER+ Sasha used 38 red stickers and 22 blue stickers. Show how you can break apart the addends to find how many stickers Sasha used.

38 → ____ + ____

+22 → ____ + ____

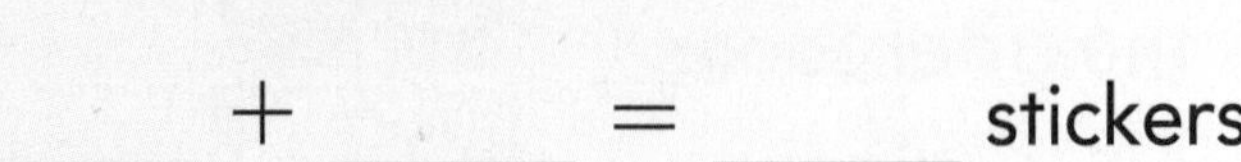

____ + ____ = ____ stickers

TAKE HOME ACTIVITY • Write 32 + 48 on a sheet of paper. Have your child break apart the numbers and find the sum.

Name ______________________

Break Apart Addends as Tens and Ones

Common Core **COMMON CORE STANDARD—2.NBT.B.5**
Use place value understanding and properties of operations to add and subtract.

Break apart the addends to find the sum.

1. 18 → ___ + ___
+ 21 → ___ + ___

___ + ___ = ___

2. 33 → ___ + ___
+ 49 → ___ + ___

___ + ___ = ___

Problem Solving

Choose a way to solve.
Write or draw to explain.

3. Christopher has 28 baseball cards. Justin has 18 baseball cards. How many baseball cards do they have together?

_____ baseball cards

4. WRITE Math Explain how to break apart the addends to find the sum of 25 + 16.

____

____

Lesson Check (2.NBT.B.5)

1. What is the sum?

$$\begin{array}{r} 27 \\ +\ 12 \\ \hline \end{array}$$

2. What is the sum?

$$\begin{array}{r} 17 \\ +\ 35 \\ \hline \end{array}$$

Spiral Review (2.OA.B.2, 2.NBT.A.1, 2.NBT.A.3, 2.NBT.B.5)

3. What is the value of the underlined digit?

   2<u>5</u>

   ____

4. What number has the same value as 12 tens?

   ____

5. Ally has 7 connecting cubes. Greg has 4 connecting cubes. How many connecting cubes do they have?

   ____ cubes

6. Juan painted a picture of a tree. First he painted 15 leaves. Then he painted 23 more leaves. How many leaves did he paint?

   ____ leaves

FOR MORE PRACTICE GO TO THE Personal Math Trainer

Name ______________________________

Model Regrouping for Addition

Essential Question When do you regroup in addition?

Common Core **Number and Operations in Base Ten—2.NBT.B.5**
MATHEMATICAL PRACTICES
MP1, MP5, MP7

Listen and Draw

Use tens and ones blocks to model the problem.
Draw quick pictures to show what you did.

Tens	Ones

MATHEMATICAL PRACTICES 5

Use Tools Describe how you made a ten in your model.

FOR THE TEACHER • Read the following problem. Brandon has 24 books. His friend Mario has 8 books. How many books do they have?

Model and Draw

Add 37 and 25.

Step 1 Look at the ones. Can you make a ten?

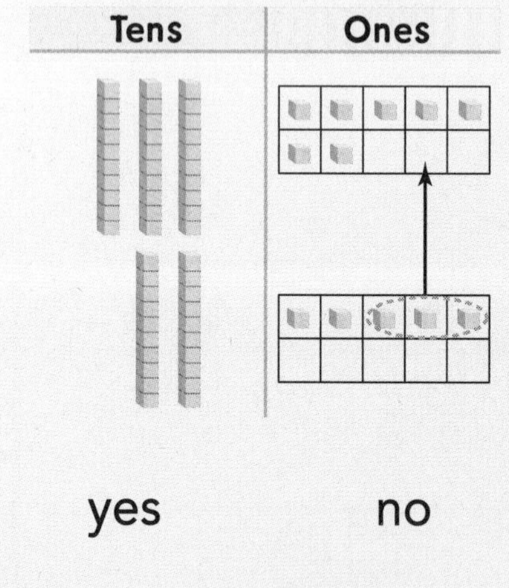

yes no

Step 2 If you can make a ten, **regroup**.

Tens | Ones

Trade 10 ones for 1 ten to regroup.

Step 3 Write how many tens and ones. Write the sum.

Tens | Ones

_____ tens _____ ones

_____

Share and Show

Draw to show the regrouping. Write how many tens and ones are in the sum. Write the sum.

1. Add 47 and 15.

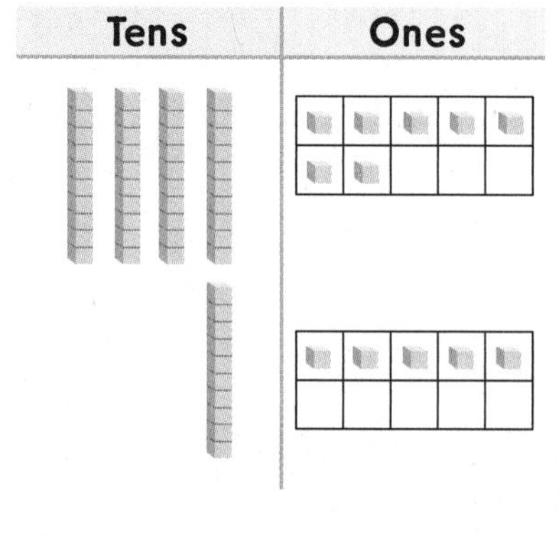

_____ tens _____ ones

_____

2. Add 48 and 8.

Tens | Ones

_____ tens _____ ones

_____

3. Add 26 and 38.

Tens | Ones

_____ tens _____ ones

_____

Name ______________________________

On Your Own

Draw to show if you regroup. Write how many tens and ones are in the sum. Write the sum.

4. Add 79 and 6.

Tens	Ones

_____ tens _____ ones

____

5. Add 18 and 64.

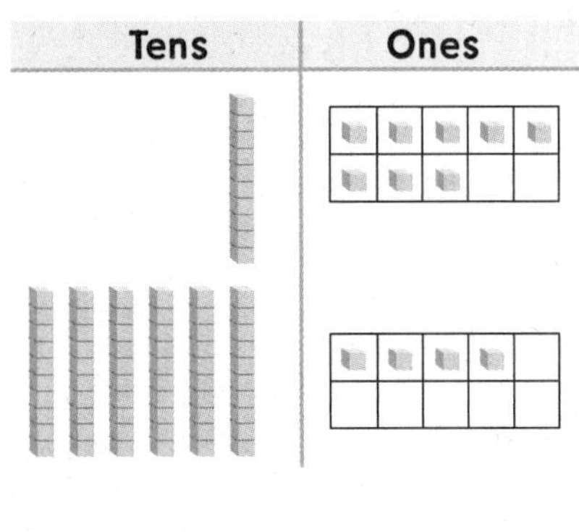

_____ tens _____ ones

____

6. Add 23 and 39.

Tens	Ones

_____ tens _____ ones

____

7. Add 54 and 25.

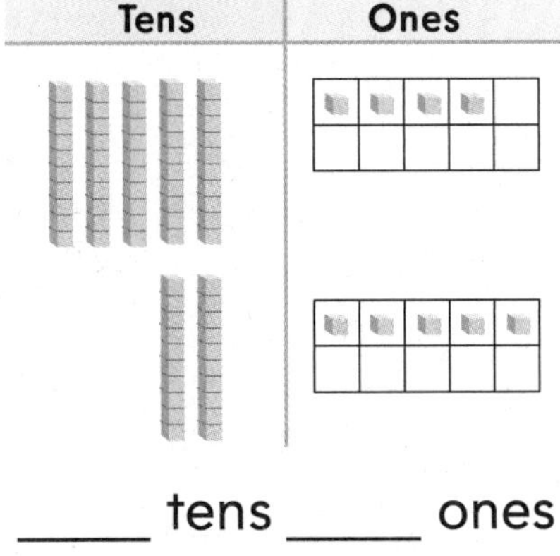

_____ tens _____ ones

____

8. Add 33 and 7.

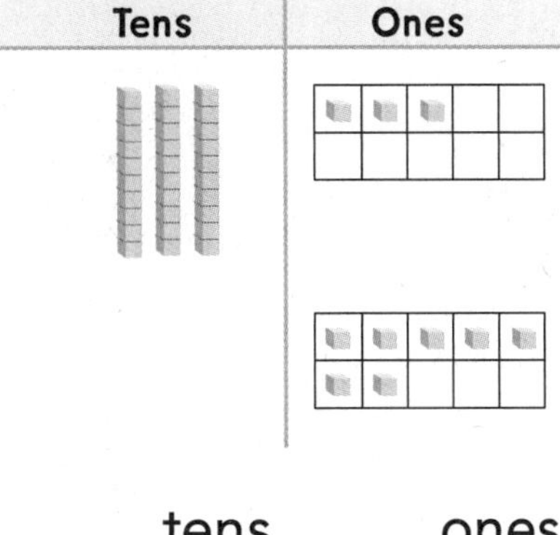

_____ tens _____ ones

____

9. Add 27 and 68.

Tens	Ones

_____ tens _____ ones

____

10. THINK SMARTER Kara has 25 toy animals and 12 books. Jorge has 8 more toy animals than Kara has. How many toy animals does Jorge have?

_____ toy animals

Problem Solving • Applications

Write or draw to explain.

11. MATHEMATICAL PRACTICE 1 **Make Sense of Problems** Mrs. Sanders has two fish tanks. There are 14 fish in the small tank. There are 27 fish in the large tank. How many fish are in the two tanks?

_______ fish

12. THINKSMARTER Charlie climbed 69 steps. Then he climbed 18 more steps. Show two different ways to find how many steps Charlie climbed.

Charlie climbed _______ steps.

TAKE HOME ACTIVITY • Ask your child to write a word problem with 2-digit numbers about adding two groups of stamps.

Name ______________________________

Model Regrouping for Addition

Draw to show the regrouping. Write how many tens and ones in the sum. Write the sum.

Common Core **COMMON CORE STANDARD—2.NBT.B.5** *Use place value understanding and properties of operations to add and subtract.*

1. Add 63 and 9.

Tens	Ones

_____ tens _____ ones

_____

2. Add 25 and 58.

Tens	Ones

_____ tens _____ ones

_____

3. Add 58 and 18.

Tens	Ones

_____ tens _____ ones

_____

4. Add 64 and 26.

Tens	Ones

_____ tens _____ ones

_____

5. Add 17 and 77.

Tens	Ones

_____ tens _____ ones

_____

6. Add 16 and 39.

Tens	Ones

_____ tens _____ ones

_____

Problem Solving

Choose a way to solve. Write or draw to explain.

7. Cathy has 43 leaves in her collection. Jane has 38 leaves. How many leaves do the two children have?

_____ leaves

8. WRITE Math Suppose you are adding 43 and 28. Will you regroup? Explain.

____

Lesson Check (2.NBT.B.5)

1. Add 27 and 48. What is the sum?

Tens	Ones

____

Spiral Review (2.OA.B.2, 2.OA.C.3, 2.NBT.B.5)

2. What is the sum?

$7 + 7 =$ ____

3. Circle the odd number.

6 12 21 22

4. What is the sum?

$39 + 46 =$ ____

5. What is the sum?

$5 + 3 + 4 =$ ____

FOR MORE PRACTICE GO TO THE **Personal Math Trainer**

Name ____________________

Model and Record 2-Digit Addition

Essential Question How do you record 2-digit addition?

Common Core Number and Operations in Base Ten—2.NBT.B.5 *Also 2.NBT.B.9*
MATHEMATICAL PRACTICES
MP1, MP4, MP6

Listen and Draw Real World

Use to model the problem.
Draw quick pictures to show what you did.

Tens	Ones

MATHEMATICAL PRACTICES 6

Make Connections Did you trade blocks in your model? Explain why or why not.

FOR THE TEACHER • Read the following problem. Mr. Riley's class collected 54 cans for the food drive. Miss Bright's class collected 35 cans. How many cans did the two classes collect?

Model and Draw

Trace over the quick pictures in the steps.

Step 1 Model 37 + 26. Are there 10 ones to regroup?

Tens	Ones
□	
3	7
+ 2	6

Step 2 Write the regrouped ten. Write how many ones are in the ones place now.

Tens	Ones
1	
3	7
+ 2	6
	3

Step 3 How many tens are there? Write how many tens are in the tens place.

Tens	Ones
1	
3	7
+ 2	6
6	3

Share and Show

Draw quick pictures to help you solve. Write the sum.

1.

Tens	Ones
□	
2	6
+ 3	2

Tens	Ones

2.

Tens	Ones
□	
5	8
+ 2	4

Tens	Ones

Name ______________________________

On Your Own

Draw quick pictures to help you solve. Write the sum.

3.

	Tens	Ones
	☐	
	3	4
+		9

Tens	Ones

4.

	Tens	Ones
	☐	
	2	7
+	2	4

Tens	Ones

5.

	Tens	Ones
	☐	
	3	5
+	2	3

Tens	Ones

6.

	Tens	Ones
	☐	
	5	9
+		6

Tens	Ones

7. THINK SMARTER Tim has 36 stickers. Margo has 44 stickers. How many more stickers would they need to have 100 stickers altogether?

_______ more stickers

8. GO DEEPER A baker wants to sell 100 muffins. So far the baker has sold 48 corn muffins and 42 bran muffins. How many more muffins does the baker need to sell?

_______ more muffins

Problem Solving • Applications  

Write or draw to explain.

9. MATHEMATICAL PRACTICE 1 **Make Sense of Problems** Chris and Bianca got 80 points in all in the spelling contest. Each child got more than 20 points. How many points could each child have gotten?

Chris: ________ points

Bianca: ________ points

Personal Math Trainer

10. THINKSMARTER+ Don built a tower with 24 blocks. He built another tower with 18 blocks. How many blocks did Don use for both towers? Draw quick pictures to solve. Write the sum.

Tens	Ones

_____ blocks

Did you regroup to find the answer? Explain.

____

____

____

TAKE HOME ACTIVITY • Write two 2-digit numbers and ask your child if he or she would regroup to find the sum.

Name ______________________

Model and Record 2-Digit Addition

COMMON CORE STANDARD—2.NBT.B.5
Use place value understanding and properties of operations to add and subtract.

Draw quick pictures to help you solve. Write the sum.

1.

	Tens	Ones
	□	
	3	8
+	1	7

Tens	Ones

2.

	Tens	Ones
	□	
	5	8
+	2	6

Tens	Ones

3.

	Tens	Ones
	□	
	4	2
+	3	7

Tens	Ones

4.

	Tens	Ones
	□	
	5	3
+	3	8

Tens	Ones

Problem Solving Real World

Choose a way to solve.
Write or draw to explain.

5. There were 37 children at the park on Saturday and 25 children at the park on Sunday. How many children were at the park on those two days?

_____ children

6. WRITE Math Explain why you should record a 1 in the Tens column when you regroup in an addition problem.

____

____

Lesson Check (2.NBT.B.5)

1. What is the sum?

	Tens	Ones
	☐	
	3	4
+	2	8

2. What is the sum?

	Tens	Ones
	☐	
	4	3
+	2	7

Spiral Review (2.OA.B.2)

3. Adam collected 14 pennies in the first week and 9 pennies in the second week. How many more pennies did he collect in the first week than in the second week?

$14 - 9 =$ ____ pennies

4. What is the sum?

$3 + 7 + 9 =$ ____

5. Janet has 5 marbles. She finds double that number of marbles in her art box. How many marbles does Janet have now?

$5 +$ ____ $=$ ____ marbles

6. What is the difference?

$13 - 5 =$ ____

FOR MORE PRACTICE GO TO THE Personal Math Trainer

Name ___________________________

2-Digit Addition

Essential Question How do you record the steps when adding 2-digit numbers?

Common Core **Number and Operations in Base Ten—2.NBT.B.5, 2.NBT.B.9**
MATHEMATICAL PRACTICES
MP1, MP3, MP6

Draw quick pictures to model each problem.

Tens	Ones

Tens	Ones

FOR THE TEACHER • Read the following problem and have children draw quick pictures to solve. Jason scored 35 points in one game and 47 points in another game. How many points did Jason score? Repeat the activity with this problem. Patty scored 18 points. Then she scored 21 points. How many points did she score in all?

Math Talk MATHEMATICAL PRACTICES 1

Analyze Relationships Explain why regrouping works.

Model and Draw

Add 59 and 24.

Step 1 Add the ones.

$9 + 4 = 13$

Tens	Ones
☐	
5	9
+ 2	4

Step 2 Regroup.
13 ones is the same as 1 ten 3 ones.

Tens	Ones
1	
5	9
+ 2	4
	3

Step 3 Add the tens.

$1 + 5 + 2 = \mathbf{8}$

Tens	Ones
1	
5	9
+ 2	4
8	3

Share and Show

Regroup if you need to. Write the sum.

1.

Tens	Ones
☐	
4	2
+ 2	9

✓ 2.

Tens	Ones
☐	
3	1
+ 1	4

✓ 3.

Tens	Ones
☐	
2	7
+ 4	5

Name ___________________________

On Your Own

Regroup if you need to. Write the sum.

4.

	Tens	Ones
	□	
	4	8
+		7

5.

	Tens	Ones
	□	
	3	5
+	4	2

6.

	Tens	Ones
	□	
	7	3
+	2	0

7.

	3	3
+	2	7

8.

	5	2
+		5

9.

	3	6
+	5	8

10.

	6	4
+	2	5

11.

	3	5
+	3	8

12.

	3	8
+	5	2

Solve. Write or draw to explain.

13. THINKSMARTER Jin has 31 books about cats and 19 books about dogs. He gives 5 books to his sister. How many books does Jin have now?

_______ books

Problem Solving • Applications

14. GO DEEPER Abby used a different way to add. Find the sum using Abby's way.

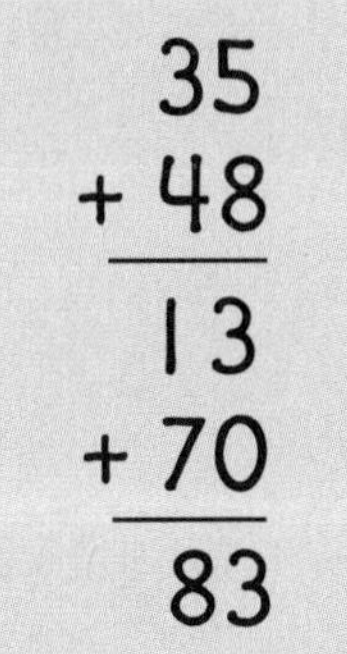

$$\begin{array}{r} 35 \\ +\ 48 \\ \hline 13 \\ +\ 70 \\ \hline 83 \end{array}$$

$$\begin{array}{r} 5\ 7 \\ +\ 2\ 9 \\ \hline \\ \hline \end{array}$$

15. MATHEMATICAL PRACTICE 3 **Verify the Reasoning of Others** Explain why Abby's way works.

____

____

____

16. THINK SMARTER Melissa saw 14 sea lions and 29 seals. How many animals did she see? Write a number sentence to find the total number of animals that she saw.

____

Explain how the number sentence shows the problem.

____

____

TAKE HOME ACTIVITY • Ask your child to show you two ways to add 45 and 38.

Name ______________________________

2-Digit Addition

Practice and Homework
Lesson 4.6

Common Core **COMMON CORE STANDARD—2.NBT.B.5**
Use place value understanding and properties of operations to add and subtract.

Regroup if you need to. Write the sum.

1.
$$\begin{array}{r|l} 4 & 7 \\ +2 & 5 \\ \hline & \end{array}$$

2.
$$\begin{array}{r|l} 3 & 3 \\ +1 & 8 \\ \hline & \end{array}$$

3.
$$\begin{array}{r|l} 2 & 8 \\ +6 & 4 \\ \hline & \end{array}$$

4.
$$\begin{array}{r|l} 1 & 3 \\ +6 & 5 \\ \hline & \end{array}$$

5.
$$\begin{array}{r|l} 1 & 7 \\ +2 & 6 \\ \hline & \end{array}$$

6.
$$\begin{array}{r|l} 3 & 6 \\ +5 & 3 \\ \hline & \end{array}$$

7.
$$\begin{array}{r|l} 5 & 8 \\ +2 & 5 \\ \hline & \end{array}$$

8.
$$\begin{array}{r|l} 3 & 7 \\ +4 & 9 \\ \hline & \end{array}$$

Problem Solving

Solve. Write or draw to explain.

9. Angela drew 16 flowers on her paper in the morning. She drew 25 more flowers in the afternoon. How many flowers did she draw?

_____ flowers

10. WRITE Math How is Exercise 5 different from Exercise 6? Explain.

____

____

Lesson Check (2.NBT.B.5)

1. What is the sum?

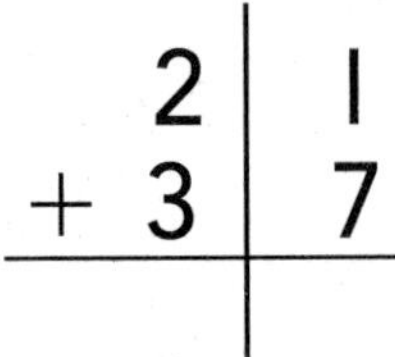

2. What is the sum?

	3	8
+	5	2

Spiral Review (2.OA.A.1, 2.NBT.A.3, 2.NBT.B.8)

3. What is the next number in the counting pattern?

103, 203, 303, 403, ____

4. Rita counted 13 bubbles. Ben counted 5 bubbles. How many fewer bubbles did Ben count than Rita?

$13 - 5 =$ ____ bubbles

5. Which number is 100 more than 265?

____

6. Write 42 as a sum of tens and ones.

____ + ____

FOR MORE PRACTICE GO TO THE **Personal Math Trainer**

Name ______________________________

Practice 2-Digit Addition

Essential Question How do you record the steps when adding 2-digit numbers?

Common Core Number and Operations in Base Ten—2.NBT.B.5 *Also 2.NBT.B.7*

MATHEMATICAL PRACTICES
MP1, MP6, MP7

Listen and Draw Real World

Choose one way to solve the problem.
Draw or write to show what you did.

FOR THE TEACHER • Read the following problem. There were 45 boys and 53 girls who ran in the race. How many children ran in the race?

Math Talk MATHEMATICAL PRACTICES 6

Explain why you chose your way of solving the problem.

Model and Draw

Mrs. Meyers sold 47 snacks before the game. Then she sold 85 snacks during the game. How many snacks did she sell?

Step 1 Add the ones.

$7 + 5 = 12$

Regroup 12 ones as 1 ten 2 ones.

$$\begin{array}{r} {}^{1} \\ 47 \\ +\ 85 \\ \hline 2 \end{array}$$

Step 2 Add the tens.

$1 + 4 + 8 = 13$

$$\begin{array}{r} {}^{1} \\ 47 \\ +\ 85 \\ \hline 2 \end{array}$$

Step 3 13 tens can be regrouped as 1 hundred 3 tens. Write the hundreds digit and the tens digit in the sum.

$$\begin{array}{r} {}^{1} \\ 47 \\ +\ 85 \\ \hline 132 \end{array}$$

Share and Show

Write the sum.

1. $\begin{array}{r} 38 \\ +\ 94 \\ \hline \end{array}$

2. $\begin{array}{r} 45 \\ +\ 52 \\ \hline \end{array}$

3. $\begin{array}{r} 83 \\ +\ 76 \\ \hline \end{array}$

4. $\begin{array}{r} 56 \\ +\ 35 \\ \hline \end{array}$

✓5. $\begin{array}{r} 63 \\ +\ 51 \\ \hline \end{array}$

✓6. $\begin{array}{r} 74 \\ +\ 49 \\ \hline \end{array}$

Name ____________________

On Your Own

Write the sum.

7.
$$\begin{array}{r} 52 \\ +\ 37 \\ \hline \end{array}$$

8.
$$\begin{array}{r} 88 \\ +\ 21 \\ \hline \end{array}$$

9.
$$\begin{array}{r} 74 \\ +\ 67 \\ \hline \end{array}$$

10.
$$\begin{array}{r} 93 \\ +\ 54 \\ \hline \end{array}$$

11.
$$\begin{array}{r} 92 \\ +\ 78 \\ \hline \end{array}$$

12.
$$\begin{array}{r} 56 \\ +\ 16 \\ \hline \end{array}$$

13.
$$\begin{array}{r} 31 \\ +\ 45 \\ \hline \end{array}$$

14.
$$\begin{array}{r} 43 \\ +\ 72 \\ \hline \end{array}$$

15. THINK SMARTER Without finding the sums, circle the pairs of addends for which the sum will be greater than 100.

Explain how you decided which pairs to circle.

73 18	54 71
47 62	36 59

____

____

____

____

TAKE HOME ACTIVITY • Tell your child two 2-digit numbers. Have him or her write the numbers and find the sum.

Name ______________________

Mid-Chapter Checkpoint

Concepts and Skills

Break apart ones to make a ten.
Then add and write the sum. (2.NBT.B.5)

1. $37 + 8 =$ ______

2. $55 + 7 =$ ______

Break apart the addends to find the sum. (2.NBT.B.5)

3.
27 → ______ + ______
+36 → ______ + ______
______ + ______ = ______

Write the sum. (2.NBT.B.5)

4.
$$\begin{array}{r} 28 \\ +\ 57 \\ \hline \end{array}$$

5.
$$\begin{array}{r} 67 \\ +\ 31 \\ \hline \end{array}$$

6.
$$\begin{array}{r} 71 \\ +\ 19 \\ \hline \end{array}$$

7. THINK SMARTER Julia collected 25 cans to recycle. Dan collected 14 cans. How many cans did they collect? (2.NBT.B.5)

______ cans

Name ______________________

Practice 2-Digit Addition

COMMON CORE STANDARD—2.NBT.B.5
Use place value understanding and properties of operations to add and subtract.

Write the sum.

1.
  58
+ 17
____

2.
  44
+ 86
____

3.
  36
+ 13
____

4.
  49
+ 72
____

5.
  58
+ 87
____

6.
  32
+ 59
____

Problem Solving

Solve. Write or draw to explain.

7. There are 45 books on the shelf. There are 37 books on the table. How many books are on the shelf and the table?

_____ books

8. WRITE Math Describe how you regroup when you find the sum of 64 + 43.

____

____

Lesson Check (2.NBT.B.5)

1. What is the sum?

$$\begin{array}{r} 56 \\ +\ 35 \\ \hline \end{array}$$

2. What is the sum?

$$\begin{array}{r} 74 \\ +\ 15 \\ \hline \end{array}$$

Spiral Review (2.OA.A.1, 2.OA.B.2, 2.NBT.A.1, 2.NBT.A.3)

3. What is the value of the underlined digit?

$\underline{5}26$

____

4. Mr. Stevens wants to put 17 books on the shelf. He put 8 books on the shelf. How many more books does he need to put on the shelf?

17 − 8 = ____ books

5. What is the difference?

11 − 6 = ____

6. Write 83 as a sum of tens and ones.

____ + ____

FOR MORE PRACTICE GO TO THE Personal Math Trainer

Name ___________________________

Rewrite 2-Digit Addition

Essential Question What are two different ways to write addition problems?

Common Core **Number and Operations in Base Ten—2.NBT.B.5**

MATHEMATICAL PRACTICES
MP1, MP6, MP7

Listen and Draw (Real World)

Write the numbers for each addition problem.

+ ______	+ ______
+ ______	+ ______

Math Talk MATHEMATICAL PRACTICES 7

Look for Structure
Explain why it is important to line up the digits of these addends in columns.

FOR THE TEACHER • Read the following problem and have children write the addends in vertical format. Juan's family drove 32 miles to his grandmother's house. Then they drove 14 miles to his aunt's house. How many miles did they drive? Repeat for three more problems.

Model and Draw

Add. 28 + 45 = ?

Step 1 For 28, write the tens digit in the tens column.

Write the ones digit in the ones column.

Repeat for 45.

$$\begin{array}{r} 2\ 8 \\ +\ 4\ 5 \\ \hline \end{array}$$

Step 2 Add the ones.

Regroup if you need to.

Add the tens.

$$\begin{array}{r} 2\ 8 \\ +\ 4\ 5 \\ \hline \end{array}$$

Share and Show

Rewrite the addition problem. Then add.

1. 25 + 8

+

2. 37 + 10

+

3. 25 + 45

+

4. 38 + 29

+

5. 20 + 45

+

6. 63 + 9

+

7. 15 + 36

+

8. 74 + 18

+

Name ___________________________

On Your Own

Rewrite the addition problem. Then add.

9. 27 + 54

10. 34 + 30

11. 26 + 17

12. 48 + 38

13. 50 + 32

14. 61 + 38

15. 37 + 43

16. 79 + 17

17. 45 + 40

18. 21 + 52

19. 17 + 76

20. 68 + 29

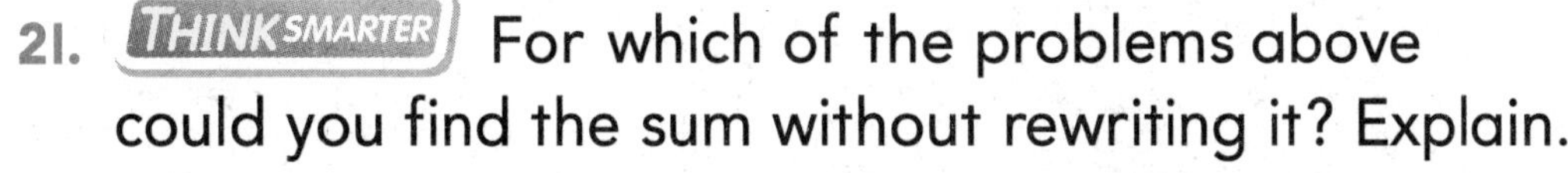

21. THINK SMARTER For which of the problems above could you find the sum without rewriting it? Explain.

____

____

____

Problem Solving • Applications  

Use the table.
Write or draw to show how you solved the problem.

Points Scored This Season	
Player	**Number of Points**
Anna	26
Lou	37
Becky	23
Kevin	19

22. MATHEMATICAL PRACTICE 1 **Analyze Relationships** Which two players scored 56 points in all? Add to check your answer.

_________ and _________

23. THINKSMARTER Shawn says he can find the sum of 20 + 63 without rewriting it. Explain how to find the sum using mental math.

____

____

____

____

TAKE HOME ACTIVITY • Have your child write and solve another problem, using the table above.

Name ______________________

Rewrite 2-Digit Addition

Common Core **COMMON CORE STANDARD—2.NBT.B.5**
Use place value understanding and properties of operations to add and subtract

Rewrite the numbers. Then add.

1. 27 + 19

   \+ ______

2. 36 + 23

   \+ ______

3. 31 + 29

   \+ ______

4. 48 + 23

   \+ ______

5. 53 + 12

   \+ ______

6. 69 + 13

   \+ ______

7. 24 + 38

   \+ ______

8. 46 + 37

   \+ ______

Problem Solving 

Use the table. Show how you solved the problem.

9. How many pages did Sasha and Kara read together?

   ____ pages

Pages Read This Week	
Child	**Number of Pages**
Sasha	62
Kara	29
Juan	50

10. WRITE Math Explain what can happen if you line up the digits incorrectly when you rewrite addition problems.

____

____

____

Lesson Check (2.NBT.B.5)

1. What is the sum of 39 + 17?

$+$ ____

2. What is the sum of 28 + 16?

$+$ ____

Spiral Review (2.OA.C.4, 2.NBT.A.1, 2.NBT.A.3, 2.NBT.B.6)

3. What number is another way to write 60 + 4?

____

4. The classroom has 4 desks in each row. There are 5 rows. How many desks are there in the classroom?

____ desks

5. A squirrel collected 17 acorns. Then the squirrel collected 31 acorns. How many acorns did the squirrel collect?

____ acorns

6. What number can be written as 3 hundreds 7 tens 5 ones?

____

FOR MORE PRACTICE GO TO THE Personal Math Trainer

Name ______________________________

Problem Solving • Addition

Essential Question How can drawing a diagram help when solving addition problems?

Operations and Algebraic Thinking—2.OA.A.1 *Also 2.NBT.B.5*

MATHEMATICAL PRACTICES
MP1, MP2, MP4

Kendra had 13 crayons. Her dad gave her some more crayons. Then she had 19 crayons. How many crayons did Kendra's dad give her?

Unlock the Problem

What do I need to find?

how many crayons
____
Kendra's dad gave her

What information do I need to use?

She had ________ crayons.
After he gave her some more crayons, she had ________ crayons.

Show how to solve the problem.

There are 19 crayons in all.

13	____

19

13 + ■ = 19
____

________ crayons

HOME CONNECTION • Your child used a bar model and a number sentence to represent the problem. These help show what the missing amount is in order to solve the problem.

Try Another Problem

Label the bar model. Write a number sentence with a ▒ for the missing number. Solve.

- What do I need to find?
- What information do I need to use?

1. Mr. Kane has 24 red pens. He buys 19 blue pens. How many pens does he have now?

____	____

____

________________ ____ pens

2. Hannah has 10 pencils. Jim and Hannah have 17 pencils altogether. How many pencils does Jim have?

____	____

____

________________ ____ pencils

Math Talk MATHEMATICAL PRACTICES 2

Explain how you know if an amount is a part or the whole in a problem.

Name ______________________

Share and Show 

Label the bar model. Write a number sentence with a ▒ for the missing number. Solve.

✓ 3. Aimee and Matthew catch 17 crickets in all. Aimee catches 9 crickets. How many crickets does Matthew catch?

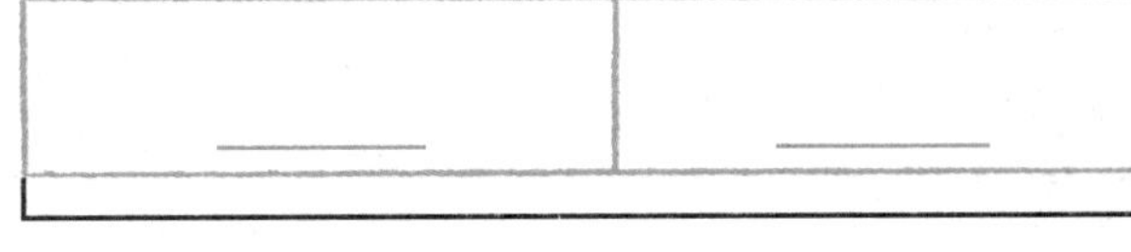

_______ crickets

____

✓ 4. Percy counts 16 grasshoppers at the park. He counts 15 grasshoppers at home. How many grasshoppers does Percy count?

_______ grasshoppers

____

5. THINKSMARTER There are three groups of owls. There are 17 owls in each of the first two groups. There are 47 owls in all. How many owls are in the third group?

_______ owls

On Your Own

WRITE Math

Write or draw to explain.

6. There are 37 paper clips in the box and 24 paper clips on the table. How many paper clips are there in all?

_______ paper clips

7. MATHEMATICAL PRACTICE 1 **Make Sense of Problems** Jeff has 19 postcards and 2 pens. He buys 20 more postcards. How many postcards does he have now?

_______ postcards

8. GO DEEPER There are a total of 41 chickens on the farm. There are 13 chickens in each of the 2 cages in the barn. The rest of the chickens are outside. How many chickens are outside?

_______ chickens

9. THINK SMARTER There are 23 books in a box. There are 29 books on a shelf. How many books are there?

_______ books

TAKE HOME ACTIVITY • Ask your child to explain how to solve one of the problems above.

Name ______

Problem Solving • Addition

Common Core **COMMON CORE STANDARD—2.OA.A.1**
Represent and solve problems involving addition and subtraction.

Label the bar model. Write a number sentence with a ■ for the missing number. Solve.

1. Jacob counts 37 ants on the sidewalk and 11 ants on the grass. How many ants does Jacob count?

   ______ ants

2. There are 14 bees in the hive and 17 bees in the garden. How many bees are there?

   ______ bees

3. WRITE Math Describe how you labeled the bar model and wrote a number sentence to solve Exercise 2.

Lesson Check (2.OA.A.1)

1. Sean and Abby have 23 markers altogether. Abby has 14 markers. How many markers does Sean have?

____	____

   ____

2. Mrs. James has 22 students in her class. Mr. Williams has 24 students in his class. How many students are in the two classes?

____	____

   ____

Spiral Review (2.OA.B.2, 2.NBT.A.2)

3. What is the difference?

   $15 - 9 =$ ____

4. What is the sum?

   $7 + 5 =$ ____

5. Jan has 14 blocks. She gives 9 blocks to Tim. How many blocks does Jan have now?

   $14 - 9 =$ ____ blocks

6. What is the next number in the counting pattern?

   29, 39, 49, 59, ____

FOR MORE PRACTICE GO TO THE Personal Math Trainer

Name ______________________________

Algebra • Write Equations to Represent Addition

Essential Question How do you write a number sentence to represent a problem?

Common Core **Operations and Algebraic Thinking—2.OA.A.1** *Also 2.NBT.B.5*

MATHEMATICAL PRACTICES
MP2, MP5, MP6

Listen and Draw Real World

Draw to show how you found the answer.

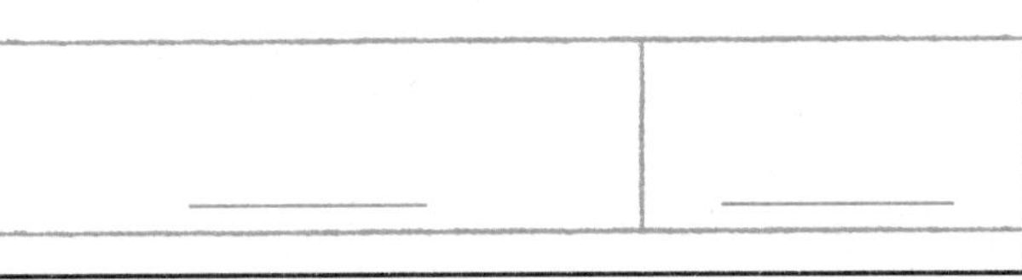

FOR THE TEACHER • Read the following problem and have children choose their own methods for solving. There are 15 children on the bus. Then 9 more children get on the bus. How many children are on the bus now?

Math Talk MATHEMATICAL PRACTICES 5

Communicate Explain how you found the number of children on the bus.

Model and Draw

You can write a number sentence to show a problem.

Sandy has 16 pencils. Nancy has 13 pencils. How many pencils do the two girls have?

THINK:

	16 pencils
+	13 pencils
	29 pencils

The two girls have ______ pencils.

Share and Show

MATH BOARD

Write a number sentence for the problem. Use a ▢ for the missing number. Then solve.

1. Carl sees 25 melons at the store. 15 are small and the rest are large. How many melons are large?

____

______ melons

2. 83 people went to a movie on Thursday. 53 of them were children and the rest were adults. How many adults were at the movie?

____

______ adults

Name ___________________________

On Your Own

Write a number sentence for the problem. Use a ■ for the missing number. Then solve.

3. Jake had some stamps. Then he bought 20 more stamps. Now he has 56 stamps. How many stamps did Jake have to start?

___________________ ________ stamps

4. THINKSMARTER Braden's class went to the park. They saw 26 oak trees and 14 maple trees. They also saw 13 cardinals and 35 blue jays. Compare the number of trees and the number of birds that the class saw.

________ ◯ ________

5. MATHEMATICAL PRACTICE 6 **Explain** Amy needs about 70 paper clips. Without adding, circle 2 boxes that would be close to the amount that she needs.

70 clips	81 clips	54 clips
19 clips	35 clips	32 clips

Explain how you made your choices.

____

____

____

Problem Solving • Applications

6. MATHEMATICAL PRACTICE 1 **Make Sense of Problems**
Mr. Walton baked 24 loaves of bread last week. He baked 28 loaves of bread this week. How many loaves of bread did he bake in the two weeks?

_______ loaves of bread

7. THINK SMARTER Denise saw these bags of oranges at the store.

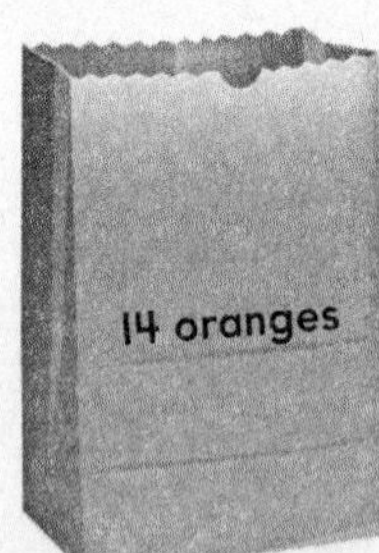

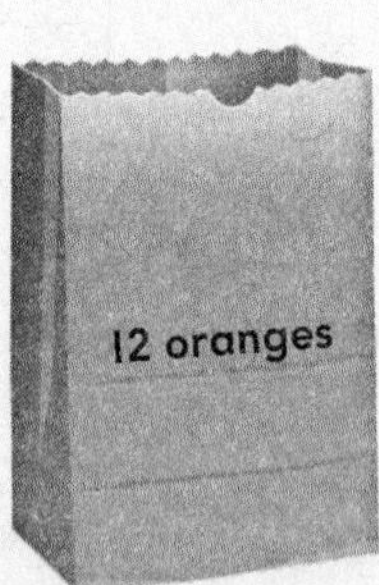

Denise bought 26 oranges. Which two bags of oranges did she buy?
Draw or write to show how you solved the problem.

Explain how you found the numbers that have a sum of 26.

____

____

____

TAKE HOME ACTIVITY • Have your child explain how he or she writes a number sentence to stand for a problem.

Name ______________________

Algebra • Write Equations to Represent Addition

Common Core **COMMON CORE STANDARD—2.OA.A.1**
Represent and solve problems involving addition and subtraction.

Write a number sentence for the problem. Use a ■ for the missing number. Then solve.

1. Emily and her friends went to the park. They saw 15 robins and 9 blue jays. How many birds did they see?

____

____ birds

2. Joe has 13 fish in one tank. He has 8 fish in another tank. How many fish does Joe have?

____

____ fish

Problem Solving

Solve.

3. There are 21 children in Kathleen's class. 12 of the children are girls. How many children in her class are boys?

____ boys

4. WRITE Math Explain how you decided what number sentence to write for Exercise 1.

____

____

____

____

Lesson Check (2.OA.A.1)

1. Clare has 14 blocks. Jasmine has 6 blocks. How many blocks do they have?

   14 + 6 = ____ blocks

2. Matt finds 16 acorns at the park. Trevor finds 18 acorns. How many acorns do they find?

   16 + 18 = ____ acorns

Spiral Review (2.OA.A.1, 2.OA.B.2, 2.OA.C.3, 2.OA.C.4)

3. Leanne counted 19 ants. Gregory counted 6 ants. How many more ants did Leanne count than Gregory?

   19 − 6 = ____ ants

4. What is the sum?

   4 + 3 + 6 = ____

5. Ms. Santos puts seashells into 4 rows. She puts 6 seashells in each row. How many seashells are there altogether?

   ____ seashells

6. Circle the even number.

   9　　14　　17　　21

FOR MORE PRACTICE GO TO THE **Personal Math Trainer**

Name ______________________________

Algebra • Find Sums for 3 Addends

Essential Question What are some ways to add 3 numbers?

Common Core **Number and Operations in Base Ten—2.NBT.B.6**

MATHEMATICAL PRACTICES
MP1, MP4, MP8

Listen and Draw Real World

Draw to show each problem.

MATHEMATICAL PRACTICES 1

Which numbers did you add first in the first problem? **Explain** why.

FOR THE TEACHER • Read the following problem and have children draw to show it. Mr. Kim bought 5 blue balloons, 4 red balloons, and 5 yellow balloons. How many balloons did Mr. Kim buy? Repeat for another problem.

Model and Draw

There are different ways to add three numbers.

How can you add 23, 41, and 17?

Think of different ways to choose digits in the ones **column** to add first.

You can make a ten first. Then add the other ones digit. Then add the tens.

```
  23
  41
+ 17
```

3 + 7 = 10
10 + 1 = 11

Add from top to bottom. First add the top two digits in the ones column, then add the next digit. Then add the tens.

```
  23
  41
+ 17
```

3 + 1 = 4
4 + 7 = 11

Share and Show MATH BOARD

Add.

1.	2.	3.	4.
33 34 + 32	47 21 + 7	65 13 + 15	58 27 + 22

5.	6.	7.	8.
12 22 + 36	10 42 + 36	31 21 + 16	30 29 + 48

Name ______________________________

On Your Own

Add.

9. 22 + 27 + 18 = ____

10. 26 + 31 + 19 = ____

11. 24 + 11 + 53 = ____

12. 33 + 43 + 4 = ____

13. 40 + 17 + 32 = ____

14. 25 + 25 + 25 = ____

15. 19 + 65 + 24 = ____

16. 73 + 4 + 16 = ____

17. GO DEEPER Mrs. Carson is making food for a party. She makes 20 ham sandwiches, 34 turkey sandwiches, and 38 tuna salad sandwiches. How many sandwiches does she make for the party?

_______ sandwiches

18. THINK SMARTER Sophia had 44 marbles. She bought 24 more marbles. Then John gave her 35 marbles. How many marbles does Sophia have now?

_______ marbles

Problem Solving • Applications

Solve. Write or draw to explain.

19. MATHEMATICAL PRACTICE 1 **Evaluate** Mrs. Shaw has 23 red notebooks, 15 blue notebooks, and 27 green notebooks. How many notebooks does she have?

_______ notebooks

20. MATHEMATICAL PRACTICE 4 **Model Mathematics** Write a story problem that could be solved using this number sentence.

$$12 + 28 + \blacksquare = 53$$

____

____

____

____

21. THINKSMARTER Mr. Samson gave his students 31 yellow pencils, 27 red pencils, and 25 blue pencils. How many pencils did he give to his students?

_______ pencils

TAKE HOME ACTIVITY • Ask your child to show you two ways to add 17, 13, and 24.

Name ______________________

Algebra • Find Sums for 3 Addends

COMMON CORE STANDARD—2.NBT.B.6
Use place value understanding and properties of operations to add and subtract.

Add.

1.
$$\begin{array}{r} 23 \\ 20 \\ +25 \\ \hline \end{array}$$

2.
$$\begin{array}{r} 15 \\ 22 \\ +38 \\ \hline \end{array}$$

3.
$$\begin{array}{r} 13 \\ 52 \\ +34 \\ \hline \end{array}$$

4.
$$\begin{array}{r} 27 \\ 40 \\ +19 \\ \hline \end{array}$$

5.
$$\begin{array}{r} 31 \\ 45 \\ +24 \\ \hline \end{array}$$

6.
$$\begin{array}{r} 34 \\ 11 \\ +28 \\ \hline \end{array}$$

7.
$$\begin{array}{r} 42 \\ 36 \\ +11 \\ \hline \end{array}$$

8.
$$\begin{array}{r} 18 \\ 22 \\ +34 \\ \hline \end{array}$$

9.
$$\begin{array}{r} 53 \\ 19 \\ +25 \\ \hline \end{array}$$

Problem Solving

Solve. Write or draw to explain.

10. Liam has 24 yellow pencils, 15 red pencils, and 9 blue pencils. How many pencils does he have altogether?

_____ pencils

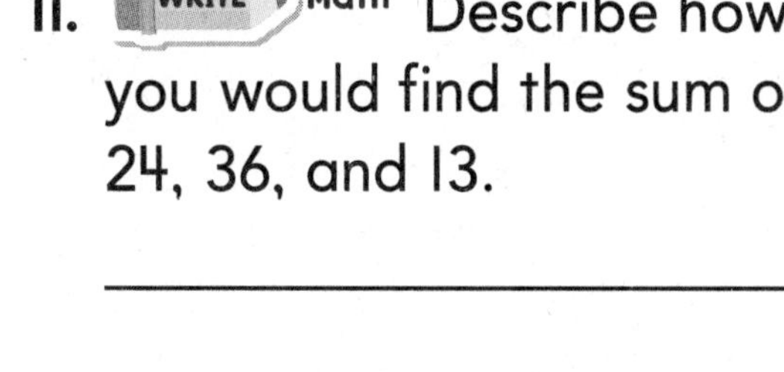

11. WRITE Math Describe how you would find the sum of 24, 36, and 13.

____

____

Lesson Check (2.NBT.B.6)

1. What is the sum?

$$\begin{array}{r} 22 \\ 31 \\ +\ 16 \\ \hline \end{array}$$

2. What is the sum?

$$\begin{array}{r} 17 \\ 26 \\ +\ 30 \\ \hline \end{array}$$

Spiral Review (2.OA.A.1, 2.OA.C.4, 2.NBT.A.3, 2.NBT.B.8)

3. What number is 10 more than 127?

____

4. Mr. Howard's phone has 4 rows of buttons. There are 3 buttons in each row. How many buttons are on Mr. Howard's phone?

____ buttons

5. Bob tosses 8 horseshoes. Liz tosses 9 horseshoes. How many horseshoes do they toss?

8 + 9 = ____ horseshoes

6. What number can be written 3 hundreds 1 ten 5 ones?

____

Name ___________________________________

Algebra • Find Sums for 4 Addends

Essential Question What are some ways to add 4 numbers?

Common Core **Number and Operations in Base Ten—2.NBT.B.6**

MATHEMATICAL PRACTICES
MP1, MP6, MP8

Listen and Draw Real World

Show how you solved each problem.

MATHEMATICAL PRACTICES 6

Describe how you found the answer to the first problem.

FOR THE TEACHER • Read this problem and have children choose a way to solve it. Shelly counts 16 ants in her ant farm. Pedro counts 22 ants in his farm. Tara counts 14 ants in her farm. How many ants do the 3 children count? Repeat for another problem.

Model and Draw

You can add digits in a column in more than one way. Add the ones first. Then add the tens.

Find a sum that you know. Then add to it.

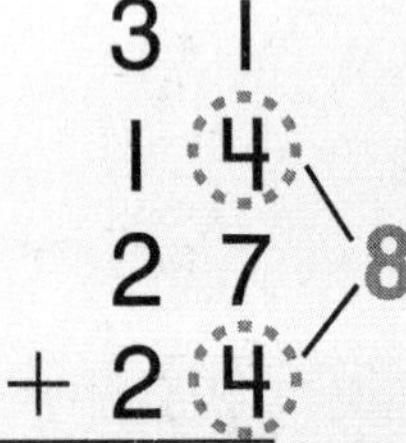

THINK:
8 + 1 = 9, then add on 7 more. The sum of the ones is 16 ones.

Add pairs of digits first. Then add these sums.

```
  3 1 \
  1 4 / 5
  2 7 \
+ 2 4 / 11
```

THINK:
5 + 11 = 16, so there are 16 ones in all.

Share and Show

Add.

1.
$$\begin{array}{r} 23 \\ 11 \\ 22 \\ +31 \\ \hline \end{array}$$

2.
$$\begin{array}{r} 30 \\ 15 \\ 3 \\ +25 \\ \hline \end{array}$$

3.
$$\begin{array}{r} 13 \\ 26 \\ 54 \\ +12 \\ \hline \end{array}$$

4.
$$\begin{array}{r} 27 \\ 2 \\ 23 \\ +13 \\ \hline \end{array}$$

✅5.
$$\begin{array}{r} 45 \\ 14 \\ 35 \\ +51 \\ \hline \end{array}$$

✅6.
$$\begin{array}{r} 32 \\ 21 \\ 15 \\ +30 \\ \hline \end{array}$$

Name ______________________

On Your Own

Add.

7.
```
  36
  12
  21
+ 26
----
```

8.
```
  14
  23
  20
+ 11
----
```

9.
```
  22
  13
  15
+ 27
----
```

10.
```
  45
  12
  41
+ 22
----
```

11.
```
  59
  31
  51
+ 73
----
```

12.
```
  34
  10
  31
+ 22
----
```

13. GO DEEPER Some friends need 100 bows for a project. Sara brings 12 bows, Angela brings 50 bows, and Nora brings 34 bows. How many more bows do they need?

_______ more bows

Solve. Write or draw to explain.

14. THINK SMARTER Laney added four numbers which have a total of 128. She spilled some juice over one number. What is that number?

22 + 43 +  + 30 = 128

____

Problem Solving • Applications 

Use the table.
Write or draw to show how you solved the problems.

Shells Collected at the Beach	
Child	**Number of Shells**
Katie	34
Paul	15
Noah	26
Laura	21

15. MATHEMATICAL PRACTICE 1 **Evaluate** How many shells did the four children collect at the beach?

_______ shells

16. GO DEEPER Which two children collected more shells at the beach, Katie and Paul, or Noah and Laura?

____

17. THINK SMARTER There were 24 red beads, 31 blue beads, and 8 green beads in a jar. Then Emma put 16 beads into the jar. Write a number sentence to show the number of beads in the jar.

____

TAKE HOME ACTIVITY • Have your child explain what he or she learned in this lesson.

Name ________________________

Algebra • Find Sums for 4 Addends

Common Core **COMMON CORE STANDARD—2.NBT.B.6**
Use place value understanding and properties of operations to add and subtract.

Add.

1.
$$\begin{array}{r} 18 \\ 32 \\ 23 \\ +\ \ 3 \\ \hline \end{array}$$

2.
$$\begin{array}{r} 45 \\ 31 \\ 29 \\ +72 \\ \hline \end{array}$$

3.
$$\begin{array}{r} 24 \\ 62 \\ 70 \\ +33 \\ \hline \end{array}$$

4.
$$\begin{array}{r} 83 \\ 32 \\ 61 \\ +22 \\ \hline \end{array}$$

5.
$$\begin{array}{r} 37 \\ 15 \\ 31 \\ +12 \\ \hline \end{array}$$

6.
$$\begin{array}{r} 21 \\ 13 \\ 96 \\ +18 \\ \hline \end{array}$$

Problem Solving

Solve. Show how you solved the problem.

7. Kinza jogs 16 minutes on Monday, 13 minutes on Tuesday, 9 minutes on Wednesday, and 20 minutes on Thursday. What is the total number of minutes she jogged?

_____ minutes

8. WRITE Math Describe two different strategies you could use to add 16 + 35 + 24 + 14.

____

Lesson Check (2.NBT.B.6)

1. What is the sum?

$$\begin{array}{r} 12 \\ 33 \\ 56 \\ +\ 32 \\ \hline \end{array}$$

2. What is the sum?

$$\begin{array}{r} 41 \\ 74 \\ 43 \\ +\ 20 \\ \hline \end{array}$$

Spiral Review (2.OA.A.1, 2.NBT.B.5)

3. Laura had 6 daisies. Then she found 7 more daisies. How many daisies does she have now?

   6 + 7 = ____ daisies

4. What is the sum?

$$\begin{array}{r} 52 \\ +27 \\ \hline \end{array}$$

5. Alan has 25 trading cards. He buys 8 more. How many cards does he have now?

   25 + 8 = ____ cards

6. Jen saw 13 guinea pigs and 18 gerbils at the pet store. How many pets did she see?

   13 + 18 = ____ pets

FOR MORE PRACTICE GO TO THE Personal Math Trainer

Name ______________________________

✓ Chapter 4 Review/Test

Personal Math Trainer
Online Assessment and Intervention

1. Beth baked 24 carrot muffins. She baked 18 apple muffins. How many muffins did Beth bake?

Label the bar model. Write a number sentence with a ■ for the missing number. Solve.

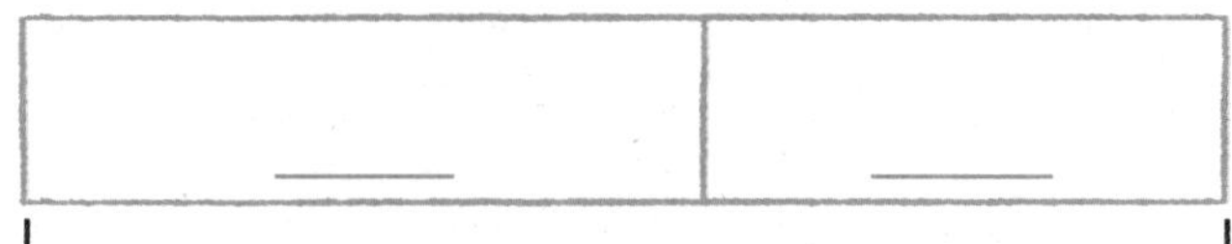

____

______________ ______ muffins

2. Carlos has 23 red keys, 36 blue keys, and 44 green keys. How many keys does he have? Circle your answer.

Carlos has [67 / 80 / 103] keys.

3. Mike sees 17 blue cars and 25 green cars. Choose all the ways you can use to find how many cars he sees. Then solve.

○ $\begin{array}{r} 17 \\ +\ 25 \\ \hline \end{array}$ ○ $\begin{array}{r} 25 \\ -\ 17 \\ \hline \end{array}$ ○ $\begin{array}{r} 25 \\ +\ 17 \\ \hline \end{array}$ ○ $\begin{array}{r} 17 \\ +\ 17 \\ \hline \end{array}$

Mike sees ______ cars.

Describe how you solved the problem.

____

____

4. Jerry has 53 pencils in one drawer. He has 27 pencils in another drawer.

Draw a picture or write to explain how to find the number of pencils in both drawers.

Jerry has _______ pencils.

Personal Math Trainer

5. THINK SMARTER + Lauren sees 14 birds. Her friend sees 7 birds. How many birds do Lauren and her friend see? Draw quick pictures to solve. Write the sum.

Tens	Ones

_______ birds

Did you regroup to find the answer? Explain.

____

____

6. Matt says he can find the sum of 45 + 50 without rewriting it. Explain how you can solve this problem using mental math.

____

____

Name ______________________________

7. Ling sees the three signs at the theater.

Section A	Section B	Section C
35 seats	43 seats	17 seats

Which two sections have 78 seats?

Explain how you made your choices.

____

____

8. Leah put 21 white marbles, 31 black marbles, and 7 blue marbles in a bag. Then her sister added 19 yellow marbles.

Write a number sentence to show the number of marbles in the bag.

____

9. Nicole made a necklace. She used 13 red beads and 26 blue beads. Show how you can break apart the addends to find how many beads Nicole used.

13 → ______ + ______

+ 26 → ______ + ______

______ + ______ = ______

10. GO DEEPER Without finding the sums, does the pair of addends have a sum greater than 100?
Choose Yes or No.

51 + 92	○ Yes	○ No
42 + 27	○ Yes	○ No
82 + 33	○ Yes	○ No
62 + 14	○ Yes	○ No

Explain how you decided which pairs have a sum greater than 100.

____

____

____

11. Leslie finds 24 paper clips in her desk. She finds 8 more paper clips in her pencil box. Choose all the ways you can use to find how many paper clips Leslie has in all.

○ 24 + 8

○ 24 − 8

○ 24 + 6 + 2

12. Mr. O'Brien visited a lighthouse. He climbed 26 stairs. Then he climbed 64 more stairs to the top. How many stairs did he climb at the lighthouse?

_______ stairs

Chapter 5

2-Digit Subtraction

Curious about Math

There are hundreds of different kinds of dragonflies. If 52 dragonflies are in a garden and 10 fly away, how many dragonflies are left? How many are left if 10 more fly away?

Name ______________________________

Subtraction Patterns

Subtract 2. Complete each subtraction sentence. (1.OA.A.1)

1. 7 − 2 = 5
2. 6 − ____ = ____
3. 5 − ____ = ____
4. 4 − ____ = ____
5. 3 − ____ = ____
6. 2 − ____ = ____

Subtraction Facts

Write the difference. (1.OA.C.6)

7. $\begin{array}{r} 8 \\ -\ 5 \\ \hline \end{array}$

8. $\begin{array}{r} 14 \\ -\ 6 \\ \hline \end{array}$

9. $\begin{array}{r} 9 \\ -\ 6 \\ \hline \end{array}$

10. $\begin{array}{r} 16 \\ -\ 7 \\ \hline \end{array}$

11. $\begin{array}{r} 12 \\ -\ 6 \\ \hline \end{array}$

12. $\begin{array}{r} 10 \\ -\ 8 \\ \hline \end{array}$

Tens and Ones

Write how many tens and ones are in each model. (1.NBT.B.2b)

13. 54

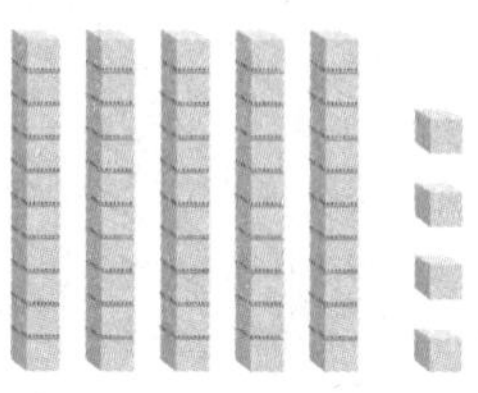

____ tens ____ ones

14. 45

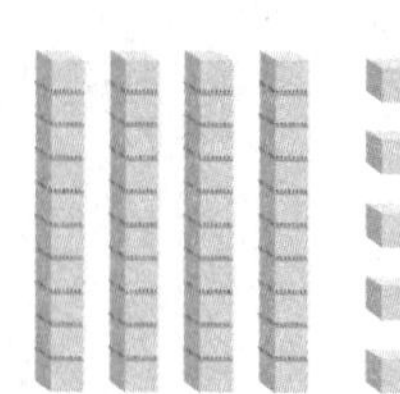

____ tens ____ ones

This page checks understanding of important skills needed for success in Chapter 5.

Name ______________________________

Vocabulary Builder

Review Words
difference
regroup
tens
ones
digit

Visualize It

Fill in the boxes of the graphic organizer.

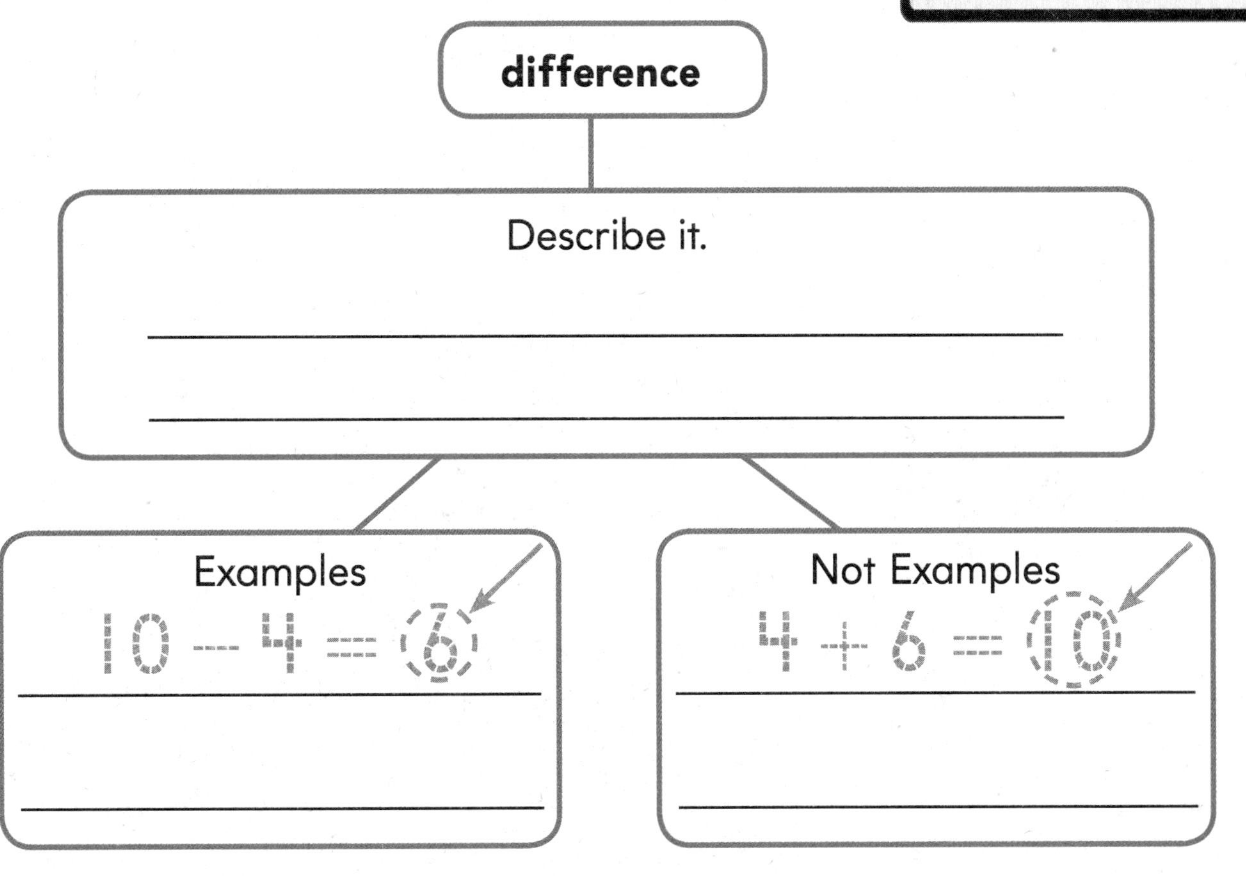

Understand Vocabulary

Draw a line to complete the sentence.

1. A **digit** can be •   • as 2 **tens**.
2. You can **regroup** •   • 0, 1, 2, 3, 4, 5, 6, 7, 8, or 9.
3. 20 **ones** are the same •   • to trade 10 ones for 1 ten.

GO DIGITAL • Interactive Student Edition • Multimedia eGlossary

Chapter 5

Game Subtraction Search

Materials

- 3 sets of number cards 4–9
- 18 ●

Play with a partner.

1. Shuffle all the cards. Place them face down in one stack.
2. Take one card. Find a square with a subtraction problem with this number as the difference. Your partner checks your answer.
3. If you are correct, place a ● on that square. If there is no match, skip your turn.
4. Take turns. The first player to have ● on all the squares wins.

Player 1

12 − 5	9 − 2	10 − 5
16 − 7	13 − 7	17 − 9
7 − 3	11 − 5	18 − 9

Player 2

8 − 3	15 − 7	11 − 6
17 − 8	9 − 3	16 − 8
13 − 9	6 − 2	14 − 7

Chapter 5 Vocabulary

addend sumando 1	**column** columna 7
difference diferencia 14	**digit** dígito 15
is equal to (=) es igual a 33	**ones** unidades 45
regroup reagrupar 56	**ten** decena 61

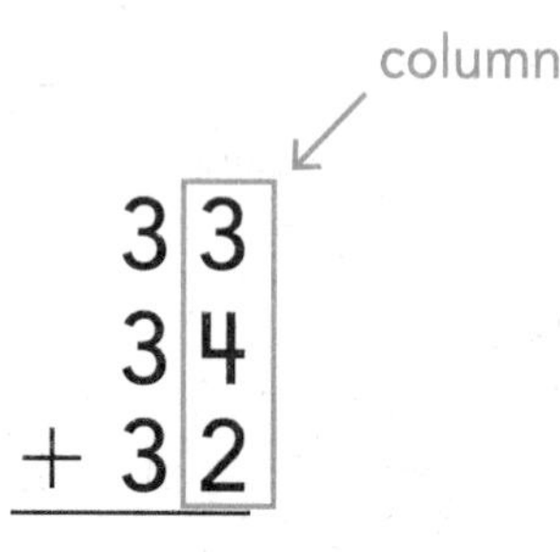

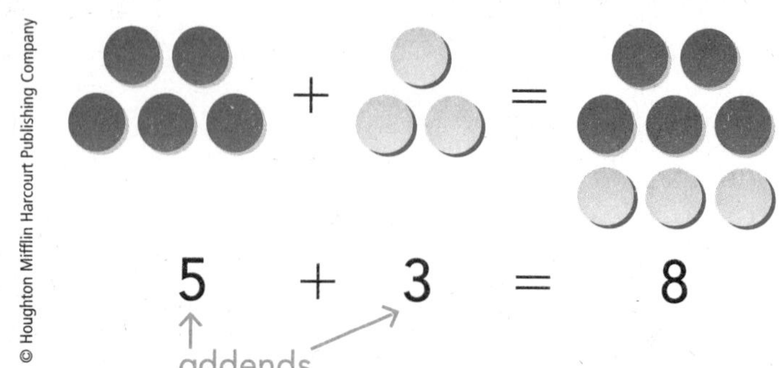

0, 1, 2, 3, 4, 5, 6, 7, 8, and 9 are **digits**.

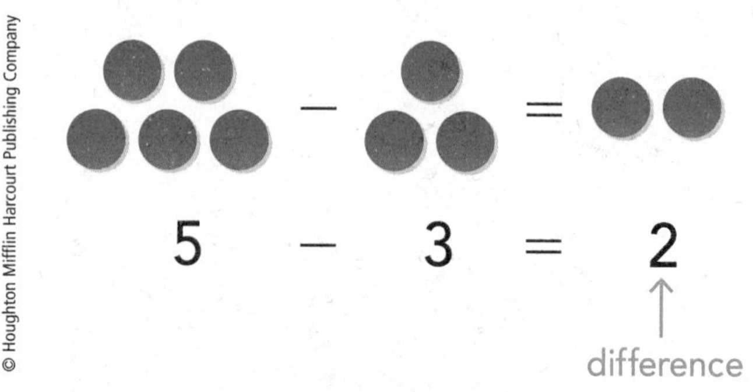

10 ones = 1 ten

2 plus 1 is equal to 3

$2 + 1 = 3$

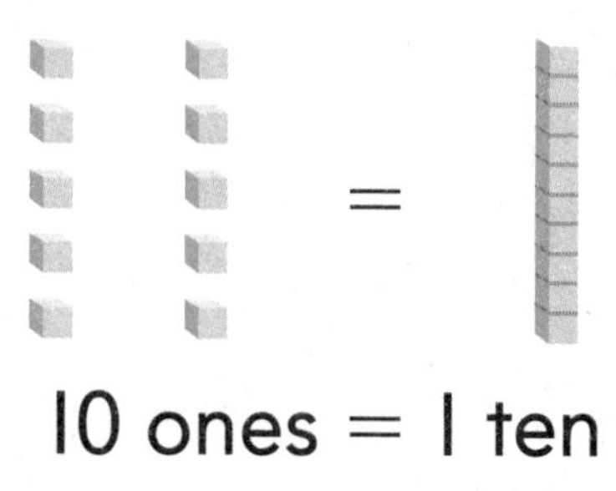

10 ones = 1 ten

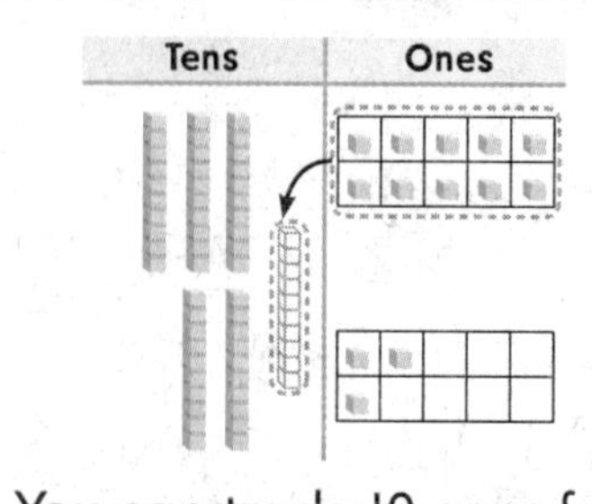

You can trade 10 ones for 1 ten to **regroup**.

Bingo

Word Box
addend
column
difference
digit
is equal to (=)
ones
regroup
ten

For 3 to 6 players

Materials

- 1 set of word cards
- 1 bingo board for each player
- game markers

How to Play

1. The caller chooses a word card and reads the word. Then the caller puts the word card in a second pile.
2. Players put a marker on the word each time they find it on their bingo boards.
3. Repeat steps 1 and 2 until a player marks 5 boxes in a line going down, across, or on a slant and calls "Bingo."
4. Check the answers. Have the player who said "Bingo" read the words aloud while the caller checks the word cards in the second pile.

The Write Way

Reflect

Choose one idea. Write about it in the space below.

- Explain how drawing quick pictures helps you subtract 2-digit numbers.
- Tell about all the different ways you can subtract 2-digit numbers.
- Write about a time that you helped explain something to a classmate. What was your classmate having trouble with? How did you help him or her?

Name ______________________

Algebra • Break Apart Ones to Subtract

Essential Question How does breaking apart a number make subtracting easier?

Common Core **Number and Operations in Base Ten—2.NBT.B.5**
MATHEMATICAL PRACTICES MP1, MP5, MP6

Listen and Draw

Write two addends for each sum.

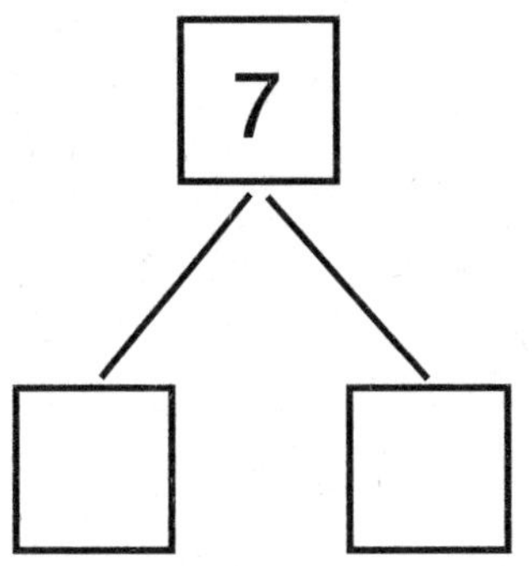

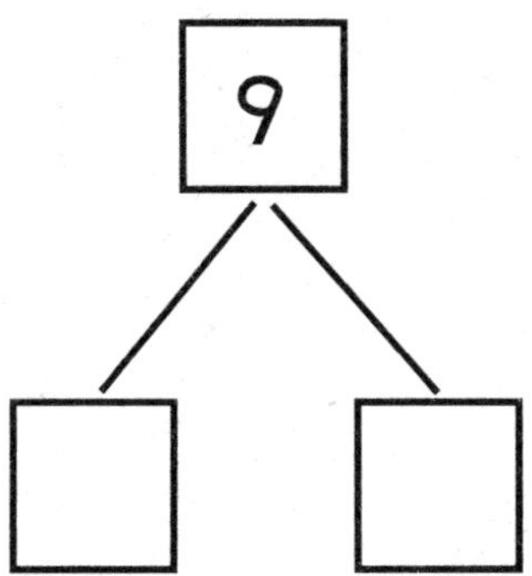

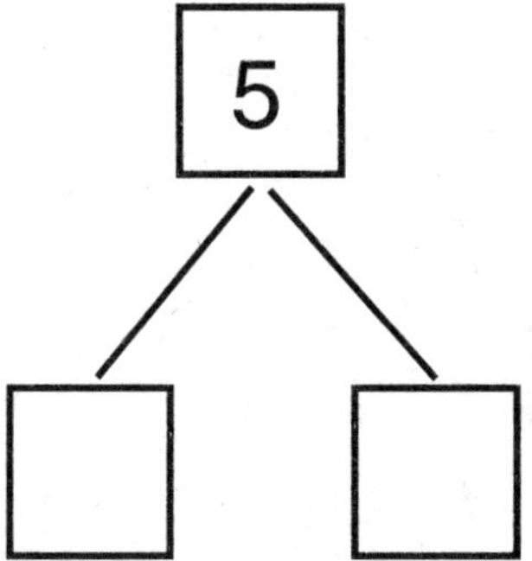

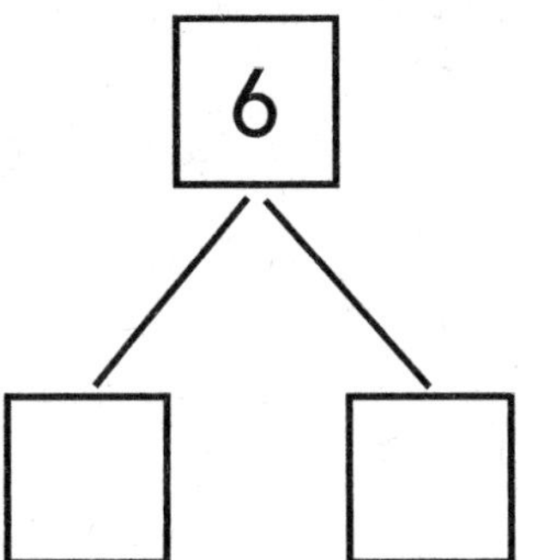

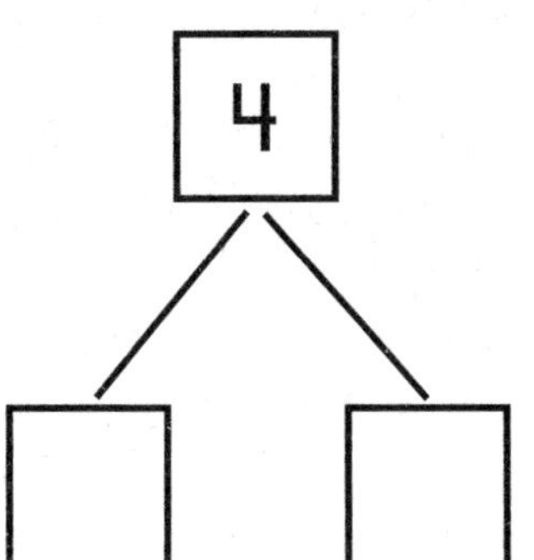

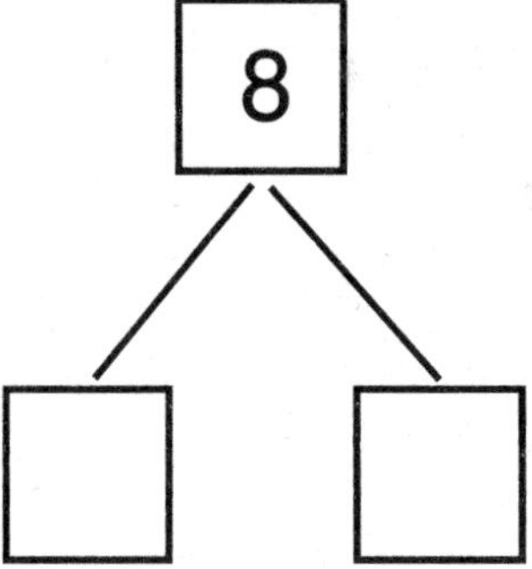

MATHEMATICAL PRACTICES 6

Describe how you chose addends for each sum.

FOR THE TEACHER • After children have recorded addends for each sum, have a class discussion about the different facts that children represented on their papers.

Model and Draw

Break apart ones. Subtract in two steps.

63 − 7 = ■

3 4

Start at 63. Subtract 3 to get to 60. Then subtract 4 more.

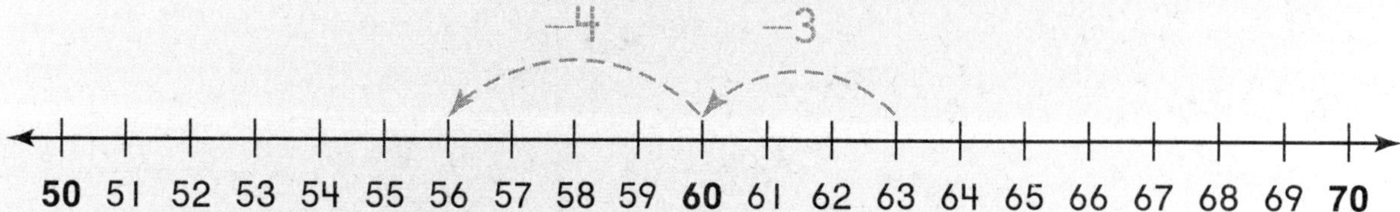

So, 63 − 7 = ______.

Share and Show

Break apart ones to subtract. Write the difference.

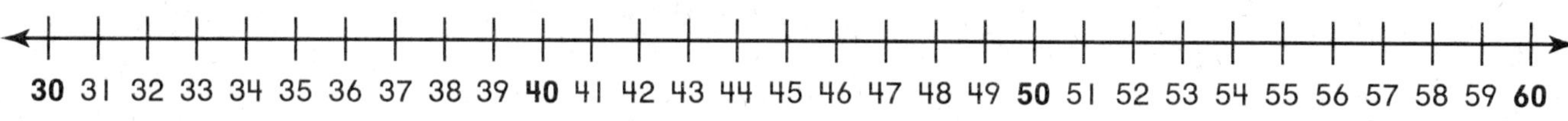

1. 55 − 8 = ______

5 3

2. 42 − 5 = ______

2 3

3. 41 − 9 = ______

4. 53 − 6 = ______

5. 44 − 7 = ______

6. 52 − 8 = ______

Name ___________________________

On Your Own

Break apart ones to subtract. Write the difference.

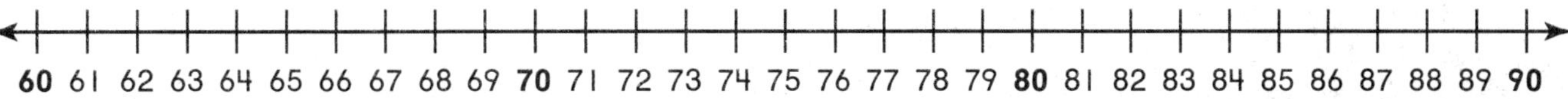

7. 75 − 7 = ______

8. 86 − 8 = ______

9. 82 − 5 = ______

10. 83 − 7 = ______

11. 72 − 7 = ______

12. 76 − 9 = ______

13. 85 − 8 = ______

14. 71 − 6 = ______

15. THINKSMARTER Cheryl brought 27 bagels for the bake sale. Mike brought 24 bagels. They sold all but 9 of them. How many bagels did they sell?

______ bagels

16. MATHEMATICAL PRACTICE 1 **Analyze** Lexi has 8 fewer crayons than Ken. Ken has 45 crayons. How many crayons does Lexi have?

______ crayons

Problem Solving • Applications

Write or draw to explain.

17. Cheryl built a toy train with 27 train cars. Then she added 18 more train cars. How many train cars are on the toy train now?

_______ train cars

18. MATHEMATICAL PRACTICE 1 **Analyze** Samuel had 46 marbles. He gave some marbles to a friend and has 9 marbles left. How many marbles did Samuel give to his friend?

_______ marbles

19. THINKSMARTER Matthew had 73 blocks. He gave 8 blocks to his sister. How many blocks does Matthew have now?

Draw or write to show how to solve the problem.

Matthew has _______ blocks now.

TAKE HOME ACTIVITY • Ask your child to describe how to find 34 − 6.

Name ______________________

Algebra • Break Apart Ones to Subtract

COMMON CORE STANDARD—2.NBT.B.5
Use place value understanding and properties of operations to add and subtract.

Break apart ones to subtract.
Write the difference.

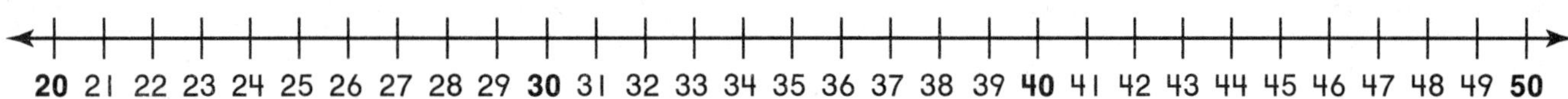

1. 36 − 7 = _____
2. 35 − 8 = _____
3. 37 − 9 = _____
4. 41 − 6 = _____
5. 44 − 5 = _____
6. 33 − 7 = _____
7. 32 − 4 = _____
8. 31 − 6 = _____

Problem Solving

Choose a way to solve. Write or draw to explain.

9. Beth had 44 marbles. She gave 9 marbles to her brother. How many marbles does Beth have now?

_____ marbles

10. WRITE Math Draw a number line and show how to find the difference for 24 – 6 using the break apart method in this lesson.

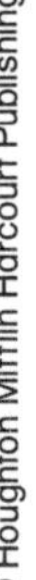

Lesson Check (2.NBT.B.5)

1. What is the difference?

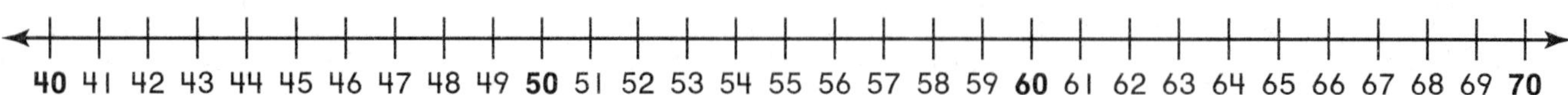

$58 - 9 =$ ____

Spiral Review (2.OA.B.2, 2.NBT.B.6)

2. What is the difference?

$14 - 6 =$ ____

3. What is the sum?

$3 + 6 + 2 =$ ____

4. What is the sum?

$64 + 7 =$ ____

5. What is the sum?

$56 + 18 =$ ____

FOR MORE PRACTICE GO TO THE **Personal Math Trainer**

Name ______________________________

Algebra • Break Apart Numbers to Subtract

Essential Question How does breaking apart a number make subtracting easier?

Common Core Number and Operations in Base Ten—2.NBT.B.5
MATHEMATICAL PRACTICES MP1, MP5, MP6

Listen and Draw Real World

Draw jumps on the number line to show how to break apart the number to subtract.

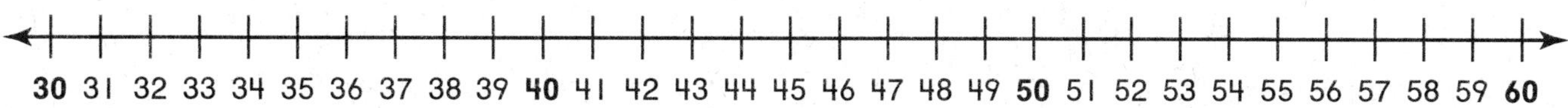

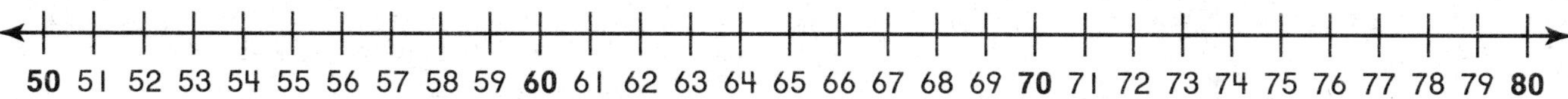

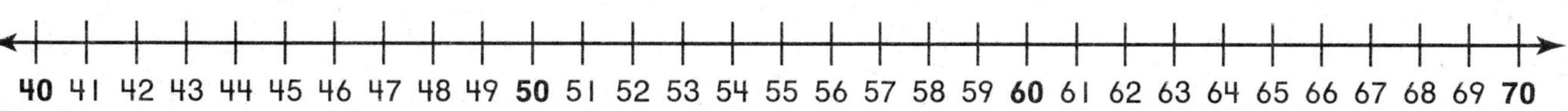

FOR THE TEACHER • Read the following problem. Have children draw jumps on the number line to solve. Mrs. Hill had 45 paintbrushes. She gave 9 paintbrushes to students in her art class. How many paintbrushes does Mrs. Hill have now? Repeat the same problem situation for 72 − 7 and 53 − 6.

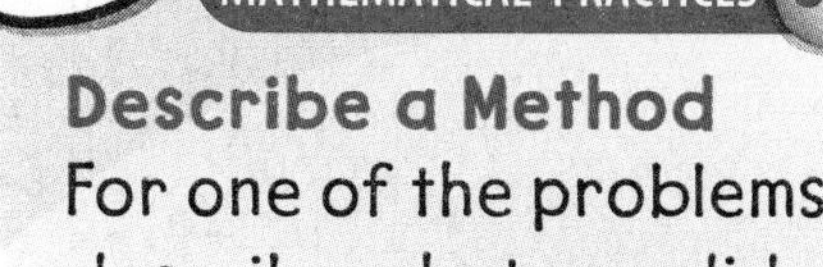

Describe a Method
For one of the problems, describe what you did.

Model and Draw

Break apart the number you are subtracting into tens and ones.

Subtract 10.
Next, subtract 2 to get to 60.
Then subtract 5 more.

$72 - 17 = \blacksquare$

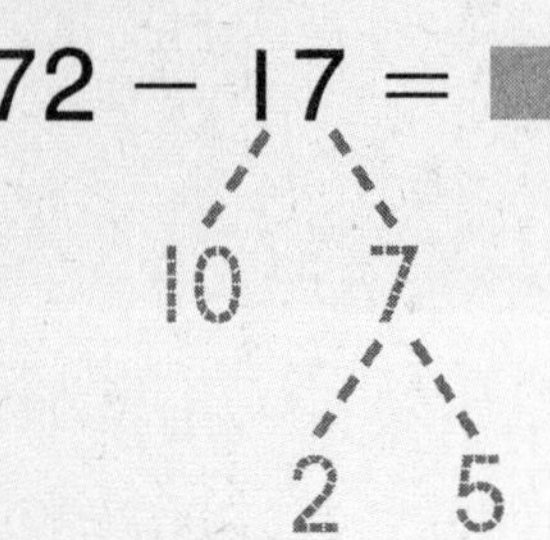

$10 + 2 + 5 = 17$

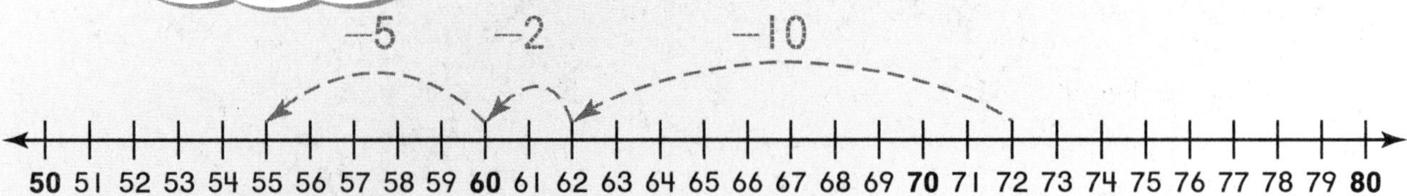

So, $72 - 17 =$ ______.

Share and Show

MATH BOARD

Break apart the number you are subtracting. Write the difference.

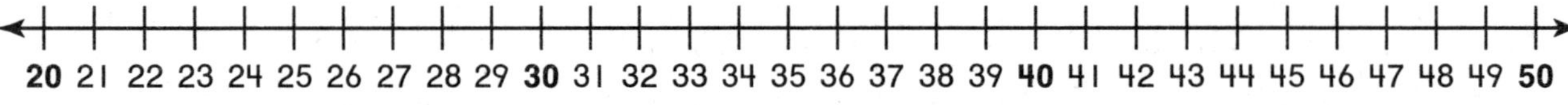

1. $43 - 18 =$ ______

2. $45 - 14 =$ ______

10 4

3. $46 - 17 =$ ______

4. $44 - 16 =$ ______

Name ____________________

On Your Own

Break apart the number you are subtracting. Write the difference.

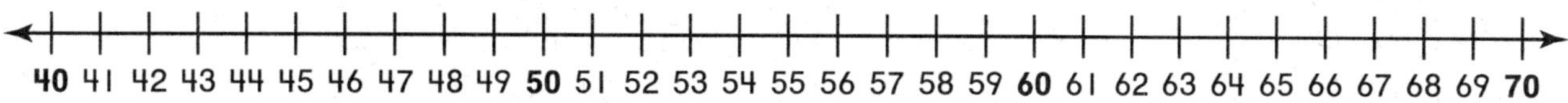

5. 57 − 15 = ______

6. 63 − 17 = ______

7. 68 − 19 = ______

8. 61 − 18 = ______

9. THINK SMARTER Jane has 53 toys in a box. She takes some toys out. Now there are 36 toys in the box. How many toys did Jane take out of the box?

______ toys

10. GO DEEPER Look at Tom's steps to solve a problem. Solve this problem in the same way.

42 − 15 = ?

Tom
35 − 18 = ?
35 − 10 = 25
25 − 5 = 20
20 − 3 = (17)

Problem Solving • Applications

11. 38 people are in the library. Then 33 more people go into the library. How many people are in the library now?

_______ people

12. MATHEMATICAL PRACTICE 1 **Analyze** Alex has 24 toys in a chest. He takes some toys out of the chest. Then there are 16 toys in the chest. How many toys did he take out of the chest?

_______ toys

13. THINKSMARTER Gail has two piles of newspapers. There are 32 papers in the first pile. There are 19 papers in the second pile. How many more papers are in the first pile than in the second pile?

_______ more papers

Write or draw to explain how you solved the problem.

TAKE HOME ACTIVITY • Ask your child to write a subtraction story that uses 2-digit numbers.

Name ______________________________

Algebra • Break Apart Numbers to Subtract

Common Core

COMMON CORE STANDARD—2.NBT.B.5
Use place value understanding and properties of operations to add and subtract.

Break apart the number you are subtracting. Write the difference.

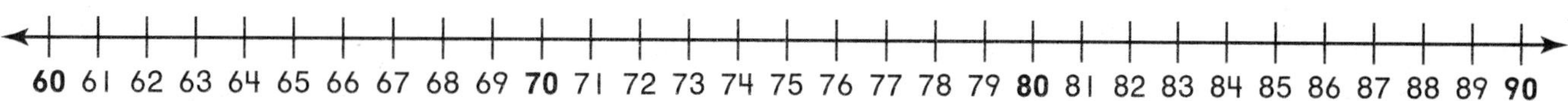

1. 81 − 14 = _____
2. 84 − 16 = _____
3. 77 − 14 = _____
4. 83 − 19 = _____
5. 81 − 17 = _____
6. 88 − 13 = _____
7. 84 − 19 = _____
8. 86 − 18 = _____

Problem Solving

Solve. Write or draw to explain.

9. Mr. Pearce bought 43 plants. He gave 14 plants to his sister. How many plants does Mr. Pearce have now?

_____ plants

10. WRITE Math Draw a number line and show how to find the difference for 36 − 17 using the break apart method in this lesson.

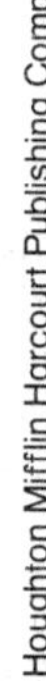

Lesson Check (2.NBT.B.5)

1. What is the difference?

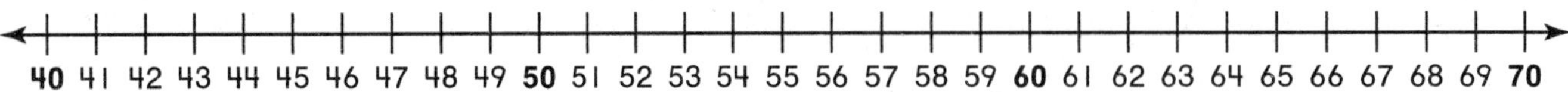

$63 - 19 = \_\_\_\_$

Spiral Review (2.OA.A.1, 2.OA.B.2, 2.NBT.B.6)

2. What is the sum?

$$\begin{array}{r} 14 \\ +\ 23 \\ \hline \end{array}$$

3. What is the sum?

$8 + 7 = \_\_\_\_$

4. Write a related subtraction fact for $6 + 8 = 14$.

____

5. John has 7 kites. Annie has 4 kites. How many kites do they have altogether?

____ kites

FOR MORE PRACTICE GO TO THE Personal Math Trainer

Name ___________________________

Model Regrouping for Subtraction

Essential Question When do you regroup in subtraction?

Common Core **Number and Operations in Base Ten—2.NBT.B.5**
MATHEMATICAL PRACTICES
MP5, MP6, MP7

Listen and Draw

Real World · Hands On

Use [tens block] [ones block] to model the problem.
Draw quick pictures to show your model.

Tens	Ones

Math Talk MATHEMATICAL PRACTICES 6

Describe why you traded a tens block for 10 ones blocks.

FOR THE TEACHER • Read the following problem. Michelle counted 21 butterflies in her garden. Then 7 butterflies flew away. How many butterflies were still in the garden?

Model and Draw

How do you subtract 26 from 53?

Step 1 Show 53. Are there enough ones to subtract 6?

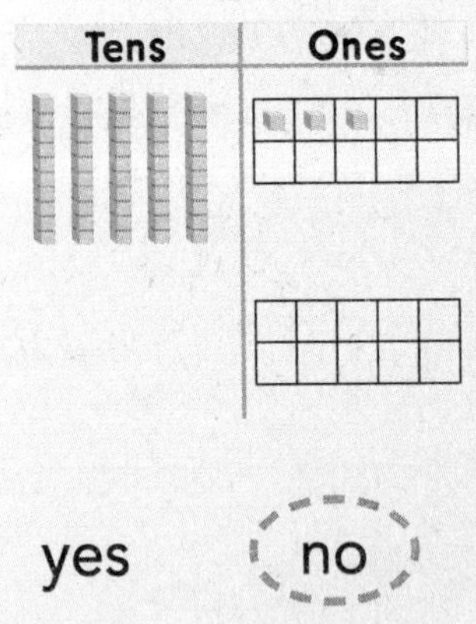

yes no

Step 2 If there are not enough ones, regroup 1 ten as 10 ones.

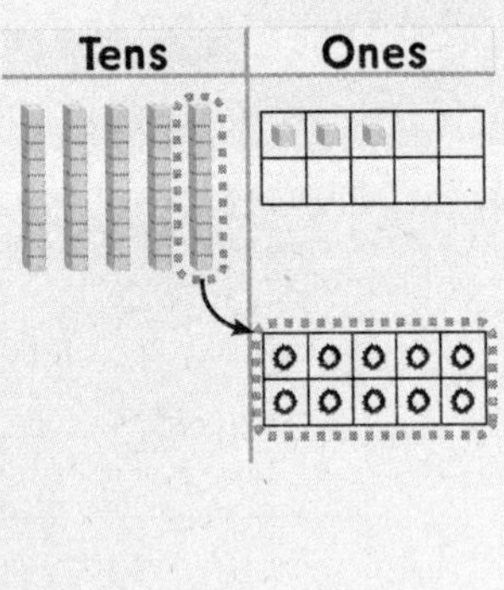

Step 3 Subtract 6 ones from 13 ones.

Tens | Ones

Step 4 Subtract the tens. Write the tens and ones. Write the difference.

Tens | Ones

____ tens ____ ones

____

Share and Show MATH BOARD

Draw to show the regrouping. Write the difference two ways. Write the tens and ones. Write the number.

1. Subtract 13 from 41.

Tens | Ones

_____ tens _____ ones

____

2. Subtract 9 from 48.

Tens | Ones

_____ tens _____ ones

____

3. Subtract 28 from 52.

Tens | Ones

_____ tens _____ ones

____

Name ______________________________

On Your Own

Draw to show the regrouping. Write the difference two ways. Write the tens and ones. Write the number.

4. Subtract 8 from 23.

Tens	Ones

_____ ten _____ ones

____

5. Subtract 36 from 45.

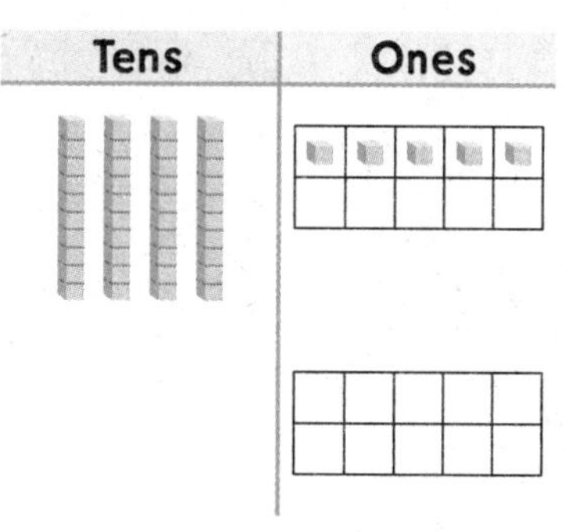

Tens	Ones

_____ tens _____ ones

____

6. Subtract 6 from 43.

Tens	Ones

_____ tens _____ ones

____

7. Subtract 39 from 67.

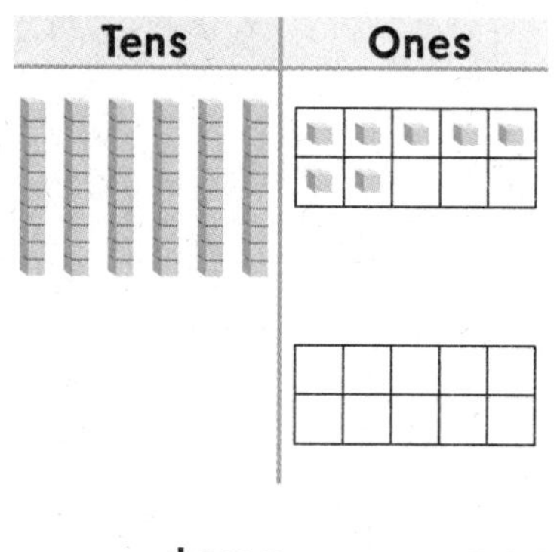

Tens	Ones

_____ tens _____ ones

____

8. Subtract 21 from 50.

Tens	Ones

_____ tens _____ ones

____

9. Subtract 29 from 56.

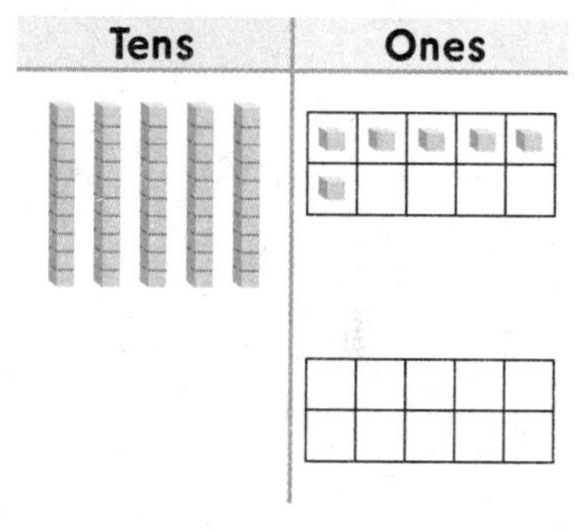

Tens	Ones

_____ tens _____ ones

____

10. GO DEEPER Draw to find what number was subtracted from 53.

Subtract _______ from 53.

3 tens 4 ones

34

Tens	Ones

Problem Solving • Applications 

Write or draw to explain.

11. THINK SMARTER Billy has 18 fewer marbles than Sara. Sara has 34 marbles. How many marbles does Billy have?

_______ marbles

12. THINK SMARTER + There are 67 toy animals in the store. Then the clerk sells 19 toy animals. How many toy animals are in the store now?

Draw to show how to find the answer.

Tens	Ones
6 tens	7 ones

_______ toy animals

Describe how you solved the problem.

____

____

____

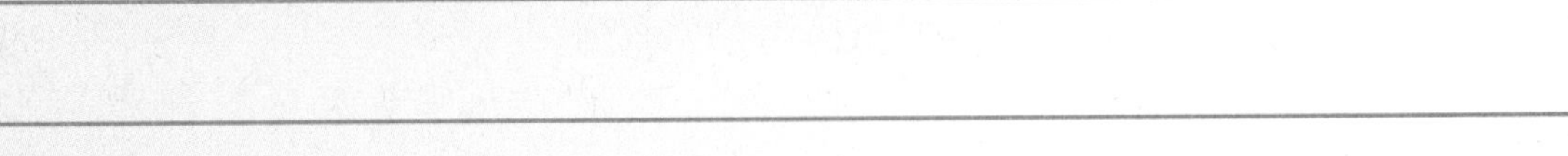

TAKE HOME ACTIVITY • Ask your child to write a subtraction story and then explain how to solve it.

Name ______________________

Model Regrouping for Subtraction

Practice and Homework
Lesson 5.3

Common Core **COMMON CORE STANDARD—2.NBT.B.5**
Use place value understanding and properties of operations to add and subtract.

Draw to show the regrouping.
Write the difference two ways.
Write the tens and ones. Write the number.

1. Subtract 9 from 35.

Tens	Ones

_____ tens _____ ones

_____

2. Subtract 14 from 52.

Tens	Ones

_____ tens _____ ones

_____

Problem Solving

Choose a way to solve. Write or draw to explain.

3. Mr. Ortega made 51 cookies. He gave 14 cookies away. How many cookies does he have now?

_____ cookies

4. WRITE Math Draw a quick picture for 37. Draw to show how you would subtract 19 from 37. Write to explain what you did.

____

____

____

Lesson Check (2.NBT.B.5)

1. Subtract 9 from 36.
   What is the difference?

Tens	Ones

____

2. Subtract 28 from 45.
   What is the difference?

Tens	Ones

____

Spiral Review (2.NBT.B.5, 2.NBT.B.6)

3. What is the difference?

$51 - 8 = \_\_\_\_$

40 41 42 43 44 45 46 47 48 49 **50** 51 52 53 54 55 56 57 58 59 **60**

4. What is the sum?

$38 + 35 = \_\_\_\_$

5. What is the sum?

$$\begin{array}{r} 63 \\ 18 \\ +\ 9 \\ \hline \end{array}$$

Name ___

Model and Record 2-Digit Subtraction

Essential Question How do you record 2-digit subtraction?

Common Core **Number and Operations in Base Ten—2.NBT.B.5** *Also 2.NBT.B.9*

MATHEMATICAL PRACTICES
MP1, MP4, MP6

Listen and Draw

Real World · Hands On

Use [tens and ones blocks] to model the problem.
Draw quick pictures to show your model.

Tens	Ones

Math Talk MATHEMATICAL PRACTICES 6

Explain a Method
Did you trade blocks in your model? Explain why or why not.

FOR THE TEACHER • Read the following problem. Mr. Kelly made 47 muffins. His students ate 23 of the muffins. How many muffins were not eaten?

Model and Draw

Trace over the quick pictures in the steps.

Subtract. $\begin{array}{r} 56 \\ -19 \\ \hline \end{array}$

Step 1 Show 56. Are there enough ones to subtract 9?

Tens	Ones
5	6
− 1	9

Step 2 If there are not enough ones, regroup 1 ten as 10 ones.

Tens	Ones
4	16
~~5~~	~~6~~
− 1	9

Step 3 Subtract the ones. 16 − 9 = 7

Tens	Ones
4	16
~~5~~	~~6~~
− 1	9
	7

Step 4 Subtract the tens. 4 − 1 = 3

Tens	Ones
4	16
~~5~~	~~6~~
− 1	9
3	7

Share and Show

Draw a quick picture to solve. Write the difference.

1.

Tens	Ones
4	7
− 1	5

2.

Tens	Ones
3	2
− 1	8

Name ____________________

On Your Own

Draw a quick picture to solve. Write the difference.

3.

	Tens	Ones
	☐	☐
	3	5
−	2	9

Tens	Ones

4.

	Tens	Ones
	☐	☐
	2	8
−		5

Tens	Ones

5.

	Tens	Ones
	☐	☐
	5	3
−	2	6

Tens	Ones

6.

	Tens	Ones
	☐	☐
	3	2
−	1	3

Tens	Ones

7. GO DEEPER There are 16 robins in the trees. 24 more fly in. Then 28 robins fly away. How many robins are still in the trees?

______ robins

Problem Solving • Applications

8. THINKSMARTER Claire's puzzle has 85 pieces. She has used 46 pieces so far. How many puzzle pieces have not been used yet?

_______ puzzle pieces

9. MATHEMATICAL PRACTICE 1 **Analyze** There were some people at the park. 24 people went home. Then there were 19 people at the park. How many people were at the park before?

_______ people

10. THINKSMARTER Mr. Sims has a box of 44 erasers. He gives 28 erasers to his students. How many erasers does Mr. Sims have now?

Show how you solved the problem.

_______ erasers

TAKE HOME ACTIVITY • Write 73 − 28 on a sheet of paper. Ask your child if he or she would regroup to find the difference.

Name ______________________________

Model and Record 2-Digit Subtraction

Common Core **COMMON CORE STANDARD—2.NBT.B.5**
Use place value understanding and properties of operations to add and subtract.

Draw a quick picture to solve. Write the difference.

1.

	Tens	Ones
	☐	☐
	4	3
−	1	7

Tens	Ones

2.

	Tens	Ones
	☐	☐
	3	8
−	2	9

Tens	Ones

Problem Solving

Solve. Write or draw to explain.

3. Kendall has 63 stickers.
Her sister has 57 stickers.
How many more stickers does Kendall have than her sister?

_______ more stickers

4. WRITE Math Draw a quick picture to show the number 24. Then draw a quick picture to show 24 after you have regrouped 1 ten as 10 ones. Explain how both pictures show the same number, 24.

____

____

____

Lesson Check (2.NBT.B.5)

1. What is the difference?

	Tens	Ones
	☐	☐
	4	7
−	1	8

2. What is the difference?

	Tens	Ones
	☐	☐
	3	3
−	2	9

Spiral Review (2.OA.B.2, 2.NBT.B.5, 2.NBT.B.6)

3. What is the difference?

$10 - 6 =$ ____

4. What is the sum?

$16 + 49 =$ ____

5. What is the sum?

$28 + 8 =$ ____

6. What is the difference?

$52 - 6 =$ ____

FOR MORE PRACTICE GO TO THE **Personal Math Trainer**

Name ______________________________

2-Digit Subtraction

Essential Question How do you record the steps when subtracting 2-digit numbers?

Number and Operations in Base Ten—2.NBT.B.5
Also 2.NBT.B.9
MATHEMATICAL PRACTICES
MP2, MP6, MP8

Listen and Draw (Real World)

Draw a quick picture to model each problem.

Tens	Ones

Tens	Ones

FOR THE TEACHER • Read the following problem. Devin had 36 toy robots on his shelf. He moved 12 of the robots to his closet. How many robots are on the shelf now? Repeat the activity with this problem: Devin had 54 toy cars. He gave 9 of them to his brother. How many cars does Devin have now?

Math Talk MATHEMATICAL PRACTICES 2

Use Reasoning Explain why regrouping works.

Model and Draw

Subtract. $\begin{array}{r} 42 \\ -15 \\ \hline \end{array}$

Step 1 Are there enough ones to subtract 5?

Tens	Ones
☐	☐
4	2
− 1	5

Step 2 Regroup 1 ten as 10 ones.

Tens	Ones
3	12
~~4~~	~~2~~
− 1	5

Step 3 Subtract the ones.

$12 - 5 = 7$

Tens	Ones
3	12
~~4~~	~~2~~
− 1	5
	7

Step 4 Subtract the tens.

$3 - 1 = 2$

Tens	Ones
3	12
~~4~~	~~2~~
− 1	5
2	7

Share and Show

Regroup if you need to. Write the difference.

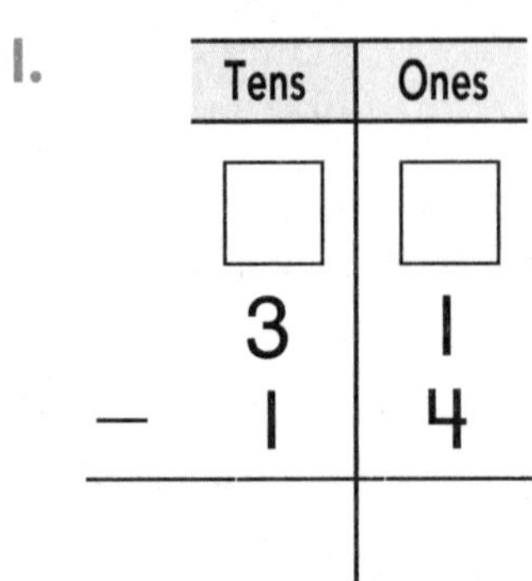

1.

Tens	Ones
☐	☐
3	1
− 1	4

2.

Tens	Ones
☐	☐
5	6
− 2	1

3.

Tens	Ones
☐	☐
7	2
− 3	5

Name ______________________________

On Your Own

Regroup if you need to. Write the difference.

4.

	Tens	Ones
	☐	☐
	2	3
−	1	4

5.

	Tens	Ones
	☐	☐
	8	7
−	5	7

6.

	Tens	Ones
	☐	☐
	3	4
−	1	8

7.

	Tens	Ones
	☐	☐
	6	1
−	1	3

8.
$$\begin{array}{r|l} 4 & 5 \\ -\ 1 & 8 \\ \hline & \end{array}$$

9.
$$\begin{array}{r|l} 5 & 2 \\ -\ 3 & 6 \\ \hline & \end{array}$$

10.
$$\begin{array}{r|l} 3 & 2 \\ -\ 1 & 3 \\ \hline & \end{array}$$

11.
$$\begin{array}{r|l} 7 & 5 \\ -\ 4 & 3 \\ \hline & \end{array}$$

12.
$$\begin{array}{r|l} 5 & 6 \\ -\ 2 & 7 \\ \hline & \end{array}$$

13.
$$\begin{array}{r|l} 9 & 4 \\ -\ 2 & 9 \\ \hline & \end{array}$$

14.
$$\begin{array}{r|l} 8 & 7 \\ -\ 3 & 9 \\ \hline & \end{array}$$

15.
$$\begin{array}{r|l} 8 & 3 \\ -\ 4 & 6 \\ \hline & \end{array}$$

16. THINKSMARTER Spencer wrote 5 fewer stories than Katie. Spencer wrote 18 stories. How many stories did Katie write?

_______ stories

17. MATHEMATICAL PRACTICE 6 **Explain a Method**
Circle the problems below that you could use mental math to solve.

54 − 10 = ____ 63 − 27 = ____ 93 − 20 = ____

39 − 2 = ____ 41 − 18 = ____ 82 − 26 = ____

Explain when to use mental math.

____

____

____

18. THINK SMARTER+ There are 34 chickens in the barn. If 16 chickens go outside into the yard, how many chickens will still be in the barn?

Circle the number from the box to make the sentence true.

There are [8 / 18 / 28] chickens still in the barn.

TAKE HOME ACTIVITY • Ask your child to write a 2-digit subtraction problem with no regrouping needed. Have your child explain why he or she chose those numbers.

Name ____________________

2-Digit Subtraction

Common Core **COMMON CORE STANDARD—2.NBT.B.5** *Use place value understanding and properties of operations to add and subtract.*

Regroup if you need to.
Write the difference.

1.

Tens	Ones
☐	☐
4	7
− 2	8

2.

Tens	Ones
☐	☐
3	3
− 1	8

3.

Tens	Ones
☐	☐
2	8
− 1	4

4.

Tens	Ones
☐	☐
6	6
− 1	9

5.

7	7
− 2	6

6.

5	8
− 3	4

7.

5	2
− 2	5

8.

8	7
− 4	9

Problem Solving Real World

Solve. Write or draw to explain.

9. Mrs. Paul bought 32 erasers. She gave 19 erasers to students. How many erasers does she still have?

_____ erasers

10. WRITE Math Write a few sentences about different ways to show subtraction for a problem like 32 − 15.

____

____

Lesson Check (2.NBT.B.5)

1. What is the difference?

	4	8
−	3	9

2. What is the difference?

	8	4
−	6	6

Spiral Review (2.OA.A.1, 2.OA.B.2, 2.NBT.B.5)

3. What is the difference?

	Tens	Ones
	☐	☐
	3	2
−	1	9

4. Write an addition fact that will give the same sum as 8 + 7.

10 + ____

5. 27 boys and 23 girls go on a field trip to the museum. How many children go to the museum?

____ children

6. There were 17 berries in the basket. Then 9 berries are eaten. How many berries are there now?

____ berries

FOR MORE PRACTICE GO TO THE Personal Math Trainer

Name ______________________________

Practice 2-Digit Subtraction

Essential Question How do you record the steps when subtracting 2-digit numbers?

Common Core **Number and Operations in Base Ten—2.NBT.B.5**
MATHEMATICAL PRACTICES
MP1, MP3, MP7

Listen and Draw Real World

Choose one way to solve the problem.
Draw or write to show what you did.

MATHEMATICAL PRACTICES 1

Describe a different way that you could have solved the problem.

FOR THE TEACHER • Read the following problem and have children choose their own methods for solving it. There are 74 books in Mr. Barron's classroom. 19 of the books are about computers. How many of the books are not about computers?

Model and Draw

Carmen had 50 game cards. Then she gave 16 game cards to Theo. How many game cards does Carmen have now?

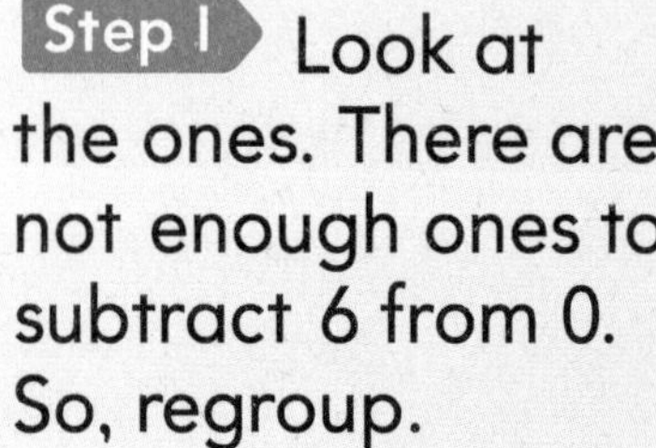

Step 1 Look at the ones. There are not enough ones to subtract 6 from 0. So, regroup.

$$\begin{array}{r} \scriptstyle 4\ 10 \\ \not{5}\ \not{0} \\ -\ 1\ 6 \\ \hline \end{array}$$

Step 2 Subtract the ones.

$10 - 6 = 4$

$$\begin{array}{r} \scriptstyle 4\ 10 \\ \not{5}\ \not{0} \\ -\ 1\ 6 \\ \hline 4 \end{array}$$

Step 3 Subtract the tens.

$4 - 1 = 3$

$$\begin{array}{r} \scriptstyle 4\ 10 \\ \not{5}\ \not{0} \\ -\ 1\ 6 \\ \hline 3\ 4 \end{array}$$

Share and Show

Write the difference.

1. $\begin{array}{r} 38 \\ -\ 19 \\ \hline \end{array}$

2. $\begin{array}{r} 65 \\ -\ 32 \\ \hline \end{array}$

3. $\begin{array}{r} 50 \\ -\ 12 \\ \hline \end{array}$

4. $\begin{array}{r} 23 \\ -\ 4 \\ \hline \end{array}$

✓5. $\begin{array}{r} 70 \\ -\ 38 \\ \hline \end{array}$

✓6. $\begin{array}{r} 52 \\ -\ 17 \\ \hline \end{array}$

Name ___________________________

On Your Own

Write the difference.

7.
$$\begin{array}{r} 41 \\ -\,24 \\ \hline \end{array}$$

8.
$$\begin{array}{r} 58 \\ -\,16 \\ \hline \end{array}$$

9.
$$\begin{array}{r} 60 \\ -\,13 \\ \hline \end{array}$$

10.
$$\begin{array}{r} 52 \\ -\,47 \\ \hline \end{array}$$

11.
$$\begin{array}{r} 72 \\ -\,46 \\ \hline \end{array}$$

12.
$$\begin{array}{r} 37 \\ -\,6 \\ \hline \end{array}$$

13.
$$\begin{array}{r} 74 \\ -\,46 \\ \hline \end{array}$$

14.
$$\begin{array}{r} 90 \\ -\,18 \\ \hline \end{array}$$

15. GO DEEPER Write the missing numbers in the subtraction problems. The regrouping for each problem is shown.

$$\begin{array}{r} 6\ 15 \\ \_\ \_ \\ -\ \_\ \_ \\ \hline 4\ 7 \end{array} \qquad \begin{array}{r} 7\ 13 \\ \_\ \_ \\ -\ \_\ \_ \\ \hline 2\ 5 \end{array}$$

16. THINK SMARTER Adam takes 38 rocks out of a box. There are 23 rocks left in the box. How many rocks were in the box to start?

_____ rocks

TAKE HOME ACTIVITY • Ask your child to show you one way to find 80 − 34.

Name ______________________________

Concepts and Skills

Break apart the number you are subtracting. Use the number line to help. Write the difference. (2.NBT.B.5)

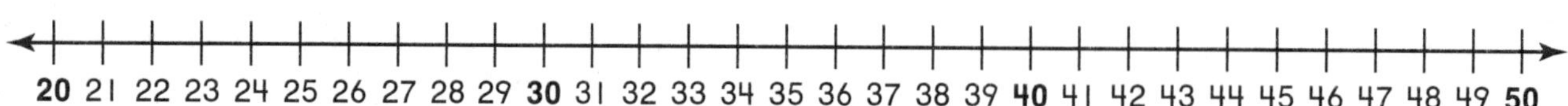

1. 34 − 8 = ______

2. 45 − 17 = ______

Draw a quick picture to solve. Write the difference. (2.NBT.B.5)

3.

	Tens	Ones
	☐	☐
	4	2
−	2	9

Tens	Ones

4.

	Tens	Ones
	☐	☐
	5	4
−	2	3

Tens	Ones

Write the difference. (2.NBT.B.5)

5.
$$\begin{array}{r} 78 \\ -\,43 \\ \hline \end{array}$$

6.
$$\begin{array}{r} 60 \\ -\,26 \\ \hline \end{array}$$

7.
$$\begin{array}{r} 85 \\ -\,37 \\ \hline \end{array}$$

8. THINK SMARTER Marissa had 51 toy dinosaurs. She gave 14 toy dinosaurs to her brother. How many toy dinosaurs does she have now? (2.NBT.B.5)

________ toy dinosaurs

Name ______________________________

Practice 2-Digit Subtraction

Common Core **COMMON CORE STANDARD—2.NBT.B.5**
Use place value understanding and properties of operations to add and subtract.

Write the difference.

1.

$$\begin{array}{r} 50 \\ -\ 18 \\ \hline \end{array}$$

2.

$$\begin{array}{r} 43 \\ -\ 17 \\ \hline \end{array}$$

3.

$$\begin{array}{r} 75 \\ -\ 18 \\ \hline \end{array}$$

4.

$$\begin{array}{r} 22 \\ -\ \ 6 \\ \hline \end{array}$$

5.

$$\begin{array}{r} 60 \\ -\ 35 \\ \hline \end{array}$$

6.

$$\begin{array}{r} 42 \\ -\ 34 \\ \hline \end{array}$$

Problem Solving

Solve. Write or draw to explain.

7. Julie has 42 sheets of paper. She gives 17 sheets to Kari. How many sheets of paper does Julie have now?

_____ sheets of paper

8. WRITE Math Draw and write to explain how these two problems are different: 35 − 15 = ________ and 43 − 26 = ________.

____

Lesson Check (2.NBT.B.5)

1. What is the difference?

$$\begin{array}{r} 73 \\ -\ 47 \\ \hline \end{array}$$

2. What is the difference?

$$\begin{array}{r} 54 \\ -\ 13 \\ \hline \end{array}$$

Spiral Review (2.OA.B.2, 2.NBT.B.6)

3. What is the sum?

$9 + 9 =$ ____

4. What is the difference?

$14 - 7 =$ ____

5. What is the sum?

$36 + 25 =$ ____

6. What is the sum?

$7 + 2 + 3 =$ ____

FOR MORE PRACTICE GO TO THE Personal Math Trainer

Name ______________________

Rewrite 2-Digit Subtraction

Essential Question What are two different ways to write subtraction problems?

Common Core **Number and Operations in Base Ten—2.NBT.B.5**
MATHEMATICAL PRACTICES
MP6, MP7

Write the numbers for each subtraction problem.

− ______	− ______
− ______	− ______

Math Talk **MATHEMATICAL PRACTICES 6**

Explain why it is important to line up the digits of the numbers in columns.

FOR THE TEACHER • Read the following problem. Have children write the numbers in vertical format. There were 45 children at a party. Then 23 children went home. How many children were still at the party? Repeat for three more problems.

Model and Draw

What is 81 − 36?
Rewrite the subtraction problem.
Then find the difference.

Step 1 For 81, write the tens digit in the tens column.

Write the ones digit in the ones column.

Repeat for 36.

Step 2 Look at the ones. Regroup if you need to.

Subtract the ones.
Subtract the tens.

Share and Show

MATH BOARD

Rewrite the subtraction problem. Then find the difference.

1. 37 − 4
2. 48 − 24
3. 85 − 37
4. 63 − 19
5. 62 − 37
6. 51 − 27
7. 76 − 3
8. 95 − 48

Name ________________________________

On Your Own

Rewrite the subtraction problem. Then find the difference.

9. 49 − 8

10. 85 − 47

11. 63 − 23

12. 51 − 23

13. 60 − 15

14. 94 − 58

15. 47 − 20

16. 35 − 9

17. 78 − 10

18. 54 − 38

19. 92 − 39

20. 87 − 28

21. THINK SMARTER For which of the problems above could you find the difference without rewriting it? Explain.

____

____

____

Problem Solving • Applications

Read about the class trip. Then answer the questions.

Pablo's class went to the art museum. They saw 26 paintings done by children. They saw 53 paintings done by adults. They also saw 18 sculptures and 31 photographs.

22. How many more paintings were done by adults than by children?

_______ more paintings

23. GO DEEPER How many more paintings than sculptures did they see?

_______ more paintings

24. THINK SMARTER Tom drew 23 pictures last year. Beth drew 14 pictures. How many more pictures did Tom draw than Beth?

Fill in the bubble next to all the ways to show the problem.

○ $\begin{array}{r} 23 \\ -\ 14 \\ \hline \end{array}$ ○ $\begin{array}{r} 23 \\ +\ 14 \\ \hline \end{array}$ ○ $23 - 14$ ○ $23 + 14$

_______ more pictures

TAKE HOME ACTIVITY • Ask your child to write and solve a subtraction problem about a family trip.

Name ______________________________

Rewrite 2-Digit Subtraction

Common Core **COMMON CORE STANDARD—2.NBT.B.5**
Use place value understanding and properties of operations to add and subtract.

**Rewrite the subtraction problem.
Then find the difference.**

1. 35 − 19	**2.** 47 − 23	**3.** 55 − 28
− ______	− ______	− ______

Problem Solving 

Solve. Write or draw to explain.

4. Jimmy went to the toy store. He saw 23 wooden trains and 41 plastic trains. How many more plastic trains than wooden trains did he see?

_____ more plastic trains

5. WRITE Math Is it easier to subtract when the numbers are written above and below each other? Explain your answer.

____

____

____

____

Lesson Check (2.NBT.B.5)

1. What is the difference for $43 - 17$?

$-$ ______

2. What is the difference for $50 - 16$?

$-$ ______

Spiral Review (2.OA.B.2, 2.NBT.B.5, 2.NBT.B.6)

3. What is the sum?

$$\begin{array}{r} 29 \\ 4 \\ 25 \\ +\ 16 \\ \hline \end{array}$$

4. What is the sum of $41 + 19$?

______

5. Write an addition fact that will give the same sum as $5 + 9$.

$10 +$ ______

6. What is the difference?

$45 - 13 =$ ______

FOR MORE PRACTICE GO TO THE **Personal Math Trainer**

Name ______________________________

Add to Find Differences

Essential Question How can you use addition to solve subtraction problems?

Common Core **Number and Operations in Base Ten—2.NBT.B.5**
MATHEMATICAL PRACTICES
MP1, MP5, MP8

Listen and Draw Real World

Draw pictures to show the problem.
Then write a number sentence for your drawing.

______________________ ________ markers

Now draw pictures to show the next part of the problem. Write a number sentence for your drawing.

______________________ ________ markers

Describe what happens when you add back the number that you had subtracted.

FOR THE TEACHER • Have children draw pictures to represent this problem. Sophie had 25 markers. She gave 3 markers to Josh. How many markers does Sophie have now? Then ask children: How many markers will Sophie have if Josh gives the 3 markers back to her?

Model and Draw

Count up from the number you are subtracting to find the difference.

$45 - 38 = \blacksquare$

Start at 38. Count up to 40.

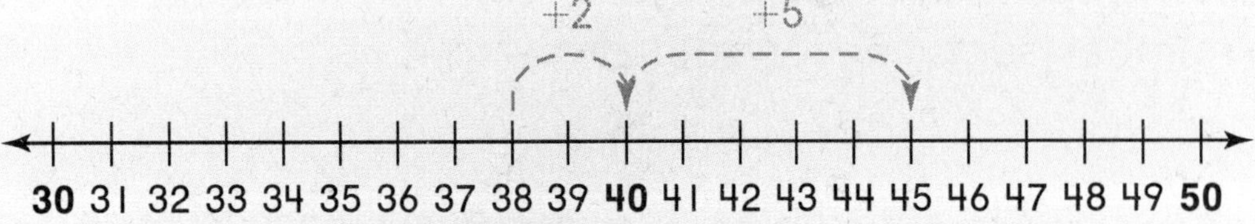

Then count up 5 more to 45.

So, $45 - 38 =$ ______.

Share and Show

MATH BOARD

Use the number line. Count up to find the difference.

1. $36 - 27 =$ ______

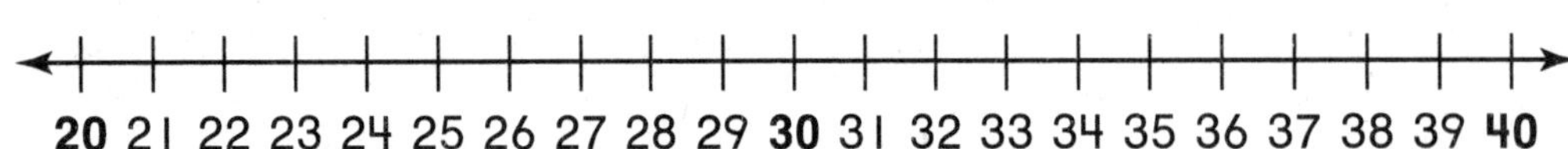

2. $56 - 49 =$ ______

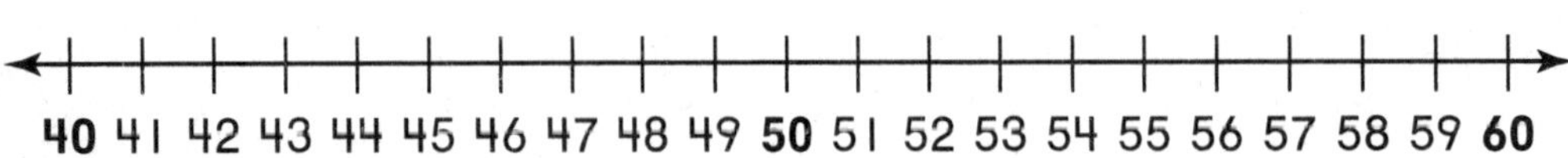

3. $64 - 58 =$ ______

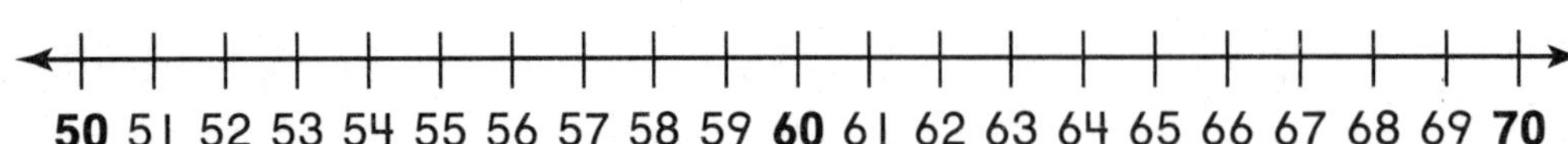

Name ______________________________

On Your Own

Use the number line. Count up to find the difference.

4. 33 − 28 = _____

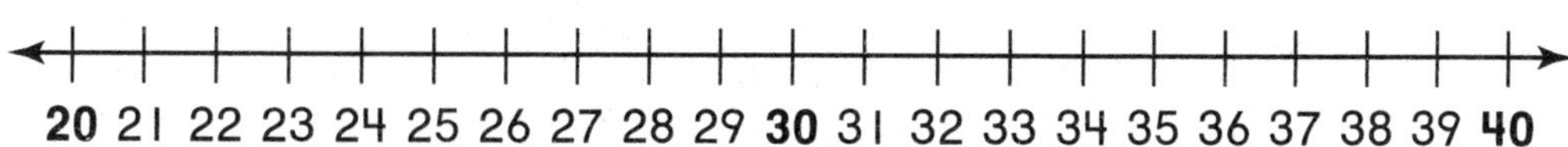

5. 45 − 37 = _____

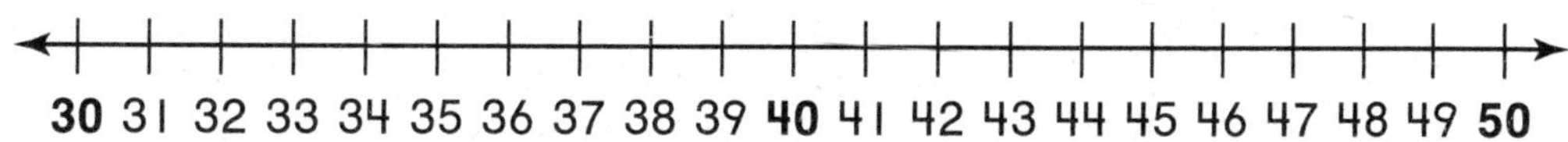

6. 58 − 49 = _____

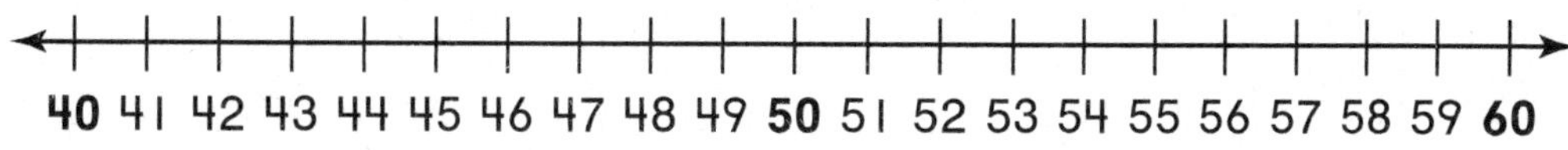

7. THINK SMARTER There were 55 books on the table. Sandra picked up some of the books. Now there are 49 books on the table. How many books did Sandra pick up?

40 41 42 43 44 45 46 47 48 49 50 51 52 53 54 55 56 57 58 59 60

_____ books

Problem Solving • Applications

Solve. You may wish to use the number line to help.

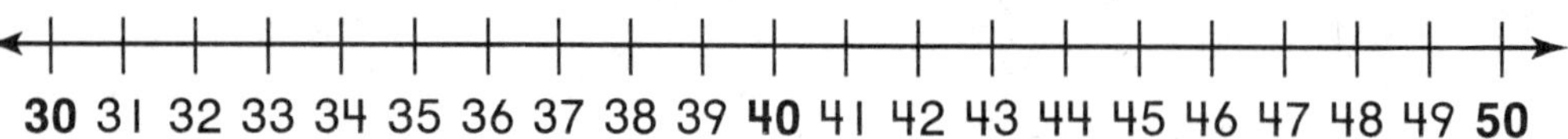

8. There are 46 game pieces in a box. Adam takes 38 game pieces out of the box. How many game pieces are still in the box?

_______ game pieces

9. THINKSMARTER Rachel had 27 craft sticks. Then she gave 19 craft sticks to Theo. How many craft sticks does Rachel have now?

Circle the number from the box to make the sentence true.

Rachel has [6 / 7 / 8] craft sticks now.

Explain how you can use addition to solve the problem.

___

___

TAKE HOME ACTIVITY • Have your child describe how he or she used a number line to solve one problem in this lesson.

Name ______________________________

Add to Find Differences

Common Core COMMON CORE STANDARD—2.NBT.B.5
Use place value understanding and properties of operations to add and subtract.

Use the number line. Count up to find the difference.

1. 36 − 29 = ____

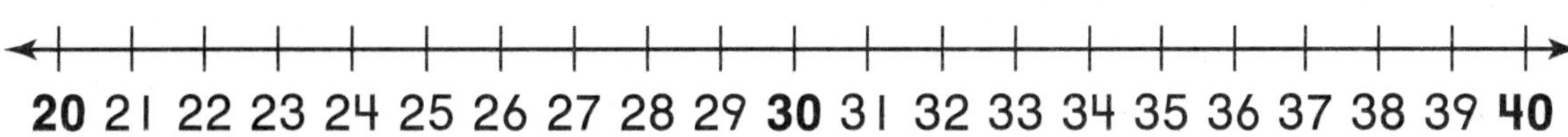

2. 43 − 38 = ____

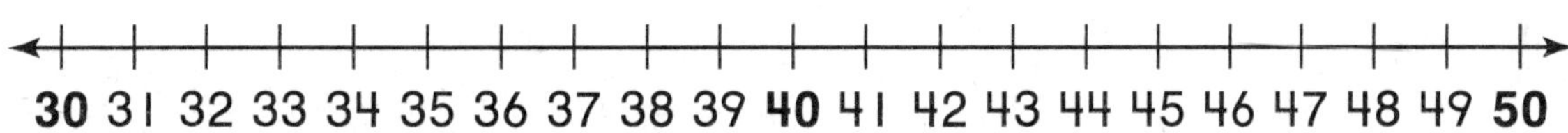

Problem Solving

Solve. You may wish to use the number line.

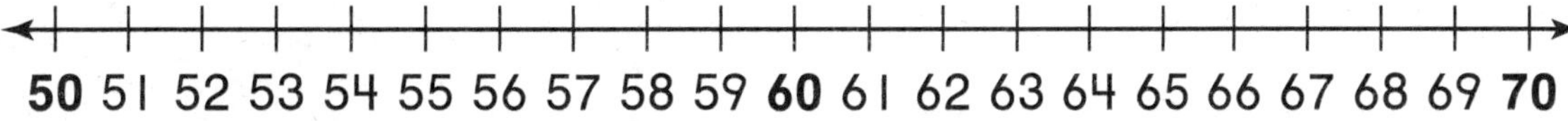

3. Jill has 63 index cards. She uses 57 of them for a project. How many index cards does Jill have now?

____ index cards

4. WRITE Math Explain how a number line can be used to find the difference for 34 − 28.

____

____

Lesson Check (2.NBT.B.5)

Use the number line. Count up to find the difference.

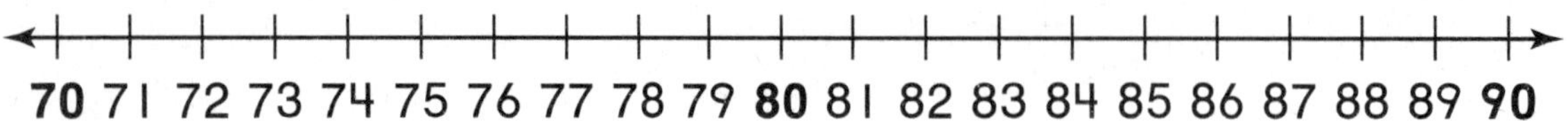

1. 82 − 75 = ____

2. 90 − 82 = ____

Spiral Review (2.OA.A.1, 2.OA.C.4, 2.NBT.B.5)

3. Jordan has 41 toy cars at home. He brings 24 cars to school. How many cars are at home?

____ cars

4. Pam has 15 fish. 9 are goldfish and the rest are guppies. How many fish are guppies?

____ guppies

5. What is the sum?

	3	5
+	1	9

6. Each table has 5 pencils. There are 3 tables. How many pencils are there altogether?

____ pencils

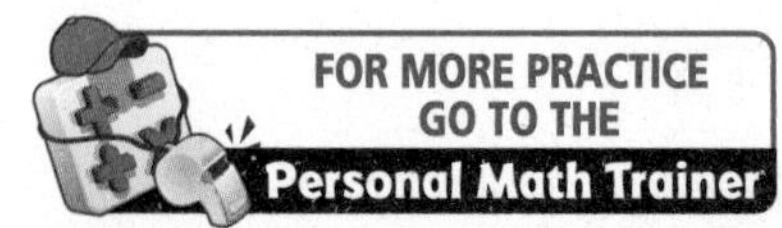

Name ____________________

Problem Solving • Subtraction

Essential Question How can drawing a diagram help when solving subtraction problems?

Common Core **Operations and Algebraic Thinking—2.OA.A.1;** *Also 2.NBT.B.5*
MATHEMATICAL PRACTICES
MP1, MP2, MP4

Jane and her mom made 33 puppets for the craft fair. They sold 14 puppets. How many puppets do they still have?

Unlock the Problem

What do I need to find?

how many puppets
they still have

What information do I need to use?

They made ______ puppets.

They sold ______ puppets.

Show how to solve the problem.

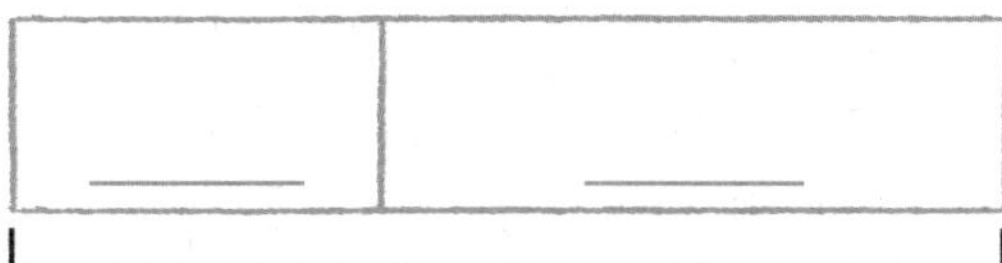

______

33 − 14 = ■

______ puppets

HOME CONNECTION • Your child used a bar model and a number sentence to represent the problem. Using a bar model helps show what is known and what is needed to solve the problem.

Try Another Problem

Label the bar model. Write a number sentence with a ■ for the missing number. Solve.

- What do I need to find?
- What information do I need to use?

1. Carlette had a box of 46 craft sticks. She used 28 craft sticks to make a sailboat. How many craft sticks were not used?

______________ ____ craft sticks

2. Rob's class made 31 clay bowls. Sarah's class made 15 clay bowls. How many more clay bowls did Rob's class make than Sarah's class?

______________ ____ more clay bowls

MATHEMATICAL PRACTICES 1

Explain how you know that Exercise 1 is a take-away problem.

Name ______________________________

Share and Show

Label the bar model. Write a number sentence with a ■ for the missing number. Solve.

3. Mr. Hayes makes 32 wooden frames. He gives away 15 frames as gifts. How many frames does he still have?

_____ frames

____

4. Wesley has 21 ribbons in a box. He has 15 ribbons on the wall. How many more ribbons does he have in the box than on the wall?

_____ more ribbons

____

5. THINK SMARTER Jennifer wrote 9 poems at school and 11 poems at home. She wrote 5 more poems than Nell. How many poems did Nell write?

_____ poems

On Your Own

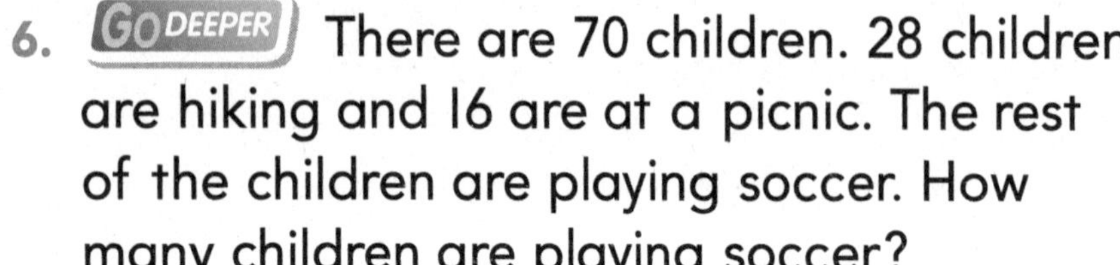

6. GO DEEPER There are 70 children. 28 children are hiking and 16 are at a picnic. The rest of the children are playing soccer. How many children are playing soccer?

Draw a model with bars for the problem. Describe how your drawing shows the problem. Then solve the problem.

____

____

____

7. THINK SMARTER There are 48 crackers in a bag. The children eat 25 crackers. How many crackers are still in the bag?

Circle the bar model that can be used to solve the problem.

25	23
48	

48	25
73	

73	48
25	

Write a number sentence with a ■ for the missing number. Solve.

____

________ crackers

TAKE HOME ACTIVITY • Ask your child to explain how he or she solved one of the problems on this page.

Name ____________________

Problem Solving • Subtraction

Common Core **COMMON CORE STANDARD—2.OA.A.1**
Represent and solve problems involving addition and subtraction.

Label the bar model. Write a number sentence with a ■ for the missing number. Solve.

1. Megan picked 34 flowers. Some of the flowers are yellow and 18 flowers are pink. How many of the flowers are yellow?

____ yellow flowers

____

2. Alex had 45 toy cars. He put 26 toy cars in a box. How many toy cars are not in the box?

____ toy cars

____

3. WRITE Math Explain how a bar model can be used to show a subtraction problem.

____
____
____
____

Lesson Check (2.OA.A.1)

1. There were 39 pumpkins at the store. Then 17 of the pumpkins were sold. How many pumpkins are still at the store?

   _____ pumpkins

2. There were 48 ants on a hill. Then 13 of the ants marched away. How many ants are still on the hill?

   _____ ants

Spiral Review (2.OA.A.1, 2.OA.B.2, 2.NBT.B.5, 2.NBT.B.6)

3. Ashley had 26 markers. Her friend gave her 17 more markers. How many markers does Ashley have now?

   _____ markers

4. What is the sum?

$$\begin{array}{r} 46 \\ +\ 24 \\ \hline \end{array}$$

5. Write a subtraction fact that will give the same difference as 15 − 7.

   10 − _____

6. What is the sum?

   34 + 5 = _____

Name ______________________

Algebra • Write Equations to Represent Subtraction

Essential Question How do you write a number sentence to represent a problem?

Common Core **Operations and Algebraic Thinking—2.OA.A.1** *Also 2.NBT.B.5*
MATHEMATICAL PRACTICES
MP1, MP2, MP3, MP4

Listen and Draw Real World

Draw to show the problem. Write a number sentence. Then solve.

____

MATHEMATICAL PRACTICES 4

Describe how your drawing shows the problem.

FOR THE TEACHER • Read this problem to children. Franco has 53 crayons. He gives some crayons to Courtney. Now Franco has 38 crayons. How many crayons did Franco give to Courtney?

Model and Draw

You can write a number sentence to show a problem.

Liza has 65 postcards. She gives 24 postcards to Wesley. How many postcards does Liza have now?

THINK:
65 postcards
−24 postcards
41 postcards

Liza has ______ postcards now.

Share and Show

Write a number sentence for the problem. Use a ■ for the missing number. Then solve.

1. There were 32 birds in the trees. Then 18 birds flew away. How many birds are in the trees now?

____

______ birds

2. Carla read 43 pages in her book. Joe read 32 pages in his book. How many more pages did Carla read than Joe?

____

______ more pages

Name ______________________________

On Your Own

Write a number sentence for the problem.
Use a ■ for the missing number. Then solve.

3. There were 40 ants on a rock. Some ants moved to the grass. Now there are 26 ants on the rock. How many ants moved to the grass?

______________________ ________ ants

4. THINK SMARTER Keisha had a bag of ribbons. She took 29 ribbons out of the bag. Then there were 17 ribbons still in the bag. How many ribbons were in the bag to start?

______________________ ________ ribbons

5. GO DEEPER There are 50 bees in a hive. Some bees fly out. If fewer than 20 bees are still in the hive, how many bees could have flown out?

________ bees

Use subtraction to prove your answer.

Problem Solving • Applications

6. MATHEMATICAL PRACTICE 6 **Make Connections** Brendan made this number line to find a difference. What was he subtracting from 100? Explain your answer.

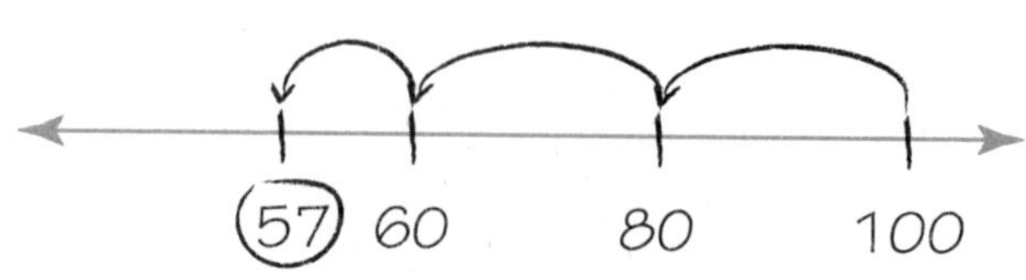

____

____

____

____

7. THINKSMARTER There are 52 pictures on the wall. 37 are wild cats and the rest are birds. How many of the pictures are birds?

Use the numbers and symbols on the tiles to write a number sentence for the problem.

15	25	37	52	−	+	=

____

________ birds

TAKE HOME ACTIVITY • Have your child explain how he or she solved one problem in this lesson.

Name ______________________________

Algebra • Write Equations to Represent Subtraction

COMMON CORE STANDARD—2.OA.A.1
Represent and solve problems involving addition and subtraction.

Write a number sentence for the problem. Use a ■ for the missing number. Then solve.

1. 29 children rode their bikes to school. After some of the children rode home, there were 8 children with bikes still at school. How many children rode their bikes home?

____

_____ children

Problem Solving

Solve. Write or draw to explain.

2. There were 21 children in the library. After 7 children left the library, how many children were still in the library?

_____ children

3. WRITE Math Describe different ways that you can show a story problem. Use one of the problems in this lesson as your example.

____

____

____

____

Lesson Check (2.OA.A.1)

1. Cindy had 42 beads. She used some beads for a bracelet. She has 14 beads left. How many beads did she use for the bracelet?

   _____ beads

2. Jake had 36 baseball cards. He gave 17 cards to his sister. How many baseball cards does Jake have now?

   _____ cards

Spiral Review (2.OA.B.2, 2.NBT.B.5)

3. What is the sum?

   $6 + 7 =$ _____

4. What is the difference?

   $16 - 9 =$ _____

5. What is the difference?

	4	6
−	3	9

6. Write an addition fact that will give the same sum as 6 + 8.

   10 + _____

FOR MORE PRACTICE GO TO THE Personal Math Trainer

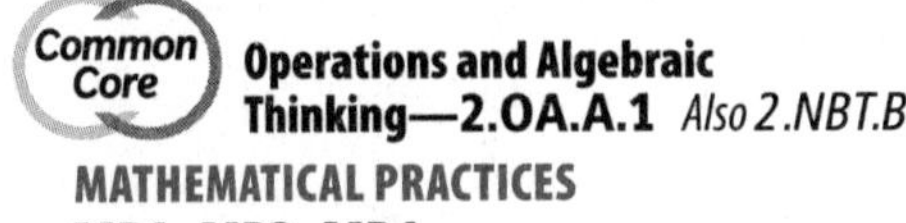

Name ______

Solve Multistep Problems

Essential Question How do you decide what steps to do to solve a problem?

Common Core **Operations and Algebraic Thinking—2.OA.A.1** *Also 2.NBT.B.5*
MATHEMATICAL PRACTICES
MP1, MP2, MP4

Label the bar model to show each problem. Then solve.

MATHEMATICAL PRACTICES

Describe how the two bar models are different.

FOR THE TEACHER • Read this 1st problem for children. Cassie has 32 sheets of paper. She gives Jeff 9 sheets of paper. How many sheets of paper does Cassie have now? After children solve, read this 2nd problem. Cassie draws 18 pictures. Jeff draws 16 pictures. How many pictures do they draw?

Model and Draw

Bar models help you know what to do to solve a problem.

Ali has 27 stamps. Matt has 38 stamps. How many more stamps are needed so they will have 91 stamps?

27	38

_____

They have ________ stamps now.

First, find how many stamps they have now.

_____	_____

91

They need ________ more stamps.

Next, find how many more stamps they need.

Share and Show

Complete the bar models for the steps you do to solve the problem.

THINK: What do you need to find first?

✓1. Jen has 93 beads. Ana has 46 red beads and 29 blue beads. How many more beads does Jen have than Ana?

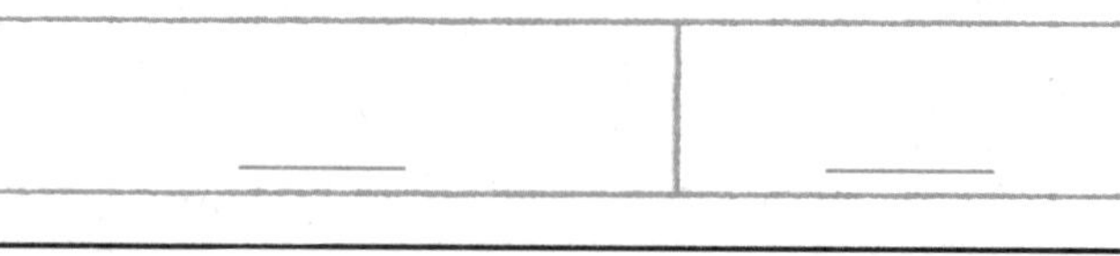

_____

_____

_____ _____

________ more beads

Name ______________________________

On Your Own

Complete the bar models for the steps you do to solve the problem.

2. Max has 35 trading cards. He buys 22 more cards. Then he gives 14 cards to Rudy. How many cards does Max have now?

_______ cards

3. Drew has 32 toy cars. He trades 7 of those cars for 11 other toy cars. How many toy cars does Drew have now?

_______ toy cars

4. Marta and Debbie each have 17 ribbons. They buy 1 package with 8 ribbons in it. How many ribbons do they have now?

_______ ribbons

Problem Solving • Applications

5. THINKSMARTER Shelby had 32 rocks. She finds 33 more rocks at the park and gives 28 rocks to George. How many rocks does she have now?

_______ rocks

6. GO DEEPER Benjamin finds 31 pinecones at the park. Together, Jenna and Ellen find the same number of pinecones as Benjamin. How many pinecones could each girl have found?

Jenna: _______ pinecones

Ellen: _______ pinecones

7. THINKSMARTER Tanya finds 22 leaves. Maurice finds 5 more leaves than Tanya finds. How many leaves do the children find in all?

Draw or write to show how you solve the problem.

_______ leaves

TAKE HOME ACTIVITY • Have your child explain how he or she would solve Exercise 6 if the number 31 was changed to 42.

Name ______________________

Solve Multistep Problems

COMMON CORE STANDARD—2.OA.A.1
Represent and solve problems involving addition and subtraction.

Complete the bar models for the steps you do to solve the problem.

1. Greg has 60 building blocks. His sister gives him 17 more blocks. He uses 38 blocks to make a tower. How many blocks are not used in the tower?

___	___

___

___	___

___

_____ blocks

Problem Solving

Solve. Write or draw to explain.

2. Ava has 25 books. She gives away 7 books. Then Tom gives her 12 books. How many books does Ava have now?

_____ books

3. WRITE Math Choose one of the problems on this page. Describe how you decided what steps were needed to solve the problem.

____

____

____

____

Lesson Check (2.OA.A.1)

1. Sara has 18 crayons. Max has 19 crayons. How many more crayons do they need to have 50 crayons altogether?

_____ crayons

2. Jon has 12 pennies. Lucy has 17 pennies. How many more pennies do they need to have 75 pennies altogether?

_____ pennies

Spiral Review (2.OA.A.1, 2.NBT.B.5, 2.NBT.B.6)

3. What is the difference?

58 − 13 = _____

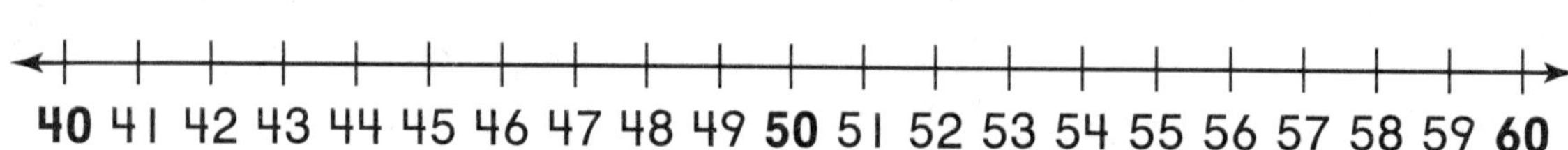

4. What is the sum?

4	7
+ 1	5

5. There are 26 cards in a box. Bryan takes 12 cards. How many cards are still in the box?

_____ cards

FOR MORE PRACTICE GO TO THE Personal Math Trainer

Name ____________________

Chapter 5 Review/Test

1. Do you need to regroup to subtract? Choose Yes or No.

65 − 23	○ Yes	○ No
50 − 14	○ Yes	○ No
37 − 19	○ Yes	○ No
77 − 60	○ Yes	○ No

2. Use the number line. Count up to find the difference.

52 − 48 = ______

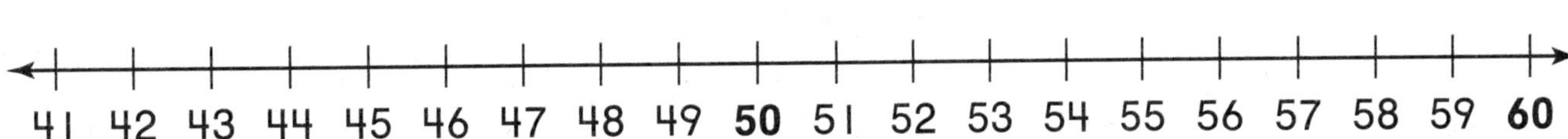

3. Ed has 28 blocks. Sue has 34 blocks. Who has more blocks? How many more? Label the bar model. Solve.

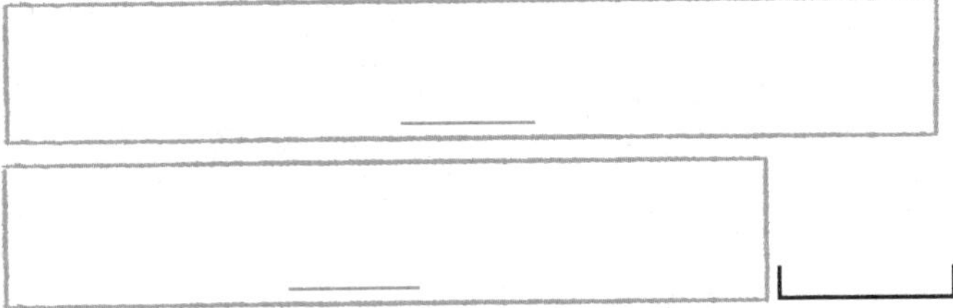

Circle the word and number from each box to make the sentence true.

Ed / Sue	has	6 / 16 / 52	more blocks.

GO DIGITAL Assessment Options Chapter Test

Break apart the number you are subtracting.
Write the difference.

4. 42 − 8 = ______

5. 53 − 16 = ______

---

6. What is 33 − 19? Use the numbers on the tiles to rewrite the subtraction problem. Then find the difference.

14	19	33	52

______
− ______
______

---

7. GO DEEPER Jacob's puzzle has 84 pieces. Jacob puts together 27 pieces in the morning. He puts together 38 more pieces in the afternoon. How many pieces does Jacob need to put together to finish the puzzle?

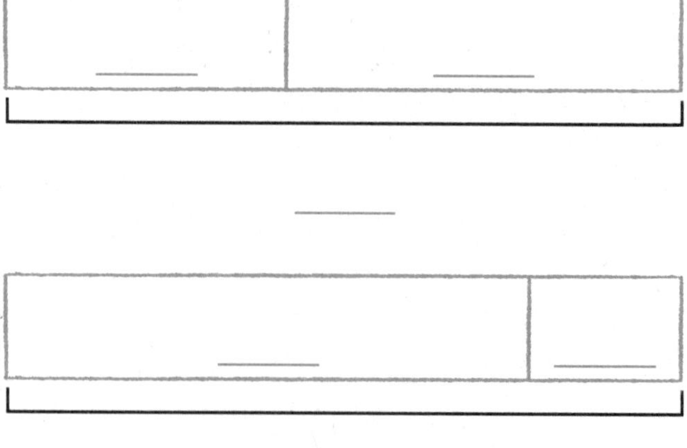

Complete the bar models for the steps you do to solve the problem.

______ more pieces

Name ______________________________

Regroup if you need to. Write the difference.

8.

	Tens	Ones
	☐	☐
	5	5
−	2	8

9.

	Tens	Ones
	☐	☐
	3	2
−	1	2

---

10. Find the difference.

$$\begin{array}{r} 90 \\ -\ 62 \\ \hline \end{array}$$

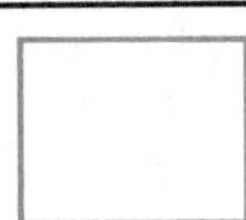

Fill in the bubble next to one number from each column to show the difference.

Tens	Ones
○ 2	○ 1
○ 3	○ 2
○ 5	○ 8

---

11. There are 22 children at the park. 5 children are on the swings. The rest of the children are playing ball. How many children are playing ball?

○ 13 ○ 23 ○ 17 ○ 27

12. THINK SMARTER + Subtract 27 from 43. Draw to show the regrouping. Fill in the bubble next to all the ways to write the difference.

- ○ 1 ten 6 ones
- ○ 66
- ○ 6 tens 1 one
- ○ 16

13. Jill collects stamps. Her stamp book has space for 64 stamps. She needs 18 more stamps to fill the book. How many stamps does Jill have now?

Write a number sentence for the problem.

Use a ■ for the missing number. Then solve.

____

Jill has ________ stamps.

14. Draw a quick picture to solve. Write the difference.

	Tens	Ones
	□	□
	6	2
−	2	5

Tens	Ones

Explain what you did to find the difference.

____

____

3-Digit Addition and Subtraction

Curious about Math

Monarch butterflies roost together during migration.

If you count 83 butterflies on one tree and 72 on another, how many butterflies have you counted altogether?

Name ______________________

Show What You Know

Model Subtracting Tens

Write the difference. (1.NBT.C.6)

1. 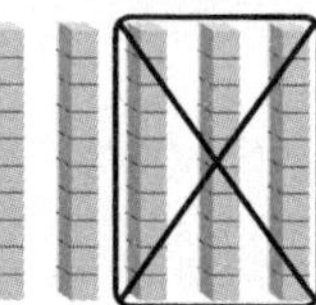

5 tens − 3 tens = ____ tens

50 − 30 = ____

2. 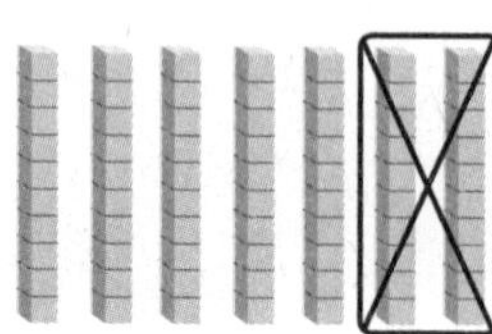

7 tens − 2 tens = ____ tens

70 − 20 = ____

2-Digit Addition

Write the sum. (2.NBT.B.6)

3. $\begin{array}{r} 54 \\ +\ 25 \\ \hline \end{array}$

4. $\begin{array}{r} 35 \\ +\ 18 \\ \hline \end{array}$

5. $\begin{array}{r} 82 \\ +\ 67 \\ \hline \end{array}$

6. $\begin{array}{r} 29 \\ +\ 81 \\ \hline \end{array}$

Hundreds, Tens, and Ones

Write the hundreds, tens, and ones shown. Write the number. (2.NBT.A.1)

7. 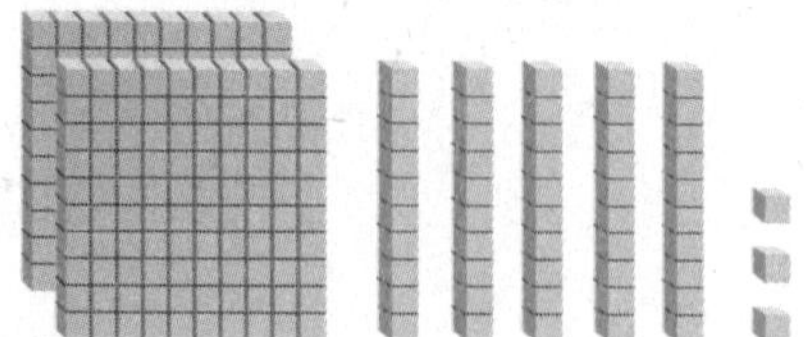

Hundreds	Tens	Ones

______

8. 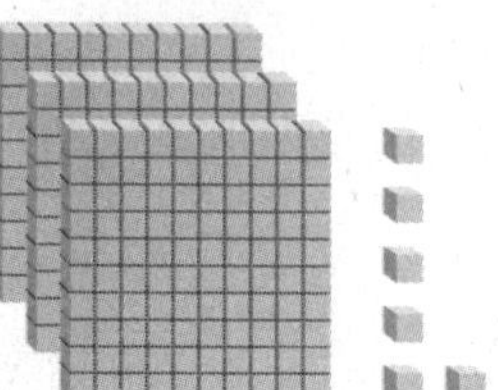

Hundreds	Tens	Ones

______

This page checks understanding of important skills needed for success in Chapter 6.

Name ________________________________

Review Words
regroup
sum
difference
hundreds

Vocabulary Builder

Visualize It

Fill in the graphic organizer by writing examples of ways to **regroup**.

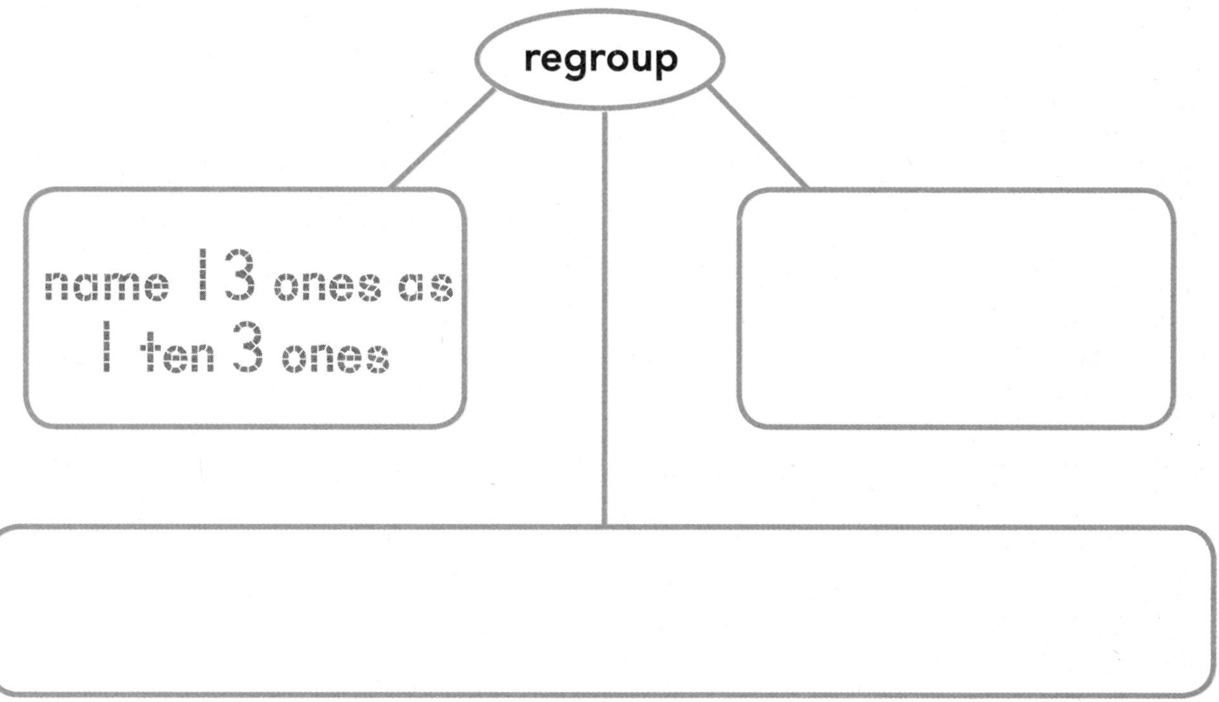

Understand Vocabulary

1. Write a number that has a **hundreds** digit that is greater than its tens digit. ________

2. Write an addition sentence that has a **sum** of 20. ________________

3. Write a subtraction sentence that has a **difference** of 10. ________________

GO DIGITAL • Interactive Student Edition • Multimedia eGlossary

Game 2-Digit Shuffle

Materials

- number cards 10–50
- 15  • 15

Play with a partner.

1. Shuffle the number cards. Place them face down in a pile.
2. Take two cards. Say the sum of the two numbers.
3. Your partner checks your sum.
4. If your sum is correct, place a counter on a button. If you regrouped to solve, place a counter on another button.
5. Take turns. Cover all the buttons. The player with more counters on the board wins.
6. Repeat the game, saying the difference between the two numbers for each turn.

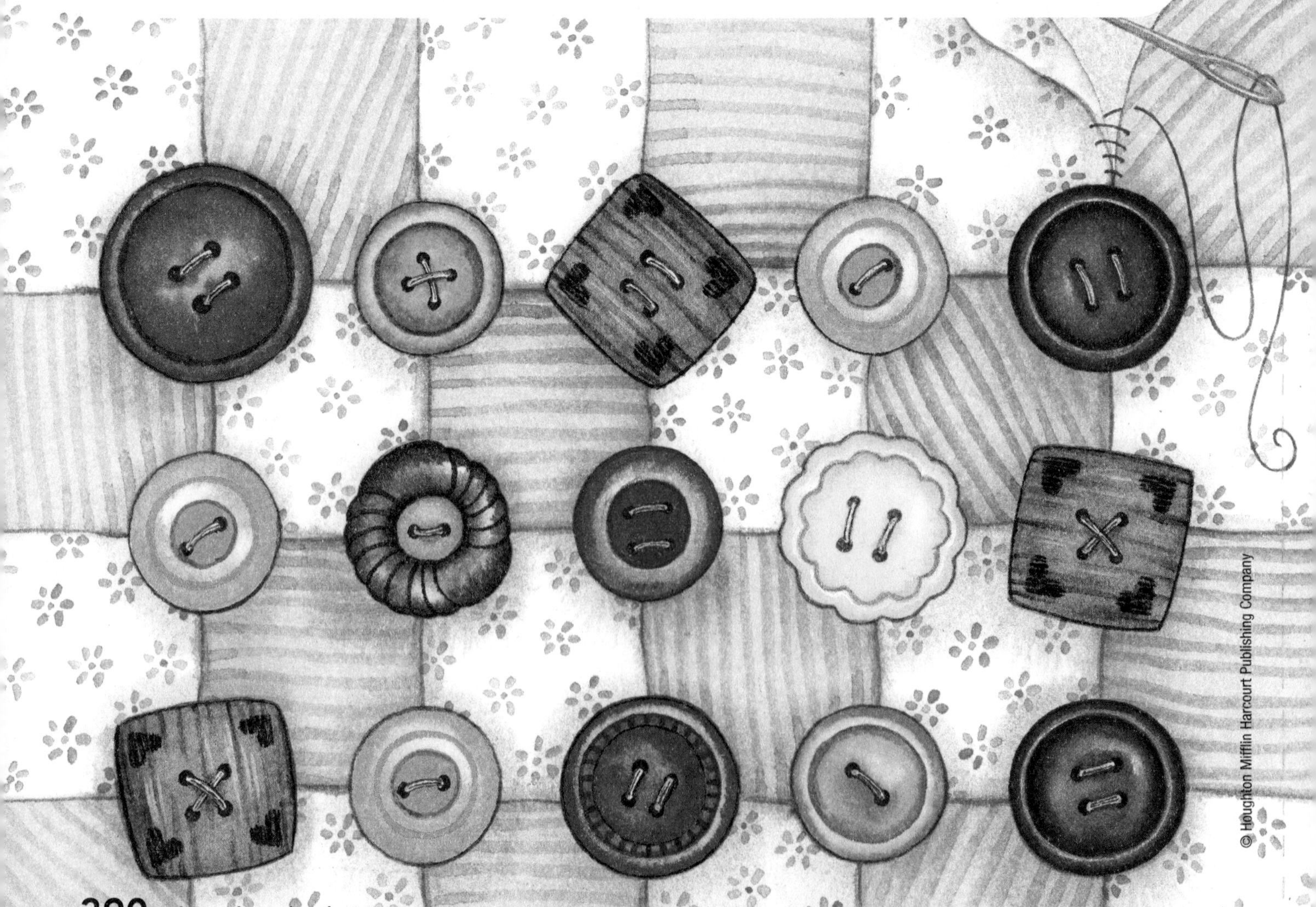

Chapter 6 Vocabulary

addend sumando 1	**column** columna 7
difference diferencia 14	**digit** dígito 15
hundred centena 31	**is equal to (=)** es igual a 33
regroup reagrupar 56	**sum** suma o total 59

column

$$\begin{array}{r} 33 \\ 34 \\ +32 \\ \hline \end{array}$$

5 + 3 = 8

addends

0, 1, 2, 3, 4, 5, 6, 7, 8, and 9 are digits.

5 − 3 = 2

difference

2 plus 1 is equal to 3

2 + 1 = 3

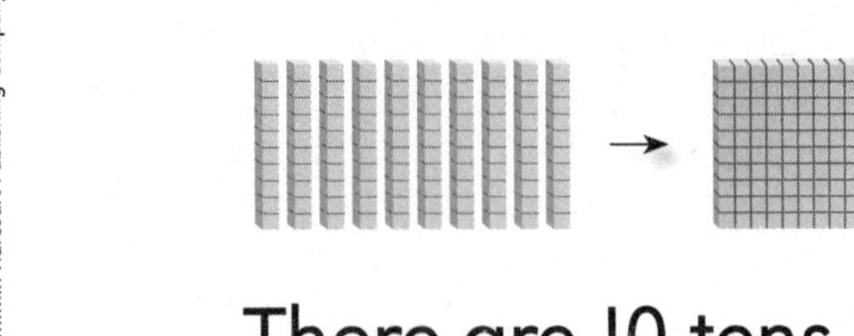

There are 10 tens in 1 **hundred**.

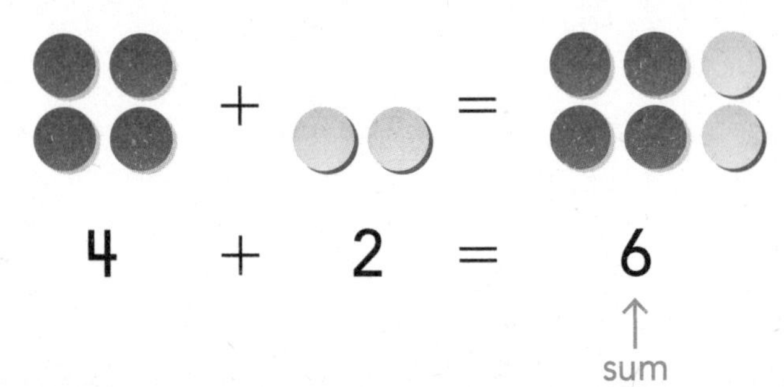

4 + 2 = 6

sum

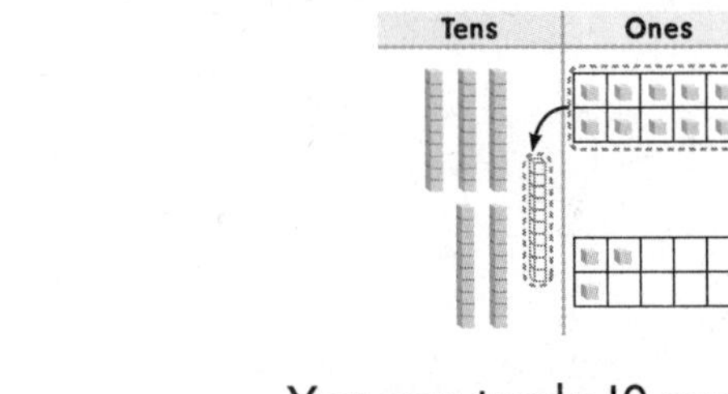

You can trade 10 ones for 1 ten to **regroup**.

Picture It

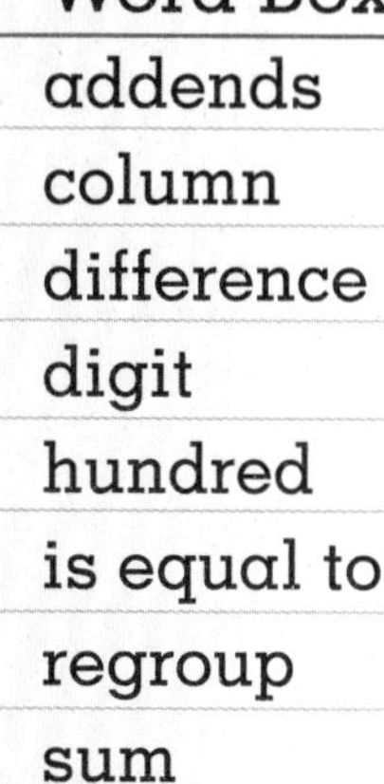

Word Box
addends
column
difference
digit
hundred
is equal to
regroup
sum

For 3 to 4 players

Materials

- timer
- sketch pad

How to Play

1. Take turns to play.
2. Choose a math word from the Word Box. Do not say the word.
3. Set the timer for 1 minute.
4. Draw pictures and numbers to give clues about the math word.
5. The first player to guess the word gets 1 point. If he or she uses the word in a sentence, they get 1 more point. That player gets the next turn.
6. The first player to score 5 points wins.

The Write Way

Reflect

Choose one idea. Write about it on the lines below.

- Tell how to solve this problem.

$$42 - 25 = \_\_\_\_$$

- Write a paragraph that uses at least **three** of these words.

addends **digit** **sum** **hundred** **regroup**

- Explain something you know about regrouping.

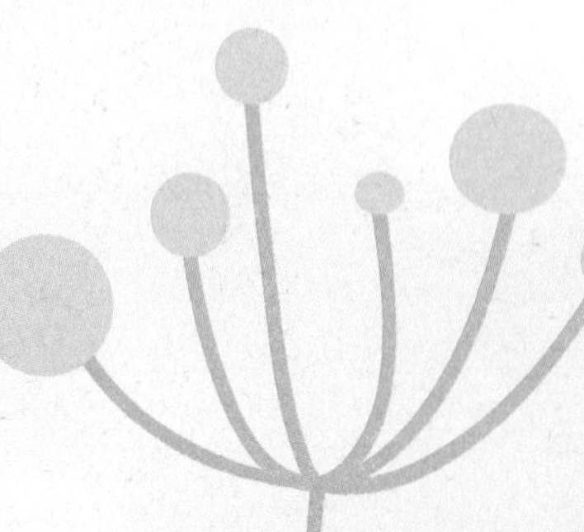

Name ______________________

Draw to Represent 3-Digit Addition

Essential Question How do you draw quick pictures to show adding 3-digit numbers?

Common Core **Number and Operations in Base Ten—2.NBT.B.7**
MATHEMATICAL PRACTICES
MP2, MP5, MP6

Listen and Draw Real World

Draw quick pictures to model the problem.
Then solve.

Tens	Ones
	________ pages

MATHEMATICAL PRACTICES 5

Use Tools Explain how your quick pictures show the problem.

FOR THE TEACHER • Read this problem to children. Manuel read 45 pages in a book. Then he read 31 more pages. How many pages did Manuel read? Have children draw quick pictures to solve the problem.

Model and Draw

Add 234 and 141.

Hundreds	Tens	Ones

3 hundreds 7 tens 5 ones

375

Share and Show

MATH BOARD

Draw quick pictures. Write how many hundreds, tens, and ones in all. Write the number.

1. Add 125 and 344.

Hundreds	Tens	Ones

____ hundreds ____ tens ____ ones

____

2. Add 307 and 251.

Hundreds	Tens	Ones

____ hundreds ____ tens ____ ones

____

Name ______________________________

On Your Own

Draw quick pictures. Write how many hundreds, tens, and ones in all. Write the number.

3. Add 231 and 218.

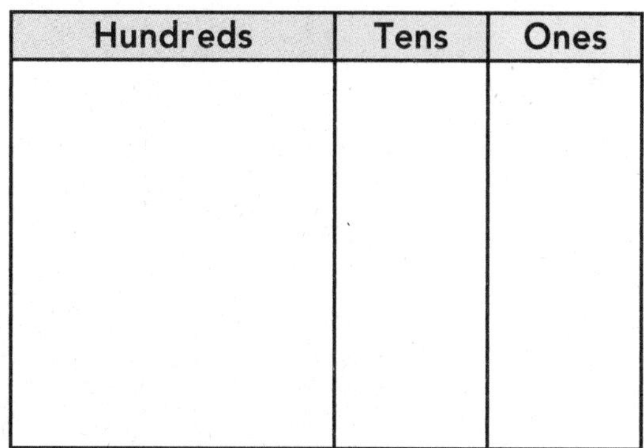

Hundreds	Tens	Ones

_____ hundreds _____ tens _____ ones

____

4. Add 232 and 150.

Hundreds	Tens	Ones

_____ hundreds _____ tens _____ ones

____

5. THINK SMARTER Use the quick pictures to find the two numbers being added. Then write how many hundreds, tens, and ones in all. Write the number.

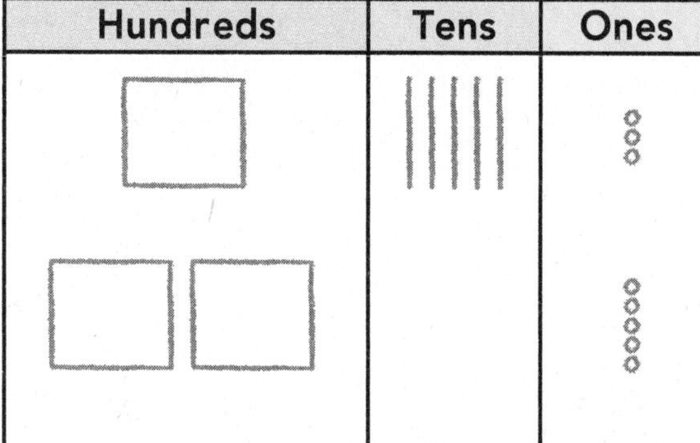

Hundreds	Tens	Ones

Add _____ and _____.

_____ hundreds _____ tens _____ ones

____

Problem Solving • Applications

6. MATHEMATICAL PRACTICE 2 **Represent a Problem**
There are 125 poems in Carrie's book and 143 poems in Angie's book. How many poems are in these two books?

Draw a quick picture to solve.

_______ poems

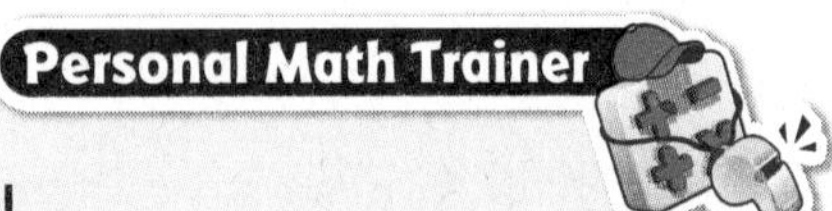

7. THINKSMARTER+ Rhys wants to add 456 and 131.

Help Rhys solve this problem. Draw quick pictures. Write how many hundreds, tens, and ones in all. Write the number.

Hundreds	Tens	Ones

_____ hundreds _____ tens _____ ones

____

TAKE HOME ACTIVITY • Write 145 + 122. Have your child explain how he or she can draw quick pictures to find the sum.

Name ______________________

Draw to Represent 3-Digit Addition

Common Core
COMMON CORE STANDARD—2.NBT.B.7
Use place value understanding and properties of operations to add and subtract.

Draw quick pictures. Write how many hundreds, tens, and ones in all. Write the number.

1. Add 142 and 215.

Hundreds	Tens	Ones

____ hundreds ____ tens ____ ones

____

Problem Solving

Solve. Write or draw to explain.

2. A farmer sold 324 lemons and 255 limes. How many pieces of fruit did the farmer sell altogether?

_______ pieces of fruit

3. WRITE Math Draw quick pictures and write to tell how you would add 342 and 416.

____

____

____

Lesson Check (2.NBT.B.7)

1. Ms. Carol sold 346 child tickets and 253 adult tickets. How many tickets did Ms. Carol sell?

   _______ tickets

2. Mr. Harris counted 227 gray pebbles and 341 white pebbles. How many pebbles did Mr. Harris count?

   _______ pebbles

Spiral Review (2.OA.C.4, 2.NBT.B.5, 2.NBT.B.6)

3. Pat has 3 rows of shells. There are 4 shells in each row. How many shells does Pat have?

   ____ shells

4. Kara counted 32 red pens, 25 blue pens, 7 black pens, and 24 green pens. How many pens did Kara count?

   ____ pens

5. Kai had 46 blocks. He gave 39 blocks to his sister. How many blocks does Kai have left?

   $46 - 39 =$ ____ blocks

6. A shop has 55 posters for sale. 34 posters show sports. The rest of the posters show animals. How many posters show animals?

   ____ posters

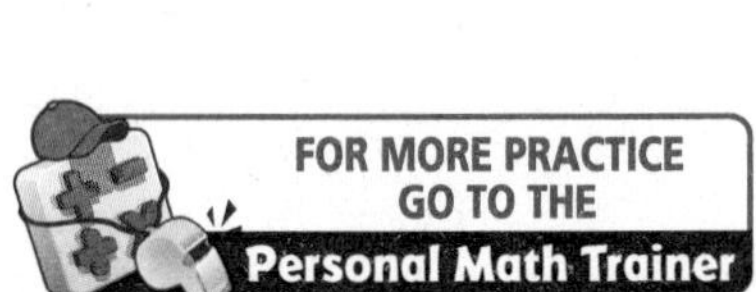

Name ____________________

Break Apart 3-Digit Addends

Essential Question How do you break apart addends to add hundreds, tens, and then ones?

Common Core **Number and Operations in Base Ten—2.NBT.B.7**
MATHEMATICAL PRACTICES MP6, MP8

Listen and Draw

Write the number. Draw a quick picture for the number. Then write the number in different ways.

______

____ hundreds ____ tens ____ ones

______ + ______ + ______

______

____ hundreds ____ tens ____ ones

______ + ______ + ______

MATHEMATICAL PRACTICES 6

Make Connections
What number can be written as 400 + 20 + 9?

FOR THE TEACHER • Have children write 258 on the blank in the left corner of the first box. Have children draw a quick picture for this number and then complete the other two forms for the number. Repeat the activity for 325.

Model and Draw

Break apart the addends into hundreds, tens, and ones. Add the hundreds, the tens, and the ones. Then find the total sum.

538	→	500 + 30 + 8
+216	→	200 + 10 + 6
		700 + ___ + ___ = _____

Share and Show

Break apart the addends to find the sum.

1. 321 → ___ + ___ + ___
   +457 → ___ + ___ + ___
   ___ + ___ + ___ = ___

✓2. 744 → ___ + ___ + ___
   +162 → ___ + ___ + ___
   ___ + ___ + ___ = ___

✓3. 254 → ___ + ___ + ___
   +536 → ___ + ___ + ___
   ___ + ___ + ___ = ___

Name ______________________________

On Your Own

Break apart the addends to find the sum.

4. 374 → ______ + ______ + ______

+518 → ______ + ______ + ______

______ + ______ + ______ = ______

5. 425 → ______ + ______ + ______

+232 → ______ + ______ + ______

______ + ______ + ______ = ______

6. 849 → ______ + ______ + ______

+123 → ______ + ______ + ______

______ + ______ + ______ = ______

7. THINKSMARTER Mr. Jones has many sheets of paper. He has 158 sheets of blue paper, 100 sheets of red paper, and 231 sheets of green paper. How many sheets of paper does he have?

______ sheets of paper

Problem Solving • Applications Real World

8. GO DEEPER Wesley added in a different way.

```
  327
+ 468
-----
  700    7 hundreds
   80    8 tens
+  15    15 ones
-----
  795
```

Use Wesley's way to find the sum.

```
  539
+ 247
-----
```

9. THINK SMARTER There are 376 children at one school. There are 316 children at another school. How many children are at the two schools?

376	⟶	300 + 70 + 6
+ 316	⟶	300 + 10 + 6

Select one number from each column to solve the problem.

Hundreds	Tens	Ones
○ 2	○ 4	○ 2
○ 4	○ 8	○ 3
○ 6	○ 9	○ 6

TAKE HOME ACTIVITY • Write 347 + 215. Have your child break apart the numbers and then find the sum.

Name ____________________

Break Apart 3-Digit Addends

Common Core
COMMON CORE STANDARD—2.NBT.B.7
Use place value understanding and properties of operations to add and subtract.

Break apart the addends to find the sum.

1. 518 → ____ + ____ + ____
+ 221 → ____ + ____ + ____

____ + ____ + ____ = ____

2. 438 → ____ + ____ + ____
+ 142 → ____ + ____ + ____

____ + ____ + ____ = ____

Problem Solving

Solve. Write or draw to explain.

3. There are 126 crayons in a bucket. A teacher puts 144 more crayons in the bucket. How many crayons are in the bucket now?

____ crayons

4. WRITE Math Draw quick pictures and write to explain how to break apart addends to find the sum of 324 + 231.

____

Lesson Check (2.NBT.B.7)

1. What is the sum?

$$\begin{array}{r} 218 \\ +\ 145 \\ \hline \end{array}$$

2. What is the sum?

$$\begin{array}{r} 664 \\ +\ 223 \\ \hline \end{array}$$

Spiral Review (2.OA.B.2, 2.NBT.B.5, 2.NBT.B.6, 2.NBT.B.9)

3. Ang found 19 berries and Barry found 21 berries. How many berries did they find altogether?

$19 + 21 =$ ____ berries

4. Write a subtraction fact related to $9 + 6 =$

____

5. There are 25 goldfish and 33 betta fish. How many fish are there?

$25 + 33 =$ ____ fish

6. Subtract 16 from 41. Draw to show the regrouping. What is the difference?

Tens	Ones

____

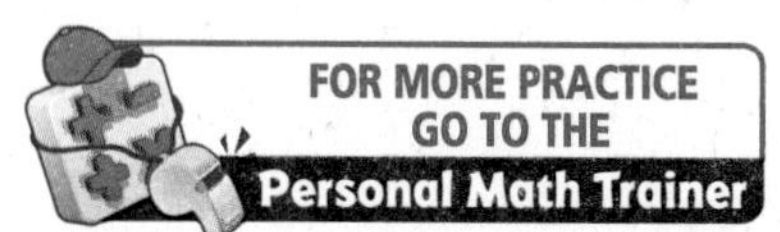

Name ______________________________

3-Digit Addition: Regroup Ones

Essential Question When do you regroup ones in addition?

Common Core **Number and Operations in Base Ten—2.NBT.B.7**

MATHEMATICAL PRACTICES
MP4, MP6, MP8

Listen and Draw

Real World · Hands On

Use [hundred flat, ten rod, one cube] to model the problem.
Draw quick pictures to show what you did.

Hundreds	Tens	Ones

FOR THE TEACHER • Read the following problem and have children model it with blocks. There were 213 people at the show on Friday and 156 people at the show on Saturday. How many people were at the two nights? Have children draw quick pictures to show how they solved the problem.

Math Talk MATHEMATICAL PRACTICES 6

Describe how you modeled the problem.

Model and Draw

Add the ones.
6 + 7 = 13

Regroup 13 ones as 1 ten 3 ones.

Hundreds	Tens	Ones
	1	
2	4	6
+ 1	1	7
		3

Hundreds	Tens	Ones

Add the tens.

1 + 4 + 1 = 6

Hundreds	Tens	Ones
	1	
2	4	6
+ 1	1	7
	6	3

Hundreds	Tens	Ones

Add the hundreds.

2 + 1 = 3

Hundreds	Tens	Ones
	1	
2	4	6
+ 1	1	7
3	6	3

Hundreds	Tens	Ones

Share and Show

Write the sum.

1.

Hundreds	Tens	Ones
	☐	
3	2	8
+ 1	3	4

2.

Hundreds	Tens	Ones
	☐	
4	4	5
+	2	3

Name ______________________________

On Your Own

Write the sum.

3.

	Hundreds	Tens	Ones
		☐	
	5	2	6
+	1	0	3

4.

	Hundreds	Tens	Ones
		☐	
	3	4	8
+		1	9

5.

	Hundreds	Tens	Ones
		☐	
	6	2	8
+	3	4	7

6.

	Hundreds	Tens	Ones
		☐	
	2	3	5
+	2	5	7

7.

	Hundreds	Tens	Ones
		☐	
	5	6	2
+	3	2	9

8.

	Hundreds	Tens	Ones
		☐	
	1	4	7
+	1	2	5

9. THINK SMARTER On Thursday, there were 326 visitors at the zoo. There were 200 more visitors at the zoo on Friday than on Thursday. How many visitors were at the zoo on both days?

__________ visitors

Problem Solving • Applications

Solve. Write or draw to explain.

10. MATHEMATICAL PRACTICE 4 **Model with Mathematics** The gift shop is 140 steps away from the zoo entrance. The train stop is 235 steps away from the gift shop. How many total steps is this?

_______ steps

11. THINK SMARTER Katina's class used 249 noodles to decorate their bulletin board. Gunter's class used 318 noodles. How many noodles did the two classes use?

_______ noodles

Did you have to regroup to solve? Explain.

TAKE HOME ACTIVITY • Ask your child to explain why he or she regrouped in only some of the problems in this lesson.

Name ____________________

3-Digit Addition: Regroup Ones

Common Core **COMMON CORE STANDARD—2.NBT.B.7**
Use place value understanding and properties of operations to add and subtract.

Write the sum.

1.

	Hundreds	Tens	Ones
		☐	
	1	4	8
+	2	3	4

2.

	Hundreds	Tens	Ones
		☐	
	3	2	1
+	3	1	8

3.

	Hundreds	Tens	Ones
		☐	
	4	1	4
+	1	7	9

4.

	Hundreds	Tens	Ones
		☐	
	6	0	2
+	2	5	8

Problem Solving

Solve. Write or draw to explain.

5. In the garden, there are 258 yellow daisies and 135 white daisies. How many daisies are in the garden altogether? ________ daisies

6. WRITE Math Find the sum of 136 + 212. Explain why you did or did not regroup.

____

Lesson Check (2.NBT.B.7)

1. What is the sum?

Hundreds	Tens	Ones
	☐	
4	3	5
+ 1	4	6

2. What is the sum?

Hundreds	Tens	Ones
	☐	
4	3	6
+ 3	0	6

Spiral Review (2.OA.B.2, 2.NBT.B.5, 2.NBT.B.6, 2.NBT.B.7)

3. What is the difference?

$9 - 4 =$ ____

4. What is the sum?

$$\begin{array}{r} 82 \\ +\ 59 \\ \hline \end{array}$$

5. What is the sum?

$26 + 7 =$ ____

6. Add 243 and 132. How many hundreds, tens, and ones are there in all?

____ hundreds ____ tens

____ ones

FOR MORE PRACTICE GO TO THE Personal Math Trainer

Name ____________________

3-Digit Addition: Regroup Tens

Essential Question When do you regroup tens in addition?

Common Core **Number and Operations in Base Ten—2.NBT.B.7**
MATHEMATICAL PRACTICES
MP6, MP8

Listen and Draw

Real World · Hands On

Use [hundred block] [ten rod] [one cube] to model the problem.
Draw quick pictures to show what you did.

Hundreds	Tens	Ones

FOR THE TEACHER • Read the following problem and have children model it with blocks. On Monday, 253 children visited the zoo. On Tuesday, 324 children visited the zoo. How many children visited the zoo those two days? Have children draw quick pictures to show how they solved the problem.

Math Talk MATHEMATICAL PRACTICES 6

Explain how your quick pictures show what happened in the problem.

Model and Draw

Add the ones.

2 + 5 = 7

Hundreds	Tens	Ones
□	□	
1	4	2
+ 2	8	5
		7

Hundreds	Tens	Ones

Add the tens.

4 + 8 = 12
Regroup 12 tens as 1 hundred 2 tens.

Hundreds	Tens	Ones
1	□	
1	4	2
+ 2	8	5
	2	7

Hundreds	Tens	Ones

Add the hundreds.

1 + 1 + 2 = 4

Hundreds	Tens	Ones
1	□	
1	4	2
+ 2	8	5
4	2	7

Hundreds	Tens	Ones

Share and Show

Write the sum.

1.

Hundreds	Tens	Ones
□	□	
3	4	7
+ 2	9	1

✓ 2.

Hundreds	Tens	Ones
□	□	
1	6	5
+ 3	5	4

✓ 3.

Hundreds	Tens	Ones
□	□	
5	3	8
+ 1	4	0

Name ______________________________

On Your Own

Write the sum.

4.

Hundreds	Tens	Ones
☐	☐	
1	5	6
+	4	2

5.

Hundreds	Tens	Ones
☐	☐	
7	6	4
+ 1	5	3

6.

Hundreds	Tens	Ones
☐	☐	
3	7	2
+ 1	8	5

7.

2	2	4
+ 1	5	7

8.

3	1	4
+ 4	3	5

9.

7	5	3
+ 1	5	2

10. GO DEEPER In a bowling game, Jack scored 116 points and 124 points. Hal scored 128 points and 134 points. Who scored more points? How many more points were scored?

________ ________ more points

MATHEMATICAL PRACTICE 6 **Attend to Precision**
Rewrite the numbers. Then add.

11. 760 + 178

+
______

12. 216 + 346

+
______

13. 423 + 285

+
______

Problem Solving • Applications

14. THINKSMARTER These lists show the pieces of fruit sold. How many pieces of fruit did Mr. Olson sell?

Mr. Olson	Mr. Lee
257 apples	314 pears
281 plums	229 peaches

_______ pieces of fruit

15. GO DEEPER Who sold more pieces of fruit?

____

How many more?

_______ more pieces of fruit

16. THINKSMARTER At the city park theater, 152 people watched the morning play. Another 167 watched the afternoon play.

How many people watched the two plays? _______ people

Fill in the bubble next to each true sentence about how to solve the problem.

- ○ You need to regroup the tens as 1 ten and 9 ones.
- ○ You need to regroup the tens as 1 hundred and 1 ten.
- ○ You need to add 2 ones + 7 ones.
- ○ You need to add 1 hundred + 1 hundred + 1 hundred.

TAKE HOME ACTIVITY • Have your child choose a new combination of two fruits on this page and find the total number of pieces of the two types of fruit.

Name ______________________

3-Digit Addition: Regroup Tens

COMMON CORE STANDARD—2.NBT.B.7
Use place value understanding and properties of operations to add and subtract.

Write the sum.

1.

Hundreds	Tens	Ones
☐	☐	
1	8	7
+ 2	3	2

2.

Hundreds	Tens	Ones
☐	☐	
3	2	2
+ 3	5	6

3.

Hundreds	Tens	Ones
☐	☐	
2	8	5
+ 5	3	1

4.

4	4	5
+	3	4

5.

6	2	0
+ 2	8	8

6.

5	5	7
+ 1	8	0

Problem Solving Real World

Solve. Write or draw to explain.

7. There are 142 blue toy cars and 293 red toy cars at the toy store. How many toy cars are there?

_______ toy cars

8. WRITE Math Find the sum of 362 + 265. Explain why you did or did not regroup.

____

____

Lesson Check (2.NBT.B.7)

1. What is the sum?

$$\begin{array}{r} 472 \\ +\ 255 \\ \hline \end{array}$$

2. Annika has 144 pennies and Yahola has 284 pennies. How many do they have altogether?

$$\begin{array}{r} 144 \\ +\ 284 \\ \hline \end{array}$$

Spiral Review (2.OA.B.2, 2.NBT.B.5, 2.NBT.B.7)

3. What is the sum?

$$\begin{array}{r} 56 \\ +\ 38 \\ \hline \end{array}$$

4. What is the sum?

$$\begin{array}{r} 326 \\ +\ 139 \\ \hline \end{array}$$

5. Francis had 8 toy cars, then his brother gave him 9 more. How many toy cars does Francis have now?

$8 + 9 =$ ____ cars

6. What is the difference?

$$\begin{array}{r} 82 \\ -\ 34 \\ \hline \end{array}$$

FOR MORE PRACTICE GO TO THE Personal Math Trainer

Name ______________________________

Addition: Regroup Ones and Tens

Essential Question How do you know when to regroup in addition?

Common Core **Number and Operations in Base Ten—2.NBT.B.7** *Also 2.NBT.B.9*

MATHEMATICAL PRACTICES
MP1, MP6, MP8

Listen and Draw

Use mental math. Write the sum for each problem.

$$\begin{array}{r} 40 \\ +\ 20 \\ \hline \end{array} \qquad \begin{array}{r} 200 \\ +\ 700 \\ \hline \end{array} \qquad \begin{array}{r} 70 \\ +\ 30 \\ \hline \end{array} \qquad \begin{array}{r} 500 \\ +\ 300 \\ \hline \end{array}$$

10 + 30 + 40 = ______

100 + 400 + 200 = ______

10 + 50 + 40 = ______

600 + 300 = ______

MATHEMATICAL PRACTICES 1

Analyze Were some problems easier to solve than other problems? Explain.

FOR THE TEACHER • Encourage children to do these addition problems quickly. You may wish to first discuss the problems with children, noting that each problem is limited to just adding tens or just adding hundreds.

Model and Draw

Sometimes you will regroup more than once in addition problems.

$$\begin{array}{r} \scriptstyle 1\;\,1\;\;\; \\ 2\;5\;9 \\ +\;4\;7\;6 \\ \hline 7\;3\;5 \end{array}$$

9 ones + 6 ones = 15 ones, or 1 ten 5 ones

1 ten + 5 tens + 7 tens = 13 tens, or 1 hundred 3 tens

1 hundred + 2 hundreds + 4 hundreds = 7 hundreds

THINK:
Are there 10 or more ones?
Are there 10 or more tens?

Share and Show

Write the sum.

1. $\begin{array}{r} 1\;8\;4 \\ +\;3\;2\;9 \\ \hline \end{array}$

2. $\begin{array}{r} 5\;4\;6 \\ +\;2\;7\;8 \\ \hline \end{array}$

3. $\begin{array}{r} 3\;2\;7 \\ +\;3\;5\;3 \\ \hline \end{array}$

4. $\begin{array}{r} 2\;3\;4 \\ +\;1\;5\;2 \\ \hline \end{array}$

5. $\begin{array}{r} 3\;7\;5 \\ +\;2\;7\;2 \\ \hline \end{array}$

6. $\begin{array}{r} 1\;8\;9 \\ +\;6\;2\;3 \\ \hline \end{array}$

Name ______________________________

On Your Own

Write the sum.

7.
$$\begin{array}{r} 574 \\ +\ 281 \\ \hline \end{array}$$

8.
$$\begin{array}{r} 416 \\ +\ 483 \\ \hline \end{array}$$

9.
$$\begin{array}{r} 346 \\ +\ 597 \\ \hline \end{array}$$

10.
$$\begin{array}{r} 365 \\ +\ 283 \\ \hline \end{array}$$

11.
$$\begin{array}{r} 647 \\ +\ 109 \\ \hline \end{array}$$

12.
$$\begin{array}{r} 546 \\ +\ 356 \\ \hline \end{array}$$

13.
$$\begin{array}{r} 348 \\ +\ 631 \\ \hline \end{array}$$

14.
$$\begin{array}{r} 455 \\ +\ 139 \\ \hline \end{array}$$

15.
$$\begin{array}{r} 563 \\ +\ 245 \\ \hline \end{array}$$

16. THINK SMARTER Miko wrote these problems. What are the missing digits?

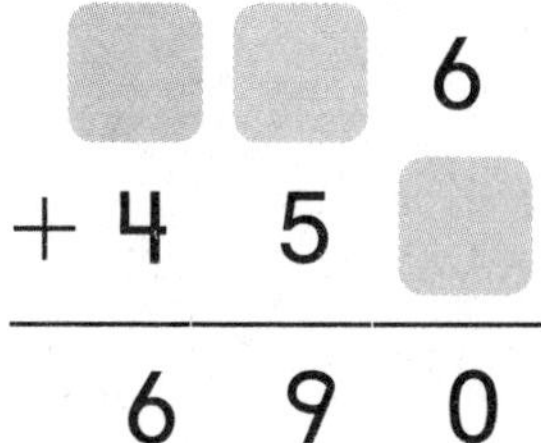

$$\begin{array}{r} \square\ \square\ 6 \\ +\ 4\ 5\ \square \\ \hline 6\ 9\ 0 \end{array}$$

$$\begin{array}{r} 6\ \square\ 7 \\ +\ 2\ 3\ \square \\ \hline \square\ 6\ 2 \end{array}$$

TAKE HOME ACTIVITY • Have your child explain how to solve 236 + 484.

Name ______________________________

Mid-Chapter Checkpoint

Concepts and Skills

Break apart the addends to find the sum. (2.NBT.B.7)

1. 567 → ______ + ______ + ______
   +324 → ______ + ______ + ______

   ______ + ______ + ______ = ______

Write the sum. (2.NBT.B.7)

2.
$$\begin{array}{r} 2\ 4\ 8 \\ +\ 3\ 4\ 6 \\ \hline \end{array}$$

3.
$$\begin{array}{r} 6\ 3\ 7 \\ +\ 2\ 6\ 4 \\ \hline \end{array}$$

4.
$$\begin{array}{r} 3\ 9\ 1 \\ +\ 5\ 3\ 7 \\ \hline \end{array}$$

5. THINK SMARTER There are 148 small sand dollars and 119 large sand dollars on the beach. How many sand dollars are on the beach? (2.NBT.B.7)

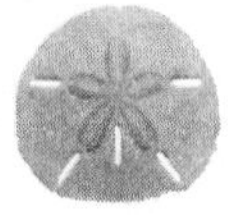

______ sand dollars

Name ______________________________

Addition: Regroup Ones and Tens

Common Core

COMMON CORE STANDARD—2.NBT.B.7
Use place value understanding and properties of operations to add and subtract.

Write the sum.

1.
$$\begin{array}{r} 547 \\ +\ 435 \\ \hline \end{array}$$

2.
$$\begin{array}{r} 367 \\ +\ 284 \\ \hline \end{array}$$

3.
$$\begin{array}{r} 485 \\ +\ 456 \\ \hline \end{array}$$

4.
$$\begin{array}{r} 187 \\ +\ 306 \\ \hline \end{array}$$

5.
$$\begin{array}{r} 647 \\ +\ 128 \\ \hline \end{array}$$

6.
$$\begin{array}{r} 523 \\ +\ 174 \\ \hline \end{array}$$

Problem Solving

Solve. Write or draw to explain.

7. Saul and Luisa each scored 167 points on a computer game. How many points did they score together?

_______ points

8. WRITE Math Write the addition problem for 275 plus 249 and find the sum. Then draw quick pictures to check your work.

____

Lesson Check (2.NBT.B.7)

1. What is the sum?

$$\begin{array}{r} 348 \\ +\ 272 \\ \hline \end{array}$$

2. What is the sum?

$$\begin{array}{r} 123 \\ +\ 217 \\ \hline \end{array}$$

Spiral Review (2.OA.A.1, 2.OA.B.2, 2.NBT.B.6, 2.NBT.B.9)

3. Write an addition fact that has the same sum as 9 + 4.

   10 + ____

4. What is the sum?

$$\begin{array}{r} 32 \\ 15 \\ +\ 46 \\ \hline \end{array}$$

5. Add 29 and 35. Draw to show the regrouping. What is the sum?

   Tens | Ones

   ____

6. Tom had 25 pretzels.
   He gave away 12 pretzels.
   How many pretzels does Tom have left?

   25 − 12 = ____ pretzels

Name ______________________________

Problem Solving • 3-Digit Subtraction

Essential Question How can making a model help when solving subtraction problems?

Common Core Number and Operations in Base Ten—2.NBT.B.7
MATHEMATICAL PRACTICES MP1, MP4, MP6

There were 436 people at the art show. 219 people went home. How many people stayed at the art show?

Unlock the Problem  

What do I need to find?

how many people
____
stayed at the art show

What information do I need to use?

________ people were at the art show.

Then, ________ people went home.

Show how to solve the problem.

Make a model. Then draw a quick picture of your model.

________ people

HOME CONNECTION • Your child used a model and a quick picture to represent and solve a subtraction problem.

Try Another Problem

Make a model to solve. Then draw a quick picture of your model.

- What do I need to find?
- What information do I need to use?

1. There are 532 pieces of art at the show. 319 pieces of art are paintings. How many pieces of art are not paintings?

_______ pieces of art

2. 245 children go to the face-painting event. 114 of the children are boys. How many of the children are girls?

_______ girls

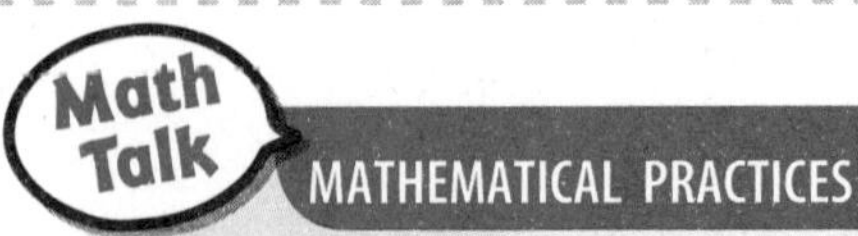

Explain how you solved the first problem on this page.

Name ______

Share and Show

Make a model to solve. Then draw a quick picture of your model.

3. There were 237 books on the table. Miss Jackson took 126 books off the table. How many books were still on the table?

______ books

4. There were 232 postcards on the table. The children used 118 postcards. How many postcards were not used?

______ postcards

5. THINK SMARTER 164 children and 31 adults saw the movie in the morning. 125 children saw the movie in the afternoon. How many fewer children saw the movie in the afternoon than in the morning?

______ fewer children

On Your Own

MATHEMATICAL PRACTICE 1 **Make Sense of Problems**

6. There were some grapes in a bowl. Clancy's friends ate 24 of the grapes. Then there were 175 grapes in the bowl. How many grapes were in the bowl before?

_______ grapes

7. THINK SMARTER At Gregory's school, there are 547 boys and girls. There are 246 boys. How many girls are there?

Draw a quick picture to solve.

Circle the number that makes the sentence true.

There are [201 / 301 / 793] girls.

TAKE HOME ACTIVITY • Ask your child to choose one of the problems in this lesson and solve it in a different way.

Name ___________________________

Problem Solving • 3-Digit Subtraction

COMMON CORE STANDARD—2.NBT.B.7
Use place value understanding and properties of operations to add and subtract.

Make a model to solve. Then draw a quick picture of your model.

1. On Saturday, 770 people went to the snack shop. On Sunday, 628 people went. How many more people went to the snack shop on Saturday than on Sunday?

   ________ more people

2. There were 395 lemon ice cups at the snack shop. People bought 177 lemon ice cups. How many lemon ice cups are still at the snack shop?

   ________ cups

3. There were 576 bottles of water at the snack shop. People bought 469 bottles of water. How many bottles of water are at the snack shop now?

   ________ bottles

4. WRITE Math Draw quick pictures to show how to subtract 314 and 546.

Lesson Check (2.NBT.B.7)

1. There are 278 math and science books. 128 of them are math books. How many science books are there?

_______ books

2. A book has 176 pages. Mr. Roberts has read 119 pages. How many pages does he have left to read?

_______ pages

Spiral Review (2.OA.B.2, 2.NBT.B.5, 2.NBT.B.6, 2.NBT.B.7)

3. What is the sum?

$1 + 6 + 2 = \_\_\_\_$

4. What is the difference?

$54 - 8 = \_\_\_\_$

5. What is the sum?

$$\begin{array}{r} 356 \\ +\ 174 \\ \hline \end{array}$$

6. What is the sum?

$$\begin{array}{r} 22 \\ +\ 16 \\ \hline \end{array}$$

FOR MORE PRACTICE GO TO THE Personal Math Trainer

Name ______________________________

3-Digit Subtraction: Regroup Tens

Essential Question When do you regroup tens in subtraction?

Common Core **Number and Operations in Base Ten—2.NBT.B.7**

MATHEMATICAL PRACTICES
MP1, MP6, MP8

Use [blocks] to model the problem.
Draw a quick picture to show what you did.

Hundreds	Tens	Ones

Math Talk MATHEMATICAL PRACTICES 1

Describe what to do when there are not enough ones to subtract from.

FOR THE TEACHER • Read the following problem and have children model it with blocks. 473 people went to the football game. 146 people were still there at the end of the game. How many people left before the end of the game? Have children draw quick pictures of their models.

Model and Draw

$354 - 137 = ?$

Are there enough ones to subtract 7?

yes **no**

Regroup 1 ten as 10 ones.

Hundreds	Tens	Ones
	4	14
3	~~5~~	~~4~~
− 1	3	7

Hundreds	Tens	Ones

Now there are enough ones.

Subtract the ones.

$14 - 7 = 7$

Hundreds	Tens	Ones
	4	14
3	~~5~~	~~4~~
− 1	3	7
		7

Hundreds	Tens	Ones

Subtract the tens.

$4 - 3 = 1$

Subtract the hundreds.

$3 - 1 = 2$

Hundreds	Tens	Ones
	4	14
3	~~5~~	~~4~~
− 1	3	7
2	1	7

Hundreds	Tens	Ones

Share and Show

Solve. Write the difference.

1.

Hundreds	Tens	Ones
	☐	☐
4	3	1
− 3	2	6

2.

Hundreds	Tens	Ones
	☐	☐
6	5	8
− 2	3	7

Name ______________________________

On Your Own

Solve. Write the difference.

3.

Hundreds	Tens	Ones
	☐	☐
7	2	8
− 1	0	7

4.

Hundreds	Tens	Ones
	☐	☐
4	5	2
− 2	1	6

5.

Hundreds	Tens	Ones
	☐	☐
9	6	5
− 2	3	8

6.

Hundreds	Tens	Ones
	☐	☐
4	8	9
− 1	4	9

7. GO DEEPER A bookstore has 148 books about people and 136 books about places. Some books were sold. Now there are 137 books left. How many books were sold?

_______ books

8. THINK SMARTER There were 287 music books and 134 science books in the store. After some books were sold, there are 159 books left. How many books were sold?

_______ books

Problem Solving • Applications

Make Sense of Problems

Solve. Write or draw to explain.

9. There are 235 whistles and 42 bells in the store. Ryan counts 128 whistles on the shelf. How many whistles are not on the shelf?

_______ whistles

Personal Math Trainer

10. THINKSMARTER+ Dr. Jackson had 326 stamps.

He sells 107 stamps. How many stamps does he have now?

_______ stamps

Would you do these things to solve the problem?
Choose Yes or No.

Subtract 107 from 326.	○ Yes	○ No
Regroup 1 ten as 10 ones.	○ Yes	○ No
Regroup the hundreds.	○ Yes	○ No
Subtract 7 ones from 16 ones.	○ Yes	○ No
Add 26 + 10.	○ Yes	○ No

TAKE HOME ACTIVITY • Ask your child to explain why he or she regrouped in only some of the problems in this lesson.

Name ________________

3-Digit Subtraction: Regroup Tens

Common Core

COMMON CORE STANDARD—2.NBT.B.7
Use place value understanding and properties of operations to add and subtract.

Solve. Write the difference.

1.

	Hundreds	Tens	Ones
		☐	☐
	7	7	4
−	2	3	6

2.

	Hundreds	Tens	Ones
		☐	☐
	5	5	1
−	1	1	3

3.

	Hundreds	Tens	Ones
		☐	☐
	4	8	9
−	2	7	3

4.

	Hundreds	Tens	Ones
		☐	☐
	7	7	2
−	2	5	4

Problem Solving

Solve. Write or draw to explain.

5. There were 985 pencils. Some pencils were sold. Then there were 559 pencils left. How many pencils were sold?

_______ pencils

6. WRITE Math Choose one exercise from above. Draw quick pictures to check your work.

Lesson Check (2.NBT.B.7)

1. What is the difference?

$$\begin{array}{r} 346 \\ -\ 127 \\ \hline \end{array}$$

2. What is the difference?

$$\begin{array}{r} 568 \\ -\ 226 \\ \hline \end{array}$$

Spiral Review (2.OA.A.1, 2.OA.C.4, 2.NBT.B.5, 2.NBT.B.7)

3. What is the difference?

45 − 7 = ____

4. Leroy has 11 cubes. Jane has 15 cubes. How many cubes do they have altogether?

____ cubes

5. Mina puts 5 flowers in each vase. How many flowers will she put in 3 vases?

____ flowers

6. Mr. Hill had 471 pencils. He gave away 164 pencils. How many pencils did he keep?

________ pencils

FOR MORE PRACTICE GO TO THE Personal Math Trainer

Name ____________________

3-Digit Subtraction: Regroup Hundreds

Essential Question When do you regroup hundreds in subtraction?

Common Core Number and Operations in Base Ten—2.NBT.B.7, 2.NBT.B.9

MATHEMATICAL PRACTICES
MP1, MP3, MP8

Listen and Draw Real World

Draw quick pictures to show the problem.

Hundreds	Tens	Ones

Math Talk MATHEMATICAL PRACTICES 1

Describe what to do when there are not enough tens to subtract from.

FOR THE TEACHER • Read the following problem and have children model it with quick pictures. The Reading Club has 349 books. 173 of the books are about animals. How many books are not about animals?

Model and Draw

$428 - 153 = ?$

Subtract the ones.

$8 - 3 = 5$

	Hundreds	Tens	Ones
	☐	☐	☐
	4	2	8
−	1	5	3
			5

There are not enough tens to subtract from.

Regroup 1 hundred.
4 hundreds 2 tens is now 3 hundreds 12 tens.

	Hundreds	Tens	Ones
	3	12	☐
	~~4~~	~~2~~	8
−	1	5	3
			5

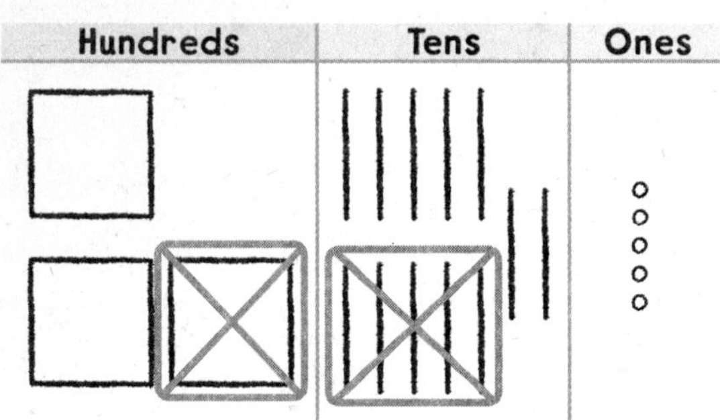

Subtract the tens.

$12 - 5 = 7$

Subtract the hundreds.

$3 - 1 = 2$

	Hundreds	Tens	Ones
	3	12	☐
	~~4~~	~~2~~	8
−	1	5	3
	2	7	5

Share and Show

Solve. Write the difference.

1.

	Hundreds	Tens	Ones
	☐	☐	☐
	4	7	8
−	3	5	6

2.

	Hundreds	Tens	Ones
	☐	☐	☐
	8	1	4
−	2	6	3

Name ______________________________

On Your Own

Solve. Write the difference.

3.

	Hundreds	Tens	Ones
	☐	☐	☐
	6	2	9
−	4	8	2

4.

	Hundreds	Tens	Ones
	☐	☐	☐
	9	3	6
−	1	7	3

5.

	4	3	5
−	1	9	2

6.

	3	8	7
−		4	7

7.

$$\begin{array}{r} 588 \\ -\ 450 \\ \hline \end{array}$$

8.

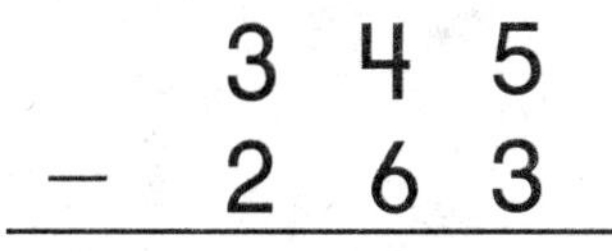

$$\begin{array}{r} 345 \\ -\ 263 \\ \hline \end{array}$$

MATHEMATICAL PRACTICE 3 **Make Arguments**

9. Choose one exercise above. Describe the subtraction that you did. Be sure to tell about the values of the digits in the numbers.

____

____

____

____

Problem Solving • Applications

10. THINKSMARTER Sam made two towers. He used 139 blocks for the first tower. He used 276 blocks in all. For which tower did he use more blocks? ________________

Explain how you solved the problem.

____

____

11. THINKSMARTER This is how many points each class scored in a math game.

Mrs. Rose	Mr. Chang	Mr. Pagano
444 points	429 points	293 points

How many more points did Mr. Chang's class score than Mr. Pagano's class? Draw a picture and explain how you found your answer.

_______ more points

TAKE HOME ACTIVITY • Have your child explain how to find the difference for 745 − 341.

Name ______________________

3-Digit Subtraction: Regroup Hundreds

COMMON CORE STANDARD—2.NBT.B.7
Use place value understanding and properties of operations to add and subtract.

Solve. Write the difference.

1.

	Hundreds	Tens	Ones
	☐	☐	☐
	7	2	7
−	2	5	6

2.

	Hundreds	Tens	Ones
	☐	☐	☐
	9	6	7
−	1	5	3

3.

	6	3	9
−	4	7	2

4.

	4	4	8
−	3	6	3

Problem Solving

Solve. Write or draw to explain.

5. There were 537 people in the parade. 254 of these people were playing an instrument. How many people were not playing an instrument?

_______ people

6. WRITE Math Write the subtraction problem for 838 − 462 and find the difference. Then draw quick pictures to check your difference.

____

Lesson Check (2.NBT.B.7)

1. What is the difference?

$$\begin{array}{r} 538 \\ -\ 135 \\ \hline \end{array}$$

2. What is the difference?

$$\begin{array}{r} 218 \\ -\ 126 \\ \hline \end{array}$$

Spiral Review (2.OA.B.2, 2.NBT.B.5, 2.NBT.B.6, 2.NBT.B.7)

3. What is the difference?

52 − 15 = ____

4. Wallace has 8 crayons and Alma has 7. How many do the have together?

8 + 7 = ____ crayons

5. What is the sum?

$$\begin{array}{r} 47 \\ +\ 26 \\ \hline \end{array}$$

6. Mrs. Lin's class read 392 books in February. Mr. Hook's class read 173 books. How many more books did Mrs. Lin's class read?

$$\begin{array}{r} 392 \\ -\ 173 \\ \hline \end{array}$$

books

Name ______________________

Subtraction: Regroup Hundreds and Tens

Essential Question How do you know when to regroup in subtraction?

Common Core **Operations and Algebraic Thinking—2.NBT.B.7** *Also 2.NBT.B.8*

MATHEMATICAL PRACTICES
MP1, MP6, MP8

Listen and Draw Real World

Use mental math. Write the difference for each problem.

50	600	80	900
− 20	− 400	− 30	− 300
____	____	____	____

90 − 40 = ______

700 − 500 = ______

70 − 60 = ______

800 − 300 = ______

MATHEMATICAL PRACTICES 6

Were some problems easier to solve than other problems? **Explain.**

FOR THE TEACHER • Encourage children to do these subtraction problems quickly. You may wish to first discuss the problems with children, noting that each problem is limited to just subtracting tens or just subtracting hundreds.

Model and Draw

Sometimes you will regroup more than once in subtraction problems.

Regroup 2 tens 5 ones as 1 ten 15 ones. Subtract the ones.

↓

Regroup 7 hundreds 1 ten as 6 hundreds 11 tens. Subtract the tens.

↓

Subtract the hundreds.

		11	
	6	~~1~~	15
	~~7~~	~~2~~	~~5~~
−	3	4	9
	3	7	6

Share and Show

Solve. Write the difference.

1. $\begin{array}{r} 421 \\ -\ 138 \\ \hline \end{array}$

2. $\begin{array}{r} 274 \\ -\ 182 \\ \hline \end{array}$

3. $\begin{array}{r} 546 \\ -\ 267 \\ \hline \end{array}$

4. $\begin{array}{r} 859 \\ -\ 57 \\ \hline \end{array}$

✓5. $\begin{array}{r} 747 \\ -\ 159 \\ \hline \end{array}$

✓6. $\begin{array}{r} 938 \\ -\ 370 \\ \hline \end{array}$

Name ___________________________

On Your Own

Solve. Write the difference.

7.
$$\begin{array}{r} 342 \\ -\ 138 \\ \hline \end{array}$$

8.
$$\begin{array}{r} 463 \\ -\ 281 \\ \hline \end{array}$$

9.
$$\begin{array}{r} 855 \\ -\ 497 \\ \hline \end{array}$$

10.
$$\begin{array}{r} 657 \\ -\ 384 \\ \hline \end{array}$$

11.
$$\begin{array}{r} 521 \\ -\ 146 \\ \hline \end{array}$$

12.
$$\begin{array}{r} 758 \\ -\ 537 \\ \hline \end{array}$$

13.
$$\begin{array}{r} 542 \\ -\ 168 \\ \hline \end{array}$$

14.
$$\begin{array}{r} 823 \\ -\ 673 \\ \hline \end{array}$$

15.
$$\begin{array}{r} 947 \\ -\ 579 \\ \hline \end{array}$$

16. THINKSMARTER Alex wrote these problems. What are the missing digits?

$$\begin{array}{rrrr} & & 4 & 15 \\ & 9 & \square & \square \\ - & 6 & 2 & 8 \\ \hline & 3 & 2 & 7 \end{array}$$

$$\begin{array}{rrrr} & 7 & 13 & \\ & \square & \square & 7 \\ - & 1 & 5 & \square \\ \hline & 6 & 8 & 1 \end{array}$$

Problem Solving • Applications

17. GO DEEPER This is how Walter found the difference for 617 − 350.

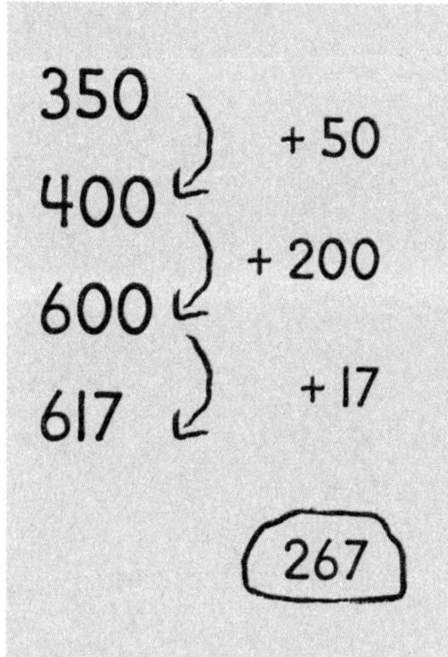

Find the difference for 843 − 270 using Walter's way.

18. MATHEMATICAL PRACTICE 1 **Analyze** There are 471 children at Caleb's school. 256 children ride buses to get to school.

How many children do not ride buses to get to school?

__________ children

19. THINK SMARTER Mrs. Herrell had 427 pinecones. She gave 249 pinecones to her children.

How many pinecones does she still have?

__________ pinecones

TAKE HOME ACTIVITY • Ask your child to find the difference when subtracting 182 from 477.

Name ____________________

Subtraction: Regroup Hundreds and Tens

COMMON CORE STANDARD—2.NBT.B.7
Use place value understanding and properties of operations to add and subtract.

Solve. Write the difference.

1.

$$\begin{array}{r} 816 \\ -\ 345 \\ \hline \end{array}$$

2.

$$\begin{array}{r} 932 \\ -\ 163 \\ \hline \end{array}$$

3.

$$\begin{array}{r} 796 \\ -\ 468 \\ \hline \end{array}$$

Problem Solving

Solve.

4. Mia's coloring book has 432 pages. She has already colored 178 pages. How many pages in the book are left to color?

_______ pages

5. WRITE Math Draw quick pictures to show how to subtract 546 from 735.

Lesson Check (2.NBT.B.7)

1. What is the difference?

$$\begin{array}{r} 349 \\ -\ 187 \\ \hline \end{array}$$

2. What is the difference?

$$\begin{array}{r} 336 \\ -\ 178 \\ \hline \end{array}$$

Spiral Review (2.OA.A.1, 2.OA.B.2, 2.NBT.B.5, 2.NBT.B.7)

3. What is the sum?

$$\begin{array}{r} 246 \\ +\ 533 \\ \hline \end{array}$$

4. What is the difference?

$$\begin{array}{r} 38 \\ -\ 14 \\ \hline \end{array}$$

5. What is the difference?

$17 - 9 =$ ____

6. Lisa had 15 daisies. She gave away 7 daisies. Then she found 3 more daisies. How many daisies does Lisa have now?

________ daisies

Name ____________________

Regrouping with Zeros

Essential Question How do you regroup when there are zeros in the number you start with?

Common Core **Number and Operations in Base Ten—2.NBT.B.7**
MATHEMATICAL PRACTICES
MP1, MP6, MP8

Draw or write to show how you solved the problem.

Describe another way that you could solve the problem.

FOR THE TEACHER • Read the following problem and have children solve. Mr. Sanchez made 403 cookies. He sold 159 cookies. How many cookies does Mr. Sanchez have now? Encourage children to discuss and show different ways to solve the problem.

Model and Draw

Ms. Dean has a book with 504 pages in it. She has read 178 pages so far. How many more pages does she still have to read?

$$\begin{array}{r} 504 \\ -\ 178 \\ \hline \end{array}$$

Step 1 There are not enough ones to subtract from.

Since there are 0 tens, regroup 5 hundreds as 4 hundreds 10 tens.

$$\begin{array}{rrrr} & 4 & 10 & \\ & \not{5} & \not{0} & 4 \\ - & 1 & 7 & 8 \\ \hline \end{array}$$

Step 2 Next, regroup 10 tens 4 ones as 9 tens 14 ones.

Now there are enough ones to subtract from.

14 − 8 = 6

$$\begin{array}{rrrr} & & 9 & \\ & 4 & \not{10} & 14 \\ & \not{5} & \not{0} & \not{4} \\ - & 1 & 7 & 8 \\ \hline & & & 6 \end{array}$$

Step 3 Subtract the tens.

9 − 7 = 2

Subtract the hundreds.

4 − 1 = 3

$$\begin{array}{rrrr} & & 9 & \\ & 4 & \not{10} & 14 \\ & \not{5} & \not{0} & \not{4} \\ - & 1 & 7 & 8 \\ \hline & 3 & 2 & 6 \end{array}$$

Share and Show

Solve. Write the difference.

1.
$$\begin{array}{rrrr} & 3 & 0 & 8 \\ - & 2 & 5 & 9 \\ \hline \end{array}$$

2.
$$\begin{array}{rrrr} & 7 & 5 & 5 \\ - & 4 & 3 & 8 \\ \hline \end{array}$$

3.
$$\begin{array}{rrrr} & 8 & 0 & 1 \\ - & 3 & 7 & 5 \\ \hline \end{array}$$

Name ____________________

On Your Own

Solve. Write the difference.

4.
$$\begin{array}{r} 563 \\ -\,182 \\ \hline \end{array}$$

5.
$$\begin{array}{r} 904 \\ -\,568 \\ \hline \end{array}$$

6.
$$\begin{array}{r} 705 \\ -\,231 \\ \hline \end{array}$$

7.
$$\begin{array}{r} 603 \\ -\,328 \\ \hline \end{array}$$

8.
$$\begin{array}{r} 442 \\ -\,238 \\ \hline \end{array}$$

9.
$$\begin{array}{r} 901 \\ -\,675 \\ \hline \end{array}$$

10.
$$\begin{array}{r} 702 \\ -\,426 \\ \hline \end{array}$$

11.
$$\begin{array}{r} 684 \\ -\,219 \\ \hline \end{array}$$

12.
$$\begin{array}{r} 479 \\ -\,137 \\ \hline \end{array}$$

13. THINK SMARTER Miguel has 125 more baseball cards than Chad. Miguel has 405 baseball cards. How many baseball cards does Chad have?

______ baseball cards

Problem Solving • Applications

14. MATHEMATICAL PRACTICE 1 **Analyze** Claire has 250 pennies. Some are in a box and some are in her bank. There are more than 100 pennies in each place. How many pennies could be in each place?

_______ pennies in a box

_______ pennies in her bank

Explain how you solved the problem.

____

____

____

____

15. THINKSMARTER There are 404 people at the baseball game. 273 people are fans of the blue team. The rest are fans of the red team. How many people are fans of the red team?

Does the sentence describe how to find the answer? Choose Yes or No.

Regroup 1 ten as 14 ones.	○ Yes	○ No
Regroup 1 hundred as 10 tens.	○ Yes	○ No
Subtract 3 ones from 4 ones.	○ Yes	○ No
Subtract 2 hundreds from 4 hundreds.	○ Yes	○ No

There are _______ fans of the red team.

TAKE HOME ACTIVITY • Ask your child to explain how he or she solved one of the problems in this lesson.

Name ______________________________

Regrouping with Zeros

COMMON CORE STANDARD—2.NBT.B.7
Use place value understanding and properties of operations to add and subtract.

Solve. Write the difference.

1.
$$\begin{array}{r} 806 \\ -\ 345 \\ \hline \end{array}$$

2.
$$\begin{array}{r} 902 \\ -\ 783 \\ \hline \end{array}$$

3.
$$\begin{array}{r} 794 \\ -\ 268 \\ \hline \end{array}$$

4.
$$\begin{array}{r} 687 \\ -\ 144 \\ \hline \end{array}$$

5.
$$\begin{array}{r} 505 \\ -\ 167 \\ \hline \end{array}$$

6.
$$\begin{array}{r} 307 \\ -\ 154 \\ \hline \end{array}$$

Problem Solving

Solve.

7. There are 303 students.
There are 147 girls.
How many boys are there?

_______ boys

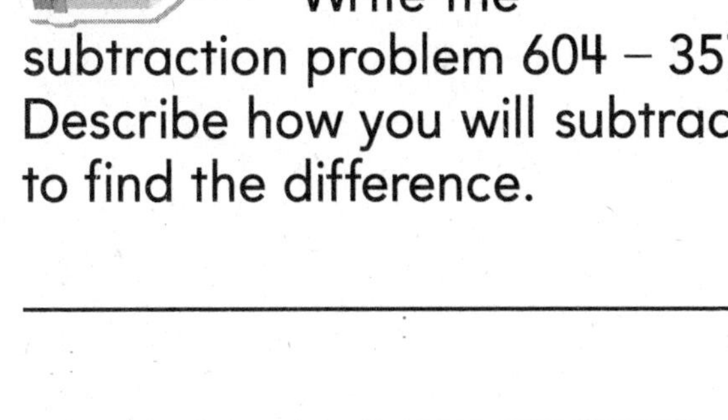

8. Write the subtraction problem 604 – 357. Describe how you will subtract to find the difference.

____

____

Lesson Check (2.NBT.B.7)

1. What is the difference?

$$\begin{array}{r} 301 \\ -\ 187 \\ \hline \end{array}$$

2. What is the difference?

$$\begin{array}{r} 406 \\ -\ 268 \\ \hline \end{array}$$

Spiral Review (2.OA.B.2, 2.NBT.B.5, 2.NBT.B.7)

3. What is the sum?

$$\begin{array}{r} 35 \\ +\ 79 \\ \hline \end{array}$$

4. There are 555 students at Roosevelt Elementary School and 282 students at Jefferson Elementary. How many students are at the two schools altogether?

$$\begin{array}{r} 555 \\ +\ 282 \\ \hline \end{array}$$

students

5. What is the difference?

$10 - 2 =$ ____

6. Gabriel's goal is to read 43 books this year. So far he has read 11 books. How many books does he have left to meet his goal?

$$\begin{array}{r} 43 \\ -\ 11 \\ \hline \end{array}$$

books

FOR MORE PRACTICE GO TO THE Personal Math Trainer

Name ____

Chapter 6 Review/Test

1. Mr. Kent had 948 craft sticks. His art class used 356 craft sticks. How many craft sticks does Mr. Kent have now?

   ______ craft sticks

---

2. At the library, there are 668 books and magazines. There are 565 books at the library. How many magazines are there?

   Circle the number that makes the sentence true.

   There are [13 / 103 / 1,233] magazines.

---

3. There are 176 girls and 241 boys at school. How many children are at school?

$$\begin{array}{r} 176 \\ +\ 241 \\ \hline \end{array} \longrightarrow \begin{array}{r} 100 + 70 + 6 \\ 200 + 40 + 1 \\ \hline \end{array}$$

   Select one number from each column to solve the problem.

Hundreds	Tens	Ones
○ 2	○ 1	○ 3
○ 3	○ 3	○ 5
○ 4	○ 4	○ 7

Personal Math Trainer

4. THINK SMARTER + Anna wants to add 246 and 132.

Help Anna solve this problem. Draw quick pictures. Write how many hundreds, tens, and ones in all. Write the number.

Hundreds	Tens	Ones

____ hundreds ____ tens ____ ones

______

5. Mrs. Preston had 513 leaves. She gave 274 leaves to her students. How many leaves does she still have? Draw to show how you found your answer.

______ leaves

6. A farmer has 112 pecan trees and 97 walnut trees. How many more pecan trees does the farmer have than walnut trees?

Fill in the bubble next to all the sentences that describe what you would do.

- ○ I would regroup the hundreds.
- ○ I would add 12 + 97.
- ○ I would subtract 7 ones from 12 ones.
- ○ I would regroup the tens.

Name ___________________________

7. Amy has 408 beads. She gives 322 beads to her sister. How many beads does Amy have now?

Does the sentence describe how to find the answer? Choose Yes or No.

Regroup 1 ten as 18 ones.	○ Yes	○ No
Regroup 1 hundred as 10 tens.	○ Yes	○ No
Subtract 2 tens from 10 tens.	○ Yes	○ No

Amy has ________ beads.

---

8. GO DEEPER Raul used this method to find the sum 427 + 316.

$$\begin{array}{r} 427 \\ +\ 316 \\ \hline 700 \\ 30 \\ +\ 13 \\ \hline 743 \end{array}$$

Use Raul's method to find this sum.

$$\begin{array}{r} 229 \\ +\ 313 \\ \hline \end{array}$$

Describe how Raul solves addition problems.

____

____

9. Sally scores 381 points in a game. Ty scores 262 points. How many more points does Sally score than Ty?

○ 121 ○ 643 ○ 129 ○ 119

---

10. Use the numbers on the tiles to solve the problem.

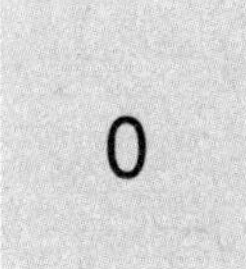

3 6

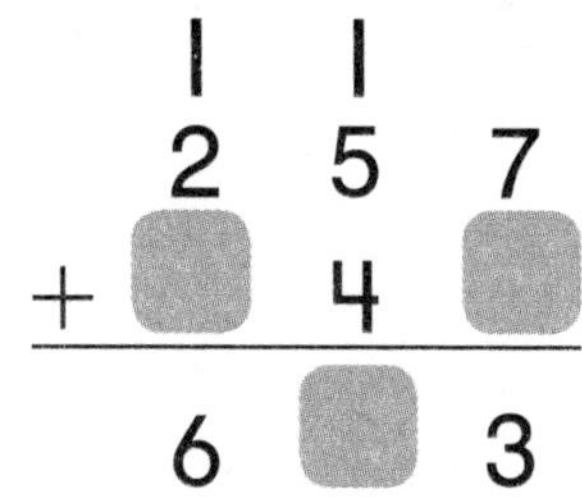

Describe how you solved the problem.

____

____

____

____

Picture Glossary

addend sumando

5 + 8 = 13

addends

a.m. a.m.

Times after midnight and before noon are written with **a.m.**

11:00 a.m. is in the morning.

angle ángulo

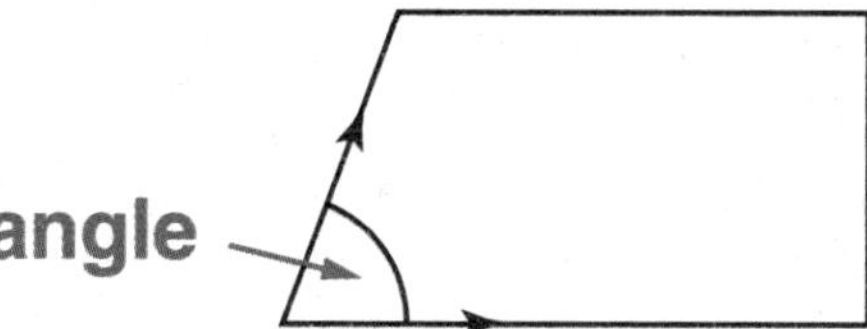

bar graph gráfica de barras

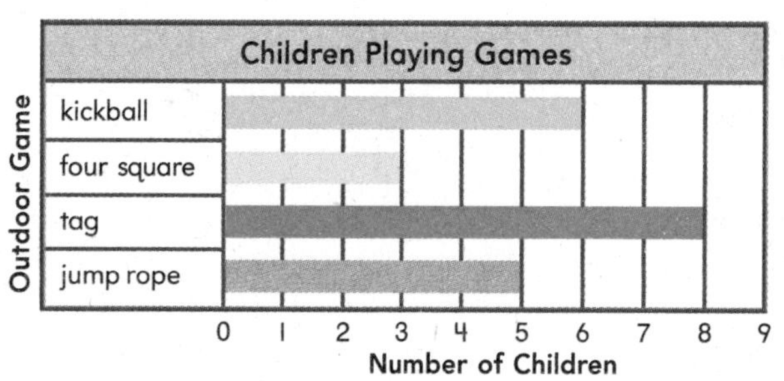

cent sign símbolo de centavo

53¢

cent sign

centimeter centímetro

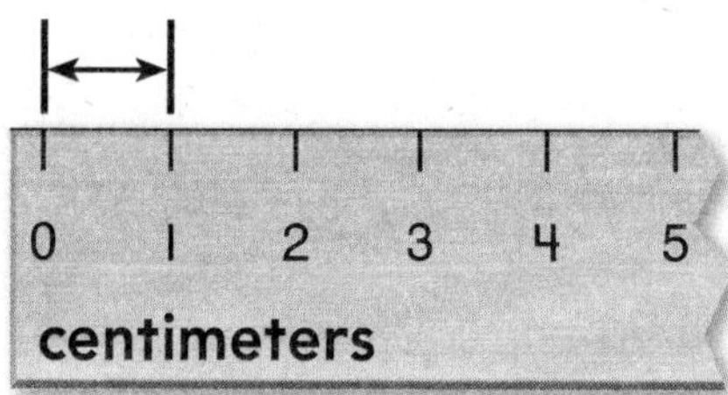

column columna

column

$$\begin{array}{r} 33 \\ 34 \\ +32 \\ \hline \end{array}$$

compare comparar

Use these symbols when you **compare**: $>$, $<$, $=$.

$241 > 234$

$123 < 128$

$247 = 247$

compare comparar

Compare the lengths of the pencil and the crayon.

The pencil is longer than the crayon.

The crayon is shorter than the pencil.

cone cono

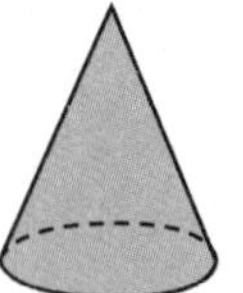

cube cubo

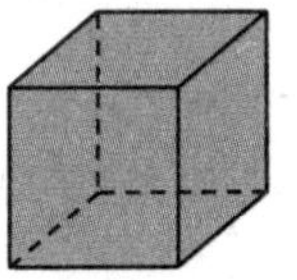

cylinder cilindro

data datos

Favorite Lunch	
Lunch	**Tally**
pizza	IIII
sandwich	~~IIII~~ I
salad	III
pasta	~~IIII~~

The information in this chart is called **data**.

decimal point punto decimal

$1.00
↑
decimal point

difference diferencia

9 − 2 = 7
↑
difference

digit dígito

0, 1, 2, 3, 4, 5, 6, 7, 8, and 9 are **digits**.

dime moneda de 10¢

A **dime** has a value of 10 cents.

dollar dólar

One **dollar** is worth 100 cents.

dollar sign símbolo de dólar

$1.00
↑
dollar sign

doubles dobles

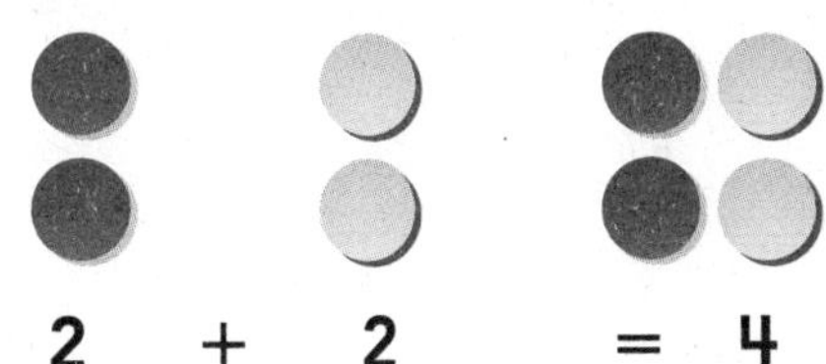

edge arista

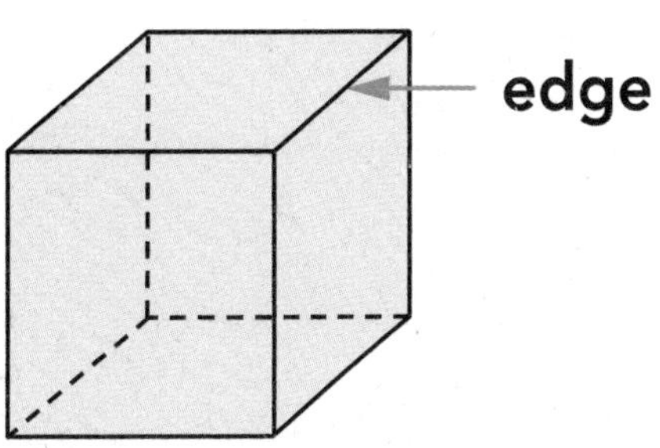

An **edge** is formed where two faces of a three-dimensional shape meet.

estimate estimación

An **estimate** is an amount that tells about how many.

even par

2, 4, 6, 8, 10, . . .

even numbers

face cara

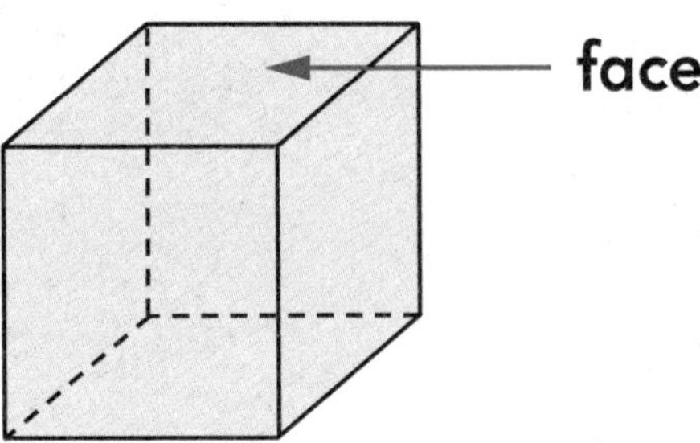

Each flat surface of this cube is a **face**.

foot pie

1 **foot** is the same length as 12 inches.

fourth of cuarto de

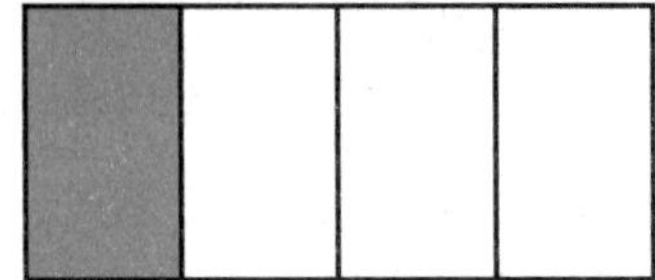

A **fourth of** the shape is green.

fourths cuartos

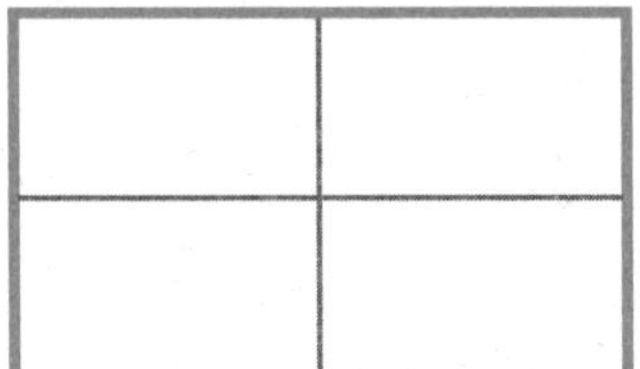

This shape has 4 equal parts. These equal parts are called **fourths**.

half of mitad de

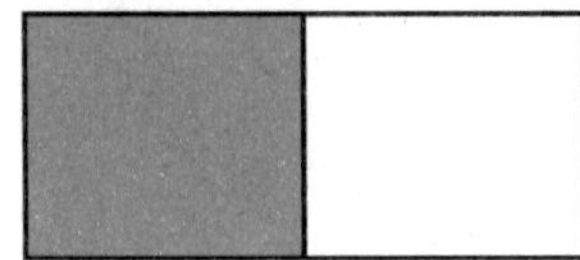

A **half of** the shape is green.

halves mitades

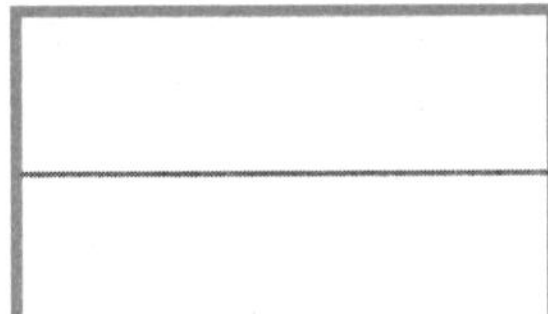

This shape has 2 equal parts. These equal parts are called **halves.**

hexagon hexágono

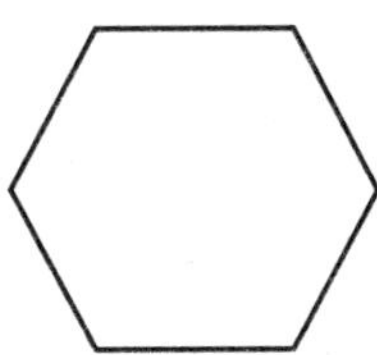

A two-dimensional shape with 6 sides is a **hexagon**.

hour hora

There are 60 minutes in 1 **hour**.

hundred centena

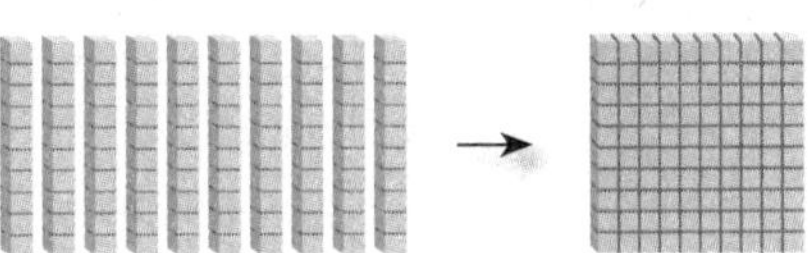

There are 10 tens in 1 **hundred.**

inch pulgada

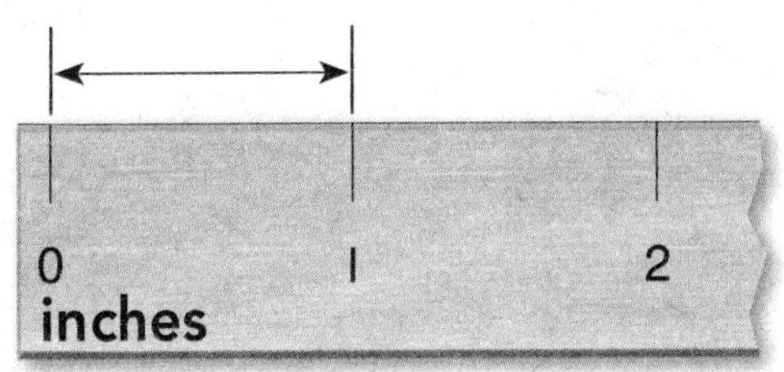

is **equal to** (=) es igual a

247 **is equal to** 247.

247 = 247

is greater than (>) es mayor que

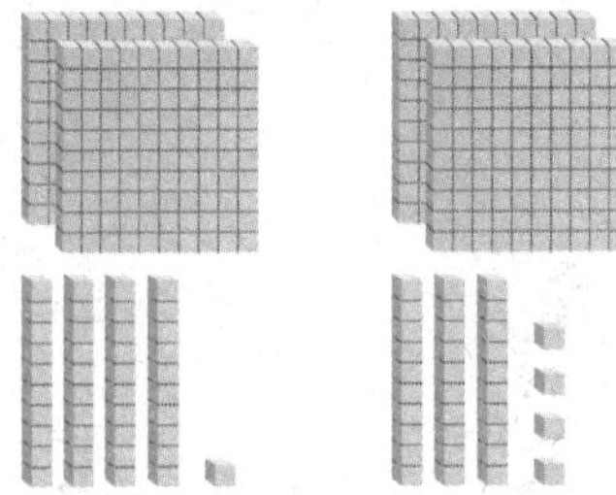

241 **is greater than** 234.

241 > 234

is less than (<) es menor que

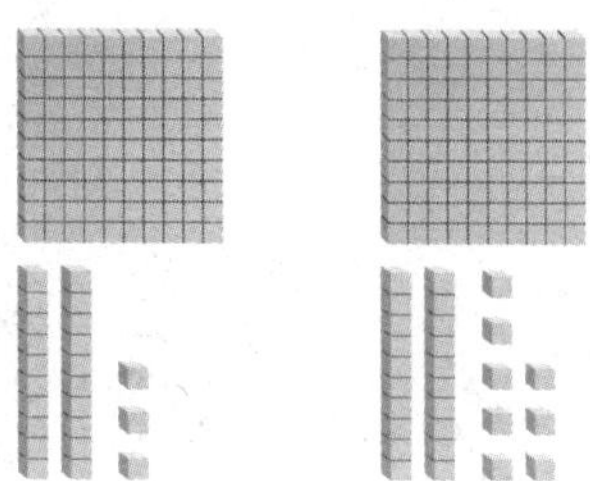

123 **is less than** 128.
$123 < 128$

key clave

Number of Soccer Games							
March	⚽	⚽	⚽	⚽			
April	⚽	⚽	⚽				
May	⚽	⚽	⚽	⚽	⚽	⚽	
June	⚽	⚽	⚽	⚽	⚽	⚽	⚽

Key: Each ⚽ stands for 1 game.

The **key** tells how many each picture stands for.

line plot diagrama de puntos

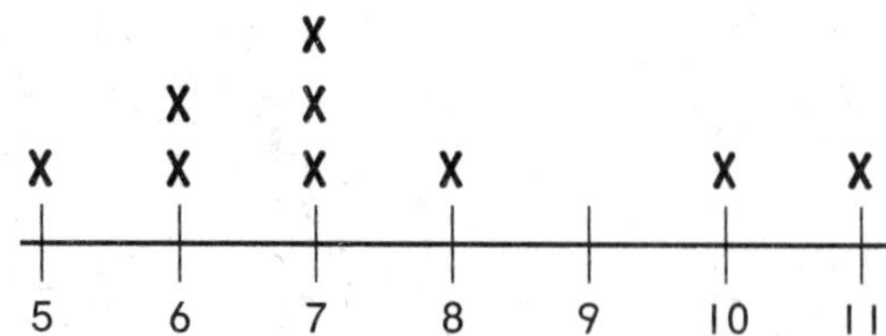

Lengths of Paintbrushes in Inches

measuring tape cinta métrica

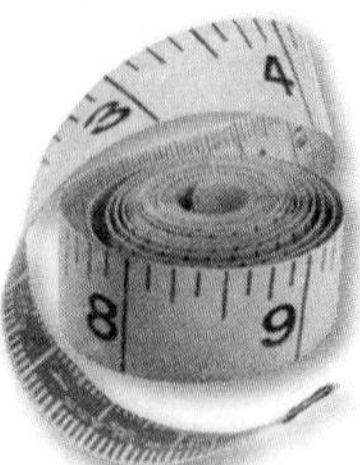

meter metro

1 **meter** is the same length as 100 centimeters.

midnight medianoche

Midnight is 12:00 at night.

minute minuto

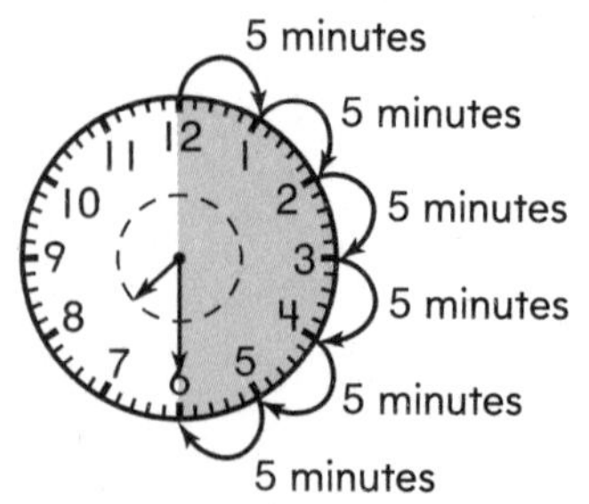

There are 30 **minutes** in a half hour.

nickel moneda de 5¢

A **nickel** has a value of 5 cents.

noon mediodía

Noon is 12:00 in the daytime.

odd impar

1, 3, 5, 7, 9, 11, . . .

odd numbers

ones unidades

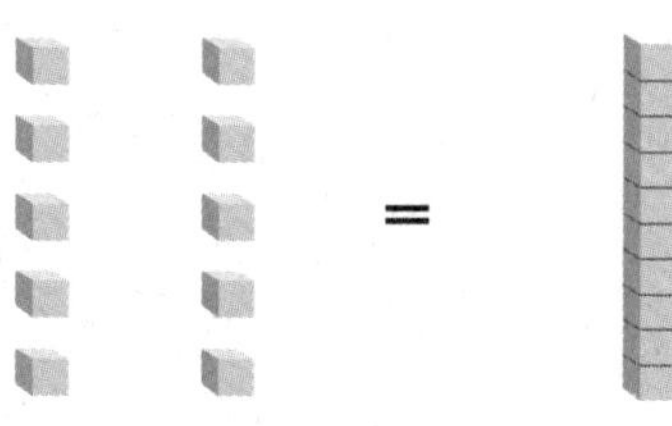

10 ones = 1 ten

penny moneda de 1¢

A **penny** has a value of 1 cent.

pentagon pentágono

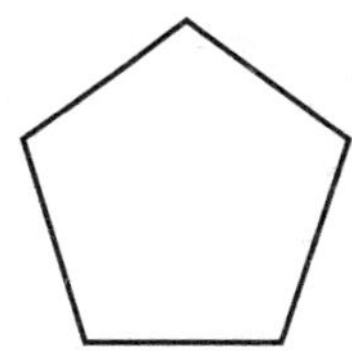

A two-dimensional shape with 5 sides is a **pentagon**.

picture graph gráfica con dibujos

Number of Soccer Games							
March	⚽	⚽	⚽	⚽			
April	⚽	⚽	⚽				
May	⚽	⚽	⚽	⚽	⚽	⚽	
June	⚽	⚽	⚽	⚽	⚽	⚽	⚽

Key: Each ⚽ stands for 1 game.

plus (+) más

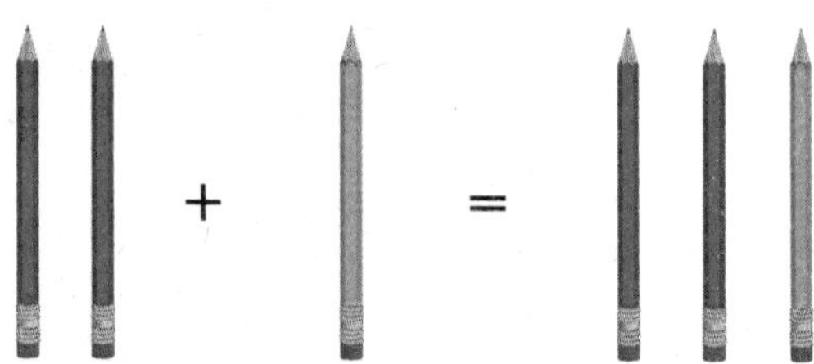

2 plus 1 is equal to 3

2 + 1 = 3

p.m. p.m.

Times after noon and before midnight are written with **p.m.**

11:00 p.m. is in the evening.

quadrilateral cuadrilátero

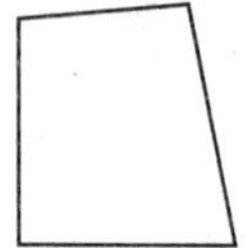

A two-dimensional shape with 4 sides is a **quadrilateral**.

quarter moneda de 25¢

A **quarter** has a value of 25 cents.

quarter of cuarta parte de

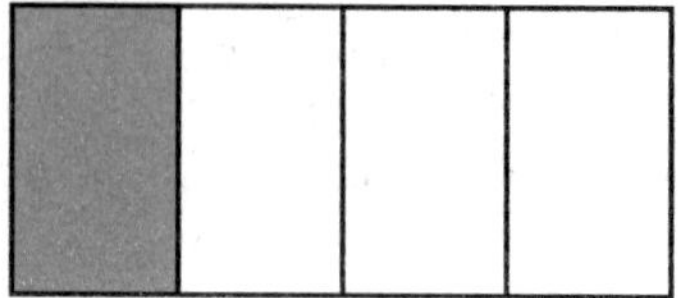

A **quarter of** the shape is green.

quarter past y cuarto

15 minutes after 8
quarter past 8

rectangular prism prisma rectangular

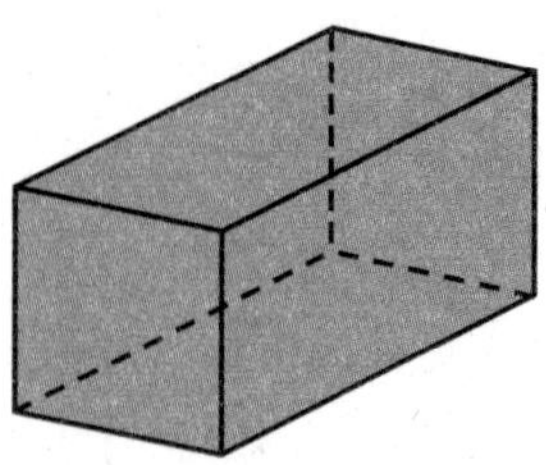

regroup reagrupar

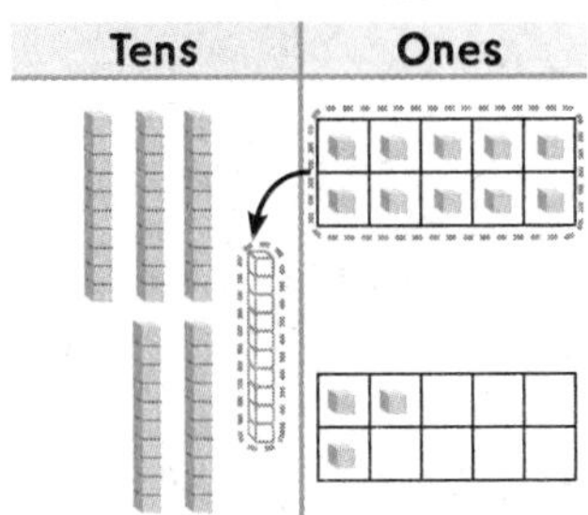

You can trade 10 ones for 1 ten to **regroup**.

side lado

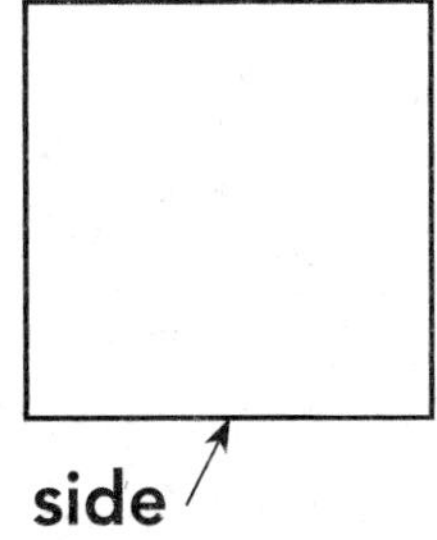

This shape has 4 **sides**.

sphere esfera

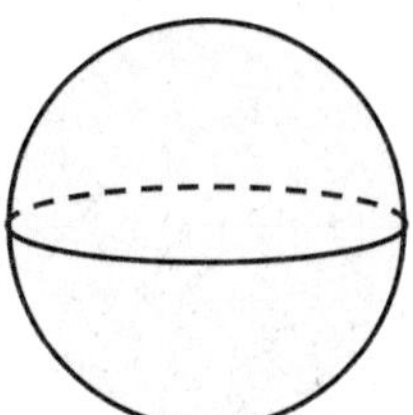

sum suma o total

9 + 6 = 15

↑ **sum**

survey encuesta

Favorite Lunch	
Lunch	**Tally**
pizza	IIII
sandwich	𝍸 I
salad	III
pasta	𝍸

A **survey** is a collection of data from answers to a question.

ten decena

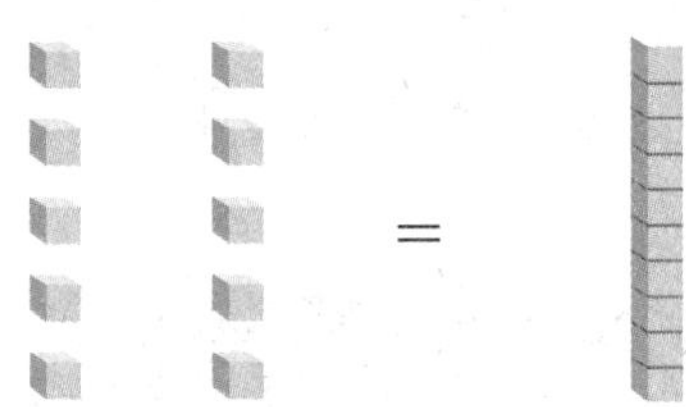

10 ones = 1 ten

third of tercio de

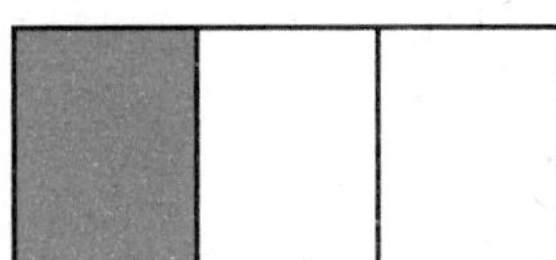

A **third of** the shape is green.

thirds tercios

This shape has 3 equal parts. These equal parts are called **thirds**.

thousand millar

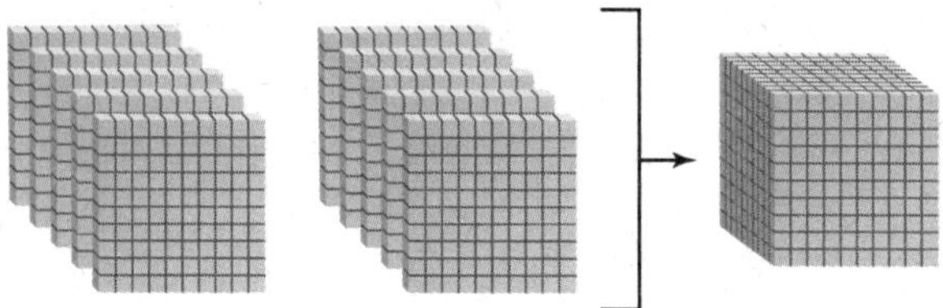

There are 10 hundreds in 1 **thousand**.

vertex/vertices
vértice/vértices

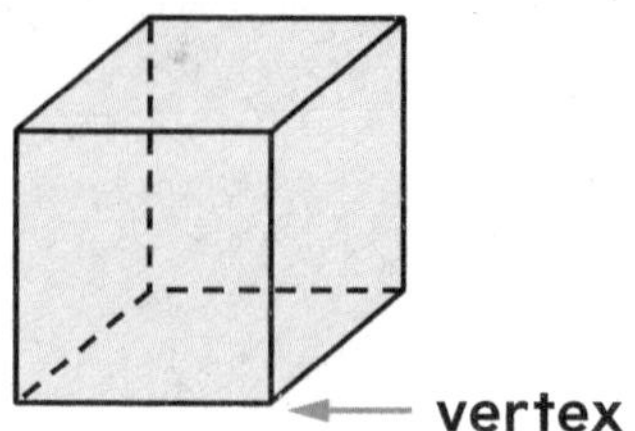

A corner point of a three-dimensional shape is a **vertex**.

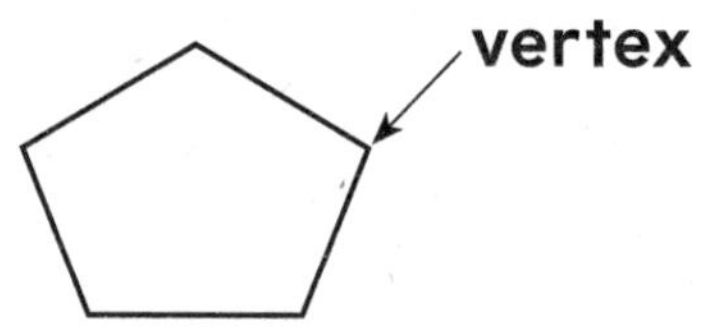

This shape has 5 **vertices**.

yardstick regla de 1 yarda

A **yardstick** is a measuring tool that shows 3 feet.

Correlations

COMMON CORE STATE STANDARDS

Standards You Will Learn

Mathematical Practices		Some examples are:
MP1	Make sense of problems and persevere in solving them.	Lessons 1.3, 1.5, 2.2, 3.2, 3.3, 4.7, 4.9, 4.11, 5.9, 5.10, 5.11, 6.7, 7.7, 8.5, 9.4, 10.1, 10.2, 10.3, 10.4, 10.6, 11.5
MP2	Reason abstractly and quantitatively.	Lessons 1.2, 2.6, 2.11, 2.12, 3.5, 3.9, 4.9, 4.10, 5.5, 5.9, 5.10, 5.11, 6.1, 8.1, 8.4, 8.5, 8.6, 9.4, 9.7, 10.2, 10.4
MP3	Construct viable arguments and critique the reasoning of others.	Lessons 1.1, 2.5, 2.8, 2.11, 4.6, 5.6, 5.10, 6.8, 8.8, 9.3, 10.5, 10.6
MP4	Model with mathematics.	Lessons 1.4, 1.7, 2.3, 2.11, 3.8, 3.9, 3.11, 4.1, 4.2, 4.5, 4.9, 4.11, 5.4, 5.9, 5.10, 5.11, 6.6, 7.3, 7.4, 7.5, 7.6, 7.7, 8.5, 8.9, 9.4, 10.1, 10.3, 10.5, 10.6, 11.3, 11.4, 11.5, 11.6, 11.10, 11.11
MP5	Use appropriate tools strategically.	Lessons 3.7, 3.10, 4.4, 5.1, 5.2, 5.3, 5.8, 6.1, 8.1, 8.2, 8.4, 8.6, 8.8, 8.9, 9.1, 9.3, 9.5, 11.2, 11.7, 11.9
MP6	Attend to precision.	Lessons 1.3, 1.5, 1.6, 2.1, 2.5, 2.7, 2.12, 3.5, 3.11, 4.1, 4.2, 4.3, 4.6, 4.8, 4.10, 4.12, 5.5, 5.7, 6.1, 6.2, 6.3, 6.4, 6.5, 6.7, 6.9, 6.10, 7.2, 7.3, 7.8, 7.9, 7.10, 7.11, 8.1, 8.2, 8.3, 8.4, 8.6, 8.7, 8.9, 9.1, 9.2, 9.3, 9.6, 9.7, 10.1, 10.2, 10.3, 10.4, 10.5, 11.1, 11.2, 11.6, 11.8, 11.9, 11.10, 11.11
MP7	Look for and make use of structure.	Lessons 1.1, 1.2, 1.6, 1.7, 1.8, 1.9, 2.1, 2.2, 2.3, 2.4, 2.5, 2.6, 2.7, 2.8, 2.9, 2.10, 3.1, 3.2, 3.3, 3.7, 3.10, 4.4, 4.7, 4.8, 5.3, 5.6, 5.7, 7.1, 7.5, 7.6, 7.11, 8.3, 8.7, 9.2, 9.5, 9.6, 11.4, 11.5

Standards You Will Learn

Mathematical Practices		Some examples are:
MP8	Look for and express regularity in repeated reasoning.	Lessons 1.2, 1.6, 2.1, 2.2, 2.4, 2.12, 3.2, 3.3, 3.4, 3.5, 3.7, 4.3, 4.11, 4.12, 5.5, 5.8, 6.2, 6.3, 6.4, 6.5, 6.7, 6.8, 6.9, 6.10, 7.2, 7.3, 7.4, 7.8, 7.9, 7.10, 8.1, 8.8, 9.1, 11.7, 11.8
Domain: Operations and Algebraic Thinking		**Student Edition Lessons**
Represent and solve problems involving addition and subtraction.		
2.OA.A.1	Use addition and subtraction within 100 to solve one- and two-step word problems involving situations of adding to, taking from, putting together, taking apart, and comparing, with unknowns in all positions, e.g., by using drawings and equations with a symbol for the unknown number to represent the problem.	Lessons 3.8, 3.9, 4.9, 4.10, 5.9, 5.10, 5.11
Add and subtract within 20.		
2.OA.B.2	Fluently add and subtract within 20 using mental strategies. By end of Grade 2, know from memory all sums of two one-digit numbers.	Lessons 3.1, 3.2, 3.3, 3.4, 3.5, 3.6, 3.7
Work with equal groups of objects to gain foundations for multiplication.		
2.OA.C.3	Determine whether a group of objects (up to 20) has an odd or even number of members, e.g., by pairing objects or counting them by 2s; write an equation to express an even number as a sum of two equal addends.	Lessons 1.1, 1.2
2.OA.C.4	Use addition to find the total number of objects arranged in rectangular arrays with up to 5 rows and up to 5 columns; write an equation to express the total as a sum of equal addends.	Lessons 3.10, 3.11

Standards You Will Learn

Standards You Will Learn		Student Edition Lessons
Domain: Number and Operations in Base Ten		
Understand place value.		
2.NBT.A.1	Understand that the three digits of a three-digit number represent amounts of hundreds, tens, and ones; e.g., 706 equals 7 hundreds, 0 tens, and 6 ones. Understand the following as special cases:	Lessons 2.2, 2.3, 2.4, 2.5
	a. 100 can be thought of as a bundle of ten tens — called a "hundred."	Lesson 2.1
	b. The numbers 100, 200, 300, 400, 500, 600, 700, 800, 900 refer to one, two, three, four, five, six, seven, eight, or nine hundreds (and 0 tens and 0 ones).	Lesson 2.1
2.NBT.A.2	Count within 1000; skip-count by 5s, 10s, and 100s.	Lessons 1.8, 1.9
2.NBT.A.3	Read and write numbers to 1000 using base-ten numerals, number names, and expanded form.	Lessons 1.3, 1.4, 1.5. 1.6, 1.7, 2.4, 2.6, 2.7, 2.8
2.NBT.A.4	Compare two three-digit numbers based on meanings of the hundreds, tens, and ones digits, using $>$, $=$, and $<$ symbols to record the results of comparisons.	Lessons 2.11, 2.12
Use place value understanding and properties of operations to add and subtract.		
2.NBT.B.5	Fluently add and subtract within 100 using strategies based on place value, properties of operations, and/or the relationship between addition and subtraction.	Lessons 4.1, 4.2, 4.3, 4.4, 4.5, 4.6, 4.7, 4.8, 5.1, 5.2, 5.3, 5.4, 5.5, 5.6, 5.7, 5.8
2.NBT.B.6	Add up to four two-digit numbers using strategies based on place value and properties of operations.	Lessons 4.11, 4.12

Standards You Will Learn

	Standards You Will Learn	Student Edition Lessons
Domain: Number and Operations in Base Ten		
Use place value understanding and properties of operations to add and subtract.		
2.NBT.B.7	Add and subtract within 1000, using concrete models or drawings and strategies based on place value, properties of operations, and/or the relationship between addition and subtraction; relate the strategy to a written method. Understand that in adding or subtracting three-digit numbers, one adds or subtracts hundreds and hundreds, tens and tens, ones and ones; and sometimes it is necessary to compose or decompose tens or hundreds.	Lessons 6.1, 6.2, 6.3, 6.4, 6.5, 6.6, 6.7, 6.8, 6.9, 6.10
2.NBT.B.8	Mentally add 10 or 100 to a given number 100–900, and mentally subtract 10 or 100 from a given number 100–900.	Lessons 2.9, 2.10
2.NBT.B.9	Explain why addition and subtraction strategies work, using place value and the properties of operations.	Lessons 4.6, 6.8
Domain: Measurement and Data		
Measure and estimate lengths in standard units.		
2.MD.A.1	Measure the length of an object by selecting and using appropriate tools such as rulers, yardsticks, meter sticks, and measuring tapes.	Lessons 8.1, 8.2, 8.4, 8.8, 9.1, 9.3
2.MD.A.2	Measure the length of an object twice, using length units of different lengths for the two measurements; describe how the two measurements relate to the size of the unit chosen.	Lessons 8.6, 9.5

Standards You Will Learn

		Student Edition Lessons
Domain: Measurement and Data		
Measure and estimate lengths in standard units.		
2.MD.A.3	Estimate lengths using units of inches, feet, centimeters, and meters.	Lessons 8.3, 8.7, 9.2, 9.6
2.MD.A.4	Measure to determine how much longer one object is than another, expressing the length difference in terms of a standard length unit.	Lesson 9.7
Relate addition and subtraction to length.		
2.MD.B.5	Use addition and subtraction within 100 to solve word problems involving lengths that are given in the same units, e.g., by using drawings (such as drawings of rulers) and equations with a symbol for the unknown number to represent the problem.	Lessons 8.5, 9.4
2.MD.B.6	Represent whole numbers as lengths from 0 on a number line diagram with equally spaced points corresponding to the numbers 0, 1, 2, ..., and represent whole-number sums and differences within 100 on a number line diagram.	Lessons 8.5, 9.4
Work with time and money.		
2.MD.C.7	Tell and write time from analog and digital clocks to the nearest five minutes, using a.m. and p.m.	Lessons 7.8, 7.9, 7.10, 7.11
2.MD.C.8	Solve word problems involving dollar bills, quarters, dimes, nickels, and pennies, using $ and ¢ symbols appropriately. *Example: If you have 2 dimes and 3 pennies, how many cents do you have?*	Lessons 7.1, 7.2, 7.3, 7.4, 7.5, 7.6, 7.7

Standards You Will Learn

		Student Edition Lessons
Domain: Measurement and Data		
Represent and interpret data.		
2.MD.D.9	Generate measurement data by measuring lengths of several objects to the nearest whole unit, or by making repeated measurements of the same object. Show the measurements by making a line plot, where the horizontal scale is marked off in whole-number units.	Lesson 8.9
2.MD.D.10	Draw a picture graph and a bar graph (with single-unit scale) to represent a data set with up to four categories. Solve simple put-together, take-apart, and compare problems using information presented in a bar graph.	Lessons 10.1, 10.2, 10.3, 10.4, 10.5, 10.6
Domain: Geometry		
Reason with shapes and their attributes.		
2.G.A.1	Recognize and draw shapes having specified attributes, such as a given number of angles or a given number of equal faces. Identify triangles, quadrilaterals, pentagons, hexagons, and cubes.	Lessons 11.1, 11.2, 11.3, 11.4, 11.5, 11.6
2.G.A.2	Partition a rectangle into rows and columns of same-size squares and count to find the total number of them.	Lesson 11.7
2.G.A.3	Partition circles and rectangles into two, three, or four equal shares, describe the shares using the words *halves, thirds, half of, a third of,* etc., and describe the whole as two halves, three thirds, four fourths. Recognize that equal shares of identical wholes need not have the same shape.	Lessons 11.8, 11.9, 11.10, 11.11

Index

A

D

E

N

Q

S